D0875436

WITHDRAWN

A Moment's Notice

Also by Carol J. Greenhouse

*Praying for Justice: Faith, Order, and Community
in an American Town*

Law and Community in Three American Towns,
coauthored with Barbara Yngvesson and David M. Engel

Carol J. Greenhouse

A Moment's Notice

Time Politics across Cultures

Cornell University Press

Ithaca and London

First published 1996 by Cornell University Press.

Library of Congress Cataloging-in-Publication Data

Greenhouse, Carol J., 1950–
    A moment's notice : time politics across cultures / Carol J.
Greenhouse.
       p. cm.
    Includes bibliographical references and index.
    ISBN 0-8014-3061-5 (cl : alk. paper).—ISBN 0-8014-8228-3 (pbk.
: alk. paper)
    1. Political anthropology. 2. Time—Social aspects. I. Title.
GN492.2.G74   1996
306.2—dc20   95-53724

Printed in the United States of America

⊛ The paper in this book meets the minimum requirements
of the American National Standard for Information Sciences—
Permanence of Paper for Printed Library Materials, ANSI Z39.48-1984.

For Hannah

Contents

Preface

*T*HIS BOOK IS about time, politics, culture, and ethnography. What Nancy D. Munn (1992) calls the "problem of time" has been more or less central to anthropology since the discipline's beginnings over a century ago, and recent theorizings of postcoloniality and postmodernity have made the braiding and unbraiding of histories, time, nationalism, and cultural practice familiar across the disciplines of anthropology, history, literature, sociology, and cultural studies. "Social time," as Emile Durkheim called it, names this long-standing inquiry into the varied means and ends people make of the logistical and existential challenges of living in the company of others. In the subject of social time anthropologists have found scope for exploring the allure and repugnance of modernism while pursuing a quintessentially modernist project themselves. In that regard, anthropology's explicit cultural relativism masked its implicit cultural critique. Specifically, Anglo-American legal ideas regarding the territorialization of identity, the cultural legitimation of law, the normative aspects of communicative orders, and the technologies of reciprocity met their limits in encounters with "the Other," to borrow Johannes Fabian's phrase, but anthropology then converted the limits of law's regulatory efficacy at home and abroad into the relativities of others' temporalities.

This book offers a reflexive analysis of the ways Western concepts of law structure ethnographic practice in domains fundamental to both classical social anthropology and the current discipline. I base my analysis on a critical cumulative reading and reinterpretation of anthropology's treatment of time, which, for reasons the book itself explains, has been a surrogate for specific questions of power, authority, and legitimacy.

The project began as a comparative study of the ethnography of "law." At the time the book took shape as a question in 1981, the anthropology of law was in an acutely self-critical moment, a climax to more than a decade of particularly fruitful ethnographic research and debate. Throughout the late sixties and seventies, the most contentious debates focused on the nature of rules and, even more so, on problems of comparison that juxtaposed Anglo-American state law and the so-called customary practices of formerly sovereign people in colonial or newly independent states. Those debates and their potential stakes for people's autonomy made the ethnology of law (that is, the cross-cultural comparison of customs and norms) seem all the more important and intriguing, yet simultaneously elusive, if not altogether moot.

While the contemporary anthropology of law is obviously no longer a unified "subdiscipline," it arguably remains a coherent project when viewed as a response to the critical legacy of the sixties and seventies, as well as to the contemporary social and political legacy of the rights debates from that same period. I would defend a continuing place for an anthropology of law, specifically, for the sake of understanding how the signs that mark cultural difference come to be attached to particular forms of conflict, how such signs circulate and operate within and across—even *as*—legal systems, and how they materialize as human vulnerability and value. The ethnography of law in this broader sense is a flourishing genre.

My interest in law and time arose in the field and in the classroom. In the early 1980s, I was in the midst of writing up an ethnographic study of law use and ideologies of social order in a U.S. town, in the course of which my questions about conflict had led to an exploration of local ideas about history and salvation (in the religious sense) as contrasting paradigms of community and "law." That experience prompted my interest in a more general question of how the cultural uses of law might be embedded in concepts of history and temporality in the United States and elsewhere. When I took this question to the classroom, it seemed to yield some productive cumulative readings, which added to my interest in exploring further.

Initially, I imagined that I might find some comparative route across the cultural variety of jural ideas and institutions by looking at social time as a conceptual matrix for the tasks of law, but time does not explain law. Pursuing the idea that time's varieties might help account for the different sorts of normative tasks societies assign themselves only made it clear to me that anthropology's typologizing rubrics of time were highly ethnocentric, and inadequate for the variety of temporal formulations known to exist. In retrospect, both the plausibility of my initial question and its failure were results of the corollary relationship between the problems of time and law in anthropology. The reason why an anthropology of time looked like it might offer a route around the comparative conundrums facing legal ethnology was that it was *already* that; my efforts to link time and law led directly back to the reflexive and comparative problems that prompted the project in the first place.

Simon Roberts (1978) had posed some of those problems in a galvanic essay titled "Do We Need an Anthropology of Law?"—to which his answer was a qualified "no." Subsequently, John Comaroff (1980) and Comaroff and Roberts (1981) developed compelling ethnographic arguments as to the undesirability of building an ethnology of law on some a priori definition of the term "law" or its presumed manifestations. A rich ethnographic literature from the 1980s and 1990s attests to the futility of any direct comparison of rules and jural institutions from an interpretive standpoint, given the potential incommensurateness of cultural epistemologies, situations, and legalities around the world, not to speak of the state legalities that exist over and against these.

By the mid-1980s, legal anthropology as such sought and found renewed engagement with its home discipline, where attention had meanwhile turned to the ethnographic implications of the variety of poststructuralist reformulations then emerging from the humanities and humanistic social sciences. Those developments in the discipline at large quickly took the shape of debates over the canons and practices of ethnographic research, so fundamentally did the new approaches seem to call into question long-standing assumptions about the nature of social order and objectivity.

Indeed, nowhere can the force of anthropology's recent intellectual developments be appreciated more fully than in the context where they were first rehearsed, that is, in the ethnography of law. There, questions of how cultural domains are defined and ordered and how these might be studied ethnographically have always had literal, practical meanings that bring into bold relief the philosophical and epistemological dilemmas that are now integral to professional ethnographic discourses. Anthropologists abandoned cross-cultural comparison first in relation to law and then more broadly, not because they lost interest in it (witness contemporary ethnographic writing on modernity and global capitalism as contexts for linking lives across cultures) but because they doubted the availability of a conceptual vocabulary that could escape circularity. In retrospect, legal anthropology's internal divisions were a harbinger of later strains in the discipline at large on precisely the same ground. Faced with the relatively sudden emergence of pressing empirical evidence of cultural, political, and normative diversity, ethnography in general felt the challenge of a "crisis of representation" (as George E. Marcus and Michael Fischer [1986] put it) well rehearsed—though in narrower terms and on a smaller scale—by legal anthropologists in the contexts of debate I have just sketched. In this book, the classic debates in legal anthropology leave their traces primarily in the narrative style of Part I.

The problem of time is not only a classic anthropological question. It is also a current dilemma in the world of events. The classic problem is organized around the paradox of difference: If mortality is the central universal of life, how and why should we take cultural differences with respect to time seriously? Can time and cultural difference both be "real"? If we say that time is "cultural," then what do we do with death? If we say that time is universal, then what do we do with culture? Can we have time *and* culture, or do interpretivism and other constructionist approaches to social phenomena defeat themselves at death's door?

The current dilemma is also about taking culture and time seriously simultaneously. Is there a vital and affirmative place for difference in the world of the future? The much-heralded "postmodern condition," like the problem of time itself, pits time and culture against each other, as politicians, activists, and academics variously assert and contest the limits of cultural diversity in relation to the future of the nation-state. Can we envision a global society that has both functioning states *and* a flourishing multiculturality, or does democracy defeat itself at the limits of homogeneity?

The link between these two renderings of the problem of time is no mere semantic parallel. They are joined by the related practices of the state, on the one hand, and ethnography, on the other, in particular through the idea of society or social structure and its derivative formulations of agency.

Anticipating what follows, I believe that much of what ethnographers have taken to be the comparative significance of social time rests on projections onto other cultural spheres of Western repertoires of state legitimation. But this projection into the spaces and idioms of people's actual lives (beyond the West, but also "within" the West) is no mere ethnocentrism; it has been part of the history of the world. Accordingly, my proposal is not to "undo" the West's influence by rolling it back to reveal some pristine cultural state but rather to take it into account as systematically as possible in my own readings. In rereading, my efforts have been vastly helped by current ethnographic and historical research on creativity, improvisation, resistance, and the potential incommensurability of knowledge practices across cultures.

Recently, anthropologists have sought new grounding in a conceptual vocabulary designed for the constantly elusive borders between order and disorder. Pierre Bourdieu's term "habitus" refers to "the system of dispositions to a certain practice" (1990b, 7)—something between codes and chaos (something like the rules of the game, in Bourdieu's own explanation) which provides a sense of what goes without saying. In other quarters, "social structure" has yielded to other politically and historically informed ethnographic approaches to discourse, agency, ideology, hegemony, and resistance. Drawing on these formulations, I explore the ways ruling or aspiring elites represent the social basis of their own legitimacy and how these representations mask contests and incommensurabilities among their (claimed) constituencies. "Representation" itself means different things in the different contexts I consider, since our familiar sense of it entails propositions about agency and identity which are also at issue in these cases.

In recent years, the axioms of anthropology—that cultures are bounded entities and social structures comprehensive wholes—have been subjected to vigorous and, in my view, convincing critique. The result has been new ethnographic and comparative questions of practice and agency, which have had the positive effect of opening up considerable new ethnographic ground around questions of power, knowledge, and meaning. In particular, institutions and aspects of life that were formerly out of bounds by virtue of their irreducible complexity—for example, the simultaneous existence of multiple (even competing) world views in a single situation, the contradictory elements of culture and cultural practice, the disruptive elements of interaction, and the highly negotiated quality of collective representation—are now well within the frame of anthropology's ethnographic projects. Former dichotomies of materiality and meaning have also dissolved, now that we know more (for example) about how cultural groups, even persons, are constituted in legalities of various kinds and degrees of force.

Some commentators, even within anthropology, shelve these developments under the label "postmodernism"; however, this is a misnomer. "Postmodern" has some value as a comparative term, but the ethnography of postmodernity is not to be confused with epistemological postmodernisms. Indeed, the impact of postmodernism on anthropological epistemologies and methodologies tends to be overrated, e.g., in the misuse of the term "postmodernism" to comprise feminisms, interpretivism, symbolic anthropology—all of which have made distinctive contributions to the ethnography of "postmodernity." This said, it is *not* an overstatement to say that anthropology's efforts to come to terms with the present world of events has profoundly—and positively—changed the field. The emergence of new ethnographic genres is just one sign of the discipline's current energy and creativity. I leave it to others to rue the so-called fragmentation of our discipline.

The scope and aims of this book and, for the most part, its form were more or less settled in 1992, although I revised the whole and added two new chapters to update the manuscript in 1994 and early 1995. Even so, readers who have been following current writing on time, power, culture, and postmodernities will quickly see where my own time horizons are, in my selection and emphasis. I have tried to make the text itself a faithful record of my intellectual debts, but unsurprisingly, footnotes capture only one dimension of the appreciation I feel for the people who made my personal experience particularly rewarding. This book has been very much a part of my shared life with colleagues, students, friends, and family. I also had the advantage of help from several individuals willing to lend their expertise to someone they had never met. For their readings, in part or in toto, I am grateful to Christopher Borstel, Robert Eno, Dorothy Greenhouse, Michael Herzfeld, John Henderson, Michael Jackson, Arthur Kleinman, Joan Kleinman, Elizabeth Mertz, and Anya Peterson Royce. Judith Bailey, as copyeditor, and the anonymous reviewers for Cornell University Press were sensitive and alert readers whose advice was especially beneficial at crucial stages. Thomas Lee, East Asia librarian at Indiana University, provided a crucial reference. Teresa Adams Lester, Cynthia Werner, Ann Reed, and Sheryl Lockridge helped with timely research and production assistance.

Over the years, countless conversations have kept me engaged with this book even when my attention was largely directed elsewhere. I am especially indebted to James Boon, Davydd J. Greenwood, Robert J. Smith, John S. Henderson, Donald Brenneis, David Engle, Alton Heinz, Mary Katzenstein, Peter Katzenstein, D. Marie Provine, William Provine, Billie Jean Isbell, Phil Parnell, Joëlle Bahloul, Paula Girshick, Beverly Stoeltje, Stephanie Kane, Jane Bachnik, Hal Barton, Elizabeth Reichel, Nancy Ries, Judy Rosenthal, Gretchen Weix, and Stacia Zabusky.

Several colleagues pointed me to key sources I would not have known to seek otherwise: Alfred Aman, Jr., Jane Bachnik, Carol Bloodworth, Paul Dillon, Robert Eno, John Henderson, Susanne Hoelgaard, David Holmberg, Paul Hyams, Billie Jean Isbell, Joan Kleinman, Elizabeth Mertz, Marie Provine, Francis Snyder, Bonnie Urciuoli, Elizabeth Zoller, the late Harold Shaddick, and anonymous reviewers.

The U.S. material in Chapters 6 and 7 has had the benefit of many castings and conversations at professional conferences and seminars, aided by hosts, organizers, commentators, and copanelists on these occasions. In these contexts, I am especially grateful to Don Brenneis, Lawrence Douglas, William Felstiner, Elizabeth Mertz, Robert Post, Marshall Shapo, Julia Lamber, Pat Baude, Loren Robel, Sally Merry, Barbara Yngvesson, Joan Vincent, Davydd Greenwood, John Comaroff, José-Antonio Fernández de Rota, Stephanie Kane, JoAnn Martin, Phil Parnell, Bonnie Urciuoli, and Austin Sarat.

This book has had a long history in conversation, but only a short one in print. I am grateful for permission to use previously published material in revised and reanalyzed form. Portions of earlier work are reprinted by permission of The Yale Law Journal Company and Fred B. Rothman &

Company from *The Yale Law Journal*, vol. 98, pages 1631–51; also, I have drawn on my earlier essays in *Anthropologie et Sociétés* 13(1): 35–50, and *Law's Violence*, ed. Austin Sarat and Thomas Kearns (Ann Arbor: University of Michigan Press, 1992).

In addition to collegial support, several institutions have contributed material support. I am very grateful to the National Endowment for the Humanities for a summer stipened at an early stage and for subsequent sabbatical and study leave support from the College of Arts and Sciences, Cornell University. At Indiana I have had the benefit of research support from the College of Arts and Sciences and the Office of Research and the University Graduate School, for which I am deeply appreciative. Without such help, it would not have been possible for me to integrate the demands of writing into my teaching and other professional commitments.

I express warm gratitude to my hosts at Wolfson College, Emmanuel College, and King's College, for their generous hospitality and for making available to me the libraries and other resources that I needed for my work during sabbatical and other periods of leave in Cambridge.

Though I have tried to make this book a record of my debts, I cannot help but be keenly aware of the ways it falls short in that regard. Nowhere has resigning myself to the inevitability of understatement been more difficult than with respect to Peter Agree, Fred Aman, and Hannah Fidell, to whom I feel unrepayable debts. For years, this book's most convincing sign of reality was as a topic of conversation with Peter Agree at Cornell University Press. He supplied the book's subtitle. In addition, I am deeply grateful to him for so generously making his critical judgment and creative expertise available to me just as I needed them. Fred Aman, my husband, has lent his scholarly imagination and zest for celebration to the cause of making me believe that he regarded this project as something other than an intrusion in our lives; of course, believing him makes any expression of thanks from me seem ludicrously thin. To Hannah, our niece, my sense of debt is of a rather different kind, though perhaps all debts are similar in that they carry one's mind toward their source, and the future. Hannah makes the prospect of the future wonderfully bright. I dedicate this book to her, with love and respect.

CAROL J. GREENHOUSE

Bloomington, Indiana

A Moment's Notice

Introduction

THE MAJOR PREMISE of this book is that time is cultural. I shall not consider here whatever it is that physicists and astronomers mean when they talk about time.[1] My focus is squarely on the ways people talk about and use representations of time in social life, ideas that developed independently of whatever "real time" might be. For this reason, I tend to refer simply to "time," unless I am talking about someone's theory of social time or stressing contingent propositions of time "in nature."

Even in a discipline as eclectic as contemporary sociocultural anthropology, it is fair to say that social time is not a subject like any other. The map of its contours leads straight to the heart of the discipline—and then, just as quickly, out again. Anthropologists know that people conceptualize time differently around the world, but they have tended to treat social time as a paradox, seeming to be both culturally relative and universal, as if mortality made a mockery of culture and its constructions. Viewed in this way, social time might seem to take anthropology, and with it all interpretive disciplines, to their epistemological limits. But social time harries the borders of humanism only if we believe that there is some cultural universal at time's core. There is not—claims of the universality of the human condition notwithstanding.

This book offers a reflexive and comparative reading of time to make a case for thinking of "social time" in fresh terms. Time might appear to "us" (whoever "we" are) to be about change and mortality, but this is only one formulation. Viewed more broadly, time articulates people's understandings of agency: literally, what makes things happen and what makes acts relevant in relation to social experience, however conceived. Our familiar preoccupations with change and individuals' life-spans are only examples of such concerns. Since cultural propositions about agency are (as we shall see) always plural, potentially incommensurate, and determinate only under particular circumstances, taking a comparative ethnographic approach to time does not mean that time is "relative" or that mortality is just a point of view, but neither does it mean that past the edge of the subject of time interpretivism inevitably defeats itself.

Overall, I maintain that the paradox of social time is the artifact of a durable and multidimensional ethnocentrism in the anthropological treatment of time and that the template for this ethnocentrism is in the cultural conventions of political self-legitimation in modern nation-states. For the most part, anthropological studies of social time have proceeded from the double assumption that linear time—"our" time—really *is* our time and really is *real*. The first assumption leads to an ethnographic error, the a priori ascription of cognitive value to all representations of time and then the according of ontological status to any temporal representation as a template for collective perception or social action on a large scale. The second assumption erroneously privileges linear time as most manifestly confirmed by universal conditions of mortality, work, and change. These assumptions are powerfully reinforced in the canons of ethnographic practice and in the temporal discourses of state nationalism.[2]

These assumptions have long cultural histories as well as lively traditions of critical debate. Their contemporary frame of reference might be viewed as a conversation between the legacies of Emile Durkheim and Karl Marx. The Durkheimian legacy emphasizes *time*, as a collective representation of social experiences in nature; social time is a matter of perception, and its value to social theory is as a methodological touchstone for affirmative experiences of social integration. Marx's legacy emphasizes *history* in its concerns with historical materialism and the progressive transformation of social forms. In modern writing, the Durkheimian inflection tends to relativize time; the Marxian inflection tries to decode time's mystifications. More often, these positions are mixed, and one of my concerns is to address current attempts to pull them apart and redefine the whole question of social time.

Among anthropologists interested in social time, these positions—Durkheimian history as time and Marxian time as history—have sometimes been debated directly, but more often they seem to account for the conventional trajectories and limits of exploration and debate. The debates are fascinating and important, since they involve terms that circulate across wide and disparate domains, only some of which are academic. But as an ethnology of time, these conventions are unnecessarily limiting, and much of what follows probes the limitations for their underlying cultural and intellectual concerns, so as to move past them. My hope is to contribute fresh questions to current debates about culture, difference, and change.

Whereas the followers of Durkheim and Marx are at odds over the question of what social time *does*, they are in tacit agreement on the question that is more central to this book, and that is the sense in which social time can be said to be "social" at all. Both traditions envision social time in relation to *whole societies*, though their notions of how the "wholes" cohere are different. From the standpoint of how social social time is, these differences over mechanics and methodology, which are major differences in some contexts, are relatively minor. At least, they are secondary to a common logic of assumptions which goes something like this: social time involves an implicit recognition of an objective and natural world in which societies exist; therefore, within societies, social time links concrete individuals to the social whole, giving societies a means of reproducing themselves over time as entities.

The gist of this logic is to allow *us* (anthropologists) to be relativists to the extent that *others* (indeed, the Others) are objectivists. It allows us to view time as social only to confirm that *they* view time as natural; relativism might be no more than objectivism deferred. As a matter of logic, Alfred Gell has pointed out, we cannot have it both ways.[3] As a practical matter, though, we evidently can and do, inasmuch as this very logic incorporates and reproduces what Marilyn Strathern, in another context, calls the "long-standing set of assumptions in Anglophone anthropology at large, namely the equation of groups with social structure and of politics with society."[4] To anticipate my argument, anthropological concepts of time and culture are indeed wedded to the time-space formulas of states, nations, and citizenship. These, in turn, incorporate and reproduce in very direct ways particular Western canons regarding the significance of mortality. Breaking apart these equations proves to be highly productive in a search for fresh possibilities for an anthropology of time.

The logical and methodological muddles surrounding the anthropology of time are interesting in themselves, but they are also compelling because so much is at stake in them in terms of the theoretical vitality of the discipline and its relevance in a world where, as Clifford Geertz put it over twenty years ago, no one is ever going to let anyone else alone ever again.[5] The muddles mean that we are currently in a position to answer both yes and no to the question that has always been at the root of anthropology's scientific, practical, and ethical relevance: Are all cultural practices and epistemologies ultimately commensurate? This is not a question of whether people can live together or of cultural or moral relativism. People are already living together, perforce. The question is whether cultural differences pose problems of communication, convenience, and style or more complicated problems of participation that cannot be so readily commodified and "costed out." I believe the evidence supports the more complicated answer, not because cultural differences alone, or even primarily, divide the world and distribute its dangers. I do not claim that social time is the only route toward such basic questions as this one, but it is one very clear route, in the sense that a rich ethnographic literature makes a broad and inviting intellectual road.

Time and Agency

The book is in two parts. Part I draws widely on secondary ethnographic sources to offer a critical rereading of the ethnological literature on time. At the outset, I concentrate on the aspects of social time which anthropologists conventionally view as confirming its natural basis, since, as I have already noted, that is where the problem of time is most theoretically charged. I find that basis not in nature but in social contest. Further, I suggest that time only seems to be about nature because Western ideas about social order, conflict, and law are so deeply embedded in the self-legitimating claims that these are "natural" formations. Specifically, what "naturalizes" social order in the West is the idea that the significance of death is universal. In social science, this idea is incorporated and reproduced most fundamentally in the notion of social structure, as well as in other domains of thought. Exploring these bodies of thought for their specific premises about relationships of time, life, and social order reveals that what passes for the natural rationality of linear time is, in fact, a set of cultural claims about the efficacy of law and specific technologies of social ordering. Death is the West's master metaphor of control and power; it is the law that presses against the seeming relativities of time in particular situations. This recognition leads to a project of *re*reading, to the extent that one can read "through" or "past" these claims, as it were, guided by the ethnographic literature itself.

My own rereading leads me to suggest that time is not about, or not first about, personal or collective experiences of change but about cultural formulations of agency and their compatability or incompatibility within specific institutional forms. "Agency" names cultural propositions about how the universe works. These are somewhat indeterminate and open-ended under ordinary circumstances and almost assuredly taken for granted. Agency has emerged as an anthropological issue in recent years primarily in response to theoretical and comparative problems of social structure and history.[6] An interpretive approach to agency—that is, to individuals' actions and their social effects—has reinvigorated the study of social change, particularly in plural contexts where cultures "intersect."

I want to stress here that "agency" itself is a cultural concept. In other words, agency is a productive area of ethnographic inquiry not only because it opens up questions about how individuals understand their own situations but, even more fundamentally, because it allows us to ask how people construe the whole question of what social relevance means. The axiomatic connection between questions of agency and individual action is deeply inscribed in what Pierre Bourdieu (1990a) calls the "officialized" representations of social structures and processes in the West, but the axiom is by no means universal, its power and wide circulation notwithstanding.

Limiting considerations of agency to individuals and collective representations of individual action risks overdetermining the meaning of "society" as the sum of individuals and their acts. This is a prime formulation by which officialized knowledge practices in the modern nation-state project the legalities of citizenship and civil life as sociological principle. From the vantage point of how people understand their *own* worlds, in the West or beyond it, it is *their* understandings of agency and their contests over it which shape the ethnographic frame, not ours. In what follows, some cultural constructions do define agency as an attribute of individuals; others limit it to only some individuals; others accord priority to nonhuman forms of agency; and so on. For now, the basic point is that other kinds of time are actually other formulations of agency, as represented by particular people under particular circumstances.

Viewed as a cultural concept rather than an analytically neutral term, agency can be seen to involve a range of substantive and formal considerations. Both are critical to social time, although I hasten to interject that I am not suggesting the formal/substantive distinction is universal. Substantive considerations involve such questions as whose acts and which acts "matter" as signs of how the universe works. We tend to assume that everyone's acts matter in this sense, though they do not, even in the West. We also tend to assume that the nature and distribution of agency itself is a settled question in the West, though it is not, as I demonstrate in Chapter 6. Agency's formal aspects primarily concern its distribution across social space. Distribution might mean many things, but I concentrate on agency's dispersal—literally, where, when, and how the social world's quickening is registered and communicated culturally.

Chapter 1 begins with the anthropological literature on social time, concentrating on how issues and debates within the discipline are shaped by broader notions beyond it, in particular, assumptions about the universality of the cultural significance of human mortality. These are at the core of the anthropological debate over the nature of the difference between cyclical and linear time. Against these assumptions, I draw on ethnographic evidence to show that ideas about life and death are not universally drawn into cultural propositions about temporality, which seems to be more consistently an arrangement of ideas about the sources and circuitry of agency in social space. The "geometry" of time (as lines or circles) is a misleading metaphor that confuses propositions about generative powers for their materializations and spatializations.

Chapter 2 explores various routes by which assumptions about the universal meanings of death are incorporated into anthropological theorizing about the intrinsic rationality of linear time. In the main, such theorizing leads to another (and, I think, prior) set of assumptions about the nature of social order as necessarily involving the problem of accommodating individuality and its analogue, cultural diversity, within social orders. The link between time and mortality is central to powerful institutions *in the West*, particularly with regard to the complex self-legitimations of the state. The significance of the difference between "the individual" and "society" emerges as the principal means by which the dynamics of individual agency are conceptually separated from the presumed stabilities of "society" itself. Social order, in these writings, implies collective and fixed meanings and settled social forms, toward or against which individual agency registers its effects.

Accordingly, I explore, by means of illustrative texts, major ethnographic areas where linear time is embedded in social practice (including anthropological theorizing). I focus on a set of distinctions that are related in that they are constituted in a common proposition linking the rationality of linear time to the presumed universal significance of death as "fixing" individual agency in the "archive" of society. In each case, the distinctions trace important legal status differentials of culture and class. These distinctions are literacy and orality (literacy held out as a technology for "fixing" individual meanings in textual form), law and legal pluralism (legal pluralism held out as "fixing" cultural meanings to social fields), gifts and official economies (gift exchange held out as "fixing" social relationships to time). My purpose in Chapter 2 is to show how specific officialized notions of life and death are incorporated into ethnographic practice through these distinctions, although in each case ethnographic practice also yields counterevidence to these notions. Thus, through their ethnographic analyses and as grounds for reflexive reading, these studies help us look at particular meanings of law, life, and temporality in the canons of Western social thought.

These are the subject of Chapter 3. Beginning with the concept of "social structure" as a prime locus where assumptions about individuality and agency, on the one hand, and death and society, on the other, are incorporated into both social science and cultural practice, I maintain that the classical formulations of social structure fail to acknowledge the variety—as ethnography has made this variety accessible—of cultural and personal formulations of agency. My goal in Chapter 3 is to make a case for moving the subject of time from its current grounding in assumptions about the universality of the significance of *death*, to new ground in the broad variability and unpredictability of *life*, or agency. Death and life turn out not to be reciprocal in this context. In my view social time is not some universal expression of a preoccupation with intervals inspired by anxiety over death; rather, it comprises very particular improvisations with the cultural meanings of agency inspired by social crises. This chapter involves a double theme, one a conception of "agency" as involving a range of issues beyond "individual action" and the other a reconsideration of some classic themes in the anthropology of law from the vantage point of agency, understood as a concept that is highly culturally charged.

The concluding proposition of Part I is that time is "about" agency and its availability as grist for political self-legitimation. "Social time" is always plural and always contested; it is *not* always existentially important. This conception might seem counterintuitive, so convincingly does convention insist that "social time" really *is* time. Convention confronts, masks, denies, or ignores various assertions of rival formulations of agency, even close to home. In the United States, for example, canonical social discourses leave room for other formulations of agency primarily in caricature or in their pejorative association with marginal or subaltern groups: creationism, laziness, superstition, witchcraft—these are just some of the noteworthy expressions of resistance to the officialized renderings of agency bound up in contemporary forms of government and its social fields. One implication of this book is that these should not be left as caricatures but read as critical, if partial, counterdiscourses of time. But counterformulations of time do not always or only emerge "from below." Commentators on "postmodernity" and "postmodernists" (also objects of caricature) have made the fragmentations and compressions of the present time into a kind of elite counterdiscourse of agency and its implied temporalities.[7]

Leaving aside for the moment the question of whether this is time-space compression or a more down-to-earth diminished scope for difference,[8] the counterdiscourse of postmodernism involves many registers. Some of these are issues for later in the book, in the chapter on the United States and in the Conclusion. Throughout, for the sake of keeping these questions of conflict, contest, and relevance open, I refer consistently to representations of time, never to concepts of time, in order to counterbalance the long-standing tendency to assume that all images of time are expressions of collective cultural mentalities.

In Part II, I apply the propositions from Part I to three extended case studies, each of which introduces further contexts and contingencies and involves explicit improvisation with the representation of time. The cases are thematically related in that they reveal the extent to which time's nature and relevance are among the fundamental concerns of people who manage the institutions of political and legal legitimacy in their respective nations.

All three cases, although in different ways, involve manifest challenges to the legitimacy of the state from below. In particular, in each case, ruling or aspiring elites address in temporal terms the political challenges from new forms of cultural diversity among their constituents. The cases show regimes concerned to develop an expression of their own moment—with the configuration of a modernity—which links the legitimacy of rule to the pluralism of the ruled. The need arises in political emergencies of various kinds. In Chapter 4 the crisis is the unification of China under the First Emperor in the third century B.C. Chapter 5 investigates early sixteenth-century Mexico to discover how Motecuhzoma addressed problems of statecraft in his expanding political sphere in ways that are memorialized (if mistakenly so) in his confrontations with Hernán Cortés. Chapter 6 outlines the processes in the late twentieth-century United States by which the political pressures of "diversity" led to an expanded discourse of representation. My focus is on the Reagan and Bush administrations' efforts to constitute the Supreme Court as a representative branch of government, as evidenced in the Robert Bork and Clarence Thomas confirmation hearings. In each case, the context of improvisations with temporal representations was a legitimacy crisis posed by new forms of cultural diversity. In current jargon, such improvisations, together with their context and stakes, are called "postmodernity."

Searching for cases comparable in scale to that of the West, with its broad hegemony and cultural influence, meant turning to other empires and their spheres of influence in other "times." There, I was guided by the availability of secondary literature and translations of primary sources in languages that I could read (English, French, and Spanish). (This factor yields important limitations, to which I return later.) To simplify matters as much as possible, I restricted my choices to contexts where the people involved were interested in calendrics, explicit in their references to time, according them some central place in indigenous elite articulations of social order. At the risk of belaboring the obvious, I do not mean that time, calendrics, and social order are "controls" in a cross-cultural experiment or that they are "comparable." I treat them not as "units" of comparison but as reasonably clear connections to modern interpretive debates in social science and specifically anthropology.

As the project developed along lines these materials made feasible for me, my concerns focused on the ways specific state processes create internal demands for fresh representations of the state among the very people who, in their official capacities, "are" the state. As Roger Chartier, a social historian, notes,

State perceptions of social phenomena are never neutral. They engender social, educational, or political strategies and practices that tend to impose one authority at the expense of others that are discredited, to lend legitimacy to a project for reform, or to justify an individual's choices and behaviour. A study of representations thus sees them as always captive within a context of rivalries and competition, the stakes of which are couched in terms of power and domination.[9]

In the case studies, crucial temporal innovations occurred in periods when ruling elites' claims to legitimacy were of necessity addressed to broad multinational constituencies that were themselves marked by new forms of cultural diversity and expanded pluralism. The expansionist politics of Motecuhzoma's regime encountered cultural diversity at both its periphery and its core, that is, at the Maya frontiers, where cultural interaction was highly dynamic, and within the Triple Alliance and its unstable factionalisms. In China the first dynasty sought means to extend administrative and ritual standards across a realm comprising previously separate kingdoms; the emperor faced issues of cultural diversity in the management of empire to an unprecedented extent. In the United States, the expansion of rights and newly active political groups—African Americans and women being just two—have redefined presidential politics in the past twenty years, as has the decentralization of the electoral process from the "smoke filled room" to state caucuses and primaries. In each case study, temporal innovation articulates and addresses particular forms of diversity arising from the cultural politics of each context.

In each case, the political regimes at issue take a strongly explicit position on the nature and uses of time as history. These three were chosen primarily because each involves a political tradition (substantially different from the others) which defines the central problem of history as that of the state. I mean that in each case, challenges of statecraft led to innovations in the identification of a principle of change which its advocates claimed had resulted in the state and in their own qualification to rule. Such principles of history are designed to involve criteria of differentiation by which the legitimacy of the state is presented against a field of less adequate alternatives. In each of the three cases in this book, that field of alternatives is indicated and defined in a variety of significant ways. My emphasis throughout is on the constant improvisation involved in the negotiation of historically based political legitimacy, as well as the breadth of the conceptual field such improvisations entail. The three chapters of Part II focus on the debates surrounding the search for a principle of history, both in the contexts of their own times (as suggested by the available evidence) and in the modern scholarship that probes their current significance.

At another level, and in another vein, the case studies are also related through the interpretive traditions that make them available to us today. I am referring to a relationship among the conventional reading of Motecuhzoma's fall, the view of the Chinese Legalists as innovators with scientific time, and current temporal negotiations in the United States. Beginning with the last, the U.S. case has its "origins" in late medieval and early modern conceptions of time in Europe; these also feature in the sixteenth-century encounter of the Spanish with the political cultures of Mesoamerica. In a sense, the institutionalization (in myth, history, anthropology, and science) of Motecuhzoma's temporal "mistake" should be understood as part of the *same* process that identified Western public institutions with linear time: sovereigns, courts, churches, and capitalist trade. Similarly, and more recently, the Western readings of the Legalists and the Ch'in regime are also bound up in distinctly Western concerns, and these in turn are heavily shaped by Han and post-Han institutionalizations of a particular reading of that regime. In the Legalists, whom subsequent traditions in China and the West made both founders and aliens, twentieth-century Western scholars discovered their own motifs: the limits of governments' rationalizing powers, the ideal of "fit" between law and culture, and the limits of law itself. Such concerns emerge most explicitly in the prevailing Western characterizations of the Legalists' alleged excesses in these terms, as described in Chapter 4.

In this book, it is the relationship among cultural diversity, political legitimacy, and the nature of temporal improvisation which makes the cases comparable, not any one of these alone. Moreover, my "comparisons" do not involve the direct juxtaposition of the three cases, but—and this is key—rereadings of the conventional assumptions about each case *in Western scholarship*. In each case, in other words, the interpretive argument of Part I yields a reinterpretation of social science conventions in Part II. Accordingly, whereas Western convention polarizes the Confucians and Legalists of China with respect to their ideas about time, law, and rationality (in the Weberian sense), my rereading of cyclical time leads me to question that polarity. Whereas Western convention makes Motecuhzoma the dupe of his own fundamentalism or perhaps of Cortés himself, I reread Motecuhzoma's actions as those of an astute politician. Whereas Western convention makes biography the natural (and naturalistic) genre for describing a life, I see biography as a nationalist idiom. I must stress that my *re*interpretive agendas are limited ones, emerging from my own efforts to reconnect contemporary ethnographic theory to some of the very cases that were part of its formulation as a modern(ist) project.

In developing these case studies, I am acutely aware of their limitations and wish to be particularly clear about these. Any comparative project involves risks, but it would be outright recklessness to imagine that the comparative lines of the project can be retraced to some rereading of the actual circumstances that gave rise to my sources.

To begin with, the case studies involve data of rather different scales. I have begun with the most "macro" case, that of the Chinese, and concluded with the U.S. case, which in some places is microscopically textual. Each case not only frames a different social field but examines it from a different focal length. In the Chinese case, my data are for the most part Western generalizations about large expanses of time and space in the Chinese past. In the case of Mesoamerica, my material has to do with the preoccupations of a particular regime. In the U.S. case, my data are the most detailed, consisting in part of the actual testimony of candidates for the federal judiciary. In the Conclusion, I return to the question of what these shifts of register and focal length might imply for understanding time, culture, history, and politics more generally.

In preparing the Chinese and Mesoamerican chapters, I relied almost exclusively on secondary sources, largely from modern Western academic traditions, partly because I have no knowledge of Chinese or Nahuatl. Translations exist of the relevant indigenous texts, but the exegetical difficulties remain such that I did not feel qualified to undertake autonomous readings of them. This serious limitation is mitigated only slightly in the Mesoamerican case by my access to Spanish materials whose original versions dated from early colonial times. Still, I have left the primary interpretation of native texts to specialists in those fields. Thus, although China, Mesoamerica, and the United States all have vibrant textual traditions in which temporal ideas relevant to this book are expressed and debated, it is only in preparing the U.S. chapter that I have used these texts extensively as primary materials and worked directly with issues of textual strategy. My ethnographic aims are, in fact, limited to the United States and perhaps other "Western" contexts.

This said, Western scholarship has used the same sources to which I have been restricted to make Mexico and China into icons of other temporalities. Thus, my purpose is, in effect to test a fresh perspective on time by applying it to the same evidence others have considered, to see whether the newer perspective takes into account a broader range of the available evidence. Challenging conventional renderings of Aztec and Chinese temporality on the basis of a reflexive critique of modern Western scholarly traditions is not the same as offering a fresh reading of those temporalities "from the ground," nor is it a direct engagement with contemporary Latin American and Asian scholarship on these and related matters.

Thus, I urge any readers who might be seeking cognitive maps of "the

Chinese" or "the Americans" to remember that the following chapters are about institutional and symbolic innovations and their immediate contexts. This is not a cultural-psychological study of time perception or of national character. Though the individuals whose acts and words I discuss did successfully claim to speak for (or against) large-scale public institutions at least some of the time, my own starting point is in the premise that such claims are intrinsically unverifiable. At the same time, I readily acknowledge that a concept of culture compels consideration of the ways in which the negotiations among and within key institutions affect people's existential realities; however, the nature of this project precludes more than an acknowledgment of this vital issue.

It is also important to remember that these texts are the work of a relatively few individuals at the very top of their respective power elites. In the chapter on China, for example, the Legalists in question are a handful of authors of canonical texts, the advisers to the ruling house of Ch'in, and their imperial followers and commentators in succeeding generations. There were not a political party, a faction, or a popular movement. We may take it as a caution against lumping them under one sociological heading that each of the leading Legalist theorists (Shang Yang, Han Fei-tzu, and Li Ssu) died a violent death at the hands of a Legalist ruler.

I also emphasize that in focusing on elites' self-legitimating claims, I do not assume that "societies" are entities and that "culture" is produced by elites and somehow suffused to the masses, or the reverse; indeed, the concept of hegemony is very much complicated by an ethnographic focus on how the state "itself" negotiates its internal "self"-representations. Still, I do not question elites' truth claims but consider them in their own right, as locally plausible, if not always convincing (even to "the natives"), constructions of reality by some people about others in their own context. I do not view such claims by elites as representative of any popular world view, except in the sense that the people whose claims they are must have expected or hoped that potential constituents would find them credible and compelling. So much for disclaimers.

I *do* assume that any political outcome might have been otherwise and that cultural analysis is about the knowledge practices that define events as events. For this reason, ethnography cannot be expected to "explain" events or predict their outcomes. "Cultural norms" are, for the most part, highly indeterminate and implicit, except to the extent that they are rendered determinate by particular institutions (either public or private) in particular circumstances. More concretely, in considering the significance of temporal representations, I have found it useful to think of representations against this backdrop of indeterminacy and silence. It is renderings of representations out of silence—in law, in the workplace, in private relationships, and in other contexts—which make ethnographic description (by anthropologists, by natives) possible; yet, the silence must somehow remain within the ethnographic frame. To put this another way, representations must remain connected to their sites of production and currency, along with the meaning of representation itself.

Of course, the cases are mutually implicated in other less abstract ways, as well, in that "the encounter" of Europe, the Americas and China had military, economic, political and other complex cultural expressions beyond what I have emphasized here. I have not addressed the transnational aspects of the cases directly, but I hope they nevertheless suggest ways in which cultural grammars of time serve as readily in a transnational syntax of authority as in contexts conceived in more local terms. At a minimum, the processes by which an official cult of history or temporality might be asserted before a diverse population—or withdrawn—can be definitely labeled "national" only in hindsight. For example, while this manuscript was being drafted, the Soviet Union and Yugoslavia ceased to exist as states, the Eastern bloc was utterly reconfigured, Germany unified, apartheid delegalized in South Africa and democracy installed, a president elected in Haiti, removed by coup, and restored again. The alliances that shaped the "Middle East" reversed several times over, and a third party—or more—appeared to be pivotal to the presidential electoral politics of the United States. The reassertions of suppressed sovereignties which might once have looked to Western observers like a characteristic of newly independent postcolonial states now proliferate in Europe, North America, and Mexico in ethnonationalist movements of various kinds. This is precisely the context of possibilities against which I view the temporal innovations of the elites I have described in this book—as central to the constant work of maintaining the cultural legitimacy of the state against a host of forces that make legitimacy provisional, even in the systems that have seemed most durable or intransigeant, even in our own times.

The case studies involve features that shape the readings and conclusions to come. To begin with, they primarily involve temporal debates in contexts of social systems explicitly represented as such in their own times. In each case temporality is represented as having some determinate form or dynamic. There are no "timeless" societies in Part II. The fact that these are states, nations, and empires further shapes the direction of the conclusions and their implications vis-à-vis the potential disconnections between offical time representations and other formulations of agency. In this sense, these features may (at least in the view of some readers) prestructure the conclusions, but I would note again that it is precisely these cases that stand as famous examples of "social time" in the literature. The Aztecs and the Chinese are especially well known, in part because of their evident skill as astronomers, the sophistication of their time-reckoning technologies, and the elaborate aesthetics in their representation of time. The imperial aspect, the allure of "lost empires," and their own historiographic evidence add to the fascination. In the annals of social time, moreover, the Legalists of China are famous for their bureaucratic innovations with rationalization, including what some say was a linear concept of time; the Aztecs for a concept of time that was so circular that Motecuhzoma is said to have mistaken Cortés for an ancient god-king; the United States for the scientific rationality of its time sense.

My own emphasis parallels others' in these respects, but where I have reinterpreted others' findings, it is in light of a distinction between representations of time and mentalities of time which other scholars have tended not to implement. Restricting my discussion to materials where this distinction was feasible was also among my considerations. In retrospect, it seems unsurprising that explicit statements regarding temporality should emerge from elite bureaucratic contexts, since that is where temporal improvisation is the most immediately and obviously charged with interests and consequences within the organization of the elites themselves.

The "need" to render agency determinate and to claim it for the state, as it were, is a particular need. The important temporal innovations in China, central Mexico and the contemporary United States can be shown to be responses by aspiring or ruling elites to manifest challenges from below, which take the shape of new forms of diversity. The representation of this diversity *as cultural* coincides with the self-legitimation of rulership *in temporal terms*.

This book links social time to legitimacy and "legitimacy crises" (to borrow from Jürgen Habermas), but legitimacy and its crises should be understood as involving different conceptualizations and contests in each case. Legitimation is not just a neutral term that applies the same way to different political offices; legitimation crises are occasions to articulate, and perhaps invent, a view of agency in terms of which aspirants or incumbents can claim effective rulership. This conception leads to another theme that is important in my overall argument, and that is the question of whom empires speak for when they define and ritualize time in the elaborate ways for which they are famous.

In response to this question, previous works on social time have tended to treat the imperial representation of time in China and among the Aztecs (for example) as expressions of popular cultural concepts, perhaps because empires are assumed to speak for the *mentalités* of their subjects. As I have already indicated, I do not share this assumption; rather, I assume that the multiculturality of former superpowers' constituencies was as potentially problematic (though in different ways) as "diversity" is in the contemporary world. Hence, I do not assume that aspiring or incumbent elites speak *for* their constituents (which may or may not include "the masses," in any case), but I do assume that their effort is to speak *to* whoever is crucial to their legitimacy, and that legitimacy itself has many meanings.

In each of the case studies there is a "postmodernity," particularly insofar as "postmodernity" spells the collapse of a difference between looking outward and looking inward, from the standpoints of the political regimes whose legitimacy is at issue. That gaze, across constituents and "others," is constituted differently in each case, and not entirely coherently in any case. Nevertheless, in each case one can see time change shape in relation to postmodern dilemmas of legitimacy. The "post-" is a misleading temporal marker, but as it is the conventional one, I use it. Again, the terminology matters less than the distinctions and, in this case, their elision in practices of rule. I have arranged the chapters in Part II according to the increasing clarity with which improvisations in temporal representations can be linked to political circumstances, closing with the chapter on the United States.

The Conclusion offers a reading across the case studies, exploring what they have to say to each other, and their implications. The relationships across pluralisms, political forms, modernities, postmodernities, and ethnographic practice come together as the main concluding themes. Social time is not about time passing but about the vulnerability of political institutions to legitimacy crises of various kinds. For social theorists, I have suggested, this proposition has implications for how we understand "postmodernity" and "postmodernism." It seems to me that from an ethnological standpoint, postmodernity is usefully understood as a legitimation crisis, not in temporal terms, as is usually assumed (e.g., "time-space compression"), but in legal and political terms. Our current *post*modernity is not post anything, except, perhaps, an era of confidence that cultural diversity was an asset to the state's self-legitimations. Postmodernity appears variously perilous and exciting because that confidence has been tested by the extent and intensity of new cultural demands for recognition and social justice. Methodological postmodernism aestheticizes these social movements and focuses on indeterminacy, fragmentation, rupture, and so forth, but the aesthetics of postmodernity are secondary to the instabilities in the cultural foundations of politics itself. This point returns us to the proximity of time and power in the West.

The Conclusion revisits the United States for one more case study in which the book's main themes can be brought together in an interpretive argument. That argument is an end in itself, but I should probably confess that one of my goals in this book is to challenge the assumptions about time, power, culture, and modernity which have tended to exclude the United States from serious anthropological discussion. Indeed, to return to the problem with which this Introduction began, the conundrums of relativism and universalism which have vexed the anthropology of time do not so much press the limits of humanism as they reveal the fallacies of anthropology's dogged exceptionalism with regard to the so-called First World.[10] More generally, still, I hope the book will be read as an appeal for some more robust ethnography at centers of power where the improvisations that are its subject define stakes that matter well beyond the moment.

I

1 Time, Life, and Society

A MONTH INTO HIS Italian journey, en route to Rome, Goethe lingered for a few days in Venice. His diary entry for October 3, 1786, describes the highlight of his tourist's itinerary that day, a trial at the Palazzo Ducale. Compared to a lackluster opera the previous evening, the trial evidently made a lively spectacle. Goethe described it as a comedy, since "everything has probably already been settled before the public performance takes place." He found the scene "amusing, informal and natural." Among the most curious amusements was bit of ritual with an hourglass:

> The clerk started reading, and only then did I realize the significance of a little man sitting on a low stool behind a little table . . . and of the hourglass he had in front of him. So long as the clerk is reading, the time is not counted, but if the advocate wishes to interrupt the reading, he is granted only a limited time. While the clerk reads, the hourglass lies on its side with the little man's hand touching it. As soon as the advocate opens his mouth, the hourglass is raised; as soon as he stops talking, it is laid down again.
>
> Therefore, when the advocate wishes to attract the attention of the public or to challenge the evidence, it requires great skill on his part to do this effectively with brief comments. When he does, the little Saturn is completely nonplussed.[1]

In this passage, the "little Saturn" is steward of more than the hourglass. Or rather, as keeper of the hourglass, he is steward of a key symbol for an amalgam of state and citizen, speech and printed text, law and litigation, ritual and the everyday, the bureaucracy of the court and (in this case) the untidy emergencies of probate. At the core of all of these is a social fact: when the state "speaks," time stops.

The courtroom spectacle replicates in miniature a core image of temporality in the West, a theological image that gives eternity to God and time to human society. The hourglass is a technology of metonymy, each tip of it an assertion of the reality of time in relation to eternity. By Goethe's day, the state had borrowed the temporality of heaven from the church and claimed it for itself. Although time has moved from the church's monopoly to broader ownership in the institutions and practices of the state and beyond, time in the West, in practice and in social science, has never entirely lost contact with the church steeple, figuratively speaking.

The idea of time that has dominated public life in the West since the thirteenth century was not indigenous; it came to Europe with Christianity.[2] Initially, it was the concern of specialists, theologians. The expansion of Christianity into Europe brought with it two ideas about time which had long roots in Jewish and autochthonous Christian tradition: first, the origin of time in creation and, second, the end of time in a day of judgment. The linearity of time derives from the geometric connection between these two end points.[3] To speak of "linear time" is to refer to the image of time as an irreversible progression of moments, yielding ordinal conceptions of past, present, and future as well as duration. Linear time has many variations—for example, as a finite segment, an infinite line, an indefinite line, a braid or multistranded line—and many rivals. "Modern" time retains this geometry and some of its medieval "logic" but treats the problematic end points as inconclusive scientific and ethical problems.

Linear time arrived as a new idea to Europe, and it is difficult to know how it affected ordinary people as they encountered it in the long process of conversion to Christianity. Jack Goody's analysis of changes in family structure and inheritance as a result of early Christian conversion efforts beginning in the fourth century implies that local populations responded to church doctrine fairly quickly.[4] Other social historians suggest that the idea of one's own lifetime as personal property and the popularization of the idea of linear time itself came much later.[5] This disagreement is not necessarily a contradiction, for there is no reason to think that the implications of linear time were uniform, stable, or fully worked out at any given moment or that they were experienced simultaneously even in particular locales. Linear time continues to be worked out and revised, even now, as we shall see.

In the late twelfth century, the popularization of linear time in Europe was greatly accelerated by profound changes in thought and public life.[6] The European invention of the mechanical clock (not the first mechanical clock in the world) in 1354 gave impetus and definition to new ideas about time.[7] The rise of capitalism and print technologies are also credited the popularizing linear time, but these are issues for later in the book. Early Christian theologians wrote about time as "a segment of eternity," eternity defined as "endless time."[8] Time was believed to belong to God, and this belief had many practical and theoretical consequences.[9] The keystone of medieval philosophy was the proposition that God is the uniquely "total being" (*totum esse*) and the uniquely "true being" (*verum esse*); inasmuch as God monopolizes all authenticity, the visible, sensible world is by definition "mere appearance."[10]

Time, which was by this definition limited to the (human) world, was a property of the world by virtue of its creation by God and its as-yet-incomplete perfection. To put this another way, time, in theory, *represented* the incompleteness of the world *in relation to God's completeness.* Individuals could aspire to completion only in salvation, that is, in joining God. The existence of God, always and uniquely total and true, was by definition outside of time, since there was nothing else for God to become and no alternative to God's reality. Linear time took shape as the segment linking creation and judgment; all time was viewed as the history of salvation. The practical meanings of linear time took shape around this logic.

Late medieval Christianity was by no means a single entity. Historians stress the prevalence and persistence of ideas of time and eternity.[11] For Christians, the very idea of duration was charged with sacred significance as a concentration of the "becoming" aspect of salvation.[12] Linear time became the constant marker of the contingency and incompleteness of human society and of every individual's life.[13] The advancement of time, always toward Judgment Day, represented the advancement of human perfectibility, again, always relative to the perfect completeness of God. Time, Etienne Gilson notes, was "a certain mode of existence proper to contingent things, unable to realize themselves all at once in the permanence of a stable present."[14] The instant was drenched in the poignancy of impossibility—the impossibility of refusing the struggle for perfection and the impossibility of succeeding in it. This irony became the very meaning, the enduring meaning, of the idea of a life*time*, which, in this sense, makes the meaning of life contingent on the significance of death.

However great the significance of the impending day of judgment and the anxiety about it, ordinary medieval Europeans were unconcerned with timekeeping and recording time.[15] Medieval timekeeping methods are not well understood today.[16] The invention of the mechanical clock occured in a context of change that reinforced the idea of the finite and measurable lifetime from many directions.[17] Although it may have been the needs of clerics that inspired the innovations in mechanical clockworks, their widespread use facilitated the laicization of time.[18] The clock rapidly became an urban phenomenon, a key symbol of secular power and a prestigious commodity in Europe and, in the early colonial period, in the New World.[19] Modern scholars' debates suggest that a connection between forms of power and technologies of time reckoning is convincing in general but controversial in detail.[20]

Be that as it may, clocks eventually moved from church steeples to the turrets and fronts of palaces and town halls as potent symbols of dominion. The ticking clock was not only a memento mori but a reminder of the ownership of time. The fact that debates over wages, interest payments, and secular government in general took place in these terms underscores the extent to which linear time calls forth a declaration of the ultimate instrumentality of time in social terms.[21] The commemorative sense of linear time derives from its representation as a line segment connecting creation to salvation *and* as a segment that is the property of God.

What Goethe observed involved a very specific appropriation from within this system of ideas and images. The bureaucrat with the hourglass did not just keep the time; he *started* it and *stopped* it. He literally *created* time and *ended* it with each intervention of the advocate. The metonymic reference is to creation itself, the simultaneous achievement of divine agency and a dispersal of agency to human society. Theologically speaking, God's act was not in time but was time itself. The symbolism of the Venetian courtroom puts the law on the side of eternity, and litigation squarely within the world, where time passes.

The linearity of time reiterates the ownership of time, and vice versa. Thus, linear time is time with a purpose, a time-for-the-sake-of-God, -state, -shop, -self, among other possibilities. Even in secular contexts, the linearity of time reproduces both the cry for redemption and the form of redemption in its basic proposition that the individual, though fundamentally alone, can find completion by participating—and only by participating—in a cosmic order through social institutions that serve the end(s) of time.

Linear time's most powerful claim is that of its own redemptive power in relation to an individual's life. For example, fulfillment always implies a passage of time in this world view. There lies the redemptive promise of linear time. There linear time provides a reservoir of symbols with which all human purposes can (and must, in theory) be hierarchically ordered and rationalized. But there is precisely where linear time must defend itself conceptually, since linear time is also a powerful rationale for *resisting* multiple and simultaneous engagements.

By representing life as a fixed (though unknown) segment of time, the language of linear time represents all human activity as a depletion of a nonrenewable and finite store of time. The very metaphors of time, which date from the late Middle Ages, claim that an individual cannot "spend" time in more than one place at a time. To translate the complexity of human engagements from the temporal "dimension" to the social domain requires a language of hierarchy, of purposes and institutions. For example, service to God becomes equated with service to the king, or service to his lords, or service to their vassals, and so on.[22] In linear time ideas of divinity, status, and social participation are in rapid circulation, even though they might *appear* to stand in fixed taxonomic orders such as these.

Linear time did not displace other time concepts in Europe so much as it dominated them in the context of the development of the new institutions that made linear time socially relevant—emerging states, industrial capitalism, new expressions of humanism, and so on. Indigenous European ideas about time were expressed in terms of binary oppositions (day/night, summer/winter, and so on) between which time "moved" in pendulum fashion.[23] As new institutional forms developed and engaged people in new relationships (employer-employee, state-citizen, contractual bonds, and so on), different forms of time multiplied as they were juxtaposed in overlapping social fields. Such proliferations continue today in the West as well as other places within its sphere of influence where different temporalities come into contact as social tensions, for example, between work and family life, the market and faith, aspiration and consolation.[24]

If linear time dominates public life in the West, then, it is because its primary efficacy is in the construction and management of dominant social institutions, not because it is the only "kind" of time that is culturally available. The meanings of linear time are inseparable from its cultural history of use. Linear time was popularized in the West by the church in an active course of conversion, by monarchs engaged in building nation-states, and eventually by other elites who found in an image of unidirectional progress the central symbol for their legitimacy.[25] Linear time is also a technology of resistance and counterresistance; Jacques Le Goff documents an early fourteenth-century struggle between French weavers and workshop owners over access to clocks, the regulation of working hours, authorization for night work, and the hourly wage.[26] The case study in Chapter 6 explores a more recent example of how linear time channels social contests as practical problems of contemporary political management.

Indeed, linear time cannot fulfill its claims to redemptive completeness without selectively canceling and borrowing from the other temporal idioms over which it claims superiority. For example, idioms of cyclical time suffuse Western concepts of private and personal life: birth and death, the generations, dust to dust, the ages of man, marriage, parenting. Linear time did not displace these, except in specific institutional contexts that required their suspension or where their suspension could be achieved.

The clearest formal competition between linear and cyclical time in the West is in the cultural domain of the individual life, which is actually a nexus of ideas about the creation of life (birth, maturity, aging, death), agency and activity, and yet other ideas about the very possibility of a "meaning" of life (let alone a meaningful life). In the West, cyclical time continues to offer the primary formal idiom of life's creation as the reciprocal of personal death. Whereas linear time makes a person's life a private segment or personal "space" in the larger progress of time toward eternity (and to some extent modern secular thinking conflates time and eternity), cyclical time emphasizes the substantiation of life forms in constant alternation between opposed and reciprocal states (for example, living and dead, youth and age). Anthropological readings of other cultural constructions of time tend to be shaped by these tensions, among others.

If the cultural history of the idea of linear time remains relevant to questions of time's meanings (in the West or anywhere), it bespeaks the continuity of the institutional forms and the forms of experience that are built and operate on its terms. As we shall see, the meanings of linear time were not fixed in the past; they are actively challenged and refashioned in the present.[27] And as we shall also see, no concrete image of time can function on its own; all time's "shapes" are technologies for suppressing and refashioning rival temporalities as well as formulations of agency conceived outside the frameworks of time.

All these issues are packed into the "little Saturn's" office, as Goethe described it. In his hands the hourglass, turned this way and that or laid still on its side, was a palpable symbol of the mutual transferability of time's mythic reality and the state's mythic charter. It will take the rest of this book to explain why time can play this symbolic role and that it does so in terms of many different formulations of agency. The linearity of time is a geometric connection between the end points of time; other formulations of the nature and distribution of agency involve other temporal formats. Whereas familiar convention makes time primarily a matter of time passing, these other formats involve other priorities and motifs. And whereas familiar convention makes the geometry of time its most telling feature, these other formats suggest that geometry is a secondary, though not irrelevant issue.

The issue of time's varieties brings us to the broader question of "social time." In the rest of this chapter, my purpose is to define some points of departure in the anthropological literature on social time, and to prepare the way for subsequent discussion of a connection between cultural ideas about time and the visions people have of their own social orders.

Social Time

Since the nineteenth century, anthropologists have investigated the variable ways, the multiple ways, in which people reckon and live time around the world. In the very earliest days of anthropology, for example, J. G. Frazer looked forward to the possibility that new survey instruments distributed among missionaries might produce some findings on the rituals and praxis of time reckoning around the world.[28] Bronislaw Malinowski stressed the relativity of time among Melanesians, while observing that time reckoning is "a practical, as well as a sentimental, necessity in every culture, however simple."[29] Martin P. Nilsson imagined that time would make an ideal testing ground of comparative methods, since, he believed, the possibilities of variation were limited.[30] The view that time's forms are finite pervades the literature, as does the view that the main comparative question lies among those differences of form.

In general, anthropology offers somewhat contradictory observations about time and how it is conceptualized, represented, and practiced around the world. These, I take as reflexive ethnological problems, that is, problems that draw our attention to people's temporal practices and, simultaneously, to anthropology's modes of inquiry in regard to them. For example, time concepts are generally interpreted as culturally relative, while time itself is seen as more or less objective fact. Time is said to have profound influence on people's world views; yet time's significance (as the frame of mortality, for example) is taken to be universal. Time is shown to be embedded in cultural experience; yet the varieties of its forms are said to be finite. Time articulates universal experiences of change; yet time concepts involve fundamentally different lexicons and meanings. And so forth. Anthropology's main interpretive and comparative questions about time arise from such contradictions.[31] The broadest area of agreement is the social aspect of time. Though the phrase "social time" can mean several things, from the coordination of social activity over time to constructions of time itself, its general reference is to the ways in which social experience defines the forms, meanings and relevance of time.

Emile Durkheim coined the term "social time" in 1915 in a footnote to a key passage in *The Elementary Forms of the Religious Life*. Since much of the classic anthropological literature on time can be read as his legacy, it is useful to review that passage here. It concerns categories of thought, time and space among them, which "correspond to the most universal properties of things." Durkheim offers such categories of thought as essentially religious in nature, inasmuch as they express "collective realities":

Religion is eminently social. Religious representations are collective representations which express collective realities; the rites are a manner of acting which take rise in the midst of the assembled groups and which are destined to excite, maintain or recreate certain mental states in these groups. So if the categories are of religious origin, they ought to participate in this nature common to all religious facts; they too should be social affairs and the product of collective thought.[32]

Time arises as an illustrative example of these propositions: "For example, try to represent what the notion of time would be without the processes by which we divide it, measure it or express it with objective signs, a time which is not a succession of years, months, weeks, days and hours! This is something nearly unthinkable. We cannot conceive of time, except on condition of distinguishing its different moments."[33]

Durkheim next asks what "the origin of this differentiation" might be. Individuals might have a "private experience" of memory, but such experiences are not "enough to constitute the notion or category of time." The category of time "is an abstract and impersonal frame which surrounds, not only our individual existence, but that of all humanity." The category of time, he continues,

is like an endless chart, where all duration is spread out before the mind, and upon which all possible events can be located in relation to fixed and determined guide lines. It is not *my time* which is thus arranged; it is time in general, such as it is objectively thought of by everybody in a single civilization. That alone is enough to give us a hint that such an arrangement ought to be collective. And in reality, observation proves that these indispensable guide lines, in relation to which all things are temporally located, are taken from social life. . . . A calendar expresses the rhythm of the collective activities, while at the same time its function is to assure their regularity.[34]

This is a complicated passage, since Durkheim has time unfolding, as it were, from two directions at once, from the private "commemoration" of prior personal "states of consciousness" *and* from "the rhythm of . . . collective activities." A footnote clarifies this distinction: "Thus we see all the difference which exists between the group of sensations and images which serve to locate us in time, and the category of time. The first are the summary of individual experiences, which are of value only for the person who experienced them. But what the category of time expresses is a time common to the group, *a social time*, so to speak."[35]

In the book's conclusion, this distinction is once again important, as Durkheim returns to the opening theme of the social nature of categories. He distinguishes again between a person's sense of temporal orientation and the category of time or the whole of time. For a line or two, the notion of time (along with all other categories) seems on the verge of dissolving into "the category *par excellence* . . . [the] very concept of *totality*,"[36] but the moment passes. Indeed, that is not Durkheim's point; his point is that categories of thought are born in social, or collective, experience. His reference to the social as "impersonal" reiterates his differentiation between personal experiences in time and the category of time.

Durkheim is insistent—and consistent—in distinguishing personal experiences in time from social time, that is, a person's sense of temporal orientation from his or her awareness of time as a category. Yet, if these are different, how can social time be said to be collective? How does social time maintain itself as a totality which, by definition, cannot be experienced by any individual? Durkheim's answer is to link "critical instants" of collective activity to "some material phenomenon, such as the regular recurrence of such or such a star or the alternation of the seasons." As he explains, "Objective signs are necessary to make this essentially social organization intelligible to all. . . . In the same way, . . . the causal relation, from the moment when it is collectively stated by the group, becomes independent of every individual consciousness; it rises above all particular minds and events. It is a law whose value depends on no person."[37] Collective social activity, then, comes to be attached to a system of signs, which both orients individuals' sense of time and confirms their knowledge of the existence of a category of time.[38]

Alfred Gell's critique of Durkheim's theory of social time takes issue most fundamentally with what he claims is Durkheim's mistake of viewing sociological categories as metaphysical principles. In general, Gell credits Durkheim with giving "imaginative stimulus . . . to perfectly valid lines of sociological and anthropological inquiry," but he also speaks of "Durkheim's malign influence as the encourager of a certain type of quasi-metaphysical sociological speculation."[39] Yet, in contrast to some of Durkheim's "successors" (as Gell calls them) and Gell himself, it would seem that Durkheim's metaphysics (quasi or otherwise) is secondary to his hermeneutics. It is a system of *signs* which makes social action on any scale (personal or collective) legible as collective action; that they are signs of something "objective," which I take to mean "in nature," is secondary to their function *as signs*. Otherwise, individual practices and categories of collective thought float somewhat apart, though obviously, in Durkheim's text, not far apart.

Durkheim links periodicity in nature to social time only through his hypothesis about the efficacy of signs. This hermeneutic wedge has tended to be lost in subsequent writing on social time, and with it, Durkheim's distinction between personal time sense and social time has also faded. The term "social time" tends nowadays to be used as a generic category for all aspects of temporality that are not "in nature," whereas Durkheim's usage was considerably narrower. Durkheim does appear to have assumed some real time in nature, but he saw it as relevant to personal and social life only in highly mediated forms. This is undoubtedly part of the significance of his association of the collective category of time with "single civilizations" as if to say that time is experienced directly in relation to social organization, not nature. This is an important qualification, since it makes one edge of the term "collective" (as in "collective representations") a distinction between the socially relative and "the universal" and, at another edge, a distinction from the personal or individual, as we have already seen. Again, the only reason to distinguish between the collective and the universal would be to preserve some contingency related to institutional organization and practice.

Both of these edges have been blurred in the course of anthropological usage in the ethnology of time. I mean that whereas Durkheim left individuals and social wholes floating separately (though in the same social space), anthropological and sociological usage tends to make individuals microcosms of the social whole. Whereas Durkheim left an implicit distinction between the collective and the universal, subsequent usage tends both to relativize and to generalize cultural formulations of time. For Durkheim, again, time in nature is relevant to social time only indirectly, as the ultimate reference point of its hermeneutics, but for others (as we shall see), the claim as to the reality of time in nature presses the cultural realm much more closely.[40]

Structural Time

Within anthropology E. E. Evans-Pritchard's analysis of Nuer society (southern Sudan) included a seminal discussion of Nuer concepts of time, which contemporary reviews singled out for special praise.[41] Evans-Pritchard saw two "kinds" of time among the Nuer, an "ecological time" and "structural time." Ecological time was implicit in Nuer expertise with regard to periodic changes in their environment and how these were related to collective activity. In particular, the requirements of cattle, the alternation of wet and dry seasons, and transhumant migration between villages and camps are central ethnographic issues in the first half of the book. Structural time occupies the more central place in Evans-Pritchard's monograph, providing the fulcrum on which descriptions of Nuer preoccupations with cattle and ecology are balanced against analysis of their politics, kinship, and age sets. As noted, time in nature, ecological time, was not Durkheim's primary concern, but Evans-Pritchard's discussion of "structural time" was very much in the Durkheimian mold.

As Evans-Pritchard notes, "structural time" is not a translation of a Nuer idea but an analytical term referring to many Nuer practices and, in particular, to Nuer ideas about social and structural distance. The Nuer define social relationships within the frameworks suggested by myths concerning the origins of their lineages and tribes. Shared ancestry provides them with their formal idiom of social solidarity and obligation in every degree of relatedness, from the mythical ancestor of a lineage linking strangers from different regions to the more immediate genealogies that connect coresidents. Evans-Pritchard interprets such evocations of intimacy as expressions of temporality, time and "social structure" thus being one and the same idea.

Structural time is in this respect comparable to the familiar meanings of ethnicity. In the United States at least, "ethnicity" is popularly understood as both a genealogical or historical connection to a homeland elsewhere and a sociological connection to other "members" of the contemporary ethnic group. Thus, a sense of ethnic identity has a temporal component (in genealogy) and a structural one (in the sociology of lived experience). Evans-Pritchard's structural time involves the same sorts of issues, including similar fictions, since neither American ethnic groups nor Nuer groups necessarily know who their common ancestors were or if, indeed, they had common ancestors.

Evans-Pritchard stresses that *The Nuer* is not a description of Nuer life but a thematic analysis of its "structural principles." Indeed, the Nuer themselves are unconcerned with time as Evans-Pritchard himself construes the term, as he notes with some poignance:

Though I have spoken of time and units of time the Nuer have no expression equivalent to "time" in our language, and they cannot, therefore, as we can, speak of time as though it were something actual, which passes, can be wasted, can be saved, and so forth. I do not think that they ever experience the same feeling of fighting against time or of having to coordinate activities with an abstract passage of time, because their points of reference are mainly the activities themselves, which are generally of a leisurely character. Events follow a logical order, but they are not controlled by an abstract system, there being no autonomous points of reference to which activities have to conform with precision. Nuer are fortunate.[42]

Working among the Ashanti of western Africa, Meyer Fortes also interpreted social structure as a temporal idiom, but differently from Evans-Pritchard, in that he saw social structure itself as a form of time*keeping*.[43] The important difference between these interpretations is that Fortes appears to have seen social structure primarily as a technology of timekeeping, whereas Evans-Pritchard left room for time itself to be constituted in the host of practices that make up social structure in his usage of the term.

Fortes differed further from Evans-Pritchard in ascribing to Ashanti social structure both a concrete reality and an enduring form.[44] In this context, Fortes saw time as having three aspects: the durational (with no determinate effect on social structure), the continuous, and the genetic. The continuous aspects were key to his view of social structure as "an arrangement of parts brought about by the operation, through a period of time, of principles of social organization which have general validity in a particular society," essentially a timekeeping device.[45]

The differences between Fortes and Evans-Pritchard are suggestive of the nature of subsequent anthropological debates about precisely what sort of difference a cultural difference over social time might be. Early on, A. Irving Hallowell took the position that "temporal concepts are always culturally constituted," pointing to the ease with which people can and do reorient their time reference points.[46] At the same time, perhaps paradoxically, he wrote that different time orientations signal "profound differences in psychological outlook."[47] The limits of human adaptation to multiple time concepts remains a point of contention among anthropologists. Classically, this controversy takes shape over the significance of the form of time. Let us consider what time's forms are supposed to be.

Time and Totalities

Ethnographic convention supplies two geometric forms of time, the cyclical and the linear. The cyclical is generally taken to be anchored in direct observation of nature, whereas linear time is said to involve more abstract reflections on the implications of social variability and change. Given cyclical time's (presumptive) basis in nature, it is often treated as the more "primitive" form of time. Linear time, constantly pressing forward, is said to provide a language and framework for understanding progress and sequence. Cyclical time is said to be about other things— the classifications that make up the world, their logical relationships as a closed system, and their constant availability for reanimation as repetitions of the cycle.

By convention, the irreversibility of linear time and the iteration built into cyclical time make these expressions of progressive and conservative outlooks. Sometimes linear time is seen as the more modern expression or the more pragmatic one. Sometimes, since time is held to be "really" progressive, linear time tends to be privileged as the more realistic and rational expression of time, whereas cyclical time is said to require more ritual support. In general, while substantive formulations of linear and cyclical time vary, they are consistently theorized as reciprocal, the one undoing the other.

Durkheim's image of the "endless chart" on which all times can be imagined simultaneously has a modern sequel in the idea that time involves the totalization of experience. Edmund Leach's and Claude Lévi-Strauss's treatments of this idea have been influential and, interestingly, are more or less each other's inverse. For Leach, time is a religious category and, as such, a reconciliation of a fundamental duality in nature and personal life: irreversibility and repetition.[48] For Lévi-Strauss, by contrast, time is an experience to be associated with the disruption of the sense of wholeness and permanence.

In his classic essay "Cronus and Chronos," Leach (like Durkheim) invites his readers to imagine in a world without timepieces:

Suppose we had no clocks and no scientific astronomy, how then should we think about time? What obvious attributes would time possess? . . . Firstly, there is the notion of repetition. Whenever we think about measuring time we concern ourselves with some kind of metronome; it may be the ticking of a clock or a pulse beat or the recurrence of days or moons or annual seasons, but always there is something which repeats.

Here, Leach is referring to what Durkheim called "the group of sensations and images" that make up an individual's experience of time.[49] The other sort of time is revealed by mortality:

Secondly, there is the notion of non-repetition. We are aware that all living things are born, grow old and die, and that this is an irreversible process.
I am inclined to think that all other aspects of time, duration for example or historical sequence, are fairly simple derivatives from these two basic experiences:
(a) that certain phenomena of nature repeat themselves
(b) that life change is irreversible.

These temporal experiences are intrinsically or logically incompatible, according to Leach; yet the tension between them calls for a resolution. Religion provides this resolution with an overarching rubric, the category of time, within which they can be joined as complementary conditions:

We treat both [repetition and irreversibility] as aspects of "one thing", *time*, not because it is rational to do so, but because of religious prejudice. . . . The notion that the time process is an oscillation between opposites—between day and night or between life and death—implies the existence of a third entity—the "thing" that oscillates, the "I" that is at one moment in the daylight and at another in the dark, the "soul" that is at one moment in the living body and at another in the tomb.[50]

Like Durkheim, then, Leach develops the idea of time as a social category, a thought category constructed through religion. Unlike Durkheim, though, Leach begins his discussion of the twin forms of time, linear and cylical, by developing them as perceptions of how repetition and irreversible change are actually experienced by individuals. Thus, time is not in nature but is the constructed totality that arises from the religious mediation of the sorts of contradictory experiences of change which nature provides.

Lévi-Strauss is also concerned with time as an experience and in relation to totalized cultural categories, but for him, time is essentially disruptive. In his famous preface (*Ouverture*) to *The Raw and the Cooked*, Lévi-Strauss compares myth to music; both, he says, are totalizing systems in that one can anticipate the whole from any part, once one is familiar with the musical or mythical forms that make up the composition. Myth, music—always experienced as totalities—provide an illusion of immortality (the "suppression" of time) until the awareness of time once again intrudes.[51]

This suspension of time is a matter of forgetting that there is such a thing as time outside the myth or the musical performance, liberating the listener to appreciate the composition in its wholeness. In Lévi-Strauss's view, mythic compositions, like musical works, can be understood only as wholes, in that every part implies the whole (and vice versa). Whether or not one has heard the composition before, knowing the cultural forms provides some ability to anticipate how chords resolve or, in myth, how transformations will unfold. But this understanding is more than an analysis of aesthetic forms. It is literally vital. For Lévi-Strauss, the totality of myth or music can outplay the natural rhythms of the body itself. In other words, the dynamic and on-going self-realization of myth (or music) provides exhilarating escape from time for audiences, by momentarily canceling their otherwise inescapable sense of physiological mortality:

This relation to time is of a rather special nature: it is as if music and mythology needed time only in order to deny it. Both, indeed, are instruments for the obliteration of time. Below the level of sounds and rhythms, music acts upon a primitive terrain, which is *the physiological time of the listener; this time is irreversible* and therefore irredeemably diachronic, yet music transmutes the segment devoted to listening to it into a synchronic totality, enclosed within itself. *Because of the internal organization of the musical work, the act of listening to it immobilizes passing time*; it catches and enfolds a cloth flapping in the wind. It follows that by listening to music, and while we are listening to music, we enter into a kind of immortality.

It can now be seen how music resembles myth, since the latter too overcomes *the contradiction between historical, enacted time and a permanent constant.*[52]

The double association between myth and the suspension of time, and their referents in mundane, progressive, physiological time, is a recurrent theme in Lévi-Strauss's writing. Whereas Leach and Lévi-Strauss resolve universal contradictions in people's experience of time (as repetition and mortality) in their respective theories of religion and myth, Clifford Geertz looks to the social order itself.

Geertz's influential and controversial "Person, Time, and Conduct in Bali" distinguishes two forms of time perception, the cyclical and the progressive. For Geertz, "cycles and supercycles are endless, unanchored, uncountable, and, as their internal order has no significance, without climax. They do not accumulate, they do not build, and they are not consumed. They don't tell you what time it is, they tell you what kind of time it is."[53] Linear time is the more familiar form of time perception, inasmuch as it is built from what Geertz claims are universal preoccupations with personal mortality. In Bali, he writes, people experience both forms of time in several simultaneous permutations in their everyday and ritual lives. The result is that any particular "moment" is "detemporalized," that is, left open to the possibilities of transformation. Geertz also outlines a larger context for this orientation toward time in Balinese attitudes toward personal names and etiquette; in these domains, too, contradiction is resolved not by mediation of a third category but by proliferation of possibilities. Thus, Geertz concludes, Balinese time concepts can be understood in terms of broader issues of Balinese visions of cosmology and social life.

In a critique of Geertz's essay, Maurice Bloch proposes that time concepts are not so fully relative as Geertz suggests. In Bloch's view, there are only two approaches to durational time in the world, the linear and the cyclical.[54] Drawing on studies of syntax, Bloch develops the idea that humans actually share a single concept of time. Otherwise, given the basic nature of time orientation in relation to social life, people would not be able to communicate, for "communication with creatures with a fundamentally different system of ideas and life is not possible."[55] He proposes that cyclical and linear times be considered two modes of cognition and communication.[56] Their differences are differences among social situations, not—or not first (as for Geertz and others)—matters of perception. For Bloch, linear time is mundane, or profane, and cyclical time is sacred. Both orientations are constantly available to people concerned to understand and change their conditions of life: "In other words, people may be extensively mystified by the static and organic imaginary models of their society which gain a shadowy phenomenological reality in ritual communication, but they also have available to them another source of concepts, the use of which can lead to the realisation of exploitation and its challenge."[57]

Bloch's essay generated debate on both the nature of his distinction between cyclical and linear time and the operation of these time concepts in various fields of social action. M. F. C. Bourdillon argued against Bloch's association of linear time with the mundane reality of the everyday and cyclical time with mystification, pointing out that nondurational concepts do operate in the realm of the mundane and that ritual does not obscure the world.[58] Leopold E. A. Howe denied Bloch's distinction altogether, insisting that duration is not the opposite of cyclical time and that cyclical time is not stationary. Time measurement and time concepts are separate issues. From Howe's perspective, then, the Balinese might not have two time concepts, as Bloch claimed, but only one, containing cyclical and linear elements; Balinese cycles do not return to the same "temporal point" but to the same "logical point."[59]

At another level, these debates over the anthropology of time join larger debates between anthropological structuralists and Marxists over the meaning of history.[60] Durkheimian social time confronts Marxist problems of history most directly, perhaps, in the debate between Geertz and Bloch (and their critiques), but the dialogue between them is also relevant more broadly. Change, social structures and social wholes, commoditization, exchange, and value have been and remain focal points of comparative questions and explanation within the anthropology of time.

So far, I have sketched approaches to time's forms which consider repetitive and noniterative experiences of time simultaneously, for example, in Lévi-Strauss's idea that myth overrides the sense of mortality, or Bloch's view of cyclical time as mystifying linear time, or Geertz's view of time as intrinsically dual. This said, there are important differences among them. For Leach and Lévi-Strauss (as for Durkheim), time's duality is not so much an ethnographic conclusion as a commonsense premise about experience. For Geertz and Bloch, time's duality (or, for Geertz, plurality) is an ethnographic finding, presented in universalistic terms. The plurality Geertz found among the Balinese, after all, has to do with technologies for communicating meaning, not the meaning of time itself. Still, for these authors (and many others), the real meaning of time, against which a culture might construe, mistake, or mystify some alternative formulation, comes from what they take to be the universal significance of mortality. In this sense, the universality of mortality would appear to belie the relativity of social time. But is social time universally about the significance of mortality?

Irreversible Mortality and "Linear" Time

Linear time, as I have noted, is generally taken to be the more mundane, profane, practical, or objectively "true" construction of time. Ultimately, this view appears to rest equally on the assumption that cyclical times celebrate repetition or reversibility and the conviction, against the logic of so-called cyclical times, that mortality is the ultimate nonreversible experience. In the next section I take up the question of whether cyclical time really *is* repetitive. For now, I want to question the assumption that the anticipation of death is universally experienced as a compelling temporal logic in favor of linear time as the more rational system.

In its anthropological guises, this assumption has two elements. The first is that death is universally an object of individual preoccupation in the double sense of being fundamentally a concern *about* individuals and a concern *of* individuals. From there, a connection between a preoccupation with death, as the ultimate and archetypal irreversible experience, and linear time is inferential. The difference between the present and some future fixed (though unknown) point in time implies a line, from this point of view.

The second element of ethnographic treatments that privilege linear time as more realistic is the claim, implicit or explicit, that death is universally perceived as natural. These two elements are related, in that the inevitability of death is predicated on its being a natural phenomenon. How can death be anything other than inevitable? It is indeed inevitable if we are only concerned with individuals; it is less obviously inevitable if we are concerned with larger social units.

According to medieval theology, the individual lifetime took its shape as the interval between birth and death by virtue of its parallels with the history of the world (also an interval between the creation and the end of the world). Whatever the private cognitive or emotional orientation toward mortality medieval Europeans might have experienced, the institutionalization of linear time as the time of public life was modeled not on the personal mortality of the individual but on the mortality of human society itself.

In orthodox doctrinal terms, then and now, God's direct agency in the creation of time derives from Creation itself and projects divine authorship onto all human events. More skeptical secular formulations of linear time posit a less direct role for God or none at all. In the orthodox view, God created the world and consigned it to human agency, that is, made human agency relevant without surrendering "ownership" of the world. In the secular view, agency is widely dispersed in the nature of human beings (as capable of intention) and natural forces (as capable of effects), but these are never settled questions. The nature and limits of human responsibility in and for the world give rise to limitless ethical, interpretive, and practical dilemmas, even (I am tempted to say "especially") where the nature of time itself seems to be least controversial, as in the

United States, where the beginnings and endings of life are highly volatile public issues.

In her study of the meanings of death in ancient Greece, S. C. Humphreys offers a general starting point along these lines: "One would expect *a priori* . . . that societies in which power is personal and labile will show a more intense interaction between the living on the occasion of death. . . . whereas those in which it is solidly anchored in corporate groups may focus their attention more on the care of the dead." Humphreys' distinction between constructions of the person (in relation to the group) and the cultural relevance of death is suggestive. It underscores the extent to which the conventional link between the inevitability of personal death and the logic of linear time is predicated on a particular construction of the person in relation to the group. Specifically, the person is assumed to be wholly integrated as a universal unit of social action and analysis. The "problem" with death, correspondingly, is absence, nonbeing, and destruction of the physical body. "The statue," said Aristotle, "like the corpse, both is and is not the deceased."[61] The problem of representation he evoked does not define death but suggests one dimension of the social nature of life and death. The problem with death is not universally conceived in this way. For example, in some cultural contexts, a person is revealed to be layered or refracted or ambiguously multiple at death.

From this perspective, death is "like" other contexts *in life* in which representation is similarly ambiguous, urgent, or problematic. One such context might be totemism, in which the person is and is not the totem. Alf Sommerfelt reports the words of an aboriginal Australian man explaining his relationship to his totem: "Picking up a photograph of himself, the Australian . . . said: I am the kangaroo in the same sense that I am this photograph."[62]

The Walbiri (Australia), M. J. Meggitt reports, also define the emergency of death in terms of totems. They "see death as something final that marks the end of each individual personality as they know it. The previously unified personality disintegrates into its basic components, and the conception- and lodge-totems return to their spirit-homes, while the matrispirit soon dissipates completely."[63] Regarding death in terms other than a conclusive point *in time* does not in any way mitigate death's finality. Meggitt observes that the Walbiri are "unable to regard the inevitability of their own or their relatives' deaths with any philosophical detachment or resignation";[64] however, the inevitability of death does not mean that time is about that or any other inevitability. In Tahiti, too, indigenous people's anxieties about death focus on the disaggregation of being, not, as familiar theory would have it, on ceasing to be in time. As Robert Levy notes of one man, "Tavana's fear of death, recognizably modern, is the fear of separation: separation from others and the kind of separation from his own self which is non-being."[65] Maurice Leenhardt sums up some of the affirmations implicit in what he calls "the Melanesian mentality." The Melanesian man "is the man of his god, or the man of his totem, or the man of some other power. But by means of these powers or these aberrant existences, he is strong, he *is*. And as he begins to be himself he puts a little order into his entire encounter with the world, starting with the group from which he comes."[66] My point in gathering these examples is to explore ways in which death is social without necessarily being temporal.

James Woodburn describes the cultural crisis brought about by the death of the social person in his cross-cultural study of the social dimensions of death among African hunters and gatherers. The mortuary rituals and expressive responses to death are different for the Hadza (Tanzania), Mbuti (Zaire), Baka (Cameroon), and !Kungsan (Botswana and Namibia); Woodburn contrasts the relatively elaborate rituals and taboos surrounding the killing of animals with the minimal ritual response to an individual human death.[67] The striking parallels among the four groups are their collective response to mourning (that is, mourning is not for the family members alone) and their practice of abandoning the site of a death.[68] Traditionally, for example, the Baka pulled the deceased person's hut down over the corpse; now, this practice has been displaced by burial.

The cultural problem of death is also clarified by Maurice Bloch in his study of responses to death among the Merina of Madagascar. For the Merina, tombs are "a central symbol," sites where ancestors are understood as "merging" with the living group and their land; "the tomb and the descent group are thought of as undifferentiated."[69] Collective responses to death involve the vocabulary and meanings of land and kinship. Bloch relates the symbolic meanings of the tomb to the high value the Merina place on endogamy as a strategy for maintaining the solidarity of ancestral lands within a community of close kin:

This simultaneous regrouping of people and of ancestral land by endogamy is paralleled by the regrouping of the dead in the ancestral tombs of the deme. . . . Merina tombs are massive megalithic structures. . . . In each ancestral area there are a large number of tombs but the fact that they are all in the same ancestral land means that the divisive aspect represented by this multiplicity is ignored in the general way tombs are thought of. All the tombs in ancestral areas are thought of as sharing the same elements and said to be "related" or even "one". Each tomb can contain an almost unlimited number of corpses and so is a symbol of community. The presence of the tombs of a certain deme in an area is what makes this area the ancestral land of that deme. This is because the tombs contain the remains of the collective ancestors placed in the earth or land. . . . The tombs are therefore the medium of the merging of ancestors, deme and land. In the same way as the land must be regrouped, so the corpses of the dead must be regrouped in the tomb so that the common substance of the deme, whether land or corpses, is not scattered. This communal aspect of tombs is underlined by the fact that when a new tomb is built a number of corpses of deme members from other tombs must be brought in before an individual can be placed there. One can never be alone in a tomb.[70]

Here is a relationship between communal solidarity and land, group and land providing a seemingly interchangeable symbolic vocabulary for expressing the sociality of both the living and the dead.

In Bloch's view of Merina perspectives, birth and death are equivalent disruptions, each representing a particularization, a division, in a society that values solidarity as an ultimate good. Bloch explains the pivotal role of women in funerary ritual, both as objects of ritual degradation and abuse during the funeral itself and, in larger symbolic terms, as agents of disruption of group solidarity. The ritual assaults on women symbolically negate the individuation associated with women, which equates death with birth, as equally threatening the established solidarity of the community.[71]

Bloch's essay is particularly suggestive for my purposes, inasmuch as it shows so clearly how death can involve social crises other than the temporal—at least as temporal is conventionally understood in the West. For the Merina, the problem is not a *disjunction* between birth and death seen as two moments, to be connected by a line or not, but rather their *union* as equal, though different, challenges to the solidarity of the group. Indeed, in moving the social question of death from autobiography to social space, Bloch refers to the "timeless order" of the Merina, which "is created by collapsing birth and death and by representing them as the same thing."[72] He develops the notion of the timeless order, the reaffirmation of fertility in the context of funerary rituals, as a comparative axis linking the Merina to West African societies (the Mossi, Sara, Dogon, and Lodagaa) and, more broadly, to "nearly all the cultures we know, [where] it is principally women who are expected to weep."[73] Nevertheless, what we see among the Merina is not timeless order but a social order whose meanings of time are not about time in our familiar sense. Rather, time is "about" the decomposition and recomposition of social groups. Death is not about the closure of an interval but the disruption of the group and a corresponding crisis in social health.[74]

The meaning of death as intrusive or violent rupture of social solidarity can also be found elsewhere, not always in association with women. Such examples underscore the social nature of death, moving death entirely from what westerners would call the natural realm to the cultural. Among the Hopi, only the very old are believed to die a natural death; otherwise, all death is murder.[75] Among the Kaluli, too, death is considered unnatural, the work of witches, and one element of grief is the yearning to kill the witch.[76] Indeed, personhood in the social sense is by no means universally associated with the "natural" processes of birth and death. For example, Tewa children acquire personhood after birth, not with it or before it; full personhood comes in a long process that is not considered finished for years. "Finishing" is a Tewa rite of passage which celebrates the personhood of children in their respective moieties when they are about ten years old.[77] But one hardly need turn elsewhere for illustrations of a point that is at the source of so much current public moral and political controversy in the United States; the question of what defines the beginning and end of life—biology or culture—is highly unsettled in the contemporary United States, as debates over abortion, suicide, and euthanasia reveal again and again.[78]

My purpose in offering ethnographic examples is not to establish a categorical distinction between "Melanesian" or "aboriginal" mentalities and Western ones but the opposite—to connect them. In the West, as elsewhere, death calls into question the cultural organization of the person, posing a variety of personal and group crises. At the same time, the examples also suggest some of the limitations of Western assumptions about the universality of the *temporal* crisis death is said to pose for (or impose on) the individual. It is the social person, not the individual-become-corpse, which is at the center of death's cultural crisis; that is, the aspects of death's meanings which call forth some cultural elaboration are not personal but more broadly social. What death or the contemplation of one's own death might mean to individuals is beyond the scope of this book. I believe, however, that the evidence (briefly adduced though it is here) is against the assumption that mortality inherently reinforces a social logic of individuation and linear time. With this possibility in mind, let us revisit the "other" forms of time—cyclical time and (so-called) timelessness—to see how they look when viewed as something other than mystification.

Time and Timelessness

Abandonment of duality as the organizing principle for the study of social time does not in itself deliver a more vigorous ethnographic engagement with the problem of time. In practice, the ethnographic discussion of so-called cyclical time remains highly colored by the conflation of social time and what are presumed to be periodicities in nature. That is, when ethnographers look for time in societies without the West's timekeeping technologies, they look for it in cultural knowledge about natural cycles. Interestingly, some of them do not find it there.

Twentieth-century ethnography contains detailed reports, luxuriant reports, of people's ability to describe and coordinate social action in terms of natural phenomena. A classic ethnographic example of indigenous constructions of cyclical time is from the Nuer, for whom, according to Evans-Pritchard, "oecological time appears to be, and is, cyclical":[79]

The oecological cycle is a year. Its distinctive rhythm is the backwards and forwards movement from villages to camps, which is the Nuer's response to the climatic dichotomy of rains and drought. The year (*ruon*) has two main seasons, *tot* and *mai*. *Tot*, from about the middle of March to the middle of September, roughly corresponds to the rise in the curve of the rainfall, though it does not cover the whole period of the rains. . . .

The movements of the heavenly bodies other than the sun and the moon, the direction and variation of winds, and the migration of some species of birds are observed by the Nuer, but they do not regulate their activities in relation to them nor use them as points of reference in seasonsal time-reckoning. The characters by which seasons are most clearly defined are those which control the movements of the people: water, vegetation, movements of fish, &c.; it being the needs of the cattle and variations in food-supply which chiefly translate oecological rhythm into the social rhythm of the year, and the contrast between modes of life at the height of the rains and at the height of the drought which provides the conceptual poles in time-reckoning.[80]

In this passage, Evans-Pritchard seems to present the social activity of ecological time as a counterpart, a highly mediated counterpart, of natural fluctuations. In *The Nuer*, he stresses that these fluctuations are not regular and that the Nuer coordinate their activities in response to their observations of nature, not some calendar deduced from them. In this, *The Nuer* provides an ethnographic paradigm for a host of other examples.

The range of distinctions people draw from the so-called natural world is impressive if one is used to the Manichean dualisms of Western cultural rhetorics. For example, we are told that the ancient Tahitians had no word for a solar day but had twenty-four sets of terms for the sun's position in the sky (though the sets were organized from native terms by the anthropologist). Other terms provided a vocabulary with which people could refer to the nature of the clouds, the quality of light, the tides, and the opening of blossoms—all in contexts involving the coordination of activity or the specification of some moment.[81] They also observed daily, monthly, seasonal, and annual cycles based on the sun, the moon, the Pleiades, the weather, and the ripening of different breadfruit varieties.[82]

But is knowing about the so-called cycles of nature the same as marshaling that knowledge as time? Evidently not. Evans-Pritchard's qualifications about the meaning of time for the Nuer and his fascination with their freedom from Western notions of time are echoed in other ethnographic works. For example, Douglas Oliver also notes that the ancient Tahitians, sophisticated though they may have been in their observations of periodicity in nature, were "unconcern[ed] with the whole dimension of time in human affairs."[83] In his study of the Canaque (Melanesia), Leenhardt finds a similar lack of concern:

Melanesian languages do not express time, which remains undifferentiated. And by a play of morphemes . . . , they situate the action: the subject toward the front—the future; toward the back—completed action. But there is really neither future nor past. . . . it is impossible for the Canaque to grasp time. . . . his effort [is] to select some moments of duration and hold them aside, because of an inherent quality they possess.[84]

In some cases, ethnographers seem to perceive a lack of concern with time when people organize their social categories and coordinate their activities in terms other than temporal duration. For example, Levy explains Tahitian verbal forms for time in terms of two sets of spatial representations. The first is a "fixed and static space, in which all events past, present, and future can be arranged. Ancient events are at the front of this space, and subsequent events are placed farther and farther back. . . . The observer watches as the present moves back over the landscape of existence."[85] The other set of terms refers to a space where "future events flow toward an individual from in front of him and drop off behind him as past events."[86] As Leenhardt cautions, in Melanesian languages "there is really neither future nor past." "The time in which [the Canaque] moves does not extend beyond that which he can feel and conceive, no more than space can extend beyond the horizons he grasps."[87] Later, Leenhardt adds: "Each time he acts he finds himself transported into all the spatiotemporal domains in which the motives determining his choice of action can be affirmed. . . . Each of the juxtaposed times into which the subject moves is a time whose character is mythic."[88]

In yet different ways, social space provides the idiom of time among the Tiv (Nigeria), as Paul Bohannan reports: "That Tiv say they increase with the passage of generations is primarily a cosmographical notion, and its spatial aspect is of vastly greater importance than its temporal aspect."[89] For the Tiv, time and population are interdependent concepts, both expressed in spatial terms.

Renato Rosaldo's study of what he calls historical narrative among the Ilongot (Philippines) offers a detailed ethnographic portrayal of how space organizes narratives of events. In Ilongot narrative locales function as "events" do in Western historical narrative. Though their lands are relatively close to the national capital and though they have been in contact with Europeans since the first Spanish missions arrived in 1565, the Ilongot have remained relatively unintegrated in, though not isolated from, the lowlands. The Ilongot remember the years before the Second World War as the *pistaim* (peacetime), roughly the years from 1919 to 1945.[90] Peacetime ended for the Ilongot in June 1945, when U.S. forces drove the Japanese into the Philippine highlands, and one-third of the Ilongot were killed amidst general and profound disruption.

The Ilongot describe peacetime in terms of two series of changes. The first of these is the movement of their own population, consolidating, dispersing, and then consolidating again. The second refers to the relative intensity of their headhunting. Until it was effectively banned by martial law in 1972, the taking of heads was an integral part of Ilongot feuding. The Ilongot remember peacetime as initially involving intense headhunting activity, then the absence of headhunting, then its gradual intensification once again.

The external source of postwar headhunting, which reached its peak in 1959–1960, might have been the "indirect result" of battles between the guerrilla movement and counterinsurgency forces.[91] At the same time, a major hydroelectric project outside the Ilongot area brought change there by displacing other upland populations, some of whom moved into this part of the country. These developments, as well as a new U.S.-based evangelical mission, altered the shape of social relations in the uplands. Relations between the uplands and the lowlands changed even more acutely: "Headhunting . . . became even more clearly than before the dominant symbol for Ilongot identity in the context of lowland/upland relations."[92]

Headhunting was a masculine activity; a man's first head was a valued and highly legible sign of his personal effectiveness. Men of roughly the same age in the same village tended to compete with each other both in headhunting and in courting. The Ilongot say that the envy that motivates men can have positive effects: "Everybody should move in loosely coordinated fashion so that each one, energized through healthy competition, will arrive at his or her equal share."[93]

Competition between coresident male peers is inevitably a collective concern, since the meanings and implications of headhunting go (or went) well beyond being some benchmark of masculine expertise. The consequences could be terrible. The Ilongot tell of times when they were afraid to go to sleep for fear of a raid in the night and of times when the scale of violence was shocking to them, out of control. Violence could relatively easily escalate beyond the senior generation's ability to contain it with alliances, since a coresident group was collectively liable for an insult or attack against an individual from another group. The Ilongot themselves contrast this form of liability with that of the police, who look for a particular individual against whom to address their violence.[94]

More preferably, the consequence of headhunting was an alliance with the adversaries, and it was these alliances that provided young men and women with their marriage partners. Marriages conventionally cut across lines of political tension. The political and ritual energies of the senior generation were aimed at preserving viable alliances against the risks of disruption. Although excessive headhunting could be disruptive from the Ilongots' point of view, headhunting itself was not, terrifying though it might be.

The Ilongots conceptualized headhunting and marriage as reciprocal movements across familiar territory. Feuding and alliance, headhunting and marriage, dispersal and consolidation continue to provide the Ilongot with their idiom of history and with a prevalent image of social change as a quick succession of moves in the same direction by peer groups. "Often imaged as spatial movement, the Ilongot sense of history can be represented, on the one hand, as a group of people walking in single file along a trail and, on the other, as an alternation between the focus of inward concentration and the diffusion of outward dispersal."[95] Accordingly, Ilongot historical narratives include the recitation of long series of place names, each one the emblem of the violence or some other event that took place there.[96] Violence is at the core of Ilongot textuality, and the "concept of the feud is a cultural construct used most often for looking back on events and making amends."[97] In Rosaldo's view their social order is the product of constant improvisation; headhunting and marriages were the improvisatory "moves" that made their social life comprehensible to them and made narratives of social life possible and essential.

Ilongot historical narrative, which dwells on the sites of episodic violence, juxtaposes violence with what the Ilongot say is its reciprocal, marriage alliances. The Ilongot preference for interpreting violence as a form of dispersal that is recovered by the in-gathering of a marriage gives feuding its textual quality. Indeed, Rosaldo himself does not insist on a distinction between feuding and feud narratives, so deftly do the Ilongot inscribe their raids on the social landscape. At the same time, the Ilongot preference for understanding and referring to violence as one element of a larger equilibrium is sometimes severely strained, sometimes past the breaking point, when they face violence that is excessive or excessively constrained.

Rosaldo's study is especially suited for exploring anthropological notions of cyclical time because he makes it clear that the feud, a social cycle par excellence in the classic literature on the anthropology of conflict,[98] does not structure Ilongot narrative alone. If Ilongot history consists of episodes, these are not defined in terms of *intervals* punctuated by alternating head-takings and marriage alliances. Rather, as Rosaldo himself makes clear, it is the places themselves that are the "units" of Ilongot history; the irregularity of the durational intervals between them is largely irrelevant, at least to the narrative structures Rosaldo explores. Thus, though one could perhaps describe Ilongot temporality as cyclical (Rosaldo does not), it is actually Ilongot spatiality that defines and is defined by contingent configurations of individual and collective agency.

For the Iraqw (Tanzania), too, social space marshals agency. In his monograph on Iraqw concepts of time, space, and culture, Robert Thornton explores other dimensions of how space "works" as a principle of social organization and narrative.[99] The Iraqw live in a dynamic frontier zone; their concepts of space are continually subjected to practical and theoretical challenges of various kinds. Thornton sees the region as a plural social system, rejecting the notion of "*societies* interacting."[100] The Iraqw "create social space" through repertoires of ritual and oral performance, which provide them with their "political means and ends."[101] Thornton distinguishes between territory as a "conceptual category" and territory as a "political bond."[102] According to his view, "Territory is the symbolic differentiation of space (topologization) and the appropriation of this topologized space into a structure of meaning by attributing shared and public values to places, directions, and boundaries such that it may be graphically, cognitively, or ritually represented as a coherent and enduring image."[103]

The organizing, or constitutive, power of such representations appears to be only partly in their demarcation or allocation of space. Thornton reports that narratives of events are "about" their situatedness in space (rather than chronology).[104] In fact, when the study turns to Iraqw time sense, this seems to have been already accounted for by Thornton's discussion of space; at least, Thornton's discussion of duration and chronology is largely in negative terms. Iraqw narrative includes no genealogies or other absolute time markers, temporal end points, creation stories, "history," nor is there much ritual or narrative attention to death or the dead. Authority is legitimated not in relation to the past (e.g., by genealogy) but by ritual and magical means. Evidently, everything the Iraqw want to know (in their own terms) about time (in our sense of the word) is accounted for in their spatial organization and distinctions, as ongoing matters for public narrative and ritual.[105]

In these examples, the narratives are inseparable from the formulations they communicate. That is, time and space are principles of both narrative organization and social organization simultaneously; the narratives' constitutive power lies partly in this conjunction. To put this another way, to separate the question of time from the question of narrative in these examples is as inconceivable as separating the narratives from their subject matter.

Diane Bell's study of aboriginal Australian "dreamtime" clarifies how narrative constitutes time and social groups simultaneously. The Australian "dreamtime" or "dreaming" is a classic theme in the ethnology of religion. Early work on the dreaming evokes the dreamtime, sometime in the mythic past, as a source of authenticity, not the beginning of chronology. The dreaming is classically presented as an ethnographic example of indifference to time, since the "interest" in the past dreamtime is less as a point of origin than as the self-evident confirmation of the authenticity of present social forms. W. E. H. Stanner remarks: "A central meaning of The Dreaming is that of a sacred, heroic time long ago when man and nature came to be as they are; but neither 'time' nor 'history' as we understand them is involved in this meaning."[106] More recently, Bell's observations of women's rituals led her to conclude that the dreaming is a literally vital and on-going connection of people to each other and the law. Bell defines "the dogma" of the dreaming this way:

At one level the *jukurrpa* [dreamtime] is an era shrouded in the mists of time, from which the people claim to be descended without actually tracing the links. . . . The shallowness of genealogical memory is not a form of cultural amnesia but rather a way of focusing on the basis of all relationships—that is, the *jukurrpa* and the land. By not naming deceased relatives, people are able to stress a relationship directly to the land. . . . At another level the *jukurrpa* is only two generations behind the present generation; moving concurrently with the present; its heritage entrusted to the "old people", to the deceased grandparents. It is this aspect of the *jukurrpa* which makes any attempt to establish an ethnographic base line a misguided endeavour. The *jukurrpa* is not a long dead and fixed point of reference. It is a living and accessible force in the lives of people today, just as it was in the past.[107]

The ritual songs, dances, painted designs on their own bodies and on the earth, and other elements open or activate a profoundly sacred circuitry of power that links the land, the women, ancestors and their contemporaries, and life force. Knowledge and ownership of both the songs and the land to which they refer are inseparable, and indispensable to women's concepts of well-being.[108]

To put this deliberately in terms inappropriate to the people whose dreamings Bell describes, the ritual acknowledgments that fuse land and well-being cancel any possibility of distinguishing between time and space. Performances of the songs are performative in the sense that the women are not merely *representing* these cosmogonic relationships but *experiencing* them. Indeed, women stress the individuality of song compositions (which they refer to as "found"), particularly in terms of the density of their very contemporary references. As songs are passed on, their frames of reference become more generic as their specific legibility is lost to the interpretive community.[109]

But beyond the efficacy of the dreaming performances as generative cultural property, the dreamtime itself fuses time and space in the comprehensiveness of its totalizing reality. To put this deliberately inappropriately again, the dreamtime totalizes time, space, and everything else that is relevant to human experience:

The dogma of dreaming states that all the world is known and can be classified within the taxonomy created by the ancestral heroes. All possible behaviour is covered by the moral code made known through the activities of the ancestral heroes. In the *jukurrpa* was established an all-encompassing Law which binds people, flora, fauna and natural phenomena into one enormous interfunctioning world. This Law and the order which the ancestral heroes established is immutable.[110]

The dreamtime established human experience as knowable and, in Bell's words, makes possible a "historical epistemology" in which the dreaming confirms "an ideologically fixed universe and a structural potential for change."[111]

The indifference to time mentioned by some ethnographers is generally taken to indicate an absence of temporal constructions altogether, meaning that neither sequence nor duration is measured or represented by the people involved. Yet, as the examples in this section show, "indifference" to time means many different things, of very different orders. In these examples, space is not an alternative to time, or its functional counterpart, or an identifiable component of a larger "spacetime." It would be far too simple to say that "their" space is "like" "our time." Rather, they show that what makes time temporal is not necessarily an arrangement of past and future but any number of other criteria. These same criteria, whatever they may be, make agency recognizable as both a subject and a principle of narrative.

Without doubt, the ethnology of time has tended to support Durkheim's view of time as social; however, as we have already seen, successive readers have tended to revise his view of social time. Durkheim separated the question of time into two parts: the personal sense of living in time and the collective representation of time as a category of thought. In his usage, the term "social time" refers only to the collective representation of time. Between the two parts of his question about time, Durkheim inserted a hermeneutic problem, in the form of "objective signs" by which social time could become accessible to personal experience.

Leach, Lévi-Strauss, and Geertz, in their different ways, follow Durkheim's general suggestion as to the nature of social time in their emphases on the totalization of time and (therefore) its intrinsic duality (or plurality, for Geertz). I want to stress that from this point of view, it is misleading to consider the relativization of time in relation to nature or some "real time." Rather, time is relative to formulations of social experience such as agency, narrative, and space. In classic anthropology, departures from Durkheim's approach to social time have focused on the nature of cyclical time—as mystification, as natural, or as ineluctably personal. While some ethnography has explicitly privileged the reality of linear time, more of it has tended to conflate personal and social time, on the basis of a priori assumptions about nature or the universal nature of certain aspects of personal and social experience.

To put this another way, anthropological writing on social time naturalizes social practice by refashioning time as the aggregate time sense (rather than the collective representation) of people who experience time the same way—as motion, moments, repetition, consciousness of mortality, and various forms of activity. These extensions of the notion of social time proceed from analogies to the mechanical clock, as if the clock were itself a materialization of some universal time sense. In this chapter, I have suggested that the duality of linear and cyclical time provides the classic ethnography of time with its dominant narrative form, and that this can be read in terms of a view of nature as the source or reference point of time. The central premises behind this idea have to do with anthropologists' assumptions that mortality has universal implications for human understandings of a variety of social processes.

The ethnographic examples in this chapter show different ways people have of totalizing their particular formulations of agency, including *not* totalizing them. Thus, at closer ethnographic range, European "linear time" depicts agency as having been created all at once and then partially distributed among individuals (yet without being depleted by this distribution). "Indifference to time" appears to mean at least two things: untotalized formulations of agency and totalizations of agency in terms other than duration. Some "cyclical times" appear to be in the former category; others fall into the latter.

The examples in this chapter also suggest points where the traditional approach to the ethnology of time—that is, the comparison of social times—has been overdetermined by particular premises about norms and narrative. Western notions of time imply that human action unfolds *in time and place*; the word "event" always connects time to place to their occupants. In this sense, time and place are treated as empty stages, awaiting human drama. Similarly, ethnographic treatment of narrative in the classic tradition reviewed here has tended to treat speech as inert, descriptive. Between these two ideas (about time/space and narrative) is a third: that social life is an enactment of intrinsically local and localizing norms. Finally, related to all these assumptions are further assumptions about the nature of representation, in oral and written texts and in other nontextual contexts. I think of these as assumptions about the nature of reading, in the broadest sense of the term.

These assumptions about reading, time, space, speech, and society have tended to flatten ethnographic evidence in systematic ways. For example, we have already seen that time is treated as a matter of form or geometry; treating it this way is both a projection of time's line into other formats (bent, broken, ignored) and an acceptance of the logic of linear time (repeating moments in an irreversible chronology) as the presumed reference point for all other times. The category of "timeless" societies is, in fact, largely a residual category for social times that are not geometric in form. Yet, the mythic celebrations of the dreamtime and the "cosmography" of the Tiv[112] (to choose just two examples more or less at random) are not "the same" except in the sense that geometric metaphors fail *us* in our efforts to represent them. The next chapter concentrates on the themes of textuality, normativity, and their temporal relationships as ethnographic domains and as reflexive problems of representation.

2 Relative Time and the Limits of Law

IN THE LAST chapter, the subject was assumptions and debates about time which have been most central in defining "social time" as an ethnographic and comparative field of inquiry. In this chapter, I explore some major ethnographic domains in which the universal reality of linear time is the presumptive basis for theorizing. These domains—literacy, legal pluralism, exchange, and ethnographic comparison—are theoretically related in their explicit reliance on particular formulations of linear time. Overall, pursuing these intersections of temporality and textuality, in the broadest sense of both terms, highlights tensions and convergences between Marxist-inflected approaches to history and Durkheimian-inflected approaches to time. More broadly, though, it is the classic position of social anthropology on the nature of "culture" which is called into question here. My aim in this chapter is to evoke the ethnographic debates where the significance of specific assumptions about the nature of time have proven to be of particular importance to the fabric of the discipline and have been, in turn, revealed by it.

My focus is on sites where time's varieties and death's universality are maintained *as contradictions* in ethnographic practice. The "real reality" of linear time and its official status, as it were, are socially reproduced against rival ideas of agency and sovereignty within and beyond the West. The contradictions are not maintained at the "level" of ethnographic data, since the data reveal highly varied formulations of time, as well as a variety of practices that may look "temporal" to "us" but may not be temporal in the views of the people in question. Rather, the contradictions are maintained at the level of the debate itself, which constantly pits nature, death, and change against the so-called relativities of culture. Here, I interrogate that confrontation. Time may seem to be about nature, but "nature" is also profoundly imbricated in Western states' self-legitimating claims in relation to the need for law and social control. Time may seem to be about death, but in the West, "death" is also part of the hermeneutics of the state, which claims the monopoly over legitimate violence—death being the West's master metaphor of power and control. Time may seem to be about change, but the ethnography that seems to confirm the "real reality" of linear time is largely

49

from contexts in which the change in question involves confrontations across lines of culture, class, and race.

Throughout this chapter, my discussion develops around illustrative examples chosen for the generative influence of the authors in question. Each of them has contributed a significant critique of the canons in his or her areas of concern, and in each case the critique has inspired and reinvigorated ethnographic endeavor. None of them writes about time per se, but all of them draw on taken-for-granted notions of temporality as a rhetorical and comparative tool for developing their central arguments. I acknowledge reading their work at deliberate cross-purposes, for the sake of exploring how particular assumptions about "real time" prestructure problems of cross-cultural comparison, including the problem of time.

Time and Literacy

The idea that mortality "lineates" time by dissociating the moment of an individual's birth from the moment of death, has interesting parallels in anthropological and other interpretations of the significance of literacy.[1] The invention of writing is credited with giving humans the technological capacity for "fixing" texts (that is, anchoring them in the moment of their creation), and with giving them the *desire* to do so, though literacy never functions alone in this regard.[2] From this perspective, literacy is said to differ from orality as a technology of communication by fixing a "base point" from which questions of history (and science) can be posed. Time is, in effect, realized as a successive disjunction from that base point.[3] Indeed, for Ong, the reality of linear time is so prevailing and so prior to social action that he hears every spoken word as an *event in time*. Every word is gone before it is even completely uttered: "The spoken word, however abstract its signification or however static the object it may represent, is of its very nature a sound, tied to the movement of life itself in the flow of time."[4]

This classic social anthropological rendering begins in the differentiation of literacy from orality. This is an important point. In classic theory, the significance of literacy inheres *primarily* in the distinction between literacy and orality. Time's passing is inescapable; hence, the key distinction is between literate cultures' knowledge of death (the exile from Eden?) as the basis for modernity, and oral cultures' celebrations of life (inevitably condemned to impermanence).

For Ong, the primary difference between literate and oral cultures is an existential association between literacy and death: "Once I have put the message into writing, it makes no difference so far as the text goes whether I am dead or alive. . . . once a literary work is written, it makes no difference whether the author is alive or dead, and indeed, ideally speaking, he is as good as dead. . . . The connection between writing and death is very deep."[5] One might ask why the association between text and death is reserved for the written word but not painting or decorated ceramics, inscribed stone, designs on textiles, or indeed any and all products of one's own labor, or even, following Ong, remembered speech, since he places speech *within* linear time.[6] Be that as it may, the relevant connection here is between the perception that a text is fixed when it is written and the notion that the resulting disjunction between author and text signals the author's mortality. Any time segment between the act of authorship and the present is cast as one part of the segment known as a lifetime—as if writing were death's rehearsal.

From this point of view, it is noteworthy that the fixing of texts is credited with the institutionalization of orthodoxy and the diffusion of textual authority in relation to that orthodoxy.[7] Literacy increases "certainty," Jack Goody notes, but also facilitates an "individual's or group's capacity to systematize normative ideas."[8] In general, literacy is associated with modernity through an amalgam of transformations in cognitive, expressive, economic, and political spheres. For example, Kathleen Gough traces the impact of literacy in Kerala since the 1880s in the following terms:

[The] period of bulk printing and modern literacy in Kerala has seen most of the features attributed by Goody and [Ian] Watt to societies with widespread literacy. They include . . . the modern distinction between myth and history; the separation of the divine and natural worlds, the growth of a secular society as a political ideal. Knowledge is now fully divided into the cognitive disciplines familiar in the West. There has been an expansion of linear codifications of reality to new areas, for example, increased interest in exact time-keeping and in scientific causality, as also in the cataloging of historical events and the setting of targets and goals.[9]

Literacy, then, appears to be both modernizing and generative. For Goody and Ong, the power of literacy appears to surge from a "space" between an individual and his/her authored (written) texts. This disjunction is at the heart of literacy's wider social relevance. The disjunction is a space of alienation, the site where an individual is separated from his or her "works." As a technique for managing this form of alienation, literacy is intrinsically modernizing, advancing the rationality (in the Weberian sense, among others) of the social order by stripping its "products" from its producers, in and as time. Later, I will have occasion to consider how a distinction between literacy and orality conceived in these terms parallels classic anthropological formulations of norms, social order, and time itself.[10]

In respect of its implications about the direction of sociocultural change, the relationship of ideology to cultural identity, the histories embedded in the idea of cultural diversity, and the normative and behavioral dimensions of "collective consciousness," the distinction conventionally drawn between orality and literacy speaks directly to the central issues of this book. In this chapter, I suggest that it is not the *fixity* which provides the basis for important strategies of large-scale social management but the experiential contexts in which some textual authorities (and their conventional media) are more powerful than others. European ideas about the sources of law, processes of change, legal reasoning, court organization, legal forms, testaments, as well as more symbolic aspects of law are among the domains and activities that lend conventional meanings to literacy, not (or not only) the other way around.[11]

The aggregate effect of literacy is manifest, Goody maintains, in an "increase [in] 'certainty'" and in an individual's or group's capacity to systematize normative ideas.[12] Ong reaches parallel conclusions but takes the inverse approach in focusing his discussion on the "psychodynamics of orality."[13] He explores the "characteristics" of orality through a series of binary oppositions between orality and literacy, stressing throughout the creative potential of orality and, more particularly, the logical and social-engineering advances literacy promises.[14] For Ong, the contrasts between orality and literacy are "additive rather than subordinative," "aggregative rather than analytic," "redundant [versus] 'copious,'" "conservative [versus] traditionalist," "close to the human life-world" (versus more remote from it?), "agonistically toned," "empathetic and participatory rather than objectively distanced," "homeostatic," "situational rather than abstract." Ong's analysis is that "literacy opens possibilities to the word and to human existence unimaginable without writing."[15] Indeed, he ultimately presents orality as a complex of deficits in relation to literacy. This hierarchical complementarity has at least two analogs elsewhere in the work—gender and civilization[16]—which add an implicit normative, even moral, weight to the attractions of literacy (from Ong's point of view) as against orality. Ong infers the appeal of literacy from what appears to be a unidirectional, consistent pattern of social change from orality to literacy. Literacy, Ong says, emerges out of orality in "the evolution of consciousness." He notes: "I have never encountered or heard of an oral culture that does not want to achieve literacy as soon as possible."[17] Ong's analysis does not extend to the circumstances under which literacy becomes urgent in this way and the nature of the advantages it provides.

These advantages emerge in competitive contexts, most vividly those in which agencies of the state are involved in the management of differ-

ences articulated along lines of race and ethnicity. James Clifford's evocation of the Mashpee Wampanoag Tribal Council's lawsuit (in 1977)
against real estate developers in the United States Federal District Court
(*Mashpee Tribe v. New Seabury*) suggests one sort of context in which the
attractions—if that is the right word—of literacy are unambiguous.[18] He
concludes from examination of courtroom interaction in relation to the
court's finding against the tribe that literacy dominates orality.[19] Yet, if
literacy dominates orality in this context, that domination is inseparable
from the context itself, in which the court rules in favor of the developers' interests over those of local residents. Indeed, Clifford's reading of
orality and literacy is precoded with signs of hierarchy: Indian-white,
individual-corporate, local-state, popular culture–elite culture. In his
characterization of the Mashpee trial as an encounter between orality and
literacy, these other hierarchical relations are already givens. His reference to the jury room, but not the judge's chambers, as "an enclave of
orality within the vast writing machine of the law"[20] is consistent in con-
flating social categories and modes of communication with more general
lines of power in the contemporary United States.

The distinction between orality and literacy undoubtedly does make a
difference to the nature of social experience, but (and this is my point)
the evidence reveals orality and literacy only in relation to particular
modes of social organization and relations of inequality. If the distinction
between orality and literacy traces the perdurance of separate cultural and
communicative traditions in the modern world, it also, even more obviously, tracks the struggles between them. Our contemporary understandings of orality and literacy are fundamentally shaped by the fact that
primarily "oral cultures" today are *former* sovereignties. The convention
that equates literacy with official law and orality with custom is similarly
precoded with signs of specifically European legal practice. I suggest that
this is not just an *example* of the orality-literacy distinction but its essential referent.[21] In medieval Europe, lawyers were instrumental in sustaining (or neglecting) the material records of history. Where such records
were maintained, history was bound up in the public symbolism of royal
legitimacy and "the kingdom," although this was not the case everywhere.[22]

There is a double time dimension embedded in Goody's and Ong's
distinctions between orality and literacy. Goody associates literacy with
linear time, in that he views the written word as anchoring a "base point"
in time, irreversibly disengaging a moment in time from time's cycles.[23]
The notion of a base point and its alienating force establishes an analogy
between literacy and death; the compelling power of death in relation to
the logic (literally, physiologic) of linear time is supposed to inhere in the

individual's perception of a future base point in relation to which his or her experience is a unique interval. The second time dimension in these formulations begins in the assumption that since literacy was "invented" at a specific time, it is therefore the newer and improved technology of communication.[24] This evolutionary view lends itself to historical analogy in the present, as if orality were, in and of itself, "traditional" and continuous, if not entirely static.

Of these two time dimensions, the idea of the base point is more fundamental. It returns us to the asymmetries in the relative power of orality and literacy to "fix" texts (against the passage of time). This idea derives from general Western cultural propositions that link custom and law, modernity and order, and most specifically, reading and the production of texts. The idea that an author is a "prior sign-producer" in relation to a reader is a fundamental and conventional representation of reading in the West. In Susan Noakes's view, it is a fundamental *mis*representation: "The author-reader dichotomy, which in various manifestations has long plagued Western analyses of reading, ceases to be a dichotomy when the two are taken to be not different things but different instances of the same thing, sign production."[25] Noakes's call for a conceptual rearrangement of the author-reader relationship, from priority to simultaneity, returns us directly to the development of European ideas relating time, law, and society.

The assumption that a mode of communication—or anything—constitutes a "mentality" obscures questions of how social experience comes to be capable of "summing up" in this way. Chartier's reconsideration of the concept of historical mentalities develops the distinction between mentalities and representations in cultural discourse.[26] The very possibility of ethnography or history implies not that things go without saying but that particular visions of the world, which are told or written, give proof by their existence of a certain hegemony (or, one might say, reality) that their description reproduces.[27] Thus, to cite the case studies in this book, Chinese, Mesomerican, or U.S. concepts of time can be described *only because* temporality is embedded in powerful institutions that actively contribute to the definition of the conditions of public life.

From this perspective perhaps it is unsurprising to observe that in many respects—its implications about the direction of sociolegal change, the relationship of legal ideology to ethnicity, the historicities embedded in the idea of "customary law," and both the normative and behavioral dimensions of "collective consciousness"—the distinction conventionally drawn between orality and literacy speaks directly to central issues in current debates over legal pluralism. The distinction between orality and literacy is basic to the long-standing tradition in Western scholarship and jurisprudence of distinguishing between custom and law.[28] Goody gives particular attention to the ways in which literacy shapes legal consciousness and defines particular social technologies, explicitly in the hope of addressing the comparative muddles that "led to the treatment of law [by anthropologists] as a fuzzy set that covers all or most forms of social control"[29] Let us investigate some of these comparative muddles.

Time, Law, and Legal Pluralism

Standard views of the association of linear time with literacy, it seems clear, borrow the meanings of literacy from law, custom, and norms. In other words, it is power that fixes meanings, not print. Emile Benveniste's analysis of Indo-European philology suggests that some connection among law, texts, and times is very ancient in European social thought. The simultaneity of cosmic order and social order was at the core of Indo-European conceptions of the monarch, law, and justice.[30] There was no common term for law, but order was a fundamental concept across the Indo-European region: "It is 'Order' that rules both the ordering of the universe, the movements of the stars, the periodicity of the seasons and years as well as the relationship between men and gods, indeed, among men. . . . without this principle, all would return to chaos."[31]

The etymology of the term for order reveals a root meaning "harmony."[32] The key terms with which Indo-European languages designated social institutions refer again and again to their essential orality and the inscription of the voice in the world. The words for law and justice are built on roots that invoke formulas, pronouncements, oaths, "the power of the voice."[33] Justice meant the application of formulas—"fixed texts"—which were *oral* and whose possession was the privilege of a select few.[34] Judgment was culturally defined less as a matter of deliberation than as possessed of such formulas. One term (*dike*) embraced both habit and rule, since "the 'usual' way of doing things is in reality a natural or conventional obligation."[35] The root of the Latin term *rex* (political/religious sovereign) refers to the extension of a straight line as the symbol and sign of the moral order.[36] From this perspective, the line that symbolically represents time can be understood as a consolidated displacement of the constant genesis of the world in the sacred cosmos. The ancient Indo-Europeans saw the world itself as the instantaneous inscription of sacred orality, or at least they had words that implied as much. Their European heirs devised a world whose textuality (as the work of God's authorship) was equally assured but whose completion awaited the end of time.

Ancient Indo-European mythic traditions stressed the reciprocal relationship of society and cosmos, the eternity of matter, the infinity of time, and the inevitability of change.[37] Within this context of structured meanings, the proximity of linear time to other time forms can be appreciated. Whereas Western representations of cyclical time make death the source of life, linear time makes God the source of time. Whereas the infinity of time is represented as an unending cyclical or pendular motion, it can also be expressed as an infinite line. Constant change can be conceptualized as cyclic, but linear time expresses a unique cycle (the world being said to have been created only once, by God, a "big bang," or whatever) which is itself a manipulation of the idea of cyclicity.

The idea that three-dimensional space has normative and moral dimensions thus appears to have long roots in the West,[38] and also wide ones. Marc Gaborieau, for example, notes the embeddedness of contemporary Nepalese Hindu concepts of time, space, and ritual order. The ritual cycle, which has no termini, at one point "opens" a third dimension, constituting a "season" in which gods and demons do battle and the dead come to life: "The end of the cycle . . . is not in time but represents an axis that communicates with eternity."[39] Postmedieval European definitions of time as a segment of eternity downplay but do not altogether suppress the spatial element of the relationship between social and cosmic orders in favor of the temporal. Familiar cultural assumptions about the significance of events, regimes, and histories provide examples of this point. Texts, death, order, time—these are mutually embedded, corollary notions, at least in the practice of power associated with states and the projections of state power both within and beyond the West.

Whether or not one is persuaded by Benveniste's philological approach, recent writing on the subject of legal pluralism confirms the central importance of these cultural associations in the present. In its classic formulations, legal anthropology examined the norms, disputes, and third-party institutions (as well as other forms of conflict resolution) in small-scale societies, largely in the colonized or formerly colonized world. By the late 1960s, an increasingly vociferous critical reaction drew attention to some highly problematic assumptions in this literature concerning cultural conceptions of order, power, and authority; the nature and coherence of normative repertoires; the translatability of legal concepts; the efficacy of disputes as artifacts of larger cultural concerns; the relevance of the state in small-scale societies; and so forth. By the late 1970s, these critiques articulated fresh ethnographic starting points, particularly around issues of legal pluralism and the permeability of legal institutions to ideas from other cultural domains. More recently, legal anthropologists have been concerned with the role of law in the cultural construction of identities and as a site of resistance.[40]

Today, sociolegal scholars and anthropologists in particular write about law as controlling without being determinative, variant but not necessarily homologously with *cultural* variation. The law/custom distinction is no longer an object of theorizing in legal anthropology, but in submerged form, it remains central to anthropological writing on legal pluralism.[41] That field is a contentious one. "Legal centralists" (as John Griffiths calls them) identify the core issues of legal pluralism in state law, either as delegations of state authority or according to less formal practices of recognition.[42] Legal pluralists look for theirs in the articulations of normative systems across social fields, seeing state law as only one modality of legal pluralism. A reference to legal pluralism in contrast to law is thus an acknowledgment (in theory) of multiple modalities of order both "inside" and "outside" official law, but conventionally it does not question the self-legitimating claims (including jurisdictional claims) of the law itself. A distinction between centralist or pluralist is moot— and, in terms of ethnography, theoretically null—unless it also involves the law's self-constitution and construction of "difference" as cultural practices meriting investigation.[43]

The boundaries within official law (for example, agencies whose authority is explicitly delegated by the state) and, even more so, beyond it (for example, modes of regulation or dispute processing associated with nonlegal institutions or cultural communities) are ultimately a map of the society at large, according to Griffiths; legal pluralism is "an empirical state of affairs in society."[44] In summarizing the literature, Griffiths relies on Sally Falk Moore's discussion of the semiautonomous social field.[45] Drawing on Moore's view that complex societies consist of multiple intersecting social bodies capable of generating and enforcing norms, Griffiths concludes that legal pluralism and "social pluralism" are congruent.[46] In a related vein, Sally E. Merry notes the widespread division of opinion about what constitutes the appropriate field of inquiry (official law versus normative orders) and recommends regarding legal pluralism more or less as cultural pluralism.[47] Implicit in the methodological equation of legal pluralism with social or cultural pluralism is a historical process that made law a sign of difference under certain conditions. In this way, the definitional issues relating to law are returned directly to the cultural geography of social fields.

Anthropological discussions of legal pluralism have tended to take as axiomatic a corollary relationship between the organization of *legal orders* and the social relevance of *cultural difference*. The origins of this idea are not within anthropology but within the organization of the modern nation-state.[48] The idea that law and cultural identity are each others' corollary is fundamental to the cultural self-legitimations of the nation-state, as well as to much older propositions about law as the inscription of social text. The equation of cultural difference with social field is central to classical and modern Western ideologies of the nation-state.[49] As Michael Herzfeld demonstrates, nationalist ideologies conflate geography (locale) with absolute moral categories, constituting the nation in a taxonomic assemblage of "cultural types."[50] As in Western nationalist rhetorics, this moral geography is temporalized as "traditions," as if a condition of modernity were a braiding of separate strands of tradition in the present (when, in fact, it is as likely to be the reverse).[51] In this sense, the anthropological conventions with respect to legal pluralism maintain and reproduce particular aspects of Western cultural traditions about social space as simultaneously differentiating and (thereby) textual, as if "cultural boundaries" were legal inscriptions.

The definitional debates over legal pluralism are only displacements of old, now-abandoned definitional debates over law itself.[52] To the extent that anthropological attention to legal pluralism is a response to these, they maintain a place for another debate that was supposed to have been settled, the recurring debate over rules and processes that *was*, to some extent, legal anthropology from Malinowski's time until the 1980s.[53] Specifically, that debate hinged on the question of whether a comparative ethnography of law should focus on substantive rules or the processes by which rules (and other outcomes) are achieved. The very question, put in these terms, presupposes that we can know what "law" is (in which case the comparative project is circular or perhaps just taxonomic); this was the subject of the "Gluckman-Bohannan debate." A more nuanced debate took shape around the question of whether "definitions" of law in anthropology were anything more than projections of the West's cultural metaphors for law onto others' cultural space. Even now, as Griffiths and Merry make clear, there is still no consensus on the question of whether "law" can be used metaphorically to refer to all social orders and their criteria of difference, or indeed whether such usages *are* metaphorical.[54]

No matter how energetically scholars search for the nuances of the law's power in everyday life or the impact of culture on the law, legal pluralism as a field of anthropological inquiry inevitably remains tied to legal centralism for its key terms so long as it maintains the *assumption* that official and unofficial law are organized by the same map that organizes culturally differentiated social fields. An alternative approach would be to focus on the processes by which particular legal practices come to be signs of cultural identity, as well as the aspects of cultural solidarity that are *not* recognized in the sign systems the offical law has at its command.

Attending to the cultural premises and social processes that distinguish social fields and to the local significance of such distinctions increases the possibility of understanding "alternative" normative repertoires as rival propositions about agency and order which are only selectively recognized in official law.[55] Though Moore does not advocate the idea in these terms, her approach to social fields as semiautonomous normative communities does emphasize their vertical linkage within hierarchies over time.[56] Whereas Griffiths and Merry make it clear that power is an issue for anthropologists concerned with legal pluralism, the emphasis on relations of power within social fields tends to obscure questions of how power circulates and materializes in the constitution of authority, epistemologies, causes, norms, and strategies.

Any congruence between legal pluralism and cultural pluralism only makes more urgent the problem of understanding how any social process comes to be normatively organized around categories of difference in the first place. Thus, one central problem in legal pluralism would seem to be the examination of when and where the fault lines among normative communities encode potential or thwarted liberations and sovereignties. Another line of investigation might explore ways in which state legal systems manage the indeterminacies and outright contradictions among the ideological charters of constituent populations. Gender, class, race, language, ethnicity, "culture"—these are not differences of the same kind, and they by no means map the world from everyone's perspective, since the cultural meanings of difference are contingent on how populations have been caught up, consolidated, divided, or expelled from specific modes of participation in state (and translocal and international) institutional regimes. Casting the debate on legal pluralism in terms of the polarity of official law and plural social fields within states overestimates the extent to which even official law serves as a stable vantage point in terms of which to conceptualize difference. Yet this is precisely the polarity that is central to the self-legitimations of the law "itself," as we shall see in Chapter 6.

Just as the discussion of the conventional distinction drawn by anthropologists between orality and literacy drew attention to a mythical cultural geography and history in precisely these terms, so does the discussion of the scholarly conventions on legal pluralism turn the Western eye toward time and space. Noakes's analysis of reading is aimed at dismantling the dichotomies whereby literacy is imbued with the power of law. It is not literacy, I repeat, that "fixes" meanings but powerful authority. It is not time, mentality, or "custom" that preserves oral traditions alongside the writtenness of the law but something deeper and more alive. Even law in the strictest sense of the term is a dynamic order in its own right, also improvising, selecting, appropriating, denying, and contesting normative ideas from a host of sources. "In order to exist," says Louis Assier-Andrieu, "the law must be constantly reinvented.[57] Representations of orality and literacy as modes of social ordering perhaps reinvent for the modern West sacred meanings of inscription which are at the heart of liberal aspirations to justice. In the contemporary West, liberal jurisprudence represents justice as impartial and inclusive in its invocations of the simultaneity of timeless principles of order and their enactment in the social sphere.[58]

Singularizations in the Economy of Time

Anthropological treatments of the distinction between literacy and orality, on the one hand, and legal pluralism, on the other, converge in specific premises about textuality and social space. In these classic (but ongoing) anthropological formulations, these are each other's corollary. What literacy is said to achieve with respect to determining readers' responses to texts, law is said to achieve with respect to determining social relations. The fusion of these two modes of ordering is in particular premises about the power of literacy and law to preserve specific social forms (whether thought or lived) from what would otherwise be their inevitable evanescence in the flux of time. In this sense, literacy and law "work" *against* social time, just as death works *against* a lifetime; at the same time, they *are* social time, lifetime.

This point brings us to three fundamental issues. First, in the usages I have outlined so far, agency is assumed to be universally allocated to individuals. Otherwise, death would have no collective social relevance as the cue of time. Thus, even though agency might be theorized as routinely alienated from the individual and cumulatively singularized as the sediment of social structure, seeing it this way only underscores its "original" (as it were) distribution and source. Second, as technologies of social inscription (i.e., fixing meanings), literacy, law, and death are rendered theoretically equivalent in fusing an individual's intentions and acts together within a unified concept of agency.[59] Third, the distribution of agency and its inevitable singularization and alienation imply some force outside society, a temporality outside of time, as it were.[60] The idea of some larger economy of time beyond time returns us directly to the theological distinction between time and eternity developed in Chapter 1, about time's "real reality."

From this perspective, literacy, law, and death are singularizations (to borrow a term from the realms of commodity exchange).[61] They are singularizations in that they are represented as withdrawing specific and disparate effects of human agency (individual or collective intentions, rules of action, meanings, and so forth) from circulation. As we have seen, it is not so much literacy or law or even death that reveals singularization as a means of addressing and checking impermanence but rather the *contrast* between literacy and orality, law and custom, mortality and eternity.

The alienation and conversion of individual agency into a social order by means of the technologies of inscriptive forms has tended to be taken for granted. As we saw in Chapter 1, "social structure" is a mode of timekeeping in classic social anthropology, and here I can add that it is conventionally assumed to be "nonagentive" even among modern theorists. It is true that, once singularized in this way, agency is alienated from the individuals concerned and appropriated into dominant institutions, at least in the conventional narrative forms of ethnography and sociological description. In those conventions, the actions of individuals are assumed to illustrate the rules of the group, but to extrapolate from Strathern's detailed analysis of Melanesian evidence, it is in fact the social bonds constitutive of particular solidarities which "make" a person, and make a person's acts signs of anything.[62]

Literacy, law, and death are, from this point of view, the same singularization in different registers. They are merely different means by which a social order can be confirmed as existing over time. Indeed, "over time" is key, since it is only over time that social structure can become the repository for the banks (as it were) of singularized agency which the classic social anthropological position requires it to be.[63] The power of inscription (in literacy, law, or death) to fix meanings already presupposes an "economy" in which fixed meanings are preferable, that is, as a meaningful form of capital. This fictional economy is itself the object of critique in current ethnographic reassessments of exchange and gift relationships.

These issues are not just abstractions; they are raised by history, politics, capitalism, and the classic social science tradition (among other things) to the level of a concrete sociological principle. They are prevalent in the "constituted" and "lived-in" bureaucratic organization of the modern state, as we shall see.[64] They are also fundamental to the colonizing projects (both theological and political) that were the specific contexts for the exchanges in which anthropologists would have first had the opportunity to lend their imaginations to the range of ethnographic issues discussed here, and from which ethnography continues to draw some of its power as cultural critique.[65]

Time and Exchange

Exchange is another ethnographic domain structured (by ethnographers) around an essentially theological fusion of reciprocity and redemption. The theological "sign," as it were, is in the assumption that reciprocity—

prestation and counterprestation—implies a temporality, or rather, confirms a temporality in which the individual life and social experience are also contained. As in the discussion of literacy, my focus is on the way the ethnography of exchange lends credence to the "real" reality of linear time.

In *Capital*, Marx considered the circulation of money in terms of a two-phase cycle, the commodity phase and the money phase. In the second volume, he introduced a third element, productive capital, to link these.[66] There is a double temporality in Marx's idea, and for my purposes, this doubling is key. The circulation of money takes place in time, but it is also time in itself. Its importance *as* time yields a view of history in terms of stages in the development of capitalism, class consciousness, and liberation. Its importance *in* time inheres in the constant creation of intervals within which various forms of relationships open and close as "value" around specific uses of capital, as labor, exchange, and use. The concept of modes of production—logics and practices of social relations around different types of work—makes time integral to the very workings of a society and meanwhile situates social formations in time in the sense of an encompassing flow of events.

This double temporality lends the problem of time both a means and an end—exchange and history, respectively. The legacy of Marx's formulation provides the major alternative to Durkheim's social time; yet in crucial respects they do not join issue. Durkheim's legacy looks for time in the hermeneutic details of collective life; Marx's legacy looks for time in the collective life itself, in the social relations of production and in the broad course of history. The differences between the two approaches play out as the question of whether the ethnology of time should be understood as *constituted within* history, or *constituting* it. Exchange and the nature of history are inseparable issues in this debate.

Appadurai and other contributors to his collection place the critical emphasis on rereading "commodities" as a strategy for reopening ethnographic consideration of the cultural pragmatics of exchanges "across cultural boundaries" or in other contexts where the subjective meaning of goods is significantly different for the trading partners.[67] Appadurai's solution is to concentrate on the commodity itself. His approach to the problem of "the production-dominated Marxian view of the commodity"[68] is to regard the commodity as entailing a career or life course, comprising its intersections with the biographies of its owners:

Let us approach commodities as things in a certain situation, a situation that can characterize many different kinds of thing, at different points in their social lives. This means looking at the commodity potential of all things rather than searching fruitlessly for the magic distinction between commodities and other sorts of things. . . . *the commodity situation in the social life of any "thing" [is] the situation in which its exchangeability (past, present, or future) for some other thing is its socially relevant feature.*[69]

In Appadurai's formulation, a commodity is merely a "commodity phase in the social life of a thing"; yet, importantly, the "commodity *candidacy* of things is less a temporal than a conceptual feature."[70] As a conceptual feature, commodity candidacy can result in an exchange in a more or less ad hoc way, within "regimes of value" attaching to the exchange itself, without cultural or subjective agreement in any depth.[71] Temporality, then, features primarily as a rhetorical means of connecting potentially incommensurate regimes.

At this juncture, it becomes clear what the reconceptualizaton of the concept of commodity is intended (by Appadurai and the other contributors) to accomplish. That is, commodity exchange (and exchange by definition "creates" commodities) potentially *transgresses* culture, to the extent that culture is presumed to be intrinsically bounded and local. Regimes of value "account for the constant transcendence of cultural boundaries by the flow of commodities, *where culture is understood as a bounded and localized system of meanings.*"[72] The notion of culture as bounded and localized carries some of the same legalistic overtones discussed in the previous section, but Appadurai's argument does not actually depend on these. Rather, cultural boundaries (like temporality) are important to his argument primarily as a rhetorical means of articulating ways in which "cultural flows" transgress and transcend specific localizing rhetorics and practices. In fact, attending to flows of commodities allows for an ethnography of pluralism which is relatively free of "cultural boundaries." For the boundedness of culture, Appadurai substitutes the notion of biography or career—that is, the *trans*local careers of exchangeable goods. The notion of a commodity's biography implies a linear conception of time, but this, too, exceeds Appadurai's interpretive requirements, which extend only to a multicultural universe in which people are willing and able to trade for one another's goods. The notion that a career, biography, or life story encompasses these exchanges does not—cannot—arise from the exchanges themselves but derives from the external conventions of ethnographic narrative applied to them. The "social lives of things" do not so much extend linear or personal temporality onto fields of exchange (as the metaphor would imply) as they underscore the extent to which this construction of temporality arises from the serial juxtaposition of potentially incompatible regimes of value. I shall return to this point.

For Bourdieu, even more than for Appadurai, the temporal dimension of exchange is a taken-for-granted reference to incommensurate institutional practices. The nature of time is not an issue in Bourdieu's discussion of exchange; it is axiomatic. It involves irreversible succession and therefore precludes totalization *except* as euphemization.[73] It is euphemization and the possibility of temporal counterdiscourses (in social practice and through ethnography) which engage him. The discussion as a whole is just one element of a larger argument marshaled against objectivism.

Bourdieu's concerns with the temporality of reciprocity focus on the *interval* between gift and countergift as "the essence of time." By virtue of its irreversibility, time is intrinsically subversive (although this is not Bourdieu's word) in relation to the "officialized," totalizing, time-suspending practices of science and state politics. "Officialization" is the process whereby a group "teaches . . . and masks from itself its own truth . . . tacitly defining the limits of the thinkable and the unthinkable."[74] Politics, for Bourdieu, is an officializing arena "par excellence,"[75] but it is not the only one; science and social science provide others. Any totalizing representation of social life—as involving timeless truths, for example—by definition masks the temporality that such representations (and their beneficiaries) must deny. Officialized, detemporalized discourses confront challenges wherever a counterdiscourse restores the temporal dimension, as *detotalization*.[76]

Anthropology offers a quintessential counterdiscourse in just this sense, in Bourdieu's assessment,[77] in that its ethnographic domains include precisely those practices that are intrinsically detotalizing by virtue of their construction in time:

So long as one only considers practices which, like rituals, derive some of their most important properties from the fact that they are "detotalized" by their unfolding in succession, one is liable to neglect those properties of practice that detemporalizing science has least chance of reconstituting, namely the *properties it owes to the fact that it is constructed in time, that time gives it its form, as the order of a succession, and therefore its direction and meaning*. This is true of all practices which, like gift exchange or the joust of honour, are defined, *at least in the eyes of the agents, as irreversible oriented sequences of relatively unpredictable acts*.[78]

Importantly for our own project of cumulative reading, Bourdieu is unambiguous in stating what time is—an irreversible succession that cannot be comprehended except as it unfolds, which is to say, always incompletely at any specific time. Reciprocity is valuable as an object of anthropological study, from this point of view, because by its very nature, it makes the officialized *de*temporalization (e.g., of whole social systems fixed in time) undeniable. Thus, for Bourdieu, time is not *built* of intervals but *revealed* by the intervals in exchange practices. Drawing on generalized ethnographic descriptions of the practical difficulties of gift exchange, Bourdieu stresses that a successful—that is, strategic—gift exchange involves risk, improvisation, and the deft management of uncertainty.

In practice—and it is practices that concern him—the social difficulties of gift exchange amount to questions of timing. The intervals between gifts are of uneven lengths. They cannot be marshaled into rules. The uncertainty as to when and how to offer the countergift requires improvisation with respect to timing. Improvisation reintroduces uncertainty into social practice (and descriptions of practice), and "to reintroduce uncertainty is to reintroduce time."[79] Thus, Bourdieu concludes:

Time derives its efficacy from the state of the structure of relations within which time comes into play. . . . The temporal structure of practice functions . . . as a screen preventing totalization. The interval inserted between the gift and the counter-gift is an instrument of denial which allows a subjective truth [the scheme of practical sense, or *habitus*] and a quite opposite objective truth [the theoretical schema] to coexist, in both individual experience and the common judgement.[80]

The theoretical schema (for example, organizing exchange practices around a code of honor) can be sustained even when, as Bourdieu says, "every case proved an exception."[81] The ethic of honor, in his example, "bears down on each agent with the weight of all the other agents,"[82] even though practice is at odds with the rule. This disparity is essential to Bourdieu's analysis of the productive subversion of detotalizing "officialized" theoretical models of society by restoring attention to temporality. Thus, Bourdieu positions gift exchange and the project of studying it ethnographically at the disjunction between rules, law, and everyday practice, and this disjunction is itself the object of official and practical denials:

Gift exchange is the paradigm of all the operations through which symbolic alchemy produces the reality-denying reality that the collective consciousness aims at as a collectively produced, sustained and maintained misrecognition of the "objective" truth. The official truth produced by the collective work of euphemization, . . . which eventually leads to the legal definition of acceptable behaviour, . . . has a practical efficacy, for . . . [even if] every case proved an exception, it would still remain a true description of such practices as are intended to be acceptable.[83]

Here, literacy, legal pluralism, and exchange converge in the encodings by which collective efforts to manage the play of circumstances in unpredictable (and always plural) social circumstances can be both known and denied. Or to put this another way, the very notion of "certainty" or "fixing meaning" can be understood, in practice, as an officialized rendering of a wide (and ultimately irreducible) array of practices. Bourdieu reminds us that such claims by definition arise in circumstances where they are contestable, although this reminder comes in the form of his assertion that euphemization is a "reality-denying reality."[84]

In that context, Bourdieu seems to have two concerns about time. One is epistemological: the irreversibility of time means that there are limits to what one can know from observation as a practical matter. Against this epistemology, officialized discourses supply the missing pieces, as it were, in a detemporalized rendering of society as a whole. From there, Bourdieu moves to an ethnographic point about exchange, that it involves simultaneous practices that people internalize and act on in the form of sanctioned representations, or codes. To focus on the practices rather than the codes, he suggests, is inevitably to contest the "reality-denying" aspects of officialized totalizations of society. In the context of his argument, these two concerns emerge as each other's corollary.

But they *are* corollaries only under certain circumstances. Only if the officialized rendering of society is as a detemporalized whole does the rupture of exchange expose the artifice of that rendering. And only if the rupture of exchange is inherent in its constitution in the interval between prestations is the subversion of exchange specifically *temporal*. Under these conditions, the epistemological point and the ethnographic one are corollaries, even redundant. To the extent that Bourdieu's argument hinges on the irreversibility of time, they are indeed redundant. The logical demands of his argument against objectivism require only that time be shown to be "rebuilt" (as it were) out of improvised actions and unpredictable intervals.

There is an interesting slippage in this logical argument, which is actually not one argument but two. Bourdieu himself stresses the *interval* between prestations as the architecture of its subversive efficacy. As he also makes clear, though, it is the *improvisatorial* and *unpredictable* aspects of exchange that account for the critical potential of exchange practices (and ethnographic descriptions of exchange) with respect to specific officialized claims about the nature of order (e.g., as a timeless reality). As the history of linear time in the West shows, there is no necessary contradiction between the ideas of eternity (= timelessness) and time which the notion of the interval itself cannot resolve. As we saw in Chapter 1, linear time "itself" is an interval, suspended in timeless eternity; any interval of linear time is both component and metonym of this time-in-eternity.

But there is a contradiction, a subversion, of another aspect of linear time once time becomes undeniably unpredictable and improvisatorial in character, and that is its aspect as ultimately owned. Bourdieu blurs the difference between these two lines of argument by taking for granted the "real" reality of linear time somewhere beyond the officialized denials. In relation to those denials, exchange practices can be viewed as disconfirming the social control of time, and this effect is irrespective of any "real" time beyond ideologies of power, authority, and accountability. From this point of view, Bourdieu's ethnographic claims about time are not based on his epistemological claims; rather, they are based on an implicit, taken-for-granted claim about the centrality of detemporalized totalizations in ruling elites' efforts at self-legitimation. To put this more accurately, exchange is about time only if elite self-legitimation is cast in temporal terms; in that case, the subversion of exchange is political in a temporal idiom, but it is not temporal in the epistemological sense that Bourdieu considers. This modification will be important later, since it offers us a way of conceiving of intervals "in time" (as it were) which are not temporal in themselves. It also prepares us to consider that the social architecture of exchange might be about things other than intervals between prestations. The interval is imported into exchange theory from its central position in official Western theories of social order and institutional practices built on them.

Bourdieu's logical need to find in gift exchange a sense of timing arises in the service of his broader theoretical concerns with other aspects of officialized social discourse and its denials: capital, hierarchy, canons, scientism. Claiming the critical ground between Marx and Lévi-Strauss, Bourdieu's double temporality (the epistemological and the ethnographic) is an example of the very doubleness he analyzes. By viewing practices as social production and ethnography as a temporalizing (detotalizing) discourse, he is able to embrace both a Marxian theory of history *and* a structuralist theory of myth.[85] It is Marxian in its enlistment of agents in the on-going succession of time, and structuralist in concentrating on agents' (always plural) schema but not their points of view.

To be fair, Bourdieu's objective here is to theorize not the nature of time but the methodological and tactical implications of people's exchange practices in contexts where elites' self-legitimations depend on representations of the social order as a detemporalized totality. This condition is a modern one—a modernist one, even—and examples abound. But as we shall see later, these examples are of a particular kind—that is, of officialized discourses of representation, arising preeminently in relation to ruling (or aspiring) elites' self-legitimations in nation-states. While these examples confirm Bourdieu's general proposition, they also underscore its limitations. Again, Bourdieu's argument succeeds as an analysis of official discourses and the counterdiscourses that together constitute the political field; however, the argument fails as soon as we leave the domain where elite self-legitimation depends on maintaining some notion of a timeless order. Exchange "reintroduces" time only to the extent that people's exchange practices are in some relation to the state, either directly or through agencies, interests, and discursive practices. It is precisely this limitation that makes it possible to treat "the problem of time" as a *theoretical* question.

Bourdieu's analysis draws attention to the embeddedness of temporal ideas in social relations of accountability, explicitly when he focuses on exchange and implicitly in his focus on officialized renderings of time. I have just suggested that Bourdieu's more implicit argument about temporality applies only to the domains where the discursive practices in question are those of the modern nation-state under conditions of (late) capitalism. These are the conditions—entailing a massive projection of controlling images of state forms of exchange to encompass local, interpersonal exchanges—which lend exchange practices such as he describes their power as critique either in practice or in ethnography. Broad though the domain of these conditions might be, it is nonetheless a limiting condition. Recent ethnographic work considers other ways in which exchange, temporality, domination, and resistance are mutually implicated inside and outside the spheres of late capitalism and state forms. In some quarters, as for Appadurai, the critical burden falls on the nature of the commodity itself, the thing exchanged. In others, the critique is aimed at the notion of reciprocity, exchange itself.

Bourdieu makes the temporal subversions of exchange practices contingent on a structure of relationships implied (and made real) in the state's self-legitimating discourses. This is too limiting as a general proposition about temporality, in that it seems to leave no room for discursive practices that are not oriented toward the state in these terms. In contrast, Appadurai makes the geographic subversions of exchange practices contingent only on the commensurability (through the market) of disparate desires for goods. Importantly, when the ground shifts from the state to the commodity as the immediate context in which exchange occurs, the issue of temporality (i.e., as linear time) also shifts. For Bourdieu, temporality arises as an issue in exchange because exchange belies conventional (officialized) denials of time. I associate this particular aspect of official discourse with the modern state, for reasons explained more fully in Chapter 6 and the Conclusion. Other aspects of Bourdieu's argument, and Appadurai's, suggest more clearly how the superficially constitutive aspect of exchange as involving intervals can be made to vanish into the cultural framework, or conceptual schemes, derived from ad hoc exchanges.

Shifting from the temporality of exchange to the commodities exchanged effectively (if by implication) converts questions of time and timing (Bourdieu) into questions of space and spacing (Appadurai), although, as I have already suggested, Bourdieu's argument is *not* about time in precisely the same way that Appadurai's is *not* about boundaries. In both cases, the intervals of time and space are "imports" from the conventions of ethnographic writing into the ethnographic frame; their ethnographic arguments, for reasons they explain themselves, do not require the background economies of real time or real cultural boundaries. Time does not enter Bourdieu's picture through the exchange of gifts, it is *already present* as the background economy of the state's self-proclaimed control. Time's disruptions, through direct reciprocity, come from contexts where the state's control is marginal, for example, among peasants and others who live by their own traditions. For Appadurai, too, officialized notions of time (as modernity) are at issue, but his critical strategy is not through time's disruptions; rather, it is his constructions of linear time—through metaphors of biography and career—that detotalize officialized claims to an exclusive hold on modernity.

In the literacy studies, time does not enter the picture with orality but as the background economy of the colonizing projects that brought literate and oral cultures together in the same space. When Ong and Goody refer to orality, their references are uniformly to people who have lost their sovereignty to Europeans. When Bourdieu characterizes gift exchange, he is referring to people who have lost control of their markets to agents and currencies from beyond their local sphere. When Appadurai characterizes the social lives of things, he is referring to people who have reclaimed some degree of agency in the local sphere through the world market. These observations suggest the possibility of some ethnographic reinstatement of the confrontations for which these background economies are surrogates: the legitimation scenarios in which temporal forms and cultural boundaries are central discursive features. To put this more simply, my task is to convert official claims about the "real reality" of time and space back to the contests over formulations of agency and politics in which these are relevant.

Rethinking Reciprocity

Ethnographic accounts of Melanesian exchange call for a reconceptualization of exchange and, with it, classic anthropological representations of "person" and "society," among other things.[86] Annette B. Weiner's critique of classic ethnographic concepts of exchange is highly suggestive in its focus on the centrality these give to "norms of reciprocity" as involving "discrete acts of giving and receiving" in a linear succession of "replacements." She argues instead for a view of exchange as "the reproduction and regeneration of persons, objects, and relationships."[87] Tellingly, Weiner's reassessment of Malinowski's canonical work on Melanesian exchange begins with an explanation of what death means to Trobriand Islanders:

Death is an antisocial event occurring sporadically and often without more than a few days' or hours' warning. At that critical moment, every person linked in some way to the deceased and to her or his spouse and father is on display. During the course of elaborate and lengthy ceremonies, the strength and parameters of each man and woman's networks by relationships undergo a dramatic public accounting. The loss of a person is a continual threat because, at that unforeseen moment, the living must gather together, disperse, recapture, and reassert all that they have in investments.[88]

This passage offers fresh points of departure for several of the issues I have raised. First, death, while perhaps conceived as natural in some sense, is not the regular "undoing" of an individual's birth which Western narrative conventions imply it universally to be; viewed across social space, death is unpredictable, unforeseen, and sporadic. It is a social emergency, for it occasions the need for particular relatives to make complex recuperative efforts on little or no notice, to call in and redistribute their investments.

With respect to the goods themselves, exchange links the donor to a communicative context that involves multiple registers, including messages about their own and others' states of mind and body.[89] The transfer of goods from one individual to another, as detachment and attachment, constitutes the recipient as a "growing" person.[90] Indeed, the importance of the gift is its regenerative power. Over the long term, over "social and cosmic time," gifts regenerate life.[91] Importantly, the regeneration of life is conceived not as a matter of descent but as social reproduction, the regenerative power of the gift. And the gift is itself gendered.[92]

In her essay on *kula* exchange among the Gawans of Melanesia, Nancy Munn also moves away from a background economy of time toward an interpretive schema more fully grounded in the ethnography itself. The kula is "a mode of action through which, over time, an actor concentrates into himself symbols of influence or control that are sedimentations and icons of the acts which produce them."[93] Thus, the exchange system both constructs a space-time and gives the actor a medium by which to control it: A "kula career . . . consists of [an actor's] ongoing reproduction of basic acts of influence" in the movement of shells across the field of action defined by the kula itself.[94] Kula exchange is not *in time*, in Munn's view; it *is* time.[95] Munn uses the term "spacetime" to refer to the ways exchange signifies social space and social time simultaneously. The spatiotemporality of exchanges is intrinsic to their relevance and reality as an intersubjective social form.[96] For Gawans, exchange simultaneously constitutes persons, social fields, and agency:

An intersubjective spacetime is a multidimensional, symbolic order and process— a spacetime of self-other relations constituted in terms of and by means of specific types of practice. A given type of act or practice forms a spatiotemporal process, a particular *mode* of spacetime. Defined abstractly, the specifically spatiotemporal features of this process consist of relations, such as those of distance, location (including geographical domains of space), and directionality; duration or continuance, succession, timing (including temporal coordination and relative speed of activities), and so forth. . . . a mode of spacetime defines a form in terms of which the world is experienced by the agents whose actions produce it. However, . . . not only do the agents produce their world in a particular form, but they may also be seen as producing themselves or aspects of themselves in the same process.[97]

Importantly, Munn's analysis of Gawan exchange is anchored in Gawan idioms of time and agency; there is no "background" economy of time, space, or agency in the ethnographic narrative. The meaning of exchange for Gawans is fundamentally in their "culturally defined types of act and practice,"[98] how these are embodied (e.g., as giving or receiving food), and the moral transformations that these acts entail. Like Bourdieu, Munn searches for critical ground between structuralism and phenomenology; however, in contrast to Bourdieu, Munn locates this ground in the ethnographic question of how Gawans ascribe different forms of agency with moral value.

As noted, Weiner and Munn explicitly offer their ethnographies as critiques of conventional anthropological formulations of knowledge, social form, exchange, time, space, and gender. Marilyn Strathern's critique takes a reflexive form; she explores the implications of "the gender of the gift" in Melanesia for anthropological understandings of society itself. The book opens with a summary description of how the gendered gift unsettles Western assumptions that acts are neutral, self-evident events, politically relevant only to the extent that they fall within someone's control:

In the conventional anthropological view, gift exchange is taken as a self-evident act, a transaction that happens to deploy items of various kinds, including male or female ones, as assets or resources at the transactor's disposal. The behavior is assumed to be categorically neutral with power residing in the control of the event and of the assets, as in the manner in which "men" control "women." But in Melanesian culture, such behavior is not construed as gender neutral: it itself is gendered, and men's and women's ability to transact with this or that item stems from the power this gendering gives some persons at the expense of others, as does the necessity and burden of carrying through transactions.[99]

From the outset, Strathern carries these observations to the double question of gender and culture which frames her study. It is a double frame in that she is concerned not only with Melanesian ideas of gender and gifting but also with the Western knowledge practices that make these difficult to understand in anthropology (which regards cultures as different, yet comparable) and feminism (which, in the formulations that most concern Strathern, makes women different, yet in universal ways). The ethical and ethnographic force behind the relativistic idea that "the same questions must be asked . . . everywhere" derives from the Western practice of viewing societies as wholes consisting of parts, and individuals as "homologues of societies."[100] Ultimately, the book dismantles this assumption by means of an ethnographically informed reflexive critique and, in so doing, becomes an essay on the limits of comparison and the potential incommensurateness of cultures. This makes for a provocative conclusion, since the book involves a juxtaposition of "Western" and "Melanesian" ideas throughout.

Strathern reflects on the specifically Western assumptions that conventionally charter the taxonomic comparisons of classic ethnology:

The notion that diverse cultural forms generate multitudinous different "societies" belongs to a premise of commodity logic, that what people make are "things" (including abstract things such as cultures and societies). "Cultural" activity is the diversification of as well as proliferation of things. This lays the trap for doubly snared perplexities of universalism and relativity.[101]

In Melanesia, however, societies "cannot be counted separately" since people view their own societies as implicated in others', just as gifts become absorbed into the bodies of their recipients, transformed and transforming there. One can "compare" under these conditions only to the extent that the societies in question embody different versions of ceremonial exchange. Thus, it is not possible, from this perspective, to "compare" Melanesian "society" to "Western society," because at no point do Melanesian social concepts yield an "entity" to be compared and because, in Western terms, Western society "itself" does not exist except as generalizations.[102] By her own account, Strathern's narrative organization reflects her understanding of Melanesian synthetic forms,[103] successively revealing what is concealed (in this case, by means of the dialogue "between" Melanesian and Western knowledge practices), but the exercise has limits:

> Taking apart the image of the commodity (things produced for exchange) uncovers the gift (things produced by exchange); but the formula rests on a Western dichotomy in the first place. The result is that the knowledge I produce about Melanesian societies is not commensurate with the form that knowledge takes there. The fact that my argument works through innumerable oppositions and contrasts, for example, is an escapable residue of a commodity logic concerned with the value or relations between things. . . . Were one to juxtapose Melanesian knowledge practices, one would instead be faced with the presentation of a (single) synthetic image. Relations would be made apparent not through the classification of its attributes, but through its decomposition into a series of other images. Men's body would be seen to contain the children of women, and looking at the maternal body would be looking at the transactions of men.[104]

Strathern's conclusion that Melanesian and Western knowledge practices are incommensurate is *the* finding that accounts for the book's central problem and its narrative organization. As the work itself demonstrates, such a finding does not defeat ethnography (in the field or in writing); rather, it *insists* on ethnography. We can consider specifically how the issue of (in)commensurability answers to the problem of the (false) economies of time and space which circulate through the ethnographic traditions surrounding literacy, legal pluralism, and exchange.

The ethnographic fields of literacy, exchange and customary law are marked out by related features. The anthropological treatments of the distinction between literacy and orality, gifts and rational economies, law and custom converge in specific premises about time, textuality, and social space. Importantly, but always tacitly, they enlist "the other" as the foil for specific renderings of modernity and its necessity.[105] In each case, that necessity is mandated by time in theory, but in each case, the relativities of time arise as the obverse of the real projections of state power over social groups at home and abroad, through law. State law is not the direct object of inquiry of any of these fields (even classic legal anthropology did not focus on official law); yet we cannot understand how these fields operate without knowing in advance how state law functions within and across them, as the reality that makes cultural difference a commentary on "our" times. In each case, we have seen that time arises not from the ethnographic ground on which it is played out as a relative question but from the temporal assumptions embedded in specific state practices—bureaucratic administration, taxation and the regulation of economic life, and through a variety of executive, legislative and judicial powers.

The fusion of the temporal and the legal, and confusion of the legal with the temporal, inhere, then, in particular premises about the power of literacy, money, and law. This power is no mere metaphor. The theorizations of social time are about historical circumstances in which state power affects particular "others" in specific situations involving their expressivity, property, and autonomy. This is why we can return to the real world dilemmas through the ethnographic debates over time.

In each case I have discussed here—literacy, exchange, and law—the theoretical conventions claim to confirm the "real reality" of linear time. It is the claimed reality of linear time that that creates the problem of time, as I explained at the outset. In each of the three areas I have discussed here, the specifically temporal element enters the picture through a specific distinction between a "them" and an "us." Linear time becomes part of the meaning of literacy through its distinction from orality. The interval becomes the subversive property of gift exchange in contrast to the self-proclaimed rationality of officialized money economies. Modernity enters the law via its distinction from custom and its associations with past times. But as is probably obvious by now, these are not neutral taxonomic differences. They are "the difference" that marks social categories with particular signs.

Habit may teach us to read the categories as if they could exist independently of their differentiating signs. That habit can mislead us into imagining that there are people whom orality frees from the knowledge of death, whose gifts make playful havoc with the weight of debt, and whose customs make sentiment sovereign. Putting the matter this way makes it clear that the issue is not *time* but the character of subaltern groups as believers, clerks, servants, laborers, tenants, and tribesmen. The theoretical formulations that claim to confirm linear time as "real" cannot do so, since they come to rest first on the "real reality" of the signs of difference associated with practices and domains among formerly sovereign people abroad and citizens at home. These precede and precode the theoretical formulas, which are part of the historical and social context in which questions of time arise in the first place.

Those contexts are legal in the administrative and regulatory sense in all three fields I have considered. It is not the universality of death which makes others' times paradoxical; it is the particularities of their encounters with state law conceived in Western terms which makes difference seem to contest death itself. It is law that carries time afield as the sign of its own power to redeem—and to control—others. The debates over the relativities of time have been the surrogate for this other topic, and that is the nature and limits of state law in relation to the lives of ordinary people at home and abroad. If time is a sign of difference, in other words, it is because death and time are signs of power in a field of practices where that power has been contested on consistently unequal terms.

Others, notably Fabian, have made the point that time marks the other in anthropology's classic tradition; however, we do not have to stop with that reflexive point.[106] And to say that linear time is not universal does not make the question of time disappear; that is only one issue that makes the problem of time so persistent. The more tenacious issue is the one I have implied throughout: the misrepresentation of "the others" as failing to grasp the significance of the cultural varieties in *their* environments. Contemporary ethnography is replete with evidence of ordinary people's alertness to the range of power practices people employ in their presence, and their own signs for these. If the reflexive critique hits the mark, so to speak, it reveals only that the theoretical question retraces a well-trodden path of real-world encounters and crossed purposes; we can look to the same ground to find new ethnographic questions.[107]

The official Western proximity of textuality and temporality with which I began this chapter is itself a subject of critique and reformulation, and these are suggestive for reconceptualizing an anthropology of time that does not presuppose what time is. In her essay on Mikhail Bakhtin's approach to literary forms, Julia Kristeva explores "the literary word" as "an *intersection of textual surfaces*," that is, as a dynamic point of contact among texts that, in use, accounts for their meanings.[108] Drawing on Bakhtin's approach, she envisions "the word" as "a dialogue among several writings: that of the writer, the addressee (or the character), and the contemporary or earlier cultural context."[109] Following Kristeva, the meanings of words are never fixed, except provisionally in practice. From this perspective, it is not literacy that fixes texts but institutionalized canons of reading, which deny readers the possibility of a dialogue with an author through the printed word. In other words, it is not time that separates an author from his or her work but other people. The relevance of Kristeva's suggestion for my purposes is its implication that rhetorical constructions of time are also animated by the ever-changing context of living institutions, practices, values, meanings, and uses.

Time might seem to stand outside social action as its ultimate framework, but in practice, that claim can be made, and made relevant, only *in* action. Kristeva's suggestion, as applied to time (which is the corollary of her concern with texts), underscores the highly improvisatory and contingent character of the very institutions whose claims to represent—to be—"society" are most convincing. Viewing time's "forms" as produced by the interplay of forces within and around social institutions draws attention to the institutional settings in which the nature of time and its meanings are asserted and contested.

In sum, the idea of "social time" as it has been handled in anthropology's long ethnographic tradition has, for the most part, made "time" a unified force that operates differently in different contexts but whose differences anthropologists, with notable exceptions, ultimately take to confirm the reality of linear time. Another starting point, less cautious but more promising, since it lends itself more readily to empirical investigation and the incommensurabilities that demand our attention, is that the meanings of "time" are themselves variable and unsettled, except to the extent that social institutions (or, more accurately, the people who claim to speak for them) can make convincing claims otherwise. At a minimum, we can surely say that time is not a property of whole societies, except to the extent (and that is inevitably limited) to which institutions of government, economy, or other disciplinary regimes are generally implicated in people's lives. Class, occupation, colonialism, and gender—all differences of different kinds—are just some of the social divisions that also divide time, and divide people from their time(s) within societies.[110]

Once time's universality is called into question on ethnographic grounds, the powers of inscription associated with agency, literacy, exchange, and law can be seen as features of particular situations affecting subordinate and subaltern populations abroad and at home. I have suggested that the ethnographic frame around these features is more accurately seen as concretely legal, not theoretically temporal. It is law, not time, that has made state law and cultural difference into corollary signs. The question of time arises in theory only because the law's control is incomplete and insecure in practice. The relativities of time and the limits of law's cultural legitimacy and efficacy emerge from this discussion as two sides of the same question: What is the place for cultural difference in the world?

3   Agency and Authority

*I*N THE COURSE of the last two chapters, I have been developing an ethnographic critique of three main propositions central to classic scholarship on "social time": that time is really linear, that variations in time are relative, and that representations of time are expressions of individual experience. There are at least two major critical issues to bring forward from that discussion: first, the intrinsic circularity of any ethnographic approach to time which presupposes that cultural formulations of time are relative to "real" time and, second, the intrinsic ethnocentrism of projecting Western conflations of "society," "culture," and law as a universal paradigm of order. With respect to the first point, on closer examination, the "reality" of time which operates in social science theorizing about time itself has proved to be cultural in highly specific ways. These cultural practices from elite Western domains are continually reintroduced into ethnographic discourse through canonical assumptions about periodicities in nature (including personal death), the nature of literacy, the efficacy of law, and the significance of commodities and exchange.

In this chapter, I deal further with the second point. By viewing culture as the means and society as the end of *production*, anthropology (and, on this point, social science more generally) has tended to restrict questions of agency to consideration of the means whereby individual effort can be seen to be lodged as (or against) "social structure." Social structure "itself" tends to be viewed in nonagentive terms. The classic formulation of this view of things is that of Anthony Giddens,[1] whose ideas on the connections between agency and social structure have been influential in anthropology and in social theory: "The making of such a connection [between structure and agency] . . . demands the following: a theory of the human agent, or of the subject; an account of the conditions and consequences of action; and an interpretation of 'structure' as somehow embroiled in both those conditions and consequences."[2] The "somehow embroiled" is key, and Giddens reviews the possibilities through a discussion of Durkheim's and Marx's views. He opts for Marx's formulation in the *Grundrisse*:

Every social item "that has a fixed form" appears as merely "a vanishing moment" in the movement of society. "The conditions and objectifications of the process,"

[Marx] continues, "are themselves equally moments of it, and its only subjects are individuals, but individuals in mutual relationships, which they equally reproduce and produce anew . . ." These comments express exactly the standpoint I wish to elaborate.[3]

This passage traces a homology between individuals in society and moments in time; the connection between these is doubly production and reproduction. Giddens further develops the proximity of time, space, agency, and structure already present in this passage. The time-space dimensions are literally crucial, in that Giddens appears to visualize time and space as literal spaces (as in his references to "time-space *intersections*").[4] Construed as space, then, time-space provides the site of agency's realization: "'Action' or agency, as I use it, thus does not refer to a series of discrete acts combined together, but to a *continuous flow of conduct*."[5] In this flow, agency emerges as temporality, realized as inscription, as in Giddens's subsequent formulation of agency as "involving 'intervention' in a potentially malleable object-world."[6] "Situated practices" (Giddens's term for "regularized acts") and "historically located modes of activity" are additional key phrases in Giddens's lexicon whereby individuals' acts are registered as social effects.

Agency, in Giddens's discussion, is not to be confused with "intentions." Agency might name the way an individual's effort is absorbed on the page of history, but Giddens observes that effort has intended and unintended consequences. The unintended effects of human action appear to be more central to Giddens's view of social reproduction,[7] although this expectation goes unexplained. It appears to be consistent with the emerging distinction in Giddens's discussion between agency as pertaining to individual efforts and structure as pertaining to the cumulative consequences of those efforts. Structure is not nonagentive strictly speaking, but its cumulativeness over time would certainly make the total structure highly disproportioned in favor of the *un*intended from any single individual's point of view. In distinguishing agency from intention, Marilyn Strathern observes that consideration of actors' motivations should be expanded to include their actions on others' behalf; individuals do not necessarily act from their own independent aims. She adds: "The concept of agency does not simply set up the question of whether people can know or determine interests for themselves, and thus whether individual wills are crushed, bent or expanded. It demands explicit attention to the contexts in which will is relevant to action; and thus to how will as such is defined."[8]

Giddens does not expand on what "will" means, but what the actor knows and how "the structure" as a whole is implicated in people's everyday life worlds are central to his formulation of social structure as distinct from (though related to) social systems. It is this distinction, further-more, that opens a route by which he is able to avoid the conflation of structure and function, which he associates with British functionalism, and the absence of the actor, which he associates with Lévi-Straussian structuralism.[9] Structural models do not explain behavior, in Giddens's view, since rules do not govern action. Rather, in social systems, that is, in functioning societies,[10] "structure has a 'virtual existence,' as instantia-tions or moments," which involve "phenomena relating to *power*."[11] These observations lead Giddens to his important statement that "'struc-ture' refers to 'structural property,' or more exactly, to 'structuring prop-erty,' structuring properties providing the 'binding' of time and space in social systems."[12] The "binding" quality is the work of rules and their transformational and normative properties. Rules and norms are the theme of much of the rest of Giddens's discussion, since it is these that account concretely for what he terms the "recursive" aspect of structure, that is, the feedback between the structure and the individual through the "social system," which for Giddens, "refers to reproduced *interdepen-dence of action*."[13] Through the notion of interdependence, Giddens main-tains an active relationship between individual agents and the structure as separate entities and an active dialectic between rules and practices, at least in the ethnographic present, where "communicative encounters" take place.[14] Institutions, by contrast, "may be regarded as practices which are deeply sedimented in time-space: that is, which are enduring and inclusive 'laterally' in the sense that they are widespread among the members of a community or society."[15] But it is clear that the "sedimen-tation" to which Giddens refers involves more than just the passage of time; furthermore, he is explicit in rejecting consensus as a property of social systems.[16] Rather, "structuration" (Giddens's term for the dialectic between agency and structure) requires constant efforts of maintenance, legitimation, and reproduction: "The norms implicated in systems of so-cial interaction have at every moment to be sustained and reproduced in the flow of social encounters."[17] This normative work is essential to the recursive aspect of of social systems, in Giddens view: "Institutions . . . 'result' from human agency: but they are the outcome of action only in so far as they are also involved recursively as the medium of its produc-tion. In the sense of 'institution' therefore, the "collective" is bound to the very phenomenon of action."[18] In this way, the cycle by which indi-vidual agency is absorbed into and fixed in social structure is completed.

Importantly for purposes of the discussion here, the cycle of agency and structure which Giddens envisions in this highly influential work involves all the elements that feature in the previous chapters: time, space, and the modes of inscription by which agency is fixed in time (death, literacy, law, commodities). That it does is not surprising, since my themes have so far emerged directly from the same classic social science traditions that concern and inform Giddens's discussion and critique. Be that as it may, the dialectic of structure and agency is entirely parallel to the distinctions—highly problematic distinctions—by which canonical assumptions about time are drawn into cultural analysis: agency and structure, orality and literacy, legal pluralism and law, improvisation and detemporalization in exchange, indeed, cultural relativity and the universality of personal death. While superficially referring to very different things, each of these pairs is congruent in that—from the space of the distinction within each pair—the so-called real reality of linear time surfaces and suffuses cultural analysis.

In Giddens's now-classic formulation, "agency" itself is effectively a form of inscription, whose effects are caught and accumulated as "structure." But as indicated in his concluding statement about institutions, "agency" in this sense is also highly derivative of a view of social systems and their component institutions as (by definition) confirming their normative and political efficacy. As is perhaps already clear from the discussion in the preceding chapter, "the individual" might be implied in these self-legitimating claims, but the individual as a social unit in this sense is a theoretical implication, not an empirical reality. Indeed, the very neutrality of the notion of agency in this context belies its association with individuals in any sense of their potential uniqueness. To put this another way, the concept of agency as outlined here is akin to that of death, or any other form of inscription as classically conceived in social science—akin to death, that is, but unfurled backward, as a "lifetime." Death fixes meaning, and agency disperses meaning; one can put the sequence this way because the meanings are in "the system."

The association of agency with inscription is central to the officialized temporality of the Western nation-state. It lends to living the significance of death, "agency" referring to the means by which an individual's actions might be "recorded" (as it were) in experience over time. Death halts this production, as we have already seen, canceling the individual's agency by singularizing it in "society," as society. The extension of death into life through the cultural meanings of agency is a subject for Chapter 6, in which official Western cultural negotiations surrounding biography and autobiography are the main focus. In this chapter, I consider the more general point that agency has other meanings, at least other representations that *suggest* other meanings.

To the extent that Giddens's view of agency is paradigmatic, it would seem that agency universally involves issues of intention (whether or not the intention originated with the actor) and will. This view of agency would seem to imply that cultural differences with respect to the meaning of agency are limited to actors' different means or instrumentalities in relation to different goals, as well as their different understandings of what intention and causality are. If this were the case, agency would be analytically neutral; however, as we have already seen, the distinction (vis-à-vis structure) that imparts putatively neutral meaning to agency is itself highly charged with a cultural view of time, person, and society which limits such questions to the contributions of individuals to social systems. To put this another way, social science concerns with agency tend to be restricted to the significance of individuals in the same way (and for the same reasons) that officialized representations of temporality logically require intervals; individuals fill the "space" of intervals. But here we encounter a problem: time is *not* universally "about" intervals. Can we consider agency as an ethnographic question without assuming in advance that what "matter" about agency are individual effects on society or that what matter about time are "moments"?

I believe the answer to this question is yes. In this chapter, I argue for a view of time as centrally involving contests over cultural formulations of agency. That is, rather than view society as a whole and agency as its "making," I start with the possibility that people's ideas of their own agency are not necessarily organized in this way and with the premise that it is people's own ideas that we are after. Inasmuch as Giddens views rules and norms as pivotal in the recursive connections of individual agency and social structure, it is helpful to consider how open-ended and indeterminate rules and normative repertoires can be in practice. Indeed, rules are unlikely to be enunciated except in contexts where they have some strategic value, and even then, rules and explicit norms do not account for behavior. The only full-length ethnographic study of the invocation of norms remains John L. Comaroff and Simon Roberts's *Rules and Processes*. Whereas the theoretical orientation of this work is congenial to Giddens's formulations of structure and agency, the authors' findings with respect to the indeterminacy of normative repertoires as formal cultural expression and flexible technologies of individual interests ultimately (if by implication) challenge a view of institutions, or structure, as the "sedimentation" of agency.[19] Any cumulative "sedimentation" of norms would be contingent on people's knowledge of normative repertoires, not to speak of their commitments to preserving them or the energy with which they introduce them in defense of their own or others' interests. Notwithstanding what may be the contrary claims of officeholders, institutional knowledge and authority (who can do what to whom in whose name) involve ad hoc questions of practice, not (or not only) constituents' individual agency in congealed form.[20]

Cultural formulations of agency are similarly indeterminate except insofar as their articulation is occasioned by particular circumstances, for example, in contests over and enactments of authority and legitimation. My thesis is that time's many forms are cultural propositions about the nature and distribution of agency across social space—cultural propositions cast as normative claims. Such claims must be interpreted in relation to the contexts in which they arise. For this reason, I view time as being primarily "about" accountability, legitimacy and criteria of social relevance. One would expect such ideas to be highly individual and idiosyncratic, and I believe they are; ideas of agency do not necessarily take on time's familiar forms, if, indeed, they can be said to have "form" at all. Concepts of agency are not necessarily "for society" (though they might be) but potentially answer to a host of other, even unanticipated questions and felt needs. Agency is not necessarily at the level of conscious choice or ideological commitment (though again, it might be), since that would only beg the question of what enables people to make the commitments they do. As Durkheim insisted, the sense of time is not the same as social time.

In contrast, when time *is* represented as having form (e.g., as a line or circle), those questions and needs are predefined; agency is already for the sake of time itself, whatever that might be. Time's forms are varied, but not nearly so much as the paradigms of agency they must encompass. Alongside these, social times entail their own characteristic calculus for individuals and groups, but these derivative formulations of agency could not possibly clear the field of alternatives. Time's forms (including its potential "formlessness") derive from the disparate formulations of agency drawn into their "making," along with the social organization and substance of the crisis in which agency is called into doubt.

Previous scholarship on social time has tended to assume that time concepts arise from societies as wholes. Where formulations of temporality are legible across societies (as in the case studies in Part II), the regimes in question expend impressive quantities of organizational energy and resources to maintain this convention. Other than such cases, I have found no ethnographic evidence to support the view that temporality is a defining hallmark of "whole" cultures or societies. Moreover, such evidence as might seem to exist emerges from the background economy by which Western representations of time are incorporated more generally into ethnographic practice. Indeed, many of what appear in the anthropology of time as "time concepts" are actually representations of time as put forward by ruling or aspiring elites faced with self-legitimation problems of various kinds. To what extent these draw on or influence people's cognition of time, I do not know. In what follows, I assume that elites attempt to speak *to* their constituencies, but I do not presume their success in speaking *for* them or even convincing them. And similarly, reorienting the problem of time from duration and succession to accountability and legitimacy does not yield some impartial ethnological bird's-eye view of cultures. What I wanted was only *another* question to ask about time.

The Forms of Time (Revisited)

I use "agency," then, to refer to the broad and highly varied meanings people attach to questions of possibility, causation, and relevance around the world. Such ultimate "why" questions are culturally variable, as are their answers; they are also ethnographically grounded. Although I cannot help but associate agency with culturally legitimated social effects, I do not assume that such cultural legitimations are collective for "societies" as "wholes," nor (more fundamentally) do I restrict "agency" to situations of individual intention, will, or even action. I question the extent to which officialized representations of time and society (for want of a better term) acknowledge individual agency in anything like these terms. And if individual wills are culturally relevant as agency, then one must also ask whose. Individual agency may be relevant in theory but not practice, or the reverse; individual agency may also be taken for granted in differing degrees. These are just some of the questions that arise once one suspends the assumption that agency may be defined a priori as individual conduct. When it is individual conduct that matters—and certainly this is the construction of agency officialized by law and much of public life in the West—questions remain as to the contingencies and conditions attached to this idea in practice.

I return to the key point that representations of agency and the sense of agency are potentially radically different. Their substantive differences might imply connections and breaks in the social organization of experience, but this this does not make them separate or even separable ethnographic domains. I am limited by the evidence I had available to formal representations of agency, but throughout, I treat these as selective commentaries on and appropriations of other formulations in the same political or performative space.

I want to explore how agency is represented as being concentrated and distributed in the human world, what agency is and who has it.[21] In some contexts, agency is represented as highly concentrated; in others, it is highly dispersed; and agency, whatever its intrinsic *potency*, involves questions of supply. We tend to take for granted the universal distribution of agency from a theoretically infinite supply, but as we shall see in Part II, this conception is not universal at all, even "at home." Supply issues, too, appear to be implicit (and sometimes explicit) in public and official discourses of possibility and accountability.

Some of the more specific issues in this chapter have to do with the multiplicity of times in single institutional contexts, time's pluralisms, and the inevitable necessity of negotiating time in the practice of everyday life. In particular, I stress connections among distributions of agency in constructions of time and political and legal authority in practice. I must emphasize that ideas of temporality inhere in institutional forms and practices, even when they are given the appearance of fixed principles. "Telling the time" always involves contestable and negotiable claims. The examples in this chapter suggest some contexts in which temporal traditions and improvisations unfold, but these aspects of temporal experience are much more fully explored in Part II. There, I have had the advantage of ethnographic and historical literatures that explore both temporality and public political and legal institutions in specific cultural contexts. Here, the evidence is more fragmentary.

But I am getting ahead of myself. Let us return briefly to the anthropological debates over the significance of the variation in the forms of time.

Anthropological debates over time tend to be framed by questions of form: does form matter, and if so, how? Only Bourdieu defines the comparative issue as one of "tempo."[22] There appears to be substantial agreement among scholars that whatever the differences between cyclical and linear time, they inhere in the geometric arrangement of time's "units," be they the classificatory schemes of cyclical time or the instants of linear time. The metaphors of geometry in time have a long history in the West, though it is certainly not only in the West that moral ideas are spatialized in tangible ways.[23] The analogy between progressive time and the geometry of the line was explicitly drawn by early Christian theologians.[24] During the Renaissance, artists and architects tried to apply Christian perspectives in graphic design, urban space, and in other contexts. Specifically, since God's sight line was conceptualized as straight, the shortest distance between two points was the "most Christian."[25] In European conceptions of linear time the line's geometry is not only a metaphoric representation of time but also the literal depiction of its central theological focus.

From the perspective of the line, cyclical time is, in effect, a *repeating* linear form. From a linear perspective, nongeometric representations of time are not times at all but (as we have already seen) "timeless" because they seem to involve no possibility of sequence (repetitive or not). But it is not only linear time that "constructs" other temporalities in its own terms. Times conventionally labeled cyclical and timeless also do so, and in equally characteristic ways. Certainly, it is not only in the West that temporal discourse posits "the other" (a proposition developed by Fabian);[26] every representation of time seems to entail some message about its limits, sometimes figured in exotic social forms or in other codes. Indeed, these are central to the business of time. Every temporal form suspends or rearranges the temporality of the "other" or others; that is what formal representations of time *are*.

Still, whatever the efficacy of geometric metaphors in relation to linear time, geometry provides only a highly selective language of comparison. At best, the geometry of circles and lines understates the diversity and permutability of the constructions of time that exist around the world. It also ultimately fails even in relation to Western conceptions of time. So-called cyclical concepts of time make a case in point, since the meanings of cyclicity vary fundamentally from context to context. In the Chinese case, the cycles involve the constant waxing and waning of dominant cosmic forces in a fixed order of "mutual production" or "mutual conquest." In ancient Mesoamerica, multiple cycles were relevant simultaneously; the calendrical cycles were of fixed length, intercalating at regular intervals. The key metaphor in relation to Chinese time cycles appears to have been succession (although scholars debate whether succession is a metaphor of sequence or conquest); however, in Mesoamerica, the main theme appears to have been rotation, represented in the calendar wheel.

In premodern Europe, the cyclicity of time appears to have involved neither sequenced phases nor rotation. Rather, indigenous Europeans, when they expressed concern for time at all, drew on the alternation of complementary opposites (e.g., day/night, summer/winter, and so on). Today, we might think of the pendulum as a metaphor for these rhythms, but that image is anachronistic. The English word *time* derives from the Anglo-Saxon *tyd* 'tide'; the rise and fall of the tides probably remains a more appropriate image of the alternating seasonality expressed in early European time concepts.[27]

The difficulty with geometric metaphors in the anthropological analysis of time, though, is less in their technical and technological failings than in their inadequacy to express the diversity of temporal constructions that ethnographers have reported. Even when cultural constructions of time rest on underlying notions of cyclicity, a cycle might be a pendulum, a static circle, a dynamic cycle, a spiral. There are many possibilities. This problem is even more severe in relation to the "timeless" societies, so called because their representations of time do not appear geometric to a Western eye. And in between these rough categories, there are other nongeometric concepts of time—Islamic "packets" of time or Navaho "pulses," among others—where the search for a geometric analogy fails to encompass the evanescent or circulatory aspects of time's formal arrangements.[28]

Another difficulty with geometric metaphors is that they build specific Western assumptions into the interpretation of world views at home and abroad. I have already discussed particular assumptions about individuality, mortality, and linear time. In addition, geometry inserts *official* representations of time in the West into the cultural analysis of everyday life (in the West and elsewhere). The universal distributions of agency which orthodox canons of linear time stipulate are by no means universal to people's views of the world. Furthermore, the spatialization of time in the West also involves tacit cultural assumptions, in particular, those that link the meanings of space to dominion.[29] Finally, the difficulty with such ethnocentrisms is that they export to other cultures a mystification essential to modern Western political thought, which is that the meanings of time exist apart from logics of power and accountability.

At this point, I can return to the conventional rubrics of linear, cyclical, and shapeless times and reconsider what these geometries are "about." "Shapeless" times are not "timeless" but express the most highly concentrated dispersals of agency. Accordingly, "timeless" times formulate agency as having been generated in a single burst apart from the social sphere of experience. So-called cyclical times are time constructs built around one or more principles of closure, distributing agency in one or more finite clusters that include the lived-in world. So-called linear time distributes agency most widely, dispersing its "original" creation (by God, or a big bang, or another potentiating force) to each individual; religious visualizations of linear time anticipate that this widely diffused agency will once more be collected by God at the end of time. I have tried to stress the importance of the continuities and combinabilities of these distributions, in contrast to the conventional geometric metaphors and the emphasis on temporal discontinuities and separateness, to the point (for some theorists) of considering them as distinct cognitive maps. I have not been able to consider cognitive questions, since formal representations of time—social time—are not direct evidence of time concepts unless one assumes a priori that they are. The standard evidence does bring to the foreground the extraordinary diversity and adaptability of people to multiple times. But as I say, the cognitive issues fade as our focus gathers on official representations of time and their referents in problems of statecraft.

Although I occasionally use the terms "cyclical" and "linear" in the remainder of this book, they are relevant from here on only as references to specific articulations of time in an ethnographic or historical context, not as rubrics of comparative analysis.

One implication of this "translation" from geometry to agency is that anthropological questions of temporality necessarily preclude a standard unit of analysis. Indeed, cross-culturally, time does not have units; rather, it has different meanings and substantiations of relevance. Another implication is that social time is not singular or stable but potentially involves multiple propositions about agency and its distribution. Part of the comparative intrigue and challenge of the problem of time is the difficulty (and often the impossibility) of achieving some interpretive reconstruction of marginal or hidden social experiences that would account for rival temporalities or for temporalities that have been suppressed, however provisionally.[30]

It is precisely this sort of variability and interpretive possibility that are lost by limiting comparative debate to issues of temporal form and, in more specific ways, by focusing the ethnographic effort on technologies of timekeeping in the Western sense. It may well be that the world's temporalities are not mutually recognizable by their adepts as being "about" time at all (though some are); nevertheless, there appears to be no limit to people's ability to incorporate multiple temporalities into their daily lives or to their ability to modify and adapt to (theoretically) different temporal principles and media. In other words, the differences among temporal constructions are significant, but not because they set limits or define cognitive orientations to time. Their relevance is elsewhere, in the struggles, including struggles of the imagination, which are "the times."

The Concentrated Agency of "Timeless" Times

"Timelessness" involves a formulation of temporality which eludes a geometrical representation that would make it easily recognizable to Western observers. In so-called timeless societies, the principal relevance of time is to divide the matrix of significance from the lived-in world. In such contexts, agency is highly concentrated in the indeterminate point of transformation (I will not say "moment") when the lived-in world could be distinguished from some other; such transformations are the subject of myths, but (as we shall see) events, too, can be transformative in this sense. With respect to myth, referring to cultures as timeless misses the significance of the contact people retain to myth. (Clocks, too, are a constant reference to the mythogenic properties of time in other contexts, but that is a subject for another chapter.) Some of the most compelling and challenging ethnographic examples of time derive from societies for which time is bound up in myth narrative in this way; yet their temporality is ethnographically presented mainly as an absence. For example, W. E. H. Stanner writes of Australian aborigines in general: "I have never been able to discover any Aboriginal word for *time* as an abstract concept."[31] Other Pacific cultures are also described as unconcerned with time, though in each case, ethnographers also report myths that address the critical disjunction between everyday life and its rhetorical decentering as a hypothetical or contingent future, when viewed, as it were, from the mythical past (for want of a better term).[32]

The relative absence of specialized timekeeping technology does not in itself mean that time is of no interest or concern. In this regard, Lévi-Strauss considers the role of origin myths, which selectively endow forms with origin not to supply their histories but to stress their importance in the present. The myths "do not really explain an origin or indicate a cause; what they do is to invoke an origin or cause (*insignificant* in itself), to make the most of some detail or to 'stress' a species. This detail in that species acquires a differential value not because of the particular origin attributed to it but just because it is endowed with an origin when other details or species are not."[33] In myth, the historical process is "a form without content. There is indeed a before and an after, *but their sole significance lies in reflecting each other*."[34] It is the interface between "a before and an after" which I identify as the dense concentration of agency in so-called timeless societies.

According to Leenhardt, the mental domains of the Canaque of Melanesia are "spatiomythic."[35] "Everything that is not empirical or technical but that corresponds to the native's deep affectivity brings with it the reality of this mythic time, in which the Melanesian finds himself, finds his personality, and in which, finally, his very existence is determined. For the Melanesian mentality, the notion of time and the notion of being are indistinguishable."[36] The "reality" of "mythic time" appears to inhere in the constructed contrast between totemic powers and personal agency; this distinction is an organizing principle in Canaque relationships and, through their own group, the world.[37] In this contrast, which is accessible all at once, the relevance of concentrated agency is manifest.

The Diffused Concentrations of "Linear" Times

In contrast, the "line" of so-called linear time is constituted in a highly diffused distribution of agency, available only incrementally and in a vastly fragmented way. The image of the line draws attention to and reifies the succession of causes according to which theorists define it;

however, in practice, this succession involves multiple forms of agency widely distributed across the human population and its institutional forms—indeed, all things. Even to those medieval (and earlier) European theologians who thought of time as a segment of eternity, that is, as belonging to God, agency was explicitly delegated to popes, sovereigns, and on down through the hierarchy to each individual. Whereas the hierarchizing dimension of linear time has become more obscure,[38] the relevance of the individual as the medium of history remains an important element of the social logic of linear time.

These symbolic relationships are somewhat clearer in the historical context in which they were first worked out than they are today. Medieval European Christian thinkers saw "time" as the interval between two points, Creation and Judgment. The birth and death of the world were conceptualized as end points of an interval, a "segment" of eternity. Similarly, the individual's birth and death marked the end points of his or her "lifetime", a small segment of time. Just as a day of judgment would mark the end of the world's history and its translation into the community of God, so would personal salvation redeem the individual's death into eternal life. The passage of time, for the individual and for the world, was supposed to be the progress of its perfection (literally: becoming perfect). Full perfection was, in effect, a perfect state of completion, but this could be envisioned only beyond experience, since, by definition, experience in the world was the sign of essential incompleteness in relation to God. While the separateness of individuals was essential to Christian notions of salvation, the metonymic relationship between individuals and the world (that is, individuals as the part that represents the whole) was equally essential to Christian commitment to the relevance of faith. The secularization of these ideas in the late Middle Ages transformed some of their content but not their form.[39]

Some of these points are illustrated by the juxtaposition of images of salvation, history, metonymy, and agency in the following example from a medieval European text, *Njal's Saga*, perhaps the most famous of the Icelandic sagas. At the end, the narrator and the characters share a problem, and that is how to end the feud whose roots and rampages are the subject of the story. For the narrator, the solution is to end the saga. The chronicle of feud and fortune in tenth-century Iceland closes, and readers are returned to their own times. But for the characters, the solution is not so simple, since they must, in effect, begin time anew. Feuds have no inherent end points; so the characters of the story instead bring their society to a provisional conclusion and begin again on new terms. This happens in a vision:

On the morning of Good Friday, it happened in Caithness that a man called Dorrud went outside and saw twelve riders approach a woman's bower and disappear inside. He walked over to the bower and peered through a window; inside, he could see women with a loom set up before them. Men's heads were used in place of weights and men's intestines for the welf and warp; a sword served as the beater, and the shuttle was an arrow. And these were the verses they were chanting:

> "Blood rains
> From the cloudy web
> On the broad loom
> Of slaughter.
> The web of man,
> Grey as armour,
> Is now being woven;
> The Valkyries
> Will cross it
> With a crimson weft. . . .
>
> "The web is now woven
> And the battlefield reddened;
> The news of disaster
> Will spread through lands.
>
> "It is horrible now to look around,
> As a blood-red cloud
> Darkens the sky.
> The heavens are stained
> With the blood of men,
> As the Valkyries
> Sing their song. . . .
>
> "Let him who listens
> To our Valkyrie song
> Learn it well
> And tell it to others.
>
> "Let us ride our horses
> Hard on bare backs,
> With swords unsheathed,
> Away from here."

Then they tore the woven cloth from the loom and ripped it to pieces, each keeping the shred she held in her hands. . . . The women mounted their horses and rode away.[40]

This vision is seen throughout the region, from Ireland to Iceland. In the final pages of the narrative, the principals of the feud end it by papal absolution, compensation, and a long period of exile. The saga ends with a brief recounting of the names of the generations that followed the epoch of carnage which fills the hundreds of pages preceding.

The vision that sweeps the North Atlantic empires contains two important elements. One is its timing, on Good Friday, the day that for Christians commemorates the death of Christ and makes possible his resurrection and his role as redeemer. The other is its content, the literal rending of the social fabric. The subsequent action of the narrative replaces the image of the loom, the preeminent image of European cyclical time,[41] with a linear genealogy. History begins anew within the Christian peace; the Valkyries are not destroyed but move away.

The Varied Concentrations of "Cyclical" Times

Between the highly concentrated "burst" of agency in "timelessness" and the highly diffused distributions of linear time, the large middle range is occupied by time concepts expressed as other degrees and patterns of concentrated agency. Here, I refer to the large umbrella category of so-called cyclical time, as well as the residual "forms" of time which are neither shapeless nor geometric. From this perspective, various constitutions of cycles, pulses, bundles, and so on can be understood as involving patterns of distribution, which is to say, different degrees of concentration around one or more principles of closure. By "closure," I mean the source or sources of agency, whether they be determinate or indeterminate, human or not. A principle of closure—and I use this term often in what follows—generates and limits the symbolic forms by which time is recognizable as such in any particular ethnographic context.

I emphasize the idea of closure, in part, to distinguish my approach to cyclical constructions of time from other views that posit the origins of such constructions in cognitive orientations toward the repetition of "natural" cycles of various kinds. Indeed, in this book, I make no claims vis-à-vis a relationship between the cultural and social logics of various temporal constructions and human cognition. In this, I depart from an interpretive tradition that views cyclical times primarily as protoscientific, rationalized purely in terms of naturally observable phenomena. The perception of cycles in nature and the representation of time around a highly limited set of principles of closure are two different subjects.

Interestingly, it seems that even where the observation of "natural" cycles represents valued social knowledge, such knowledge does not mandate the relevance of those cycles as a technology of time reckoning. In his work on ancient Tahitians, for example, Oliver stresses indigenous indifference to time in any sense familiar to Europeans.[42] He does so in spite of the fact that, for other reasons, the Maohi did have a large array of terms denoting the sun's position during the day and night.[43] The Maohi also had terms for seasonal and calendrical cycles, though calendars were the business of specialists and, in any case, were not standardized across the region.[44]

Even if one were tempted to view constructions of time as individual cognition, one would still have to address the ways time constructions generally preclude independent operationalization of their terms by ordinary individuals. Chapters 4 and 5 develop case studies in which time is a matter for state specialists; in other ethnographic contexts, too, temporality involves uncertainties of various kinds for ordinary people. In their study of time concepts among the Mursi of southwestern Ethiopia, David Turton and Clive Ruggles stress both the social determination of time concepts and their essential ambiguity vis-à-vis particular referents in the observed world, be they social or natural.[45]

Perhaps like the Maohi (and many other people around the world), the Mursi consider that using a calendar requires a demanding expertise, though in their case, the deference to specialists in a sense defers from the individual to the group the entire matter of what time it is: "However highly recommended a particular expert is, one soon gets the feeling, after talking to him for any length of time, that there is another man, even more expert, to whom one should really be talking—except that he is either dead or a long way farther off still."[46] The Mursi associate the intervals between one moon and the next with the increasing "age" of the *bergu*, their term for one round in a seasonal cycle. They count the *bergu* —or perhaps it is more accurate to say that the *bergu* have numerical names—and associate each named interval with certain prescribed activities. Individuals can recite the activities associated with these lunations with great uniformity, but there is little agreement on what *bergu* it is at any given moment. This is the question that is infinitely deferred to specialists.[47] Season markers—flood, flowers, rains, and so on—are applied "retrospectively" to adjust the counting of lunations, but there is little interest in using these observations as a basis for measuring duration. Questions of age are answered not numerically but in terms of ceremonial activity.[48]

Turton and Ruggles conclude that "the measurement of time in Mursi country is an activity in which an individual cannot engage, whether in theory or in practice, except as a member of a local community."[49] They caution against speculating too closely on connections between systems of time and the social structures needed to support them. In general, they argue against equating time perception and time measurement on the basis of their data from the Mursi, which foreground the ambiguity and multiplicity of time constructions. Although technologies of time elsewhere might enable people to know the time independently, I believe that Turton and Ruggles's conclusions concerning the profoundly social nature of time have a general validity that (among other things) draws attention to how exceptionally reliant Western time canons are on individuals having specific needs and means for reckoning time.

In these examples, agency can be seen to have many sources and many different concentrations in the human world, from highly concentrated to highly diffuse. The material is too opaque to say very much here about agency's varied meanings, but it is at least possible now to see that agency everywhere is not formulated in terms of individual action in relation to social structures or (more broadly) as inscription. Our sense of the word *time* as inevitably involving some ultimate irreversibility similarly does not apply in any obvious way to the systems of distinctions implied in other representations of time.

Multiple Times

Although I have referred to "linear time societies" or "societies whose time is shapeless," these are purely hypothetical expressions used for the sake of clarifying key terms and their context in anthropological debate. In reality, whereas one representation of time may be given privileged dominance by powerful public institutions, its alternatives, some of them rivals, are always just offstage, if not squarely on it.[50]

Temporal representations are plural in another sense, too. Not only might more than one "kind" of time be available to people, so might one kind of time involve more than one principle of closure. That is, temporal forms can subsume different principles of distribution whereby some actors are endowed with agency. Linear time is well constructed for this sort of appropriation. Since it makes *all* individuals into agents (in theory), linear time can "absorb" any principle of distribution that makes *any* individuals or social classes agents. Even "nature" and "culture" can be drawn together in this way. Superficially, they involve fundamentally different principles of distribution, but these can be linked through notions of God's authorship of both or through "human nature," charisma, and so forth. For example, late medieval concepts of kingship in Europe divided the king into two "bodies," his natural body and the body politic.[51] The natural body lived and died, but the body politic was constant, "by the grace of God" (in the modern English expression) and, until modern times, at the pleasure of the pope. By virtue of their subordination to the pope, the European monarchs were directly identified with history but only indirectly with time itself. In contrast, the Chinese emperors increasingly identified themselves with time (as opposed to history).

Whereas the multiplicity of agentive principles might be explicitly denied or simply omitted in representations of time's form, they are sometimes addressed in other registers, for example, in certain forms of ritual. Some of these are easily "read" as time (by ethnographic observers), as if the ritual itself marked a sequence *in* time; initiation rites and installation rites are classically read as a sequence of three phases (separation, liminality, and reaggregation).[52] Corinne A. Kratz's reading of Okiek girls' initiation is especially interesting in this regard.[53] Kratz departs from the classical view of initiation rites as defined by Arnold Van Gennep (and modulated by Victor Turner), who situates the rites within the temporal frame of the life course. Although Kratz does not give explicit attention to the question of Okiek temporality, I read her description of the rites as an inversion of the canonical anthropological formula which locates ritual within time. Kratz shows that Okieks construct temporality by means of both the ritual form and its contents.

In Kratz's analysis, the ritual, viewed from the perspective of its participants, is an extended narrative sequence. Kratz argues for a view of nonnarrative aspects of initiation as incorporations (literally) of a narrative process—that is, nonverbal elements within a discursive fabric. Importantly, the temporality of the ritual is less in the narrative form than in its contents. That is, the transformation of the girls' status is inherent in the ritual's *substantive* aspects, not (or not only) in the progression of the ritual sequences. Most telling in this regard is the part of the ritual devoted to *pesenweek*, the confessional recitation of childhood wrongdoing before an audience consisting of other initiates, their parents, and other supporters. Kratz stresses that the *pesenweek* recitation is "precisely the point when [the girls] leave ordinary society as children for good."[54] The girls recount incidents from their past which were occasions for parental rebuke or punishment at the time but which, in retelling, provide occasion for calling parents' intemperate reactions into question:

What creates a *pesenta* is an interaction between child and adult gone awry, but with something wrong on the part of *both* participants. The child is disobedient and disrespectful, and the adult is angry and vengeful. Through this breach *pesenweek* re-create and illustrate the expected and moral norm for adult-child interactions, but something else also happens. When so many *pesenweek* are strung together, they begin to define an alternative norm in the midst of laughter. That norm is described from the child's perspective rather than the adult's. An unofficial view comes to the fore to vie with the official view of appropriate interactions . . . , but only temporarily. This unofficial, child's perspective is controlled and dismissed by the adults' laughter along with their joint *pesenweek* blame.[55]

The *pesenweek*, at least temporarily, define "a glimpse of resistance and an undermining alternative," a "rupture of perspective" in relation to the idealized, adult order.[56] Kratz emphasizes that the transformation of the girls' status is contingent on the *multiplication* of normative orders which the *pesenweek* involves: "When shared blame is shifted onto the foregrounded adult, the child is herself treated more like a responsible adult in a joint relation. When her relations with adults start anew with *pesenweek* absolution, then, a narrative image also begins to project the more equal adult relation to come."[57] Although the initiation rites unfold according to a standard sequencing of events, the girls' transformation of status is accomplished not in time but in the new mutuality of their relationship with adults, which, to borrow Kratz's word, "flickers" in the provisional acknowledgment of alternative moral orders.[58] The ritual seals the irreversibility of that transformation, but importantly, the transformation occurs within the ritual, not as its product or outcome. To put this another way, the temporality implicit in the ritual is inherent in the multiplication of normative orders achieved through the girls' narratives of their resistance and the accommodation of these within a single ritual form.

It is evident in Kratz's account of initiation as well as otherwise disparate contexts that agency can be reclaimed and redistributed. For example, baptism and godparenting (*compadrazgo*) define a "second birth" that gives the social group the power to create a person; natural birth might be dirty and polluting, but second birth is clean, cleansing, and sacred.[59] In the United States, the "born-again" experience is explicitly defined by believers as the addition or substitution of a sacred principle of closure to secular, mundane life.[60]

Yet other examples of personal transformation around new or additional principles of closure are to be found in succession rites. Traditionally, candidates for ritual chiefship in West Africa were members of a royal or chiefly clan or lineage and were understood to be otherwise ordinary mortal men. The chiefship, on the other hand, was associated with extraordinary powers, the regulation of rains and other enduring natural cycles (that is, culturally conceived as natural). The problem of concentrating so much agency in an ordinary individual and managing that concentration was addressed in the practice of chiefship itself, as well as ritually.[61] Among the Bashu of eastern Zaire, the chiefship (as opposed to the chief) defined cycles of time. When the ritual chief died or failed to ritually protect the land, pollution, always present, accumulated along with other negative social effects, resulting in famine: "The power of chiefship . . . is thus seen as fluctuating through time. It is, in fact, viewed as an almost organic substance that grows, declines, and is reborn. . . . Thus the waxing and waning of the land, cycles of plenty and famine, are directly tied to the waxing and waning of chiefship."[62] The role of the ritual chief was complex; at its core was the necessity that he absorb the pollution that otherwise put the community at risk, by fixing it in his own body.

The installation rites of the ritual chief emphasized his role as a (temporary) purifying reservoir of the world's constantly circulating negative agency. Among the Bashu, the investiture ceremony unfolded around the central imagery of the new ritual chief's social rebirth.[63] The candidate was given a funeral and then a surrogate mother and finally a new social identity as ritual chief. Indeed, throughout central and western Africa the dominant mode of the investiture ceremony was that of the funeral; the candidate died, and the chief was born.[64] Since the installation followed the death of a ritual chief who was by definition polluted by virtue of his performance of office, that pollution had to be discharged in a purification rite that was one element of the new ritual chief's installation. Once installed, the ritual chief was directly involved in the circulation of pollution from the bush to the village and back again. In normal times, or optimal times, the ritual chief kept pollution at bay by means of his ritual expertise and his ability to absorb (literally, to incorporate) the pollution that would otherwise poison the community. At his death, this pollution would be transferred back to the bush, leading the way to his successor's purification on behalf of the community. Pollution itself could not be purified but only ritually displaced—hence the importance of maintaining the succession of ritual chiefship and the installation ritual itself.

In the Bashu example, agency is redistributed through the personal transformation of the chiefly candidate at the moment of his succession. Redistribution can also be accomplished in other ways, for instance, through images of reversibility. David Pocock writes of Vishnu in these terms; the god can move forward and back in time along an axis that crosscuts the ages of the world.[65] Hindu cosmology makes reversibility a kind of sequencing, as agency is reordered within a closed system of time.

Temporal Pluralism

We have seen how temporal constructions multiply times internally, through multiple points of departure or principles of closure.[66] Next, I turn to the related issue of temporal pluralism, the coexistence of multiple time constructions within social fields. In practice, the proliferation of times has many causes, some internal, some external. New forms of time are regularly introduced or imposed through people's participation in social institutions, such as work, school, religious or political ritual, or law. The ethnographic literature from colonial contexts offers many examples of indigenous people's adaptations to European times, ranging from the timekeeping of wage labor to new forms of consciousness of history and mortality under pressure from Christian missions, though Europe is not the only source of temporal diversity in the formerly colonial world.

A major site of first exposure to "Western" time was in wage labor. In Europe itself, the introduction of the hourly wage (displacing piece rates) was part of what E. P. Thompson calls a "radical restructuring" of early modern European society: "Just as the new time-sense of the merchants and gentry in the Renaissance appears to find one expression in the heightened awareness of mortality, so, one might argue, the extension of this sense to the working people during the industrial revolution . . . helps explain the obsessive emphasis upon death in sermons and tracts whose consumers were among the working-class."[67] In England there were campaigns against wage labor as representing an unacceptable form of alienation; its critics declared, "We can as well live under a foreign enemy working for day wages, as under our own brethren."[68] In France, fourteenth-century textile workers demanded clocks and wage labor as elite fashion taste called for increasingly complex fabric designs; however, outside of the textile factories, workers were opposed to clocks.[69] In general, there was intense conflict as the dominant mode of timekeeping shifted from agrarian to urban market models in the late Middle Ages.[70]

It is perhaps this context of contest and resistance that makes Bourdieu's term "tempo" a meaningful sign of the character of an individual's social participation: "The over-eager peasant" of Kabylia, Algeria, writes Bourdieu, "moves ahead of the collective rhythms which assign each act its particular moment of space of the day, the year, or human life; his race with time threatens to drag the whole group into the escalation of diabolic ambition."[71] The positive value on conformity which Bourdieu is concerned to understand in Kabylia is locally valued in contrast to something else, that is, what I take to be peasants' contempt for individuals who undervalue their own labor, in effect disrupting the labor market by consistently underbidding their neighbors. Bourdieu presents the tension as being between "simple reproduction" and "indefinite accumulation"; indeed, tempo would seem to be unimportant in the abstract.[72] Its importance is as a sign of the distance between rival constructions of time built around different social values, and as a symbol of the actual physical activity of work.[73]

It is possible that some of the much-vaunted "indifference to time" that anthropologists and travelers have observed around the world involves the same sort of resistance to the clocks of capitalists and administrators which Bourdieu notes in Kabylia. It is not resistance that pervades ethnographic discussions of time in colonial or postcolonial contexts, however, but adaptation. For example, Thomas O. Beidelman describes the Kaguru (Tanzania) as using "a hodgepodge of traditional and alien beliefs" in reckoning time.[74] They have been in contact with Arab and Swahili traders since about 1860 and lived under European domination after 1880. "It is hardly surprising," Beidelman writes, "that the Kaguru have absorbed many alien concepts of time. The introduction of Western education, wage labor, Christianity, and government with schedules for taxation, communal labor and other obligations, all forced the Kaguru to take cognizance of other methods of reckoning time, however alien these may have seemed."[75] Beidelman emphasizes the individuality of people's temporal amalgams but also the relationship between their personal constructions of time and the large-scale social institutions in which they participate.

Among the Tewa (southwestern United States), temporal pluralism is institutionalized and seems to provide rival moieties with a symbolic means of balancing their differences. Traditional and Western time schemes, Alfonso Ortiz observes, "together constitute a powerful integrative force in the society, for they make it almost impossible for either moiety to attain a clear-cut ritual or political supremacy."[76] The connection Ortiz draws between temporal pluralism and the management of ritual and political competition has broad relevance beyond the Tewa world. In the Tewa case, the dual construction of time is explicit, with one strand as a Spanish import. In other cultural contexts, the multiplicity of time constructions implicitly hierarchizes local points of view, different forms of time being identified as belonging to other times or places or both.

Temporal Constructions of the "Other"

As noted, formal temporal representations (i.e., representations of time which endow it with form) differ in the technologies of appropriation by which they can absorb other, potentially rival formulations of agency. We have already considered the capacity of linear time, for example, to appropriate other formulations of agency in characteristic ways, but the capacity for such appropriation is by no means limited to linear time. Any temporal form creates the rhetorical possibility of considering (and subsuming) other times and forms of time.

For example, evocations of the time of "the other"[77] and appeals to "a better, nobler past"[78] are two means of acknowledging other temporal principles while subordinating them to a local present. Such displacements potentially involve high stakes. Herzfeld's work among Cretan shepherds details the relevance of "structural nostalgia," the celebration of an imagined desirable past, in the everyday negotiations of social relationships.[79] Viewing the present as the deterioration of a nobler past, peasants ritualize gestures of mutual reassurance in exchanges of oaths when trouble arises. The symbolic vocabulary of these oaths evokes local constructions of the past in highly specific ways, as well as the local sense of unease in the present. Thus, while distrust and competition figure importantly in people's sense of the present, they mitigate their disruptions in interpersonal rituals of varying intensity. Such rhetorical and gestural evocations of a past community based on trust are "part of the symbolic management of the present."[80]

Though by no means limited to modern times, such evocations of the past in the present are a widespread feature of modern life around the world, as are the normative values attached to them. In the United States ethnographic studies of people's attitudes toward courts and court users indicate a popular association of local historical myths (stressing harmony in the towns' traditional "way of life") with resistance to newcomers and the forces of change they represent, from the "melting pot" to "big government" and global capitalism.[81] In Japan, too, local representations of the community's past have a normative character, again, critiquing specific state agencies (in the bureaucratic sense) and roles.[82]

Evocations of the past such as these stress the continuities between the present and the past, even while they constantly reiterate the different principles on which the past and present communities operate. When such evocations are directed toward the future rather than the past, they entail broader subtexts, drawing attention to external or internally disruptive (or ameliorative) sources of change in potentially specific ways. Thus, prayer, utopianism, or more ordinary-language depictions of the future involve different means of recovering alternative or rival principles of progress and change into the present.

The project of recovering mutually contesting temporal principles is not limited to contexts where past, present, and future rhetorically converge; geographic and cultural differences also provide potent idioms for "managing the present" (to return to Herzfeld's phrase). Fabian's analysis of anthropology's "invention" of the "other" through a temporal vocabulary that distances the exotic from the familiar could be extended, in different terms, to any group, it seems. At the very least, such temporal constructions of the "other" are not limited to the West.

Each of the case studies in Part II involves a double construction of the "other," in local struggles for legitimacy and in how those struggles are conventionally "read" by scholars after the fact. Both the internal and external constructions involve explicit temporal claims and contrasts. In Chapter 4 the temporal claims of the Chinese Legalists are attacked by contemporary Confucians, but also interpreted by Chinese and Western scholars throughout the two succeeding millennia. In Chapter 5 Aztecs in the late postclassic period (itself an alien and post facto construction) appear to be committed to extending the frontiers of their sphere of influence through a campaign of self-legitimation that includes temporal terms; those terms are the celebrated object of an interpretive tradition since the Spanish conquest in 1522. In Chapter 6 developments in the recent past in the United States in the area of judicial succession involve explicit negotiations over the meaning of biography; the interpretive contest is between the partisan political camps in the U.S. Senate and their ideological debates over the state's role in the social management of "diversity." In each case, one group constructs an "other" in temporal terms that exoticize it and account for its (past, present, or hypothetical) subordinate position in a hierarchy of control.

On the basis of these case studies, it would seem that any formal representation of time is built of "readings" and manipulations of other time forms. Even "timeless" time involves this alterity and multiplicity in the assertion of a mythical order (not necessarily a prior order) to which all social forms refer. From the perspective(s) of "linear" time's diffuse distributions of agency, the relatively dense concentrations of agency in so-called cyclical time systems appear static or repetitive. From the perspective(s) of "cyclical" times, it seems that the dispersals of agency through linear time are represented as disaggregations—for example, of gods, totems, and other elements of personal and collective identity.

From the vantage point of any conception of time as distributed agency, the intense concentrations of agency in myth appear as annihilations. Lévi-Strauss's view of myth as an "instrument for the obliteration of time" makes myth cancel time by presenting all categorical possibilities simultaneously, through codes composed of binary oppositions of symbols.[83] Alternatively, myth is said to generate social forms by transforming such annihilations into formal affirmations. For example, Leach introduces a mechanical metaphor in his hypothesis that cyclical time possesses an instrinsically religious quality: "Time is experienced as . . . a sequence of oscillations between polar opposites: night and day, winter and summer, drought and flood, age and youth, life and death. . . . The notion that the time process is an oscillation between opposites . . . implies the existence of a third entity—the "thing" that oscillates . . ."[84] In Leach's view, that "thing" is the "I" or the soul.[85]

In theory, the metaphorical "suppression" of time derives from the arrangement of cyclical time, which is said to preclude a progress through time, by virtue of its total (and totalizing) exposure. As Lévi-

Strauss comments, "The open character of history is secured by the innumerable ways according to which mythical cells, or explanatory cells which were originally mythical, can be arranged and rearranged."[86] To some extent, the differences between problems of arrangement as opposed to closure are at the heart of the main interpretive question in Chapter 4, on ancient China. In China and in modern rereadings of ancient texts, rival philosophies elaborated significantly different visions of history, if not of time itself. How one interprets these tensions depends heavily on prior questions of how each "camp" characterized the innovations of the other.

In some contexts, the finite (but multiple) sources of agency posited by cyclical times are made to appear iterative from a linear-time perspective, in that the principle of closure which defines time can easily be (mis)read as a rule for repetition. This is an issue in Chapter 5, which deals with the long-standing Western view of Aztec constructions of cyclical time as involving repetition and the possibilities for rereading Aztec time as involving a particular formulation of reversible agency in relation to kingship. The Aztecs' central symbol of agency in relation to royal legitimacy was the god Quetzalcoatl, the invocation of whom (in some contexts) was an assertion of legitimacy from the Aztec point of view. Apparently, however, the Spanish viewed precisely these contexts as just the opposite, a voluntary concession of the kingdom to the invaders. No doubt the Spanish reading of Aztec visualizations of Quetzalcoatl's return to the capital were colored by their own anticipation as Christians of a "second coming."

Once again, though, it is not only the West that interprets other times; interpretation goes on constantly in all social encounters. Post-Han Confucians (or perhaps Western renderings of Confucian views) emphasized (but misrepresented) the disruptions of Legalists' ideas about time, law, and society. The Aztecs appear to have deployed the Quetzalcoatl myth strategically in an effort to appeal to the foreign elites at the edges of the Aztec zone in Maya country, where Quetzalcoatl was important as a figure of historical legend. In some parts of the Maya world during the late classic and postclassic periods, new Toltecized styles including possible symbolic referents to Quetzalcoatl appear to have displaced (and literally buried) other forms of temple worship and calendrical practices; elsewhere, they operated side by side. In the modern world, the evocation of multiple forms of agency is sometimes read as confirming the irrationality of "the other" by adherents to the notion of the linear arrangement of time. Conversely, the narrative structure of linear time is the classic "voice" of enlightenment and redemption. These are the themes of the case studies in the following chapters.

Given the evidence, it is relatively more difficult to know how societies for which time is densely concentrated in mythic "becomings" read the rival times of the world. Certainly, it is evident that they themselves are read by others as indifferent to time, or timeless. For example, Sommerfelt writes that an Aranta individual "knows no true unit of time. He recognizes neither the year, nor the month, nor the week. To the extent he cares to, he reckons from the phases of the moon. He does possess certain designations for divisions of the year."[87] Similarly, Oliver refers to the ancient Tahitians' "inattention to punctuality or, for that matter, what Europeans would judge to be their relative unconcern of the whole dimension of time in human affairs."[88] Later, he observes that ancient Tahitians "did not, it seemed, respond to the acknowledged limits of their own life spans with any sense of urgency. In this connection, however, they should be characterized as atemporal rather than patient."[89]

Raymond Firth's monograph on Tikopia ritual is suggestive in the search for the returned gaze.[90] Traditionally, the Tikopia celebrated a ritual cycle ("the work of the gods"). The circulation of sacredness in the course of this round of ceremonies was of fundamental importance. The ritual was timed according to the position of stars, the development of particular forms of vegetation, bird migrations, and so on, but these did not make up a calendar.[91] I infer that they were instead signs of particular forms or concentrations of agency necessary for the efficacy of the ritual. Firth writes, "The Tikopia have no fixed calendar and no names for the months or for the days or nights of the month. They count moons or nights of the moon for specific purposes, as in estimating pregnancy or periods between events, but they use no tallies to assist them in this."[92] A seasonal shift is marked by the "alternation" of the tradewind and the monsoon.[93] Elsewhere, Firth observes that traditional Tikopia were more concerned with the relative priority of settlement in their own communities than with remote times or places per se.[94] The indigenous populations began to convert to Christianity in 1928; by the early 1950s, the traditional spirits were said to have "lost much of their power in the confrontation with the Christian God."[95] In 1956 the ritual cycle was abandoned. At least one ritual chief kept the sacred objects pertaining to the ceremony as historical relics in a makeshift museum of his own invention; Firth offers a moving account of his visit to this man.[96] The chief had literally constructed linear time (the museum itself) across the rupture in his personal repertoire of agentive forms. The museum kept the power of the gods in the present as the past, the past serving as a vehicle for the sacred signs of agency that had no obvious space for circulation under present conditions.

Elsewhere, too, transformations of self-identity are represented as temporal shifts in the circuitry of agency. Ilongot people told Renato Rosaldo about their profound sense of loss when Philippines law suppressed the feuds that were essential to their sense of time, place, and collective identity: "In 1972, martial law brought the painful rupture in the transmission from father to son of the elaborate techniques of headhunting, and Ilongots, by the time we were again living among them two years later, sometimes said that they were no longer Ilongots."[97] By their own accounts, Ilongots associate this loss of identity with abnormal accumulations of rage and grief in their own persons, where these forces pool instead of being discharged in the normal way through the taking of heads.[98] The conversion of the Ilongots to Christianity followed these developments; they turned to Christian narrative and prayer as a means of discharging some of this burden.

Without the feud, the Ilongots also lost their primary idiom for reconstructing the past; the feud was their major "cultural construct . . . for looking back on events and making amends."[99] The authenticity of what Rosaldo calls Ilongot historical narrative is, to them, self-evidently based in personal memory. Without the link to personal experience (now that the feud is abandoned), it is difficult to imagine how such ritualized narratives as these can survive or what might replace them. Presumably this loss of contact with the spatiotemporal dimensions of identity is part of what Ilongots mourn when they express grief over their loss of self-recognition. Their experience suggests the nature of the readings people give to linear time systems when they themselves see agency in radically different terms. Of course, it is not possible to disentangle the temporal encounter in this or any other ethnographic example from its broader circumstances, often including conquest and physical force. Such disentangling should not be wished for; if time has relevance, it is not separate from the disjunctions and interruptions in people's everyday commitments but integral to them.

Agency and the Self-Legitimation of Authority

What are the implications of different distributions of agency across social space, to the extent that space is implied in the dispersal of agency as time? Time does not have an explicit spatial dimension everywhere. Official time systems originating in the West, for example, claim to separate time and space as different dimensions of reality; however, their underlying unity can be recovered in the notion of "events," which situate temporal moments in social space, or "regime," which does the inverse, or even "society" itself. More generally, too, the dispersal of agency to individuals provides for a tacit "location" of time in space, although, as preceding discussion shows, the dispersal of agency to individuals is provisional given the resorption of agency into "social structure" or other formulations of collective relationships. Social inequalities reveal other ways in which distributions of agency are restricted in practice even if they are unrestricted in theory; this is a theme for the Conclusion.

In some cultural contexts, the locational aspects of time are explicit, for example, among the Tiv of Nigeria as described by Paul Bohannan in 1953. In his account, the Tiv "indicate but do not measure time."[100] "Time is implicit in Tiv thought and speech, but it is not a category of it."[101] The Tiv indicated time by associating two events, such as markets (which give each day of the five-day week its name) or moons; however, they did not correlate different genres of events (for example, markets with moons) to form a single calendar. Genealogies also involved their own "time elements."[102] Also, "myths and legends of migration and culture origins are timeless."[103] In Bohannan's view, genealogies and myths were the only two contexts in which time indicators were made to point to spans of time longer than a lifetime.[104]

Through their idiom of association, Tiv "time notions" (as Bohannan calls them) were "basic to political structure, to the study of quasi-historical myths and legends, especially those of migration, to mystical beliefs, and to studies of social change among them."[105] Constantly juxtaposing events, location, and social categories, Tiv references to time emphasized the interdependence of time, territory, and population. Genealogies, for example, were reckoned in political terms, that is, in terms of social rather than biological relationships.[106]

In the previous chapters, I had occasion to consider some of the complexities of time-space relationships in various contexts, including the Dreaming of aboriginal Australians, the social space of the Iraqw, the ceremonial exchanges of Melanesia. These constellations of time and space are unquestionably different; yet they also have something in common. At least from our point of view, their time-space is never relevant as a totality; time and space are conceived not as wholes but always and only partially, as signs of categories of relationship within and beyond the human sphere. One way of summarizing this parallel would be in the observation that social relations do not "occur" in time and space but the reverse. Time and space are ways of regarding and representing particular social relationships, not, as in official Western convention, ways of accessing social orders as wholes. Christine Hugh-Jones's study of space and time in the Vaupés region of Colombia is particularly interesting on this point: "Different phases of . . . temporal processes are associated with different spaces within and around the longhouse," and the same "'space-time' principles" organize both the cosmos and the lived-in world.[107] Evidently, these principles do not exist as some explicit normative repertoire, at least not one conceived as such. Hugh-Jones writes that Vaupés social structure does not lend itself to modeling; it "must be pieced together from a muddling mass of statements" about kinship, group names, ancestral derivations, linguistic affiliations, geographical sites and so on.[108] Time and space emerge as part of the semiotics of food exchange (hospitality), sexual intercourse, and menstrual cycles, especially as these make up the registers of an extensive ritual life for the community.[109]

Hugh-Jones writes that "time is structured by the activities of the longhouse community,"[110] but this is time in *our* sense of the term. The temporality of the Pirá-Paraná consists of horizontal and vertical orders; the horizontal order associates directionality with male creativity (east) and female potency (west), and the vertical order with various embodiments of agency in the life cycle.[111] The transection of the horizontal and vertical orders yields three temporal systems: the human body, the anaconda body, and womb systems. These are "movable" in the sense that they can be ritually "rotated" so as to make the east-west axis vertical, or to derive the horizontal order from the vertical order. Importantly, whereas Hugh-Jones uses the language of the matrix to describe indigenous knowledge, her objective is to map a system of transformations.[112] These transformations, articulated and performed in ritual, develop an analogy between the life cycle (embodied variously) and community processes. The analogy provides the symbolic and temporal vocabulary with which people encompass the cumulative growth of descent groups and the exchange of women between longhouse communities in time.[113]

The question of how time and space might "intersect" (to borrow Giddens's phrase) is, at its heart, a question of how agency is thought, shown, or claimed to animate the social universe. In practice, this question is inseparable from that of how the universe is thought amenable to being rendered in narrative form, taking "narrative" broadly to include not only speech and written texts but also the verbal and nonverbal elements of ritual. Thus, even where time does not organize space in the sense of some actual territorial domain (e.g., in the equation of geographic distance with temporal distance), the potency of transformation, encoded as temporality, inevitably implicates specific social connections. In this regard, it is useful to consider the differences among temporal forms. Familiar notions of linear time are predicated on a universal, ongoing, and infinite distribution of agency; individuals are agents from birth (or, in some people's views, from conception). The Pirá-Paraná, on the other hand, look to ritual as means of reformulating and distributing agency more selectively and episodically. Initiation and installation rites reclaim and redistribute agency in new terms for particular eligible actors. Indeed, eligibility and, as we shall see, accountability are the major "experiences" of time in practice. Given our habits of seeing, they might not appear to be temporal at all; however, this habit is conditioned by our tendency to take individual agency for granted as a theoretical matter and to represent time as history, that is, successions of events.

Law, Authority, and Time

As cultural criterion of eligibility, accountability, and potency, the distribution of agency across social space is fundamentally related to modes of authority and their limits. It is in this sense that cultural constructions of time can be appreciated as symbolic and hermeneutic reservoirs for the legitimation of social institutions. Law, politics, and sovereignty, broadly speaking, are contexts in which some of the general contours of the relationships outlined in this chapter are most readily visible. Classic legal ethnography makes much of institutions' varying scope for the resolution of overt conflict.[114] The presence or absence of a third party, and the extent of that party's authority are the main structural features I consider here.[115]

Third parties emerge as a salient comparative feature in ethnographic studies of conflict because the third party is, in effect, the figure of surplus authority, the "extra" authority a social system can generate beyond the direct influence of disputants over each other.[116] There is a deliberate perspective in this phrasing: I use the term "surplus" to connote the inadequacy of conventional theories of agency (as equally distributed to individuals) to describe even the most routine situations of authority. Sometimes in theory but always in practice the relative strength of a third party is contingent on the other principals. When this authority is weak (or to weaken authority), parties essentially organize their own outcomes. When it is strong, they may be required to comply with a verdict they do not accept, including a requirement to negotiate among themselves. All conflict situations potentially involve some form of third party, however ad hoc; indeed, the relative strength of third-party interventions varies across cultures and situations. The question of the circumstances under which surplus authority can be generated and distributed in any particular social context is an interesting and important one because it reveals so much about a group's sense of itself as a group in relation to others.

Continuing in this very general vein, the authority of third parties can be imagined along a continuum ranging from low to high. By "continuum," I mean a hypothetical range of variation, not a typological array of actual social systems. And in focusing on social distributions of authority, I do not mean to suggest that all forms of authority are the same; quite the contrary. In any situation where the third party's authority is weak, its weakness revels a paucity of means for producing or accumulating surplus agency. Such difficulties arise regularly in the practice of politics; they can also arise as emergencies, for example, under threats of violence. Strong authority, however, by definition implies a supply of agency that exceeds the usual limits of personal efficacy. Whereas no authority is autonomous in an analytical sense, strong authority is autonomous in the practical sense of potentially bringing to bear rhetorical or physical force beyond what the disputants can successfully claim to control on their own. In using the terms "weak" and "strong," I do not mean to imply some hierarchy of relative merit but rather a range of relationships between forms of authority in practice.

Indeed, what appears to be a structural feature of dispute resolution (i.e., institutionalized or ad hoc third-party authority) is only superficially so. The superficial appearance of so-called structural features is a reference to familiar canons that conflate individual agency and structure. What social science convention makes out to be structure is more productively regarded as local strategies for marshaling contending parties' formulations of agency into a composite legitimation scenario, so as to forge the "surplus" authority necessary to the demands of the situation (however temporarily). Here again, Western conventions are misleading. In Western theory an office is not a person, but a person's "double," a twin, a successor, a rebirth, a transformation, or some other formulation. This second, the office, must have "its" own agency, however agency is situationally construed; otherwise, the office would be limited to the powers of the personal incumbent. The authority (and agency) of the office is ascribed to "society." In other contexts the "surplus" is effected by the rate of agency's circulation in social space, where it is constantly subject to redirection.

These points can be illustrated and advanced by consideration of the feud, a classic theme in social anthropology and the anthropology of law in particular. Where the dominant institutionalized response to conflict is the feud, the role of the third party is precoded with the expectation that any alliance bringing a suspension of hostilities will be provisional. It is this sense of violence as an integral and given aspect of social identity which institutionalizes the feud, not some abstract preference for violence or deficit of self-control. As the Ilongot example illustrates, the feud itself represents a distribution of agency; indeed, it is the specific distribution of agency which the Ilongot conceptualize as time.

It seems that wherever people rely (or relied) primarily on the feud as an active basis of social ordering, they also constitute time as a highly concentrated form of agency, reverberating across contemporary social space as the feud, as the Ilongot apparently do. This association is also reasonably clear in the classic ethnographic literature on feuding, although the association should not be assumed to be a cause. To say that "agency" is conceived as occurring in a concentrated burst might, under some circumstances, be a reference to some mythic representation of the cosmos, or, under others, a traumatic cataclysm of violence that displaces other "distributions" of agency as implausible from local perspectives. Thus, whereas the feuds of the Bedouin, the Murngin, the Jalé, the Ilongot, the medieval Icelanders or the early modern Scots, to raise a few classic examples, were not "the same" by any means, they all draw our attention to a construction of time that concentrates agency at some point apart from experience and actualizes that agency in the feud itself.[117] Contemporary world events provide many other examples of feuds, their formulations of agency misnamed "ethnic hatreds." Traumatic events have their own capacity to make prior conventional understandings of experience look like frail fictions, whether or not feuding takes place within a myth narrative. And as current examples remind us, agency entails notions of interest; people do not risk death for the sake of their ideas about agency, but ideas of agency are constructed in relation to contests over potentially incommensurate interests. The classic anthropological literature represents feuding as reciprocal exchange of violence, placing exchange at the core of structure. The view I am developing here posits violence in relation to agency.

I do not claim a *cognitive* link between time and the feud; issues of representation, diversity, and adaptability present themselves as forcefully in these contexts as elsewhere. Nor am I implying some association of the feud with premodern social forms or with isolation from contact with the West. As I have already explained, time addresses contestation and pluralism, not only the dilemmas arising from a European presence. Although contact with Europeans may be relatively recent in some areas of the Pacific (e.g., the 1930s for the Ilongot and the 1960s for the Jalé), even the most "remote" groups have had long contact with cultures and linguistic groups other than Europeans. Most contemporary ethnographies stress the relevance of the feud as one among several major modes of resolving conflict, as well as the innovations of formerly feuding societies with courts and legal procedure.[118] In other words, the relevance of the feud is not as a mentality but as a cultural and political idiom—which returns us to the issue of agency and how it is represented in the feud.

What sorts of affirmations does the ritualized exchange of violence inherent in the feud entail? I have already suggested that it affirms a primary source of agency in some indeterminate domain apart from the one constructed as social. This indeterminate point is not necessarily specified as prior to human experience (origin myths notwithstanding). In some contemporary contexts where violent feuding rages (for example, as

I write this, in Bosnia and Rwanda), the feud is a potent and potentiat-ing reclamation of agency from the political order of particular state forms.[119]

By virtue of its affirmation of agency from a source apart, the feud is both a political expression of resistance to the paradigms of the nation-state and correspondingly a means of social control. Violent feuding af-firms the solidarity of an individual's identification with his or her group as something other than choice and intention; the vengeance aspect of the feud is mobilized on principles of collective and absolute liability. Whether one has in mind the classic ethnographic examples of feuds or studies of contemporary violence associated with ethnonationalist move-ments in some regions, the feud affirms the group as an inherently her-metic, uncontingent domain of honor, integrity, and identity (I mean these as synonyms here). Accordingly, an episode of vengeance does not punish a broken rule; rather, vengeance connects life to loss.[120] For this reason among others, political authority can be constituted in the feud.[121]

The nature of the feud as expressing a particular configuration of agency is suggested by its relationship in practice with other political and legal forms. Violent feuding appears to generate demand for state law in some contexts, the reverse in others, as I have already suggested. In the 1970s, Marie Reay and Marilyn Strathern offered detailed studies of legal innovations in the Minj and Mount Hagen areas, respectively, of Papua New Guinea.[122] Though the examples differ in interesting ways, both deal with local authorities' improvisations with the case method, the reg-ularization of sentencing, expansions of the normative repertoire in justi-fying procedure and outcomes, among other things. Both point to differ-ent ways in which such institutional innovations required potentially fundamental renegotiation of the basic terms of collective life. In the Minj area, where local authorities insisted on treating individuals "in iso-lation," one result was a "non-reciprocal pattern of individual rights and group obligations [that] has made the outbreak of traditional warfare inevitable, since it is sparked off by the provocative acts of individuals which have incurred the wrath of groups."[123] In the Mount Hagen area, the courts were limited in other ways. Recent procedural improvements of judicial efficacy at the local level were constrained by the local prefer-ence for resolving disputes with as little talk as possible, inasmuch as people believed that a dispute would be inflamed by talk.[124]

Apart from contexts where feuding is an immediate issue, the careers of legal innovations also reveal much about the relationship of legal and political mobilization to local repertoires of agency. In Tanzania, Moore's report suggests, Chagga chiefs' experiments with expanding their authority were initially successful.[125] At first, constituents were impressed by chiefs' claims to represent the authority of the German, and later the British, administrations in what was then Tanganyika. Eventually, those claims discredited the chiefs, as constituents made increasingly vocal demands for authority whose mandate could be expressed in more local, if not necessarily more traditional, terms. Chiefs expressed the local and translocal dimensions of their authority not only in direct references to their superiors in an administrative hierarchy but also in the normative repertoires with which they justified their interventions when disputes came before them. When they emphasized their local connections, they presented outcomes in terms of their factual knowledge of disputants and their causes. Their references to more abstract rules, however, were, in effect, invocations of external sources of authority. These were eventually their undoing.

The relevance of these examples is in the evidence they provide of a relationship between political authority and particular distributions of agency. State forms of authority involve their own self-legitimating claims in terms of the agency they control and distribute ("from" the social structure "to" individuals, as it were); however, even this brief discussion suggests points at which such claims face manifest challenges in the form of other constitutions and distributions of agency. More generally, political and legal authorities draw on constructions of time in the sense that they draw on time's idioms of agency and its relative concentration or dispersal as eligibility and legitimacy. Again, integral to this point is the observation that the normal conditions under which political and legal authority are exercised in practice involve contestation from various sources, in varying intensities and in relation to different objectives. Although I believe in the practical relevance of time's distributions of agency as one element of the culturality of law and politics, I repeat that this is neither a cognitive nor a causal link. Rather, it points out how cultural constructions of time serve as reservoirs of signs, symbols of political legitimacy from above or below, as well as justificatory logics for improvisatory and radical change, and vice versa. Organized forms of resistance do not exhaust formulations of agency—literally, the sense of possibility—in practice. Moreover, it is misleading to refer to "types" of social control, since social and political expressions take shape as "cross-references," not in isolation.

II

4 Time and Territory in Ancient China

MOST COMMENTATORS ON Chinese cultural history are sooner or later drawn to the observation of the extraordinary length and continuity of Chinese ideas about the cosmos, culture, political authority, and history itself. There is general agreement as to a prevailing continuum linking modern Chinese ideas of society and what commentators take to be their beginnings in the Shang dynasty, over three thousand years ago.[1] The early and enduring establishment of written Chinese, the pervasive dominance of Confucian philosophy, the successful assimilation of alien cultural groups from the north and west, and (perhaps especially fascinating for westerners) the relatively early complexity of ancient Chinese society and its large-scale institutions—these are elements of a general portrayal of the coherence and longevity of Chinese society and culture. Of particular relevance for this chapter are the continuities and discontinuities in Chinese theories of government and political legitimacy, as well as Chinese institutions of law and politics, particularly as these are viewed by Western scholars in our own times. Although the longevity of Chinese traditions is also central to historical narrative traditions in China, my purpose here is to reengage the secondary sources that have made China a famous case in the annals of social time in Western social science. It bears repeating, even so, that Western scholarship on Chinese theories of government and statecraft follows two thousand years of Chinese historical writing on the subject.

Against this backdrop of continuity, a major historiographic and narrative tradition presents two rival philosophical schools, the Confucians and the Legalists, the tensions between them being made out to be a more or less constant disruptive force, at least in some degree. Often, commentators introduce the Legalists by contrasting them to a Confucian mainstream. The Confucians are conventionally said to have dominated the institutions of government for most of Chinese history; the Legalists had their brief ascendancy during the Ch'in dynasty (221–207 B.C.) when the First Emperor consolidated the empire by means of a crushing military conquest. Against Confucian tradition the Legalists are said to have emphasized legal rules, especially penal and administrative law, as the basis of social order.[2] The starkness of the contrast varies; the two schools tend to be more sharply differentiated in later periods, especially from the Later Han (25–220 A.D.) onward, when Confucian philosophy became the state orthodoxy and institutionalized a particular representation of the Legalists and their place in history.

The depiction of the Legalists reflects the post facto representations of the Confucians, who dominated China after the Ch'in dynasty. For reasons I shall explain, the development of Confucian philosophies as a state orthodoxy after the Ch'in collapse cast Legalism and Confucianism as philosophical opposites and political rivals. As succeeding emperors tightened their self-identification with a Confucian orthodoxy in the first few centuries A.D., the characterization of the Legalists also hardened around a few key distinctions: the Confucian basis of the social order in *li* (correct behavior) versus *fa* (law) for Legalists; the Confucian view of history as cyclical versus the Legalist ideas of progressive change; the Confucian commitment to reform based on the positive example of virtuous leaders versus the Legalist reliance on administration, rewards and punishments, and so on.

Anthony Hulsewé ascribes early Western scholarship on Chinese law to the revival of Chinese scholars' interest in the Legalists and the Han period during modern periods of law reform in the nineteenth and early twentieth centuries.[3] Western scholars also bring their own concerns to the study of Legalists and Confucianists. For example, Roberto Unger draws on the Chinese "case" in trying to discover "why legal orders developed in modern Europe and, more precisely, in modern Europe alone, until taken from there to other parts of the world."[4] In a relativizing experiment designed to test his hypothesis, he finds that the Legalists came intriguingly close but ultimately failed to develop a rule of law. The case, Unger believes, "promises to deepen our insight into the complex relationship among modes of social organization, types of consciousness, and forms of normative order" which made the European experience unique. Under the Ch'in imperial state, writes Unger,

we seem to have a society that experienced a sudden growth of its reliance on public and positive rules as devices of political control. Moreover, an intense and continuing debate took place between the proponents and the critics of this new tool of social order. Yet the turn to bureaucratic law was not followed by the emergence of specialized courts, lawyers, and legal doctrines analagous to those of postfeudal Europe.[5]

Ultimately, Unger argues, "a transcendental religion and body of sacred law" are the prerequisites of a rule of law, and these China lacked, in his view.[6] Moreover, while Legalists and Confucians were "irremediably opposed" on "the problems of the age," both "tendencies were incompatible with a rule of law doctrine" in the same way.[7] For Unger, the critical factor accounting for the differences between European and Chinese legal development is that neither Legalists nor Confucians sufficiently "respected . . . individual persons."[8]

It bears repeating that what we know of Legalist ideas is complicated by historiographic canons in both China and the West, which in effect polarized Legalist and Confucian schools on questions of legal thought, ideas of time, and human nature. Hulsewé alludes to this convention in the introduction to his translation of Ch'in law codes: "The cruel laws of the cruel state of Ch'in are a byword in traditional Chinese historiography. . . . But although the iniquities of Ch'in have become proverbial, the factual grounds for this allegation are never given, except in the most general terms."[9] Yu-Lan Fung observes that "in Chinese history, the Confucianists have always accused the Legalists of being mean and vulgar, while the Legalists have accused the Confucianists of being bookish and impractical."[10] For Sybille van der Sprenkel, the Legalists and Confucians were "the two strands of what was a violently contested philosophical controversy in the fifth to third centuries B.C."[11]

Whatever colorings subsequent periods gave them, the lines between these two schools are considerably less bright—if they are visible at all— during the early period that is the subject of this chapter. With respect to the late Warring States period (463–222 B.C.) and the Ch'in dynasty (the time frame with which I am most concerned), opposing the Legalists and Confucians almost certainly overstates the differences between them.[12] In this chapter, I limit my discussion to the development of Legalist thought up to and through the Ch'in dynasty. Indeed, this chapter is, to some extent, about a "straw man," as it were, a Legalist straw man, constructed as the antithesis of the Confucians on specific grounds having to do with their respective ideas about law and time. The straw man was highly significant during the Han dynasty, which succeeded the Ch'in, and afterward, and it has a Western counterpart, for the alleged polarity of Legalists and Confucians is central to modern Western writing about Chinese ideas of history and temporality.[13]

The School of Law, as the Legalists are also known, composed its classic texts only slightly later than Confucius and Mo Tzu, in the third and fourth centuries B.C. The writers grouped together by later commentators as a "school" were not in fact a group, nor do their writings express a unified or readily identifiable ideology. For that matter, "Confucianism" is another collective term that is highly problematic.[14] Both terms are post hoc labels. It was perhaps the historian Ssu-ma Ch'ien who several centuries later tagged these writers as Legalists because of the central importance they attached to administration and the rule of law as the basis of government and social organization.[15]

Legalists are historically important primarily because they are credited with some of the strategies of statecraft that brought the Warring States period to a close. Their influence was deeply felt in the administration of the state of Ch'in, and their theories continued to be influential in the unification of China and the founding of the empire under the Ch'in. The reign of the First Emperor (221–207 B.C.) is said to be the only period in which the Legalists actually ruled China, and they left a crucial legacy in their concepts of the polity and governance, as well as an effective bureaucratic apparatus. Their downfall was dramatic.

Subsequent imperial regimes found it politic to distinguish themselves from the Legalists, and they used a variety of strategies to that end, including post hoc consolidations and characterizations of "the Legalists" themselves. In fact, however, Legalist ideas remained central to Chinese statecraft and public administration. Thus, it is vital to distinguish between pre-Ch'in and post-Ch'in sources on the relationship of Legalists or Legalist ideas to other philosophies, especially Confucianism.

The Legalists offer a double case study of how cultural constructions of time emerge and achieve prominence in public life. Not only is the Legalists' place in history an issue; so is their view of history itself. After the Ch'in dynasty, an important aspect of the representation of the Legalists had to do with their views of history and law in relation to processes of social change. The Legalists are said to have actively cast themselves in opposition to the Confucians on this point, taking particular exception to the Confucian idealization of a golden age.[16]

Like other modern scholars, I view such a sharp distinction between Legalists and other intellectual movements in pre-Ch'in and Ch'in China with skepticism. During this early period, philosophies had not been institutionalized as partisan ideologies; scholars circulated widely. Still, the distinctive character of the Ch'in dynasty and the historical brackets around it are by no means entirely the constructions of succeeding generations. The Ch'in themselves were active participants in their own myth of difference and their distinctiveness vis-à-vis philosophical and political alternatives.

In this chapter I address two main issues. First, I reconsider the construction of Legalists and Confucians as "opposites," focusing especially on continuities between the two groups. That discussion brings the question of Legalist ideas of temporality and history to the foreground, since it is these that are often said to have most sharply divided the Legalists from all other Chinese philosophies.[17] Second, I suggest that there was a modernist element in the Legalists' representations of time, not so much in the idea of progressive change as in the semiotic association of temporality itself with empire.

These two themes are connected by a discussion of how the Legalists modified the institutions of government, including the reorganization of its symbols. One of their complex symbolic innovations was to identify the emperor himself as the primary sign of time. Whether the Legalists and their patrons did this purposely is unclear, although the innovation involved explicit expressions and ritualizations. Some commentators propose that the Legalists purposely broke with Confucian conceptions in proposing a more "modern" or more "realistic" idea of time. In my view, the Legalists were less concerned with the "scientific" aspects of time (though they might also have been interested in those) than with the need to consolidate the practice of the state around principles of agency consistent with imperial rule.

Sources and Contexts of Legalist Ideas

Notwithstanding subsequent constructions of the Legalists as departing from mainstream Chinese philosophies, their program for state and society rested on old political and philosophical foundations. Some of the institutional framework of government and principles of continuity were defined at least a thousand years before the first emperor's reign. Historiographic tradition credits the Shang dynasty (beginning about 1500 B.C.) with the development of the key terms of a configuration of culture, politics, and society in China: the status of the individual within a hierarchically organized kinship system; interdependent regional polities and resource networks; an active military; the mythical and historical association of "meritorious deeds" with living rulers; literacy associated with personal genealogy, spirituality, and governance; "exclusive access to heaven and heavenly spirits" through a variety of media and means; "wealth and its aura."[18] The Shang king was the chief diviner, priest, and sacrificer. Shang practices of divination, the intercession of ancestors, and the conceptualization of the hierarchical value of seniority also remained vital to Chinese cultural and political tradition over the succeeding two millennia.[19]

The Shang state was, in the words of Hok-lam Chan, "theocratic and proto-bureaucratic."[20] The Shang kings claimed descent from a high lord, Shang-ti, a supreme deity controlling all nature, who was the source of the king's divine right. Shang-ti was also a vital force in ordinary human affairs, controlling, among other things, harvests and the outcomes of battles.[21] Shang institutions retained their efficacy in the succeeding Chou period. The Chou asserted their legitimacy in historical terms by claiming to be in contact with the Hsia (predecessors of the Shang) and the "sons of heaven," a reference to Shang-ti.[22] Their specific right to rule was also asserted in historical terms. The first Chou king, King Wu, was ritually installed at the the Shang Heavenly Shrine in a ceremony that his followers represented as the continuation of the Shang rule.[23] Their claims to having acceded to the "Mandate of Heaven" asserted both a sacred sanction and popular legitimacy.[24] The early Chou kings probably employed descendants of Shang intellectuals as historiographers,[25] continuing Shang practice that made the writing of histories integral to the political and cultural legitimation of imperial rule.[26]

The Chou dominated China from about 1045 B.C. until the Ch'in conquest in 221 B.C., a period of intense development and change. The Chou are credited with inventing a "massive feudal network," the "traditional aristocratic kinship structure," and the institutionalization of rulership based on the "Mandate of Heaven."[27] The Mandate of Heaven was a theory of accountability linking an incumbent king's legitimacy to both divine sanction and the effectiveness of his rule.[28] Since divine sanction would be withdrawn when the king failed to govern adequately, the Mandate of Heaven was both a theory of kingship and a theory of events.[29] Chan gives the Chou achievements even broader significance: "The Chou state deserves all the credit for laying the foundation of the Chinese institutional norms, the social and political order, and intellectual and cultural development."[30] In any event, by the time the Ch'in took control, these institutions had long and complicated histories of change.[31]

The Eastern Chou era, which began in about 770 B.C., is conventionally characterized in two periods, the Spring and Autumn period (722–464 B.C.) and the Warring States period (463–222 B.C.).[32] By the beginning of the Spring and Autumn period, the feudal institutions of earlier Chou had reached a critical state, when already long traditions of rule were undergoing major transformation. The Chou state was never a "purely political institution," as Cho-yun Hsu puts it; rather, the early feudal state "resembled an enlarged household."[33] Rulers' sovereignty was mitigated by what Hsu calls "familialistic government," in which ministers were the ruler's kinsmen not entirely under his control.[34] Ministers in turn relied on officials for the operations of government. In the sixth century B.C., magistrates led a series of rebellions against ministers, and Chou feudal lords were dependent on noble families, who ruled subsidiary states as "de facto" regents and eventually eclipsed the ruler.[35] These noble families cultivated popular support as means of consolidating their power in internecine struggles within the nobility.[36] These developments accelerated the collapse of old Chou feudal oligarchies and led to their replacement with meritocratic and professional bureaucracies.[37]

The rise of the administrative state was a crucial transformation of Chinese society; it was the product of widespread changes, but it also had its architects. Shen Pu-hai and others contributed toward the creation of a central government whose consolidated authority facilitated considerably tighter control over the processes of governance.[38] At its head was the *pa*, translated as "lord protector," "lord of the covenants," "chief of the feudal lords."[39] This was the political context for the expansion and institutionalization of philosophies that also characterized this period, proliferating in response to the urgent demands of turbulent and uncertain times.[40] Chuang-tzu, Confucius, Mencius, Hsun Tzu, Han Fei-tzu, Lao Tsu, and many others lived and wrote in the late Spring and Autumn and Warring States periods. These were scholar-politicians, whose travels from state to state, giving advice to patrons, remain the subject of history and legend.[41]

It is important to note that all the philosophical schools, not just the Legalists, were integrally tied to institutions charged with managing (or aspiring to manage) growing state bureaucracies as well as policy and daily affairs of the state. Confucius was personally involved in a governmental patronage system based on discipleship and careers in the bureaucracy.[42] Confucianism, Mohism, Taoism, Legalism—these are among the many post hoc names for ideas that circulated across China, borne by philosophical consultants whose clients, or patrons, faced the tactical and moral problems of statecraft on a daily basis. Thus, although Legalists are sometimes called politicians or tacticians to distinguish them from Confucian philosophers,[43] key Legalist writers were no more or less involved with practical questions of society than the leading theoreticians of other schools.[44] Thus, in the centuries leading up to unification, Legalists and others shared a political legacy that prestructured questions of rulers' legitimacy around issues of timeliness, character, and performance, among other things.[45]

The main problem to which the Legalists addressed themselves during the Warring States period was how to maintain the new central governments of the states they advised, how to defend them against collapse. The old aristocracies had broken down, and the structures that replaced them ruled with neither an adequate institutional basis nor a well-scripted theory of legitimacy. Legalist writers—Shang Yang, Li Ssu, and Han Fei-tzu, among other "theorists of the state"[46]—designed elaborate new roles for government in their rationalizing schemas for the state and everyday life and in a justification of strong, unified imperial power. The pragmatic aspects of their writings worked out ways to unify China under an emperor by means of a far-reaching administrative apparatus through which the people could experience the emperor's authority directly and uniformly.

In spite of the name later given to the Legalists, their program had less to do with the nature of substantive law than with its use; in fact, references to written law codes were minimal.[47] Rather, Legalists applied existing law codes in new ways; in particular, they wanted to promulgate the law and theatricalize punishments to enhance the deterrent effect of law among the public at large. Innovations in the application of penal law included mutual responsibility through collective liability,[48] a system of informers and mutual denunciation, secret police, and public humiliations and executions.[49] Under the Ch'in, nobles lost some of their immunity from prosecution or particular forms of sentencing. The Legalists conceived of the law primarily as a "political tool" with which to level and rationalize Chinese society under an emperor newly defined as the source of all law.[50] The idea of the ruler as the creator of law was the context for their strong advocacy of the universal application of the rule of law, and of legal education as a substitute for moral education.

For the Legalists law was no mere set of instrumentalities; they theorized law as having power to transform the nature of society. Of the Legalists of the Warring States period Bodde observes that they exalted "law as the one and only arbiter of human affairs." The Legalists meant "to create an all-powerful state authority. . . . They rejected the concept of a harmonious universe, ridiculed the Confucian ideal of government through virtue, and persistently urged the need for absolutist controls with which to curb what they regarded as the selfishness of human nature."[51] Law was to be "the great mould for the empire," according to the Legalist writer Han Fei-tzu.[52] And penal law and punishments were central to their theory.

Under Legalist influence, the Ch'in apparently developed and effectively enforced myriad new regulations governing large and small aspects of everyday life for ordinary citizens. They built roads; they standardized weights and measures all over China, including the gauges for all wheeled vehicles; they expanded the use of standard coinage as currency; they regulated agricultural prices and managed grain surpluses, issuing highly detailed rules, which they successfully enforced.[53] Hulsewé calls these attempts to regulate every minute aspect of everyday life "absurdities" but suggests that they indicate the determination of the Ch'in to extend their "influence over all spheres of the life of [the state's] inhabitants."[54] Jacques Gernet writes: "The merit of the Legalists was to have understood that the basis of the very power of the state resided in its political and social institutions; their originality lay in their desire to subject this state and its subjects to the sovereignty of law."[55] The Legalists, Randall Peerenboom says, were "pragmatic statesmen."[56]

The Legalists' conceptualization of law has been debated. Most scholars agree that their primary concerns were with administrative and penal law. Some assess the Legalist concept of law as a "real jurisprudence."[57] Others give more weight to the pragmatic or technical aspects. Even the core terminology of the Legalists involves important ambiguities. Their term for law was *fa* (hence the Chinese term for Legalists, *fa chia*), but the more important term, especially in the early period (and sometimes used interchangeably with *fa*) was *hsing*, corporal punishment. The word *fa* was used to refer to standards or models before it was applied to legal contexts.[58] The law codes, which were written on bamboo strips and assembled into books with cord, perhaps lent materiality to this pair of terms in a polysemic metaphor. Herrlee Creel states that the verb form of the character for book meant "to regulate,"[59] and confessions were elicited from offenders with lashings of bamboo cord.[60]

Etymological ambiguities and debates aside, the Legalists did not invent the concept of law they applied so rigorously. Chinese historical tradition has always given law secular origins.[61] Han attempts to portray the Legalists as heterodox perhaps revived an ancient myth, which associated law with alien origins. The myth (recorded in the fourth century B.C.) gives the Miao credit for inventing law, emphasizing that the Miao were foreigners and barbarians (later expelled from China); some considered the Ch'in themselves "un-Chinese."[62] At any rate, in the myth, Miao applications of the law were so horrible that Shang-ti exterminated them.[63]

Derk Bodde speculates that law (*fa*) may have originated in attempts of Chinese rulers to control alien tribes who did not know the traditional forms of behavior (*li*).[64] Be that as it may, penal codes were developed in the Chou dynasty, perhaps as early as the eighth century B.C.[65] The Ch'in expanded the use of written law codes in the sixth century B.C., as well as other uses of literacy in the administration of public affairs.[66] Some theorists advocated the written promulgation of law as a means by which the people could experience the new order, but this view was sharply contested. The Legalists' concern with managing legal literacy is also evident in the details of Ch'in legal procedure, such as section 5.1 of the Ch'in code: "In trying a case, if one can use the documents to track down [the evidence in] their statements, and get the facts on the parties without investigation by beating, that is considered superior; investigation by beating is considered inferior; in addition, intimidation is considered the worst [course of action]."[67] The efficacy of written law was debated from the first, and the debates continued into modern times.[68]

More broadly, the Ch'in also controlled the circulation of other texts, most notably by censorship and an aggressive program of book burning in 213 B.C.[69] Book burning was already an old practice and it would continue long after the Ch'in regime collapsed, but it is the First Emperor who "is chiefly remembered, and cursed, for this interference."[70] On the advice of the Legalist theoretician Li Ssu, the First Emperor tried to destroy collections of poetry and early historical writings that belonged to the canon of the Confucians and other Legalist rivals. Except for those of the state of Ch'in, state historical records were also to be destroyed. The penalty for noncompliance was execution. Modern commentators debate the magnitude of the losses incurred in this campaign, their assessments depending on whether they believe memorization of texts to have been standard practice at that time and how much efficacy they accord the imperial decree, among other factors.[71]

The idea of law as a means of social regulation and control and, more specifically, as a strategy for limiting the power of feudal nobles predated the rise of the state of Ch'in under the influence of the Legalists, as did concepts of the bureaucracy.[72] The ambivalence about legal rules as the basis of government also found expression long before any direct contests took place between Legalists and Confucians. From the outset, detractors viewed written law "not only as a violation of human morality, but perhaps even of the total cosmic order."[73]

Still, it is important not to minimize either the innovations of the Legalists while they were in power or the scale of the confrontation between Legalists and Confucians. The expansion and institutionalization of literacy as a medium of public life and as the medium of law were crucial developments. It is undoubtedly significant that as chancellor to the state of Ch'in, the Legalist Li Ssu advocated both the standardization of law and the standardization of written Chinese.[74] These added to and focused the Ch'in technologies of control, which were carefully designed to advertise and implement the centrality of the ruler to the functioning state. The very office of emperor was a Ch'in innovation, calculated to celebrate the superiority of the Ch'in ruler over the other states of the empire.[75] The title chosen by the First Emperor (*huang-ti*) evoked the ancient "numinous qualities" of rulership associated with the Shang and Chou dynasties.[76]

The emperor, though he drew on political tradition for the rhetorical forms of his legitimacy, nevertheless represented a major new institutional form. In accord with Legalist theory, the Ch'in emperor was both the source and the referent of law, and of a large bureaucratic and administrative machine. In theory, the purpose of regulation was to redeem the inadequacies of moral education as a basis for collective society; specifically, regulation was supposed to maintain order through fear and compliance.[77] Legalist reforms took place not only at the top of the social structure but also, crucially, at the grass roots. Certain innovations were designed to facilitate public administration. For example, to break up large coresident family units, a double tax was placed on persons with more than two adult sons at home. Also, under a fourth-century law in the state of Ch'in, a father, son, and father's brother could not share a room.[78] In addition to these rules, which T'ung-tsu Ch'ü credits with changing family structure and size, the Ch'in empire individuated land tenure, further corroding the power of the patrilineal household.[79]

Evidently, the Ch'in were anxious to suppress powerful clans, which traditionally wrote their own rules.[80] In addition to forbidding coresidence by adult married men (or making it prohibitively expensive), the Ch'in instituted collective liability among groupings of five families, presumably in an attempt to level family privilege and loyalty.[81] The Legalist regime also initiated a system of "mutual responsibility" (one of the great arms of its sociolegal program, along with punishments), organizing kinsmen and neighbors into small cells for purposes of mutual surveillance and informing.[82] The cell system was supplemented by secret police. County magistrates administered the Ch'in penal codes at the local level.[83] Hulsewé refers to the administration of law by "a complex hierarchy of officials" under the Ch'in.[84]

In particular, the Legalists are associated with the dismantling of status-based privilege under the law, the special immunities of the various ranks of nobility.[85] This provides a major point of contrast when scholars (from Han times to the present) compare Legalist and Confucian legal philosophies. Confucians, it is said, were committed to preserving a relationship between personal status and treatment under the law, a system of immunities that protected some categories of individuals from prosecution or from specific forms of punishment. For example, Chou law, much of which the Ch'in retained when they came to power, allowed accused nobles to remain absent from court and provided nobles and commoners with different styles of manacles and fetters. The determination of punishments and the punishments themselves differed for nobles and commoners; "great officers," for example, could not be mutilated.[86] It is, however, anachronistic to associate such immunities with Confucian thought at this period.[87]

The Legalists who advised the Ch'in empire are said to have advocated implementation of a single *moral* standard in the application of law. The context for "the unification of punishments" was the need to level the status of everyone but the emperor.[88] The Ch'in abolished hereditary nobility and generally sought direct control over the peasantry.[89] The Ch'in revisions of Chou doctrine and practice were highly public. They produced theatrical and humiliating punishments for nobles, for example, hanging them in the market square (a place they would have considered beneath them in life).[90]

Legalist efforts to reorganize society under the Ch'in were not restricted to the legal domain by any means. For example, they were concerned to control the conceptual relevance of hierarchy in government and society, not to eliminate it in practice.[91] Their larger efforts extended from the administration (and equalization) of taxes to innovations in public ritual to the standardization and control of written Chinese. The collapse of the empire from a series of peasant uprisings shortly after the death of the First Emperor appears to have been primarily due to excesses of control, which cost the empire money and popular support.[92]

Legalists after the Ch'in Empire

When the Han dynasty succeeded the Ch'in, the new regime proclaimed the downfall of the Legalists but kept the most significant Ch'in achievement, the unified empire itself. Legalist theorists had guided the military, administrative, and symbolic consolidation of the empire but had been thoroughly discredited even before the Han dynasty was installed.[93] Thus, the Han were in the position of dissociating themselves from the very theorists whose principles justified the continued existence of the empire. Their solution to this problem appears to have been a public denunciation of the Legalists and the retention of virtually all the Ch'in institutions of government, including the law codes.

Hulsewé voices the scholarly consensus that the "Confucianisation" of Chinese law after the Legalists' downfall was "very gradual and haphazard" and that for at least two thousand years, Legalist theory remained the dominant theory of the state, politics, and administration.[94] There were Legalists in the Han government even after Confucianism became the state philosophy and non-Confucians were barred from the civil service in the second century A.D. Confucian scholars annotated and preserved Legalist texts, as they did the texts of other schools.[95] Thus, it is possible that even contemporary claims of the extent to which Legalists had been expelled from power were exaggerated.

Most scholars of Chinese law and government date the founding of modern Chinese institutions of governance to the Han period, in part because the Han were eventually able to achieve a vital fusion of Confucian and Legalist elements. Such a fusion was institutionally possible, even given the Legalists' downfall. It is important to remember that the Ch'in defeat was not of "Legalists" by "Confucians," as some contemporary commentators claimed.[96] Han Confucianism, as Michael Loewe observes, was a "Taoist-Legalist-Confucian amalgam," and in the earlier period as well, the term "Confucian" glosses over the diversity and wide circulation of philosophical ideas associated with this movement.[97]

The discovery of Ch'in law code fragments in Hupei in 1975 reveals the extent to which the Han kept Ch'in statutes.[98] So many of them were retained that Hulsewé refers to "Ch'in-Han law."[99] Moreover, Han law maintains not only specific statutes but the Ch'in Legalists' particular union of administrative and penal law.[100] The Han also, at least initially, kept the "unified punishments" of the Ch'in though the emperor's permission was required to prosecute some categories of persons.[101] Even so, Hulsewé notes, though the "higher classes [had] a slight advantage over the commoners," the Han codes exposed nobles to punishment, and "the rule of law remained strict for all classes."[102]

Standardization of punishments was a major issue of contention for later Confucians, since it was supposed to signal the Legalists' disregard for virtue as the leading principle (and means) of social order. Hulsewé disagrees with this characterization of Legalist aims, emphasizing that the differences between Confucians and Legalists were not substantive but technical:

The so-called dispute between the Confucianists and the Legalists is . . . primarily a dispute between "rule by means of Rules of Ceremonious Behaviour" and "rule by means of law", or to put it more concretely, a dispute between differentiating and uniform rules of behaviour. The quarrel between "rule by means of virtue" . . . and "rule by means of punishments" is of relatively secondary importance. The choice of rules of behaviour is primary; whether these rules are promoted by "transformation through virtue" or by the force of punishments is a secondary problem.[103]

Hulsewé concludes that "Han Confucianism . . . was an authoritarian legalism, with the Classics as its sacred canon."[104]

The importance of these observations is that they underscore the extent to which the Legalist program itself was oriented toward means rather than results. This is a crucial point. The Legalists' symbolic innovations can be summarized as an attempt to isolate and organize social processes *as the functions of empire* and to celebrate them as such. The immediate relevance of this point is in the context of Legalists' ideas of history, to which we will return.

The Han kept Ch'in legal and political institutions, as well as the imperial religious cults surrounding the strong centralized empire that they inherited from the Ch'in.[105] They set out, however, to change other aspects of what had been Ch'in reforms. They engineered a return to a modified feudal order, for example, restoring noble families' authority and heredity, though not their autonomous territories, and stabilizing a system of classed social ranks.[106] They restored some of the local rites suppressed by the Ch'in and the Chou and elaborated the ritual and symbolic expressions of imperial legitimacy.[107] Under the Han, scholars gave renewed attention to the coincidence of natural cycles and human events, in part through innovations in calendrics, divination, and astronomy.[108]

The Han also instituted a major project of recovering canonical texts suppressed by the Ch'in.[109] In general, there were dramatic changes in cosmology from the beginning to the end of the Han period (roughly 200 B.C. to A.D. 200), shifting the ground of imperial legitimacy from military conquest to a ritual regime.[110] The traditionally dominant Chinese vocabulary of legitimacy—combining the ruler's mandate and the public recognition of his mandate—dates from Han times,[111] but the conceptual and semiotic ground for that shift was in part made possible by the Legalists' improvisations with the semiotics of empire.

The Han, like their predecessors, were adept at managing the symbolic dimensions of empire, no more so than in their representation of the Legalists and the Ch'in.[112] The traditional image of the Legalists as draconian, pragmatic and bellicose dates from Han times,[113] when the first Chinese histories were composed. Historians became integral to the politics of statecraft.[114] It was a Han historian who first devised the term "Legalists" and applied it to a group of writers, no doubt in part to consolidate their distinctions from Confucians. Confucianism itself consolidated under the Han, gradually becoming tied to the state government as the official orthodoxy and means of recruiting and evaluating for the civil service.[115]

When the Han dynasty itself began to disintegrate, there was a revival of positive interest in the Legalists and their writings. Another sort of return came in the seventh and eighth centuries A.D. during the T'ang dynasty when the overthrow of the Ch'in and the founding of the Han dynasty and other stories "contrasting the vices of the Qin [Ch'in] and the virtue of the Han" provided themes for court entertainments and in popular theater.[116] These were not the only periods that saw heightened interest—both positive and negative—in the Legalists.[117] It appears that long after their defeat, Legalist rhetoric and institutional innovations revived whenever the rulers faced severe challenges of statecraft. The unification of China, which was the enduring achievement of the Legalists and their militarist royal patrons, was repeatedly renewed in terms that the Legalists invented. From Han times onward, however, those terms were embedded in a political and moral vocabulary that insisted on fundamental distinction between Legalists and Confucians in various respects.

Confucian Principles

Before and especially after the Ch'in dynasty, legal practice gave central importance to personal status in all social affairs. The rationale was not privilege per se (as Legalists are said to have claimed) but rather a linkage of virtue with social practice. From Chou times through the Ch'ing dynasty (which ended in 1911), the Confucian-influenced conception of virtue as the foundation of social order was in turn based on two corollary ideas of time and the natural order.[118] The first of these was that time perpetually moves toward its own return, making history, in the words of William de Bary and his colleagues, "no more than a counterpart in the human sphere of the similar cycles of Heaven and earth."[119] The second principle was what Bodde calls the perfect "cosmic harmony" of what was understood as a closed system.[120] Natural cycles inscribed the cosmic and social order with categories and principles that organized the meanings of social status and their relevance in law. Accordingly, time was the system of interrelated cycles; history recorded the relationship between natural categories and events. The essential point for now is that the concept of *li* related individuals simultaneously to each other and to the principles of universal order which defined their moment and station.

The ordered universe was at the very core of Confucian concepts of social administration,[121] which held that the task of law was to conserve cosmic harmony. Indeed, its traditional basis was a concept of "rightness" or "enlightenment."[122] Therefore, the fundamental normativity of Chinese society was vested not in law (*fa*) but in *li*, "rules of behavior varying in accordance with one's status defined in the various forms of social relationships."[123] *Li* constituted both a theory and a method of social differentiation. As theory, *li* pointed to the quasi-mythical ancient sages who were said to be their authors; their antiquity gave their observers what they understood as contact with past ages, an actual experience of time's cycles.[124]

Even before the rise of the Legalists under the Ch'in and the Confucianization of Chinese law in Han times, *fa* and *li* were conceptualized as inseparably linked in a state of productive tension, which derived less from differences of substance than from their differences as technologies. *Fa* was the stuff of administration; *li* was the stuff of everyday life and its integral connection to the cosmic order. *Fa* fixed rewards and punishments to motivate subjects to appropriate actions; *li* was supposed to constitute its own motivation for doing right.[125] Later, yin-yang theorists placed *fa* and *li* in complementary opposition, *fa* having negative value and *li* positive value, but both perpetually in relation to each other.[126]

When the Legalists were discredited, following the defeat of the Ch'in by the Han, Confucian-influenced rulers heightened this contrast between *li* and *fa* as a sign of broader differences between Legalists and Confucianists. In fact, the Han by no means eliminated law but used a variety of means to contain it in interpersonal affairs. Confucian philosophy discouraged litigation, declaring it to be its own punishment. A variety of procedures were built in to maximize the unpredictability and un-

pleasantness of the court for petitioners.[127] Mediation was institutionalized as a preferable alternative to litigation, and at the same time,
other forms of private ordering—specifically, vengeance and self-help—
were forbidden.[128]

Confucians conceptualized law as equally and simultaneously the law
of nature and society. Law, embodied in the exemplary prince, simultaneously expressed both the unity and the internal differentiation of a
universal classificatory scheme. "Heaven having placed natural law in the
heart of man," writes Jean Escarra, "the role of the prince is limited to
discovering and celebrating this law in himself for the sake of imposing it
on all by his sole example. . . . The preservation of universal order is
essentially the personal fact of the prince and owes nothing to abstract
rules."[129] *Li* provided the focus of Chinese legal philosophy during the
entire period of Confucian dominance (from the Han dynasty to the end
of the Ch'ing),[130] but it was also important prior to the rise of the Ch'in.
Li, in theory, provided for a self-regulating society, animated by the innate goodness of humankind and motivated by the good witness of virtuous men and women. *Li* was supposed to be self-enforcing by the example of the emperor and, in turn, all people. *Fa*, in this context,
represented a "necessary evil."[131]

Confucian goals of social order were predicated on these notions of
the innate goodness of humans and the intrinsic appeal of virtue. By Han
times, Bodde says, *li* was conceived as "broad moral principles" that were
in accord with the human instinct for rightness.[132] As such, *li* represented
a model of social order but not a system of social control. Against this
backdrop, the Legalist program might well have seemed a radical departure, even a subversive one. Legalists voiced the premise that human
nature is not innately good but evil and self-interested, hence requiring
external regulation and active control. Still, for the Legalists, the ultimate
goal of law was not social control, though that might be the result. The
goal was to create a self-managing society in which the law and the machinery of government were of such quality that they could not be un-
dermined by inferior administrators.[133]

Confucian approaches to law relied much more heavily on the notion
of "great men," exemplars of virtue, and this view of law by definition
involved hierarchical social distinctions. As a scheme of social differentiation, Chinese law under Confucian influence (that is, after the Ch'in dynasty) represented itself as encompassing all differences with the system
of differences which was order itself. Thus, to differentiate social status,
for example, was to articulate a universal normative principle, as Bodde
notes: "Probably the most conspicuous single Confucian influence on
imperial Chinese law is the principle of legalized inequality. Prior to the

revolution of 1911, Chinese law endlessly differentiated its treatment according to individual rank, relationship, and special circumstance."[134] Not only noble ranks were distinguished in this way, but also the young, the elderly, and the infirm.[135] Clemency and amnesty for individuals—both granted by the emperor—were also an important part of Confucian legal tradition from Han times onward.[136] The Legalists, by contrast, represented such distinctions as a multiplication of moral standards and (therefore) a diminution of law.

Confucian legal philosophy enunciated the proprieties of particular dyadic relationships (for example, ruler-minister, father-son, elder brother–younger brother, and so on) and made social order the aggregate effect of the internal regulation of these relationships. The *li* assumed and preserved a pervasive social hierarchy.[137] *Li* formed an unwritten code that emphasized an individual's duties in relation to his or her station. Confucius had held that *li* were the composition of ancient sages, and as the letters exchanged by Tzu-ch'an and Shu-hsiang imply, their orality was considered to be one source of the their enduring vitality.[138] The *li* were supposed to compel intrinsically, by their rightness and by virtue of their aesthetic form. In contrast, the Confucians viewed law (*fa*) as unaesthetic, mechanistic, a mere tool; law's very writtenness made it inflexible and limited its efficacy.[139] In practice, knowledge of *li* through the long and complex oral texts was "largely an upper-class monopoly,"[140] though *li* were evidently known in popular tradition as well as among the scholarly elite. Studying *li* was considered to be an end in itself, an authentic form of contact with the sages of past times who had established them.

The *li* were not legal rules, but as norms they were integral to the social order idealized by elites, "ideally a cooperative commonwealth," Creel writes,

> in which the ruler and his officials are dedicated to the welfare of the people, and the people in turn render loyalty and willing obedience to those above them. The most potent force for causing the people to be good, Confucius repeated over and over, was proper example set for them by the rulers. The people should be positively motivated by *li*, to do that which they ought; if they are intimidated by fear of punishment they will merely strive to avoid the punishment, but will not be made good. To render justice in lawsuits is all very well, but the important thing, Confucius said, is to bring about a condition in which there will be no lawsuits.[141]

Li were said to be the work of the sages who had lived in the golden age. Indeed, their lives made it the golden age. Living by *li* in the present was in and of itself a therapeutic project of recovery. The idea of the golden age was a cornerstone of post-Ch'in Confucian philosophy, but in different expressions, it was also important to other "schools," including earlier ones.[142] In different ways, pre-Ch'in Confucians, Mohists, and Taoists conceptualized history as a story of episodic degeneration, punctuated by great sages and their revitalizing effects, culminating in the political and social upheavals of their own age, the Warring States period.[143] Legalists, however, rejected the idea of a golden age as morally invalid, politically impractical, and perhaps technically infeasible, though they shared the general view that the present times suffered from decay.[144] Their view was that "everything is conditioned by its own immediate environment."[145] They stressed the need for law to fit the times, and their own fitness as judges of the times.[146] Shang Yang's text illustrates these ideas: "For laws, which are established without examining people's conditions, do not succeed, but a government which is enacted fittingly for the times, does not offend."[147] Creel quotes from Han Fei-tzu, another Legalist theorist from the third century B.C.: "If the laws change with the times, there is good order. . . . The Sage does not seek to follow [the ways of] antiquity, nor to conform to any constant standard."[148] Han Fei-tzu also wrote: "For governing the people there is no permanent principle save that it is the laws (*fa*) and nothing else that determine the government. Let the laws roll with the times and there will be good government. Let the government accord with the age and there will be great achievement. . . . But let the times shift without any alteration in the laws and there will be disorder."[149]

Yet, even as they supply the textual evidence to distinguish between Confucians and Legalists, Creel and others caution against overstating the differences between them on this point. Confucian and Legalist notions of history itself were not fundamentally different.[150] Confucians and Legalists do, however, appear to have given history substantially different driving forces, the Confucians locating the principle of history in moral virtue, and the Legalists in the state. For Confucians, as we have already seen, the temporal connection between moral virtue and history was embedded in *li*; for Legalists, the connection between history and the state was in *fa*, law.

Signs of the Times

What did the Legalists understand by the notion of situating law in "the times"? Without doubt, such encomiums were powerful gestures toward the imperium and the timeliness of its rule, as well as toward innovation. But what were "the times"? Were the Legalists evoking linear time, as opposed to the cyclical time that some modern scholars associate with Chinese tradition? Were they hypothesizing progressive time, against

Confucian notions of reiteration?[151] Western writers tend to interpret the Legalists' temporal innovations as an experiment with linear time, possibly in part because of the parallels that are conventionally drawn between Chou-period feudalism and feudal Europe.[152] Given that European feudalism ended with the rise of humanism and a scientific revolution, some commentators see the Legalists as representatives of a warped humanism and thwarted scientific revolution in mathematics, astronomy, and law.[153] References to Legalists as "modernists" or "realists" appear to stem more directly from the movements of European cultural history than from Legalist conceptions of time.

The basic notions of time built into Chinese theories of the order of the universe involved both continuity and discontinuity. The dynamic equilibrium of yin-yang and the succession of the five agents involve both the regenerative continuity of the cycles and the discontinuity of transitions from one form of agency to the next. Similarly, pre-Han notions of the Mandate of Heaven (which the Han transformed into a principle of dynastic continuity) articulate both continuity and discontinuity in a theory of the ruler's sacred accountability. Calendars offered a technology of continuity; yet sovereignty also involved the stewardship of time, which risked depletion and required renewal. Such renewals were not only formally useful in the symbolic sense but also pointed to the substantive nature of the ruler's responsibilities for time. Significantly, as I will suggest later, the sovereign came to represent both continuous and discontinuous aspects of time, being himself both the paramount sign of the times and time's caretaker. The association of the sovereign with "the times" as an indexical sign is just that: he was neither the producer of the times nor the product of the times but the identifying sign of the agency that *in relation to others* was time. Three aspects of temporality during the Legalist period of influence—yin-yang (or the five agents), the Mandate of Heaven, and calendrics—can help to explain imperial time.

The theories of yin-yang and five agents, which emerged in the third century B.C., constitute a major theme in Chinese representations of temporality.[154] Yin-yang links temporality to agency, formulated as phases or cosmic forces. The central principle is a natural order of cycles, each dominated by one of five cosmic forces (or agents), and each one contributing to the natural balance of the universe (yin and yang).[155] Following the sinologist Marcel Granet, Haili You explains the cycles of yin and yang, their rhythmic alternation, as aspects of the Tao (Dao):

Knowing Dao means knowing how to live "in accord with the laws of yin and yang." The locus classicus of *Dao* is in *Yijing*, *The Book of Changes*, where "*Dao* is the alternation of *yin* and *yang*." Without changing its meanings, this utterance may also be translated as "*Dao* is once *yin* and once *yang*"; "*Dao* is yin and yang at once"; or "*Dao* is the cycle of *yin* and *yang*." . . . Let us invoke Joseph Needham to suggest that the idea of *Dao* can very well be related to rhythm without implying at the moment that *Dao* is rhythm proper.[156]

Later, You adds that "the notion of yin-yang signifies a worldview that conceives of the universe as rhythmically constituted."[157] Yin and yang are not classifications of *things*, but rather "yin-yang is a category of experience," the rhythm of life itself.[158]

The cosmic forces defined not calendrical cycles but the cyclicity of time itself and, with time, history.[159] As a classification system, yin-yang addressed the forms and sequencing of agency.[160] Gernet calls these formulations "spatio-temporal groups [of] fundamental properties."[161] The Chinese cycles had a prescribed order, though what that order might be was always a subject of debate, and the cycles had no fixed duration.[162] The theory of five agents provided essential principles for the reading of omens and divination, the legitimation of sovereign rule, and the organizing principles of geography, history, and more. Yin (negative forces) and yang (positive forces) provided a larger classificatory scheme within which the five agents operated. Eventually, a classificatory system developed which was simultaneously a theory of hierarchical succession and events. In effect, it provided a map of "time-space," classifying and ordering along the dimensions of time, space, and society simultaneously. Indeed, a summary description of this sort belies the fragmentary emergence of yin-yang over several centuries; it was consolidated as a unified theory only after the period that most concerns me here. Western scholars often draw post-Ch'in yin-yang into desriptions of the Legalists during pre-Ch'in and Ch'in times, and this anachronism tends to heighten the contrast between Legalists and Confucians.

The five agents theory was consolidated and appropriated by imperial rulers after the Ch'in period, but the Ch'in were the first to appreciate some facets of its symbolic map.[163] Most important, the first emperor used the five agents theory as the symbolic reservoir for his own claims to legitimacy, to justify his accession and subsequent reforms. Thus, to symbolically underscore the end of the Chou dynasty, which was associated with fire, the Ch'in emperor took the sign of water, which extinguishes fire.[164] The First Emperor's claims to rule "by virtue of a particular cosmic element" were continued by the Han, who kept the water sign but modified some of its emblems at the time of the first Han accession.[165] Thus, it was the Ch'in who established the enduring imperial tradition by which claims to legitimate rulership were presaged by particular qualities and signs (interpreted by specialists) and marked by the use of appropriately colored regalia and the commissioning of new rituals involving the regnal element.

The adoption of the five agents as symbols of imperial legitimacy reflects an important aspect of yin-yang and five agents as a theory of time. Whereas the order of the elements was fixed in theory, which element might actually be prevalent at any particular time could be decided only provisionally. Specialists, sovereigns, and others could be more or less constantly involved in the project of resolving the ambiguities of their own times. The early Han, for example, debated the regnal sign for almost a century before experimenting with a change in 105 B.C. Thus, the questions of what time was and what time it was (to play on Clifford Geertz's phrasings) were in theory the same but in practice different. The Legalists' insistence on the relevance of "the times" perhaps expressed their emphasis on this difference.

To some extent, the five agents and the Mandate of Heaven were contradictory ideas, at least in theory, though they could also be mutually reinforcing.[166] Li Ssu and Han Fei-tzu, advisers to the state of Ch'in, did not invoke the Mandate of Heaven in their justification of the Ch'in empire.[167] The Chou version of the heavenly mandate made its confirming signs available only once the sovereign was installed, but the Han shifted the signs of the mandate to the *selection* of the ruler.[168] They also made other refinements, stressing the continuity of the mandate and the impossibility of refusing it.[169] Thus, in the years following their accession, the Han ritually consolidated two formerly separate idioms of legitimacy: the Mandate of Heaven and the five agents. By consolidating them in the particular way that they did, the Han emphasized continuity.

The Ch'in evidently preferred to justify their own imperium in other terms, that is, in terms of conquest. In resisting the Mandate of Heaven, it seems to me, the Legalists may have been resisting locating the source of sovereignty outside the sovereign himself, though this suggestion is highly speculative. It seems possible that whatever the Legalists meant by "the times," their consolidation of the sovereign's mandate in the sovereign himself provided some of the institutional basis for subsequent innovations by the Han with respect to their version of the Mandate of Heaven. In the book burning of 213 B.C., the document containing the doctrine of the Mandate of Heaven was among those singled out for destruction.

The relationship of the sovereign to "the times" was not in itself a new question in the period of the Ch'in dynasty. Traditionally, the ruler was not only the sign of his times; he was also time's steward on behalf of the realm. Stewardship involved both technical and spiritual responsibilities. The founding rulers of the Hsia, Shang, and Chou dynasties were said to have changed the first month of the year; accordingly, the First Emperor of Ch'in initiated a new calendar by designating the tenth month as the first month of the new year.[170] Later, the Han continued the practice whereby, Howard J. Wechsler notes, a calendar "was seen as part of the larger operation of altering the institutions of a predecessor when a new dynasty came to power."[171] The start of a new reign was customarily dated as the first day of the following new year, and a new reign name also refreshed time.[172]

A new calendar was not only a demonstration of the new ruler's authority, Wechsler explains, but also, more fundamentally, his responsibility for time itself:

A new calendar served not simply to symbolize a new beginning. By changing the first month, *kai-shuo*, the emperor ritually regenerated time. As the *Po Hu T'ung* says, "*shuo* 'first month' means *su* 'to revive', *ke* 'to renovate'; it means that the ten thousand things are renovated at this [moment], and so will receive their [further] regulation by it." . . . By determining the *shuo*, then, the Chinese sovereign, whose sole prerogative it was, both revived and renovated time. He put an end to the calendar of a defunct dynasty or a concluded reign and began the regeneration of time in his own.[173]

The willingness of the emperor to reject the time of his lineal ancestors and improve it was a demonstration of his concern for the masses, "proof of his commitment to have time 'work' for all his people."[174]

In incorporating the stewardship of time into the imperial functions, the Ch'in built on the preimperial tradition whereby each state kept its own calendar.[175] Presumably, such calendars were an integral part of everyday life, at least for a certain segment of the population. Archaeologists have found a Chou almanac that prescribed certain activities for each day.[176] The main purpose of calendars appears to have been the regulation of everyday activities, rather than registering of duration. Dates are rare in early documents. Authors in Shang and Chou times sometimes identified the time elapsed since the beginning of a ruling sovereign's reign, but generally the sovereign himself was not named; Creel infers that long-term chronology was not of interest to archivists at this time, but it seems as likely that it was *intervals* that were uninteresting, at least inasmuch as monarchs were not their indexical signs (as they later became).[177]

The primary relevance of calendars as guides to everyday activities is also suggested by ancient practices of divination, which provide some of the earliest Chinese historical inscriptions (from the Shang period). Under the Shang, the king was the chief diviner. David N. Keightley provides recent translations of rulers' texts of "crack making," that is, reading the cracks made when animal bones are heated over fire as oracular signs.[178] Such oracle bones were one major divinatory medium. Most of the texts have to do with the timing of events.[179] Later, other principal media included the casting of stalks from the yarrow plant and reading their linear patterns, as well as reading the flow of cosmic energy in winds.[180]

By late Chou times, and certainly by Ch'in times, these divinatory practices were very ancient—and sharply contested. Han Fei-tzu opposed their use: "The *Han-fei-tzu*," Loewe comments, "includes a warning that one of the roads to the ruin of a state lies in dependence on these methods to choose a time for action, in the belief that the success of that action would thus be assured."[181]

These background observations suggest that the Legalists shared with Confucians and others a frame of reference, a cultural repertoire of complex ideas and technologies of temporal continuity and discontinuity. Confucians and Legalists were not indistinguishable, but their differences did not monopolize the field of argument. In particular, Legalists and Confucians appear to have shared a fundamental conception of the structure of time and, in general terms, an identification of the ruler with (if not *in*) time.

Nevertheless, where these ideas involved ambiguities, there is some evidence that Legalists and Confucians developed somewhat different interpretive approaches. There appear to have been two basic ambiguities in pre-Han constructions of time, as they were relevant to the public symbols of legitimacy with which I am most concerned. First, there was the constant question of what cosmic agent was in fact dominating the times. Second, there was the question of how to validate an incumbent sovereign's claims to hold the Mandate of Heaven, which was reversible in theory and practice. Thus, like the question of which of the five agents was "in force" at any particular time, questions of legitimacy could never be settled, except provisionally and in the short term.

In these two areas, the Ch'in appear to have directed their efforts toward *containing* the ambiguities within the institutions of sovereign rule: their use of the metaphor of conquest and their neglect (or perhaps outright rejection) of the theory of the Mandate of Heaven brought time's ambiguities to the ground, as it were—and to ground governed by a strong military authority. In practice, this conceptual shift meant that the emperor himself monopolized both the continuous and the discontinuous aspects of time. Later, after the Ch'in defeat, the Confucians, at least under the subsequent Han regime, located the means of resolving time's ambiguities somewhat differently. The determination of the cosmic agents became the project of imperial ritual specialists, and the Mandate of Heaven was redefined to signify the *proof* of qualification and the guarantor of succession, rather than a post hoc sign of incumbency.

In effect, the Legalists' solution to time's difficulties was consistent with their design of a military regime in that they sought to resolve those difficulties in a more or less personal cult of imperial office, *from* which "the times" were defined and expressed in law. The Confucians' subsequent solution to the same difficulties was to situate the imperial office in a more diffuse ritual context in which the necessary proofs of legitimacy could be provided *to* the emperor. Either way, the emperor was the literal sign of the times, though in relation to the "ritual regime" developed under Confucian influence, the earlier Ch'in imperial hermeneutic was more highly concentrated on the emperor's personal office as the source of the signs of the times.[182]

What sort of concept of time, then, was involved in the Legalists' notions of "the times"? Loewe, who prefers to call the Legalists "modernists," gives considerable weight to what appear to be notions of actuality or contingency, and other scholars also take this view.[183] Arthur W. Hummel, for example, implicitly contrasts Legalist modernism with Confucian traditionalism and links Legalist thinking to Western modernism:

How to reconcile the concept of a golden age in antiquity with the ideal of a developing society has been an unending problem in Chinese history. . . . The ancient legalist school of the 3rd century BC, which was the first to wrestle seriously with the problem, frankly advocated what now amounts to the western pragmatic method of minimizing the lessons of the past, and finding the real sanctions for reform in the actualities of the day.[184]

Bodde turns even more directly to modern Western political theory for a vocabulary with which to define the issues, associating *li* with natural law and *fa* with positive law.[185]

While such comparisons are seductive, they import to ancient China officialized Western representations of time as a framework of actuality which claims reality outside the institutions that are its "products." One difficulty with such comparisons is that they separate time from the institutions of sovereignty in which the rulers of the late Chou period (and subsequent generations) appear to have embedded them. In fact, neither the Confucians nor the Legalists seem to have been primarily concerned with the relationship of the present to the past or the future. Rather, they were concerned with publicly and effectively managing a large-scale social organization with the signs that their shared concept of time made available to them. The more salient contrast to modern notions of official time in the West would appear to be the differences in how each system defines and manipulates the containment of time. Elite Chinese representations elaborated time's closure in various ways; elite Western representations stress its progressive openness. Insofar as progressive change was an issue, we have seen that *both* Legalists and Confucians were concerned with social reform, challenged as they were by the conviction that past times were qualitatively better than present times. Both looked forward to progress, though the Legalists prescribed innovating in the present, and the Confucians, emulating the past.

Temporal Management under the First Emperor

With respect to his self-identification as the sign of the times, the First Emperor undertook a concerted campaign to eliminate not only the signs of other times but also signs of time that were not under his direct control. I refer to the burning of books in 213 B.C. and the subsequent years of censorship and suppression and the particular effort to annihilate the record and literature of the past. Although, as noted, it was not only the First Emperor who ordered book burnings, it is clear that his aim was to destroy the substance of the past and to sever contact with it, though contact with the past had formerly been an end in itself. In other words, it was not only the works themselves but also the emulation of the works he tried to censor.[186] Though Bodde casts doubt on some of the horrors subsequently ascribed to the First Emperor, it does appear that he executed dozens of literati and used terrorist tactics to enforce his bans. Under the Ch'in empire, the Legalists also oversaw a program of ritual suppression which had begun earlier.[187]

The principle of selection that operated in Ch'in censorship appears to have stemmed from the larger premise that notions of "past" and "present" had a geopolitical dimension for the First Emperor and his Legalist advisers. The present was defined *spatially* by unification and the consolidation of empire, whereas the past was defined as disunity.[188] The spatialization of time appears to have added a new dimension to Chinese concepts of sovereignty. Additional evidence suggests some of the ways in which the Ch'in emperor effectively linked his personal rule with both time and space. The linkage of time and space was not new in personal geography in Ch'in times, but their connection through the emperor was an innovation.

The context of the innovation was perhaps the ancient tradition that made the ruler the chief diviner; a broader and more contemporary context might have been in Taoist philosophy. Scholars disagree as to the influence of Taoism on Legalist thought. Ying-shih Yü states that Taoists had long had influence over Chinese politics by their association with the court; this association intensified during Ch'in and Han times.[189] More cautiously, Xueqin Li places Taoist philosophers in the state of Ch'in and notes that their renaissance there survived the suppression of books and literati.[190] Bodde finds the Taoist principle of "nonactivity" in Legalist ideas about the cybernetic quality of law, putting the "machinery for government" above human frailty.[191] He also associates Taoist ideals of simplicity with Han Fei-tzu's comment that "in an age of perfect tranquility, the law is like the morning dew."[192] Creel argues against interpreting Legalist thought as a product of Taoist influence.[193]

Taoist conceptions of geography envisioned the earth, heaven, and hell arrayed as core and peripheries in a horizontal, planar space, a "liturgical space" defined by four (or eight) cardinal points and their center.[194] Urban design, particularly in capitals, expressed this sacred geography in its organization around intersecting cardinal axes. The south-north axis was the "main processional axis" through the capital, as Paul Wheatley remarks, "the celestial meridian writ small."[195] The city's most important buildings were along this axis, facing south. This main avenue was designed to be experienced not as a vista (as modern Western boulevards were) but as a progressive itinerary.[196] Maps, which were common in China in the third century B.C. and later, also depict the progression of a traveler's itinerary.[197]

In the capitals particularly, the central point of intersection of the cardinal directions had special significance (especially elaborated by the Han). This site was identified with the ruler. The palace, sited by a specialist diviner, was conceived as an *axis mundi*, the central pole of the universe. Wheatley draws on a contemporary Chinese text to define the palace as the point where the earth and sky meet, where the seasons merge, where wind and rain are gathered in, and where yin and yang are in harmony, that is, as the place where time and space are one, and all forms of agency are dynamic and potent.[198] Power flowed from the royal ceremonial complex to the surrounding countryside through the city gates.[199] Within the ceremonial complex, the Temple of Ancestors and the Altar of Earth were "conceived jointly as a microcosm of the empire."[200]

Whether or not in Taoist terms, the Ch'in emperor intensified the association of the ruler with the spatial aspects of the empire in specific ways. At the beginning of his reign, the First Emperor commissioned a tomb that was to be a microcosm of the empire.[201] He also undertook a series of "progresses" through his domain, celebrated in his (or in commissioned) inscriptions at sacred sites.[202] Whereas Shang concepts of sovereignty did not emphasize or celebrate the territorial aspects of kingship, the First Emperor, both as emperor and earlier as the Ch'in king, appears to have territorialized his claims to legitimacy in these and other ways.[203]

One reason for the emperor's travels to China's east coast was his personal quest for immortality. An elixir of immortality was said to be available offshore, past some coastal islands, and the emperor's personal mysticism appears to have defined this aspect of his search for longevity. The desire for "worldly immortality" in the sense of permanent good health was an ancient Chinese tradition by the time of the Ch'in dynasty.[204] Longevity and worldly immortality were at the center of a widespread ritual and medical complex, and for pre-Ch'in princes, the search for immortality drugs was apparently "general practice."[205]

The idea of "otherworldly immortality" (*hsien*), however, was new at the end of the Ch'in dynasty.[206] In contrast to the worldly immortal with permanent social existence, the *hsien* immortal, says Yü, was "a secluded individual wandering in the sky, in no way related to the human world."[207] The First Emperor may have been the first prince to seek immortality in this sense.[208] His desire was well known, and thousands of specialists came to his court. When he failed to find immortality drugs, attending specialists diagnosed the failure as the sign of his excessive worldliness; they prescribed a life of Taoist quietism, by which he might win the particular transcendency he sought. The cult of mystery surrounding his itinerary developed partly from his attempt to follow this prescription for seclusion and withdrawal from the earthly concerns of power politics.[209] His performance of rites associated with the search for longevity or immortality is documented in contemporary historical accounts.[210]

I interpret the quest for immortality as (among other things) the search for a semiotics that would effectively blur or preclude an association of the emperor with a particular moment in time or point in space. As a *hsien* immortal, the emperor would have been identified with time itself but not with a particular era. This semiotic effort would have been consistent with the general approach Legalists took to the "problem" of time. There is additional evidence of Legalists' contributions to the emperor's dissociation from the world of events in favor of a more generalized identification with time itself. To begin with, the First Emperor developed a cult of mystery around his person and his travels. He had many palaces built, and revealing his whereabouts, even after the fact, was made a capital offense.[211] Second, the First Emperor's parentage was also, at least in legend, hedged with doubt.[212] Third, Legalist theory admonished the emperor not to be involved in disputes as a third party.[213] While these elaborations of the first emperor's personal cult of office can be interpreted in many ways, I connect them as related evidence of the Ch'in emperor's Legalist-guided efforts to remove his biography from the world of events to the realm of myth. It is especially significant that his efforts to dehistoricize his person were simultaneous with his efforts to territorialize the symbols of his rule. In practice, this strategy meant obliterating all but the monumental evidence of his personal itinerary.

Whether or not they were intentional, the emperor's manipulations of the semiotics of time and space minimized his personal place *in* history in favor of a symbolic association of his personal reign *as time itself*. The corollary of this symbolic move is the cult of imperial mystery which removed the emperor from a particular place and situated him, in effect, everywhere at once. It is important to stress the result of this corollary, and that is the emperor's symbolic centrality in literally linking time and space. It is also important to consider the emperor's symbolic role in distinguishing time from history, history being constructed as the realm of events and biography.[214]

The question remains as to what sort of distinction this might have been. By virtue of the emperor's rule, time seems to have been represented as containing all the forces or forms of agency necessary for the creation of events, including military force. Did history—conceptualized as contained or enclosed within time in this sense—have some secondary relationship to time? Those Western scholars who see the Legalists as "modernists" infer that they understood events as being produced *in* time, that is, as a succession whose links made up time. Though this might be the case, it appears that the Legalists were less concerned with problems of continuity than they were with problems of agency. Thus, I would suggest that the Legalists, to the extent that they were concerned with "events" as such, were primarily interested in the aspects that connected them to the state as manifestations of time, that is, in events *as* time.

Still, some conceptual medium would have been required to connect events (the stuff of history) to the imperial state (time itself). The Legalists' emphasis on the importance of promulgating written law takes on particular symbolic importance in this context. I have already noted the Legalists' particular insistence on the efficacy of written law as a medium of standardization and as a means of providing direct contact between the state and its inhabitants. This was a major issue of contention between Legalists and their opponents, and it remained an issue long after the Legalists themselves were discredited, with the Ch'in empire's collapse. I have also noted the Legalists' role in standardizing Chinese script and their representation of the "writtenness" of law as the self-evident proof of its standardization. One important element of their project of standardizing the law across status groups and unifying punishments was the idea that punishments should be set for categories of crime, not categories of person.[215] The rationale for this principle was an idea that Legalists shared with Confucians, "the rectification of names." This was in effect a theory of semiotics (or, more accurately, against semiotics) based on the premise that classificatory terms, or "names," should apply literally to the contents of the category. For Confucians, the rectification of names promised a means of clarifying social responsibilities; for the Legalists, it offered a syntax of social control.[216] Either way, the rectification of names and universal order were, by definition, corollaries.

The relevance of the rectification of names in a discussion of the nature of "the times" is in the possibility that Legalists saw history not as a segment in time but as a hermetic system in which all forms of agency were mutually referential. In other words, "the times" envisioned by the Legalists might have been a closed system, in which imperial edicts, the application of law, social behavior, and the organization of society were perfectly and mutually reinforcing. As noted, the Legalists envisioned their ultimate goal as the creation of a legal machinery so perfect that it would be self-sustaining, undiminished even by inferior administrators.[217] In this context, written law appears to have been conceived as the extension or projection of the emperor across his domain, a medium of contact between the emperor and his subjects. The emperor was the source of all legality.[218] From this perspective, written law was yet another metonymic expression of the emperor's personal office. Significantly, it was one that expressed his identification with the territory over which he was sovereign, as well as his simultaneous association with "the times."

If this discussion offers a plausible interpretation of Legalist conceptions of time, then it would help account for the ease with which subsequent imperial regimes retained Legalist institutions, law codes, and administrative practices even though they increasingly used Confucian terms to justify their rule. In their structure, Legalist and Confucian conceptions of time do not appear to have differed in significant ways; however, their approaches to the indeterminate aspects of those structures were significantly different. Most significant, it appears that the Legalists sought in the human sphere what Confucians and others sought in the idea of cosmic harmony. The concept of cosmic harmony conveyed the double idea that the world of human experience shares its organization and categories with heaven, and that those categories form a finite set, such that any one implies all others. As Bodde writes: They viewed the universe as a self-contained living organism which, like every organism, experiences phases of birth, growth, decline, and seeming death—. . . invariably followed by renewed generation."[219] Thus, cosmic harmony not only implied the simultaneous inscription of all categories in the world, but also provided for a principle of change in the relationship of repeating cycles that were time itself. In the Legalist version of this idea, it seems that the principle of closure containing the world (that is, the set of classifications that are the world) shifted significantly from heaven to the emperor. Accordingly, or ideally, the emperor himself was to become the central principle of time, beyond history but defining history. Legalist concepts of written law specified both the means and the ends of a concept of history that interpreted events as the extensions of the emperor's "times" across the social space of his realm.

Perhaps western scholars have sought a reflection of their own modernist commitments in the Legalists, imagining the Confucians as traditionalists. Certainly, this aim would be consistent with the view that the

Legalists, had they succeeded, would have institutionalized a concept of progressive time in China long before it has popular currency in the West. For reasons developed in this chapter, I suggest that it is not a notion of progressive time that lends the Legalists' temporal innovations their modernist feel. Rather, what makes Legalist thought seem so familiar to Western eyes is their representation of the ultimate conceptual source of legality as deriving simultaneously from the world of experience and from a universe of timeless principles. This same mediating quality is symbolically linked to justice in popular semiotics of law in the United States (see Chapter 6). In other words, it is not the Legalists' "modernism" or their "positive law" that Westerners recognize but their symbolic negotiation of the potential contradictions inherent in a concept of social order that is taken to be the workings at once of political institutions and of sacred principles, embodied in particular forms of authority.

Specifically, in the United States, and no doubt elsewhere, contemporary cultural ideas distinguish between "justice" and "politics" in ways that unwittingly evoke Legalists' efforts to identify legality simultaneously with a mortal person and with the principle that made the emperor's personal office time itself. In the American context, "history" is the domain of politics but "justice" involves rather different notions of temporality, and public institutions are constantly faced with the problem of how to manage the juxtaposition of these two temporal logics when confronted with the reality of agencies and events in everyday life.

If Western scholars have not emphasized this particular parallel in Legalist thought, it is no doubt because the West's state institutions have their own needs and means of concealing the form and substance of their temporal negotiations. I believe it is the limited parallels in Legalist and Western notions of government's role in negotiating a critical distinction between time and history which predisposes Western writers to read Legalist references to time as gestures toward the same post-Copernican scientific principles that are embedded in modern Western principles of state bureaucracy. I have presented another interpretation in this chapter because in both China and the West it appears to be the interplay of rival visions of large-scale public institutions which inspired and animated their respective constructions of time.

The context in which the Legalists guided the Ch'in state to imperial preeminence over a newly unified China was by definition one of expanding cultural and social diversity. Their vision of the emperor's personal office was responsive to the challenges of that diversity in any number of ways, from devising a title that would distinguish him from kings to introducing new institutions of government. Here, I would emphasize the efficacy of the Legalists' reconstruction of temporality itself around inclusive principles; the concepts of time I have been considering, it is important to recall, also had a spatial dimension. The efficacy of this conceptualization of the empire in time and space outlasted the Ch'in dynasty.

In the next chapter, I consider another configuration of agency which acquires form as temporality in relation to problems of statecraft. The context shifts to ancient Mesoamerica, where, until they were interrupted by the Spanish invasion, the Aztecs were actively campaigning to extend the sovereignty of the royal line over new domains. There, too, the legitimacy of the sovereign was publicly justified in temporal terms, though differently than in China. Motecuhzoma legitimated his reign in terms of a complex genealogy that connected him to both a sacred ancestor deity, Quetzalcoatl, and, through the Quetzalcoatl cult, the reigning elites of potentially subordinate statelets. That genealogy had embedded within it a principle of territoriality, in that myths surrounding the sacred ancestor deity with whom the Aztecs identified their royal line described the god's itinerary to the edge of the Mesoamerican world, and his promised return. This aspect of territoriality was embedded in Aztec concepts of royal succession. The invocation of this ancestral deity also entailed a principle of reversible time, by virtue of Quetzalcoatl's particular attributes.

In the crisis of legitimacy that exploded under pressure of the Spanish military presence in the Aztec capital, Motecuhzoma increasingly invoked the temporal principles of genesis and reversal which were inherent in the conceptualization of this deity's sacredness. In that context, as in Ch'in China, temporality is ethnographically distinguishable as a dimension of social experience to the extent that circumstances required that ruling elites articulate the conceptual bases of their claims to rule. What Motecuhzoma did and did not understand of the emergency in which he found himself in 1519 has been the subject of considerable debate, and it is that debate that introduces the next chapter.

5 Time and Sovereignty in Aztec Mexico

*T*HOUGH TRADITIONAL REPRESENTATIONS of time in China and indigenous temporal ideas in Mesoamerica are both conventionally labeled cyclical, they are fundamentally different. Most centrally, whereas Ch'in innovations with temporal representation relocated the principle of temporal closure in the emperor, the imperial Aztecs located it in the cosmos.[1] Aztec ideas of sovereignty appear to have been profoundly embedded in cosmology through a legitimating discourse that linked the ruler and regular succession to specific deities.

This is the context in which Aztec concepts of time are conventionally credited with the fall of Motecuhzoma's empire. In what follows, however, I argue that Motecuhzoma's improvisations with the semiotics of cyclical time in the face of the Spanish challenge were his political idiom of resistance and should not be read as the misguided surrender of an emperor to a man whom he mistook for a god. Mesoamerica thus provides the context for an examination of how particular constructions of cyclical time are involved in political processes, first, as the Aztecs tried to expand their own sphere of influence across the subcontinent and, later, as the invading Spanish army brought that project to an end.

Since the days of the earliest Spanish chroniclers, narratives of the closing chapter of Motecuhzoma's reign have interpreted his responses to the invasion as those of a man blinded by faith and unable to grasp the reality of his desperate circumstances. This historiographic tradition dates from the first letters Hernán Cortés wrote from Mexico to Charles V, the king of Spain.[2] Cortés relates his active collaboration in what he represents as Motecuhzoma's illusion that Charles V is a long-awaited god, whose imminent return has long been prophesied. For example, in his first letter, Cortés quotes Motecuhzoma as referring to "the great lord or king who sent you here," of whom he declares, "We believe and are certain that he is our natural lord, especially as you [Cortés] say that he has known of us for some time. So be assured that we shall obey you and hold you as our lord in place of that great sovereign of whom you speak."[3]

The conventional reading of Motecuhzoma's "mistake" goes something like this: On the coast of what is now called Mexico, Cortés and his army of four hundred men set ashore in 1519 from the waters of the

Yucatan in pursuit of new worlds and fabled movable wealth. Within two days, through an established system of runners, the Aztec head of state, Motecuhzoma, of whose existence and seat several hundred miles away Cortés was unaware, learned of his landfall. The emperor was said to be dismayed but not altogether surprised by the message. He was, in a sense, expecting the arrival of an alien from the great lake to the east, for the legend of the god-king Quetzalcoatl, exiled from ancient Tula, prophesied that he would one day return from the east, in a One-Reed year of the Aztec calendar. The year 1519 was such a year. That this strange individual arriving from afar should have followers was not inconsistent with expectation, Motecuhzoma having been raised in the Aztec cult of the god Quetzalcoatl. Thus, according to the conventional telling, Motecuhzoma mistook Cortés for Quetzalcoatl and prepared to deliver the empire to him as if he were its rightful lord.

The attributes of Quetzalcoatl are also relevant in this conventional rendering of Motecuhzoma's downfall. Quetzalcoatl was a key figure in Aztec cosmology, which included many deities or deity complexes, dynamic configurations of divine attributes which could assume many aspects.[4] It was Quetzalcoatl, as a god, whose breath first set the sun in motion, creating time, day and night. It was Quetzalcoatl, as man, priest, and king, who had reigned over Tula, site of the great renaissance of learning and ritual perfection that were the pride of Aztec civilization, which claimed to be Tula's modern heir. Quetzalcoatl ruled as the priest-king of Tollan.[5] His reign is associated with Tollan's cultural florescence, and also its reform: Quetzalcoatl replaced human sacrifice with animal sacrifice (and autosacrifice) and instituted ritual baths, asceticism, and other things. He is said to have been a culture hero, even in his own time.[6]

Even more relevant for our purposes than Quetzalcoatl's reign as king is his fateful exile and the prophecy of his return. Quetzalcoatl the king was undone by a jealous rival, the god Tezcatlipoca. Tezcatlipoca, disguised as a foreigner, plied the unsuspecting king with intoxicating drink and then offered him his own sister, beguiling them into incest. When Quetzalcoatl awoke and realized what he had done, he exiled himself from Tula, in profound shame, both victim and offender, leaving toward the east with a band of devoted followers and promising (or promised by others) to return one day. The legend ends with this promise. Some say he died, others say he vanished over the watery horizon, others still that he was apotheosized as the morning star. Tula collapsed, its glory dissipated until the Aztecs, originally a nomadic band of hunters and foragers (even in their own legends), became self-proclaimed heirs to the Toltec glory. One form of self-legitimation was their claim to descend from Quetzalcoatl. As Davíd Carrasco has written, the "irony" of Motecuhzoma's empire is that the legend that legitimated Aztec rule also contained the prescription for its undoing.[7] But all social forms are ironic in precisely this way.

In the cyclical Aztec calendar Quetzalcoatl was associated with the year One-Reed, the year of his birth. As this year returned again and again, it is conventionally said to have renewed the augury of Quetzalcoatl's return. Coincidentally, Cortés made landfall in a One-Reed year and fulfilled the oracle. So convinced was Motecuhzoma, according to the prevailing narrative, that he sent Cortès the regalia of the god Quetzalcoatl while he was still en route, and when he arrived in the capital, Motecuhzoma surrendered the realm to him in a speech before a crowd assembled in front of the great temple of Tenochtitlan.

The evidence in favor of this conventional reading of events is compelling, beginning with Cortés's letters. In addition, the sixteenth-century chronicler Father Bernardino de Sahagún recorded a narrative of the conquest translated from contemporary Nahuatl: "Thus Moctezuma thought—thus it was thought—that this was Topiltzin Quetzalcoatl who had come to land. For it was in their hearts that he would come, that he would come to land, just to find his mat, his seat. For he had traveled there [eastward] when he departed."[8] From the same source, we know that Motecuhzoma sent emissaries to the still-distant Cortés, bearing elaborate gifts including the regalia of Quetzalcoatl (presumably, priestly regalia associated with the god's rites).[9] Motecuhzoma's own final public address, face-to-face with Cortés, recounted the genealogy of the Aztec royal line and referred to the king's anticipation of a god's return: "I have watched [the throne] for thee. . . . [Thy] governors are departed . . . who yet a very short time ago had come to stand guard for thee, who had come to govern the city of Mexico."[10] Indeed, at the close of Motecuhzoma's speech, the attending lords of Tlatelolco, Tezcoco, and Tlacopan turned away in anger, apparently to go into hiding.[11] Certainly, the evidence seems to underscore the practical defects of a cyclical concept of time.

This reading of the conquest of Mexico casts Motecuhzoma in the role of the superstitious fundamentalist unable to understand the realities of his circumstances, a despot unwilling to heed others who were more skeptical. Tzvetan Todorov is sympathetic to the Aztecs, believing them to be incapable of comprehending reality through the lens of cyclical time. For them, he says,

repetition prevails over difference.

In place of this cyclical, repetitive time frozen in an unalterable sequence, where everything is always predicted in advance, where the singular event is merely the realization of omens always and already present, in place of this time dominated by the system, appears the one-directional time of apotheosis and fulfillment, as the Christians then experience it. . . . [For the Spaniards,] the conquest also confirms the Christian conception of time, which is not an incessant return but an infinite progression toward the final victory of the Christian spirit. . . .

From this collision between a ritual world and a unique event results Montezuma's incapacity to produce appropriate and effective messages. Masters in the art of ritual discourse, the Indians are inadequate in a situation requiring improvisation, and this is precisely the situation of the conquest. Their verbal education favors paradigm over syntagm, code over context, conformity-to-order over efficacity-of-the-moment, the past over the present.[12]

Todorov says that the Spaniards were relatively quick to apprehend the Aztec sign system and then to use it against the Aztecs.

In reference to this passage and Todorov's argument more generally, Gananath Obeyesekere criticizes Todorov's rendering of Aztec people as a collectivity:

Aztec culture, [Todorov] says, was "overdetermined" by signs. . . . The implication is clear that ritual is hostile to improvisation. Behind Todorov's radical antitheses lies another crucial distinction pertaining to self and society. In the cosmologically and ritually constricting world of the Aztecs, there are no *individuals* as such. The person "is merely the constitutive element of that other totality, the collectivity" [quoting Todorov 1987a: 67]. . . . If in Todorov's scheme signs (culture) and persons are bound together in this manner, it should not surprise us if there is little room for motivation, agency, or the significance of the subject in the molding of society and consciousness.[13]

Obeyesekere maintains further that Todorov's sources can be used to show that "the Aztecs were as capable of spontaneity and improvisation as the Spaniards were capable of being dupes of their improvisational understanding of Aztec culture and mentality."[14]

I agree with Obeyesekere, particularly in his insistence on the importance of considering Aztec rhetorical and political improvisations in response to Cortés. Beyond the particulars of the events leading up to the conquest, specific assumptions about the nature of cyclical time are, in my view, the more basic flaw in the conventional reading. Todorov and others who subscribe to the view that Motecuhzoma mistook Cortés for Quetzalcoatl base their reading on their preanalysis of Aztec cyclical time. Specifically, such readings make elite Aztec representations of time cycles into both a representation of reiteration and a mentality incapable of grasping unique events, and then conflate the two. A secondary difficulty derives from making cyclical time itself a generic kind of time— Todorov's "cyclical, repetitive time frozen in an unalterable sequence, where everything is predicted in advance"[15]—rather than a set of ideas that were in some creative sense Aztec. I take Todorov's analysis as an example of how a reading of cyclical time as repetitive substantially preanalyzes cultural and political situations in potentially quite misleading ways.

In this chapter I want to reassess the relationship between the Quetzalcoatl myth and the end of the Aztec empire. In my view, the Western preoccupation with what is widely taken to be Motecuhzoma's misperceptions involves at least a double misreading. First, it misreads cyclical time as a mere variant of linear time and, second, it misreads Motecuhzoma's political improvisations as ritual conservativism. On the first point, I suggest that cyclical time was not Motecuhzoma's (or anyone's) cognitive template for comprehending events but the idiom of legitimacy constitutive of (and constituted by) elite political and religious practice in his times. On the second point, I suggest a rereading of Motecuhzoma's speech as rhetorically framed by idioms of legitimacy and sovereignty which show him to have taken full measure of the emergency he faced.

Time and Space in Mesoamerica

The Western narrative tradition of the Quetzalcoatl myth of return involves elements of both time and space. The temporal element is in the prophecy of a future event and in the proposition that the meaning of this event is to be found in the past. The spatial element is expressed in both the geography of Quetzalcoatl's exile and the apparent specification that the god is to return from the particular direction of his exile, taken to be the east.

The available evidence indicates that Mesoamerican time concepts, though cyclical, involved elements of continuity and discontinuity.[16] The continuous element was expressed all over Mesoamerica as a 260-day calendar.[17] The rationale behind the construction of this calendar, which consists of thirteen cycles of twenty days each, is not known. Aztecs at the time of the conquest said that it was invented by Quetzalcoatl.[18] The prevailing modern theory holds that the numbers thirteen and twenty were culturally important for some reason.[19] Although the "counting of the days" (in Nahuatl *tonalpohualli*)[20] was not a zodiac,[21] it did have divinatory uses in agriculture, domestic life, and other domains. There is evidence that the 260-day calendar was used by itinerant consultants.[22] It was also centrally involved in domestic and public ritual, through specialists whose oracles guided the naming of children (usually named for their birthday), the interpretation of omens and dreams, medical treatments, prognoses for all undertakings, and magical countermeasures when signs were inauspicious.[23]

The 260-day count was not only associated with its own imagery (in day names such as jaguar, alligator, stag, flower, reed, death, rain, move-ment, water, and so on).[24] It was also associated with directions, colors, and animals.[25] It is beyond the scope of this chapter to present the tables of evidence for these associations and the interpretive debates over their stability and significance. It is important, nevertheless, to note that by virtue of them, temporal signs were not entirely distinguishable from signs of space or, indeed, of other attributes and activities. This point will be important later.

The 260-day count was, for both the Maya and the Aztecs, only one of a pair of calendrical cycles that together formed the calendar round. The other cycle was the 365-day "counting of the years" (in Nahuatl, *xihuitl* or *xiuhpohualli*).[26] This cycle also involved the intercalation of two interior cycles, in this case, eighteen units of twenty days each, with five sequen-tial days in addition. Again, with the exception of the five nameless days, each day of the cycle was named and associated with its own dynamic properties. It is important to note that here, too, the symbols for express-ing time connected temporality to other dimensions of social experience.

The separate countings of the days and years were conceptualized by both Maya and Aztecs as intercalating to form the "calendar round" (260 days × 365 days). Many indigenous diagrams seem to depict the union of the two cycles;[27] the Maya referred to this calendar round as *katun*, also known as the "short count" among Western scholars. In addition, at least after the third century A.D., the Maya employed a "long count," consist-ing of a series of vigesimal and other counts.[28] The Aztecs never had a long count. In Anthony Aveni's view, the Mesoamerican genius for "chronology" and "the desire to create an ornate calendar developed into an obsession perhaps unparalleled in the history of human intellectual achievement."[29] Here, too, temporality verges on pathology.

Although both the Maya and the Aztecs celebrated the succession of calendrical cycles, that very ritual elaboration suggests that it is probably not accurate to refer to the cycles as wholly continuous. Indeed, the 365-day count was punctuated by a five-day period (nameless days called *uayeb* in Maya, *nemontemi* in Nahuatl). Since the days were not dedicated to any god, they were inauspicious for beginning any new enterprise (though the Maya filled them with ceremonies).[30] Further, at least for the Aztecs, the character of those days defined the character of the entire year (e.g., quarrels during the *nemontemi* augured quarrels all year).[31] The Maya did not include the nameless days in their definition of the year; the Aztecs did, as a short, nineteenth "month."[32] The Aztecs thus placed the *nemontemi* at the end of the year, and so did the Yucatec Maya in the classic period; however, the position of the *uayeb* in the Maya calendar otherwise varied from place to place.[33]

Other elements of discontinuity were in the concept of the year itself. Calendars across Mesoamerica vary in their positioning of the year's beginning, though the new year was ritually important everywhere.[34] The Aztecs celebrated a "binding of the year" ceremony in which the years were symbolized by bundles of peeled wands, with one stick for each year.[35] Bundles representing fifty-two years were bound together and buried under altars in the context of an expiatory ritual.[36] The Aztec "new fire" ceremony at the end of the fifty-two-year calendar round also symbolically emphasized extinction, purification, and renewal.[37] In addition, imperial Aztecs celebrated the termination of other cycles and these shared a conceptual form, as Emily Umberger explains: "It is evident that in Mexica thought the ends of cycles of several types (cosmic, calendrical, human) were marked by a period of darkness (death) before beginning the new cycle, which was seen metaphorically as the birth of light."[38] To the east, the Maya, too, seem to have symbolized the passage through each calendrical unit as a depletion, to be followed by the fullness of the new unit. The Maya zero represented completion, not emptiness.[39] For the Aztecs, twenty was a "closed" or "perfect" number.[40] The Maya referred to the last day of the month as the "seating" of the succeeding one.[41] Such images suggest a variety of formulations of cycles, some disjunctive (e.g., death), others conjunctive (e.g., seating).[42]

Thus, Aztecs and Maya juxtaposed and celebrated their calendrical cycles in a variety of ways, and in neither case were these continuous or repetitive. This observation strikes directly at the conventional post-Conquest meanings of Aztec cyclical time. At the very least, Aztec ritual emphasis appears to have been on depletion and renewal rather than continuity or return. It is not known whether the Aztecs distinguished among or counted calendrical cycles;[43] similarly, it is not known how the Maya long count was understood by its indigenous readers.[44] Burr Cartwright Brundage suggests that, at least for the Aztecs, "time moved in lustral bursts, each set self-contained."[45] I stress the issue of discontinuity within calendrical cycles because later I want to suggest that the mythic titanic contest between Tezcatlipoca and Quetzalcoatl provided the Aztecs with key symbols with which to express the provisional and discontinuous aspects of social life, and that these were built into the idea of time itself.

Johanna Broda concludes her monograph on Aztec and other Mesoamerican calendars with the observation that calendars from Hidalgo and Veracruz (in Mexico) to Nicaragua shared a general structure but varied in detail.[46] Indeed, that variation is relevant in the context of the circulation of the Quetzalcoatl myth across Mesoamerican space and the project of continual translation that this must have involved. It is useful to note some of the major differences between central Mexican and Maya technologies of time. In addition to the striking absence of the long count from central Mexico and the Maya world in the postclassic period, there were other variations that seem to define differences between Aztec and Maya calendrics. Their vocabularies were different and, as we have seen, details such as the placement and content of the five nameless days varied across the region. Further, in the Maya world, the calendar was intimately tied to astronomy, especially to the cycles of Venus.[47] The Aztec calendar was fundamentally embedded in the public rituals celebrating the 360-day count.[48] Maya ceremonial space, the design of cities, was oriented around the same astronomical principles that governed the calendar;[49] Aztec ceremonial urban space also constituted a form of text[50] but emphasized more the *axis mundi*. Indeed, Mesoamerican concepts of time were, at least in part, intimately bound up with both the definition and the operation of city-states and larger regimes. Thus, while the Maya might have used time "as a vehicle to legalize and canonize the authority of their rulership to the state,[51] as Aveni says, they did so in ways that are—and, I might note, were—distinguishable from those of the Aztecs' "cosmovision."[52]

Calendrical variation was not only broadly regional; it was also local. Maya locales kept their own lunar calendars.[53] On the basis of archaeological and documentary evidence, Joyce Marcus seems to agree that calendars were local productions, at least until the very rapid standardization of the lunar calendar (in under ten years) in the classic Maya world.[54] Other scholars disagree, including Broda, who makes the case against a Mesoamerican lunar calendar altogether.[55] Diane Z. Chase and her colleagues take issue with the idea of local lunar calendars on different grounds, referring to a "unified system of lunar count" among Maya centers.[56] The debate raises the important question of the extent to which calendars were locally or regionally managed.

Whether their variation was local or broadly regional, it is important to remember that Mesoamerican calendars were "about" more than chronology as modern readers might define the term. Some analysts use the term "space-time" to connote the mutual embeddedness of indigenous concepts of temporal and spatial order.[57] As I mentioned, calendrical units were associated with different directions, among other properties. Space-time was used in the construction of social space. For example, the literal placement of pyramids, public buildings, and whole cities can be read to reveal underlying ideological principles. Aveni and Horst Hartung explore in detail the astronomical (and by inference cosmological) priorities of the Maya in their urban planning.[58]

Whatever the astronomical basis of ceremonial architecture, though, its maintenance was in the social realm.[59] Pyramids, for example, served as time markers by virtue of their orientation in space, preserving ritual cycles against degradation as astronomical calculations failed to yield perfectly accurate results over time. Thus, while astronomy might figuratively underlie Mesoamerican social space, the validation and reproduction of space were in its ritual uses. We can find confirmation in the localness of the sight lines that shaped Maya architecture.[60]

Given these textual aspects of city space, it is perhaps not surprising that Mesoamerican representations and uses of space elaborated its literally conservative qualities. Sacred space, at least, was literally conservative in that temple buildings were constructed over former temples and ritual sites. For example, the Templo Mayor of Tenochtitlan was repeatedly reconstructed, each time enclosing the older temple; this is also true of other sites. Whether this conservatism was mandated by the buildings' prior ritual use, or whether it was because the site itself had meaning as a central place,[61] is not clear.

Another aspect of the conservative capacity of space was its dimensionality. At least in the Aztec world, geography seems to have been imagined not only as an indefinite horizon but also as a three-dimensional space, thicker in some places (e.g., mountains) and thinner (or perforated) elsewhere, to the point that the earth's surface yielded access to other planes of the universe.[62] It would seem that the Aztec "mountain cult" celebrated not only the vertical height of mountains but also their volume and, possibly, their contacts with other planes of the cosmos.[63] Temple pyramids represented all these aspects of mountain space,[64] making it meaningful to conceptualize them as platforms, containers, and axes.

The Aztec world view specified a "navel" where the world's horizontal and vertical planes converge; the vertical plane comprised of three levels.[65] The upper level began at the earth and extended upward through thirteen heavens.[66] The center level was the earth. Drawing on Nahuatl sources, Eduardo Matos Moctezuma describes the underworld as a geography revealed in time, that is, as a journey beginning at two mountains and, after four years, arriving at Mictlan.[67] It is not clear from his text whether the space of heaven similarly involved its own temporality.

It is agreed that Mesoamericans had a rich "language" of location,[68] but the nature of their concepts of directionality is the subject of recent debate. Would the direction of Cortés's arrival have been significant to the Aztecs? What did direction mean to them? The idea of the fourfold universe is found throughout pre-Hispanic Mesoamerica and the western hemisphere generally.[69] In the Maya world, this idea was expressed in five directions, north, east, south, west, and *yaxkin* (the sun's zenith).[70] In the Aztec world, there were five or six directions.[71] What the representation of the universe as "fourfold" might have meant to pre-Hispanic populations is highly controversial.

The currently prevailing interpretation holds that pre-Hispanic Mesoamericans did not organize space in terms of cardinal directions.[72] Dawn Ades and Gordon Brotherston supply ethnohistorical and archaeological evidence against interpreting Mesoamerican concepts of directionality in terms of cardinal points, or at least those familiar to us. The classic period and Yucatec Maya used direction glyphs, but only the glyphs for east and west can be unambiguously identified.[73]

Especially significant for our purposes, "east" was not associated with any particular geography; it did not signify an absolute orientation or place. Instead, direction glyphs express the sequence of locations in time: "As two primary terms, east and west cannot be 'points in space' for the same reason that they cannot be separate from time."[74] Accordingly, Aztec maps depicted the order in which landscape features (e.g., rivers) would be passed from a particular starting point, and in none of these was "a glyph or native word used to indicate direction."[75] Similarly, indigenous meanings of centrality, so important to the organization of ceremonial space and, in particular, to the symbolism associated with the deity Quetzalcoatl, do not imply intersecting cardinal points. Rather, the image associated with centrality is that of a womb, or generative point of sprouting.[76] It seems that however a fourfold universe was conceptualized, it was not as a geometry of quadrants formed by cardinal lines intersecting at right angles.

Mesoamerican space-time concepts were also associated with color. Space, too, was color coded throughout Mesoamerica, though the associations were neither standard nor stable. The Maya sometimes associated centrality with green; central Mexicans sometimes associated it with black.[77] Brotherston claims that the only sure Mesoamerican color code is red for east and black for west.[78] Be that as it may, color symbolism was bound up in cosmology and state rule throughout Mesoamerica.[79]

Quetzalcoatl

Quetzalcoatl himself was not completely integrated symbolically.[80] He had even more aspects and manifestations than other Mexican deities.[81] It is not possible to separate the human from the divine figure in the myth of return.[82] Nor can that aspect of his story be separated from the breadth and depth of his larger mythic and symbolic complex. His name means "feathered serpent,"[83] and this image is found in polychromes, monuments, and architecture continuously from the period of Teotihuacan's ascendancy (nearly a thousand years before Tenochtitlan) and, ambiguously, as early as the protoclassic Izapa civilization.[84] In Aztec times, the image of the feathered serpent could be found all over Mesoamerica.[85] Whether the presence of the icon inevitably indicates the presence of the Quetzalcoatl cult is another question, to which I return later.

Quetzalcoatl had many other manifestations and emblems in addition to the feathered serpent, including the wind, the night sky, celestial waters, or the morning star. These aspects can also be found in combination and permutation with other deity complexes.[86] As the wind, Quetzalcoatl was essential to the beginning of time; Aztec creation myth gives him alone among the assembled gods credit for knowing where to look for the rising sun, and also for setting it in motion in the sky with his breath. More generally, too, in, the mythic syntax of ancient Mexico, Quetzalcoatl is a fertile, generative, and ordering principle, as Davíd Carrasco reports:

The deity Quetzalcoatl was . . . exceptionally creative. Within the unstable, dynamic, and destructive cosmic-mythic setting, which appears at times to be filled with desperate and aggressive forces, Quetzalcoatl manifested the power of creation and creative ordering. Quetzalcoatl was instrumental in the creation of the universe and the establishment of the four-quartered cosmos. Quetzalcoatl participated in the creation of human life, corn, and pulque. He was part of the dynamic that created and destroyed the ages of the world.[87]

Importantly, the creative role that Carrasco outlines here was not limited to the myth-histories of the creation of the present age or to the founding of Tenochtitlan. Quetzalcoatl was present to Mexicans as the very principle of patronage in Tenochtitlan, ancestor of the noble class, the first king, archetype of the Quetzalcoatl priests who officiated at the main shrines at Templo Mayor, as the focus of the king's installation rites (at the moment of apotheosis), and as an aspect of conception and birth, among other manifestations and roles.[88]

I cannot overemphasize the importance of this evidence of Quetzalcoatl's continual *presence* to Mexicans through myth and daily practice in a wide range of institutional domains. Indeed, though the myth of return might seem to imply Quetzalcoatl's absence, these other aspects of his myth denote his luminous and unprovisional presence. The rich evidence of the myth complexes and the ritual elaboration surrounding Quetzalcoatl suggest that he is *simultaneously* present and absent. To ears attuned to the preoccupation of linear time with sequence, the myth of return seems to stipulate a chronology. I interpret the myth of return as just one element of a larger "vocabulary" of Quetzalcoatl myths from which it cannot be meaningfully isolated. The myths refer to Quetzalcoatl's exile and return among other references to the deity's attributes.

I read references to exile and return as vehicles for signs of Quetzalcoatl's different properties, states, or "aspects," not as events. Quetzalcoatl's presence and absence do not indicate an itinerary but are attributes of the deity's particular form of agency in the cosmos and society. Quetzalcoatl, as present-absent, signifies a potentiating agency and its reversibility or closure. I base this assessment on the myth of exile and return and the ritual uses of the Quetzalcoatl figure or its elements as recorded from daily and special practices. Many sources refer to "aspects" of Quetzalcoatl in the wind or the morning star, not to different Quetzalcoatls.[89] And as already noted, Quetzalcoatl cannot even be definitively distinguished from other deities.[90] Thus, figuration of a Quetzalcoatl should not be detached from its larger field of signs. In relation to those signs, Quetzalcoatl's association with reversibility, or the provisional nature of genesis, corresponds to the elements of discontinuity, depletion, and renewal embedded in the Aztec concepts of time.

In the symbolic vocabulary of the imperial Aztecs, Quetzalcoatl had a specific relevance to the legitimation and continuity of the empire and the emperor himself. Carrasco develops a convincing reading of the Quetzalcoatl myth as central to the Aztecs' understandings of their own history and the legitimacy of their rule in central Mexico.[91] Specifically, their veneration of Quetzalcoatl as the ancestor of the noble class and the founder of their monarchy linked modern Tenochtitlan to Tollan (Tula), the premier city and site of the mythic golden age ushered in by Quetzalcoatl's sovereignty in human form. To be heirs to the great Tollan was a valued good in its own right, and was instrumental in the internal and external politics of the Aztec period.

The Quetzalcoatl myth placed the deity in a variety of roles vis-à-vis Aztec historical experience. In one variant, the Aztecs are followers of the exiled Quetzalcoatl; in another, they are his heirs, through a tactical marriage alliance with the Azcapoltzalco, a Toltecized group among whom the Aztecs lived in their migratory period, prior to their founding of Tenochtitlan in the early fourteenth century.[92] Another myth places the wandering Aztecs at Cholollan, a center of the Quetzalcoatl cult, consulting an oracle about where they should settle and receiving their answer from Quetzalcoatl himself.[93]

Quetzalcoatl's importance to the empire went well beyond issues of royal genealogy and claims to the royal seat at Tenochtitlan. His myth provided the very "paradigm of authority," as Carrasco says: "While it is clear that Quetzalcoatl was not the only symbol of sanctified authority in central Mesoamerica, he was a distinctly valued, resilient, and indispensable paradigm of authority."[94] Through the offices of the high priests, the divine sources of imperial authority and their Toltec roots were constantly accessible.[95] In Henry Nicholson's view, there was a specific link between Quetzalcoatl and kingship; he "appears to have manipulated the symbols and rituals of royal power . . . so successfully that he continued, many generations after his 'fall' and 'flight,' to be considered the fountainhead of all 'legitimate' political power in central Mexico."[96] (The quotation marks presumably indicate some reservations about the specifics of the myth of return.)

In early colonial sources, the imagery of Quetzalcoatl's legitimating role is quite specific. For example, Alvarado Tezozomoc reports a conversation between Motecuhzoma and his counselor Tlacaelel, who reminded the king of his duty to restore Quetzalcoatl's portrait carved in rock at the Garden of Chapultepec, since Quetzalcoatl would return.[97]

In Aztec times, Quetzalcoatl figured importantly in the elaborate ritual of succession for the *huey tlatoani* (monarch).[98] The ceremony, which lasted for several days, emphasized the initial disjunction of the person of the candidate and the office he was about to hold.[99] A dance, the nobles encircling the *huey tlatoani* to the beat of a great drum, came at the very end of the ceremony, when the candidate was fully invested and apotheosized.[100] The drum itself was "the very voice of the wind god," Quetzalcoatl.[101] The *huey tlatoani* claimed both descent from Quetzalcoatl and mandate by election.[102]

All in all, Quetzalcoatl appears to have offered the Aztecs the hermeneutic vocabulary with which to define the rationalizing principle of authority and empire.[103] Importantly, that principle is (among other things) a temporal one that defines the historicity of the empire as phases of initiation and closure. History connects not to Quetzalcoatl alone but to a deity who figures in a host of myths with other gods. Here, I refer to the myth of return (in which Tezcatlipoca figures importantly as the agent of Quetzalcoatl's downfall) and to a larger myth literature.

For the Aztecs, these cosmogonic and foundational myths were textualized in the very design of Tenochtitlan. As Carrasco notes, Quetzalcoatl was not the patron of the city. If there was one, it was Huitzilopochtli, whose cult the Aztecs may have brought with them from their migrations and which became preeminent during the Triple Alliance period.[104] The Quetzalcoatl cult was practiced within the sacred precinct of the Templo Mayor of Tenochtitlan, where a pyramid was dedicated to the deity and where the priestly office bore the deity's name. The pyramid stood facing, and at the symmetrical junction of, the twin pyramids dedicated to Huitzilipochtli and Tlaloc (themselves complex deities, representing multiple aspects of the sun and Venus). Carrasco and others argue convincingly that the sacred precinct was a text designed to be read, if not as a charter for the particular social and cosmic relationships essential to the empire, then as the expression of its aesthetic.[105] In this geography, the Templo Mayor was the *axis mundi*,[106] and Quetzalcoatl appears to have represented the principle of centrality. It is important to recall that Mesoamerican conceptions of the center emphasized its generative aspects, rather than its location at a convergence of planes organized around cardinal axes.[107]

Quetzalcoatl's association with centrality/genesis is suggested indirectly by Aveni's analysis of the first page of the *Codex Fejervary Mayer*, a Mexican pictorial text depicting deities arranged within the form of a Maltese cross; Aveni describes the god at the center of the cross as a source "from whom life-giving streams of blood flow."[108] Brundage links Quetzalcoatl more directly to the opening of the "navel" on the floor of the ball court, which led to the nadir of the underworld.[109] At Teotihuacan, the Temple of Quetzalcoatl was "the quintessential meeting place of cosmic levels and forces," representing the convergence of the universe's vertical and pivotal forces.[110] At Templo Mayor, Quetzalcoatl's verticality is perhaps expressed in his association with the heliacal rising of Venus in his Tlahuizcalpantecuhtli aspect.[111]

My presentation of these diverse references to Quetzalcoatl's presence in cosmic space are inconclusive but perhaps suggest some elaborations of his generative power. His centrality in the temporal sense underscores his dynamic role as the historicizing principle for the Aztecs. Everywhere, it seems, his power was not so much to create the fundamental distinctions essential to Aztec life as to make them work, to animate them. As with his mobilization of the first day, his generative animation of the universe was not *in* time but was time itself. And Quetzalcoatl "himself" was not *in* time, as the conventional reading of Motecuhzoma's "mistake" has it, but was a figuration of the temporal principle. Quetzalcoatl provided the key signs and symbols with which Aztec elites could represent their historical legitimacy as the immediate effect of Quetzalcoatl's on-going agency; indeed, it seems that the legitimating relevance of history lay not in its being past but in its confirmation of the efficacy of the signs associated with the particular forms of agency that Quetzalcoatl signified. I return shortly to the place of Quetzalcoatl in Aztec historical narrative.[112]

Aztec Historical Thought and Narrative

As we have seen, Mexicans had a durable technology for calculating and naming the progress and relationships among calendrical cycles. Their concept of history also appears to have emphasized these relationships, which linked the timing of an event and its significance. To refer to the "timing" of an event apart from its significance is undoubtedly inaccurate in the Mexican context; "timing" and "meaning" were each other's corollary. Aztec historical narrative reveals some of the expressions of the identity of time and significance. Aztec historical texts are didactic, and merge events and the interpretation of events.[113] Day names apparently served as a narrative device for aligning the past and the future.[114] The myth of Quetzalcoatl's return bears these features; indeed, approaching the myth of return *as narrative* rather than as an expression of private belief is helpful in the experimental reconsideration that follows.

The alignment of past, present, and future involved more than the cycles of day names, important though those were. As in the case of the Quetzalcoatl myth, it is difficult to distinguish among aspects or manifestations of an entity, so adept were the Aztecs at managing the proliferations and consolidations of the representations of particular agents. Thus, as noted, Quetzalcoatl as deity had multiple forms, overlapping with one another and also with aspects of other gods. At the same time, though the fact of a human Quetzalcoatl at Tula in the eighth century appears to be undisputed, the question of precisely how to disentangle the human Topilztin Quetzalcoatl and the god Ehecatl Quetzalcoatl has never been settled, in spite of the enormous scholarly effort applied to it in modern times.[115] It is not only narratives of Quetzalcoatl that demonstrate Aztec facility for fusing what we might distinguish as humans and their apotheoses; representation of the god Tlaloc also indelibly merges the deity with human predecessors.[116] In their representation, the attributes of deities and humans appear to have been more important than any particular figuration of them as an aggregate assemblage (e.g., as an individual).

Pre-Hispanic Mesoamerican narrative generally begins in medias res, rather than according to some fixed chronological principle.[117] Indeed, perhaps the quality Ades and Brotherston observe reflects Aztec preference for a narrative principle other than chronology; this, at least, would seem consistent with temporal concepts that invested categories of events, rather than sequences of events, with meaning. At any rate, examples of this quality exist in the general and particular references Aztecs made to their own "myth of migration."[118]

The Aztecs were not indigenous to the Valley of Mexico but migrated there some two hundred years before the Cortés expedition. In their own story of enlightenment and success, imperial Aztecs defined the signs of their superiority and made them available to others in the form of historical narratives that demonstrated their beginnings as nomadic hunter-gatherers in the northern part of central Mexico, their political and physical feats as mercenaries in the Valley of Mexico, and their meteoric ascendancy in the Triple Alliance period.[119] These were not just legends of a glorious past but the charter for an expansionist present in which there was continual need to assert the legitimacy of the empire generally and the imperial line specifically.[120] The narrative emphasis was on the links between the present Aztecs and the Tula, the Tollan of the golden age.

The myth of Quetzalcoatl's return was part of the myth of migration at several points. First is Quetzalcoatl's association with the initiation of Tula's golden age. It was in his reign, according to myth, that Tula became the seat of culture. Several forms of the myth of migration add detail to this association. One version has the Aztecs themselves as late followers of the exiled god, leaving Tula about fifteen years after Quetzalcoatl. Another establishes the link to Tula through a strategic marriage alliance with the Tepanecs at Azcapotzalco, for whom the migrating Aztecs served as mercenaries and against whom they later rebelled.[121] Narratives of the myth also placed the Aztecs at Cholollan (or Cholula, the primary center of a Quetzalcoatl cult), receiving authorization to settle at Tenochtitlan from Quetzalcoatl himself. All versions seem to emphasize the Aztecs' rough beginnings and to credit their extended conversion experience to Quetzalcoatl's teachings and manifest legitimacy.

An illustration of the quality of in medias res in Aztec narrative comes, in fact, from the myth of migration involving the Toltec Azcapoltzalcans. The Aztecs apparently sought access to the "sacred genealogy" of Azcapoltzalco, which would link them directly to Quetzalcoatl.[122] Diego Duran, a sixteenth-century Spanish chronicler, records the Aztecs' petition for an individual whose heritage made his marriage to an Aztec woman particularly desirable:

Great lord, we the Mexicans, your servants and vassals, shut in as we are among the reeds and rushes . . . it would not be just that we should remain without a chief or lord. . . . For this reason we come to you, knowing that among your people there are sons of our blood, related to yours, brought forth from our bodies and yours. And among those of your blood and ours we have learnt that there exists a son of Opichiztahuatzin, whose name is Acamapichtli. He is also the son of your daughter called Atotoztli. We beg that you give him to us as our lord, so that we may maintain him as is fitting, since he is of the lineage of the Mexicans and of the kings and lords of Culhuacan.[123]

Acamapichtli became the founder of the royal line that ended with Motecuhzoma. This extract of direct discourse is recorded two hundred years after the fact. As Carrasco observes, the speech describes "not only an act of social acquisition but also an act of symbolic acquisition."[124] The symbolic acquisition of the hallmarks of legitimacy is managed in the narrative form itself: the desideratum, Acamapichtli, is represented to his people as being both *alien* and *already Aztec*. Thus, though the petition is addressed to Azcapoltzalco, the narrative gives the decisive part to the mixed "blood" of Azcapoltzalco and the Aztecs; Acamapichtli is, in that sense, already among the Aztecs. Motecuhzoma, I suggest, used this same narrative tactic in an attempt to appropriate Cortés into the Aztec hegemony.

Indeed, the myth of Quetzalcoatl's return is perhaps the major example of a narrative form of sacred history which isolates the desideratum's existence outside the familiar realm in order to emphasize its immanence within that very realm. Sacred history provides the means and the rationale for distinguishing the past, present, and future in meaningful terms.[125] Just as Acamapichtli is both alien and cousin, so Quetzalcoatl, whom we encounter in the same sort of narrative form, appears to me to be both exiled and returned. These are not events but states or relationships vis-à-vis the narrative community. In the chronicles, Quetzalcoatl's absence seems to be associated with stability in the monarchy; his return appears to be symbolically expressive of the intrinsic instability of succession. It is in these terms, I believe, that Motecuhzoma referred to Quetzalcoatl during the last days of the empire.

It seems clear that the myth of Quetzalcoatl's return must be understood in the context of Aztec historical narrative forms, not, in the conventional reading, as transparent statements of belief to be taken literally. Quetzalcoatl's place in the narrative forms and meanings of empire, and specifically of succession, was also expressed in other aspects of his cult. In view of the distinctive quality of Aztec historical narrative form, it seems entirely characteristic that the migration myth would represent as a direct legacy something that was, in practical terms, alien and much desired; in this case, the desideratum was a claim to involvement in the circulation of Quetzalcoatl's agency as one sign of legitimate rule.

The Quetzalcoatl Cult in Postclassic Mesoamerica

Though the Aztec migration myth (including the myth of Quetzalcoatl's return) specifies Tula as the source of their cultural practices, the Quetzalcoatl myth and its cult were older and more widespread than Tula.[126] Indeed, both the iconography and the cult practices associated with Quetzalcoatl predate the life of the man identified as Topiltzin Quetzalcoatl, who lived in the eighth century A.D.

Although the presence of iconography associated with Quetzalcoatl (such as a serpent with feathers instead of scales) does not necessarily indicate the presence of a cult dedicated to him, archaeological evidence suggests veneration of this deity was widespread and ancient.[127] There was an active Quetzalcoatl cult at Teotihuacan, whose regional hegemony preceded Tula's by as much as five hundred years (approximately 300–800 A.D.; Tula's dominance followed from the tenth to the twelfth centuries A.D.), and Tenochtitlan's by almost a millennium.[128] The Quetzalcoatl cult at Teotihuacan was probably not founded there, either. Perhaps it came to central Mexico with the Huastecs or the proto-Maya Izapans along Mexico's Gulf Coast.[129] The feathered serpent image, at any rate, was already very old and widespread by the time the Aztecs established their seat at Tenochtitlan.

Nicholson provisionally links the feathered serpent icon to the classic lowland Maya "serpent bird" or "principal bird deity," though he notes that the feathered snake image itself appears only very late in the northern Yucatec lowlands (with the Mexican influence at Uxmal) and is entirely absent in the central Maya area during the classic period.[130] In other words, though the iconography associated with Quetzalcoatl may have a longer genealogy, the feathered serpent appeared among the Maya only with the vast wave of Toltec influence that began in the ninth century A.D. The round buildings associated with the Quetzalcoatl cult, and which are otherwise rare, began to appear in the Maya world at the same time, that is, in the early postclassic period.[131]

In Chichen Itza, a Maya capital, the archaeological evidence of a Quetzalcoatl deity is strong.[132] In Yucatec Maya, Quetzalcoatl's name was Kukulcan (though I continue to refer to Quetzalcoatl throughout, for simplicity's sake). Maya narratives of the Quetzalcoatl myth stressed both his exile from Tollan *and* his arrival at Chichen Itza. At Chichen Itza, a Toltecized site that exerted influence and power over eastern Mesoamerica during its period of ascendancy, the Quetzalcoatl icon appears with great intensity.[133] Chichen Itza had its own sacred history that lay claim to both Quetzalcoatl's presence and its own identification as Tollan.

When Tula fell, its heirs to regional prominence (in terms of power and cultural influence) in central Mexico were Cholollan (Cholula) and Xochicalco. Tula and Cholollan had inherited Teotihuacan's dominant role in the Mexican Valley; Xochicalco was also important at that earlier period.[134] After the collapse of Tula, Cholollan and Xochicalco became important centers, both of which had active contact with the Maya world.[135] Cholollan, a major ritual center dedicated to Quetzalcoatl, actually predated Teotihuacan, though it is not clear when the Quetzalcoatl cult became active there. Xochicalco also had a temple dedicated to Quetzalcoatl, on which a relief shows a personified Maya date glyph pulling an Aztec date glyph on a tump line.[136] Henderson identifies additional Maya architectural and iconographic details at Xochicalco's Quetzalcoatl temple and offers them as evidence of the "exchange of esoteric informa-

tion among priests or aristocrats" from widely dispersed areas at
Xochicalco during the postclassic period (which included the Aztecs' rise
to power in central Mexico).[137]

Indeed, by the time the Aztecs came to power in the fourteenth century, there were (or had been) active Quetzalcoatl cults at the Maya lowland capitals of Chichen Itza and Mayapan (Chichen Itza's successor) and
in central Mexico at Xochicalco and probably most notably at Cholollan,
as well as other smaller sites. The Quetzalcoatl cult appears to have traveled eastward with the spread of Toltec influence in that part of Mesoamerica, and from there, it traveled back again, though it was not lost
from central Mexico in the interim. My point is that though the Aztecs
might have correctly pointed to Tula (Hidalgo) as the source of their
own practices associated with Quetzalcoatl, Quetzalcoatl was in very
wide circulation both before and after Tula at other ritual centers. By the
time the Aztecs settled at Tenochtitlan, they could have experienced the
cult at several highly cosmopolitan centers that were in contact with and
suffused by Maya knowledge and practice of Quetzalcoatl.

Among both Maya and Aztecs, the cult appears to have been associated with elites. Only at Cholollan does Quetzalcoatl appear to have been
venerated in a popular cult.[138] Indeed, the Aztecs identified Quetzalcoatl
as the founder of the nobility through autosacrifice, as Cecilia Klein explains:

According to Aztec myth, . . . the first and most important act of autosacrifice
was performed by the god Quetzalcoatl, from whom all members of the nobility
were thought to descend. By shedding blood from his virile member over the
bones of an extinct population, Quetzalcoatl created a race described . . . as "the
vassals of the gods." The first act of bloodletting thus was presented in myth as
performed by the archetypal noble for the express purpose of creating a subser-
vient commoner class.[139]

The relationship between the aristocracy and commoners was peri-
odically replicated and renewed in the ritual bloodlettings that were part
of the Quetzalcoatl cult.[140]

In the postclassic period, forms of Toltec influence in the Maya region
included the development of a new aristocracy, or perhaps the forging of
a dependency on the part of local Maya ruling dynasties on sources of
Toltec influence.[141] Whereas earlier Maya aristocracies had been relatively
autonomous, they had apparently come to depend on their ties to
"Tollan" for legitimacy. Quetzalcoatl provided an important cultural idiom for expressing these connections. For example, Quiche and Cakchi-
quel (Guatemala) records of investiture ceremonies feature a "lord Nax-
cit" (another name for Quetzalcoatl) and his palace at "Tollan" (in this

case, Chichen Itza).[142] Earlier, in the classic period, the "wind deity" had been associated with royal legitimation at Xochicalco, Palenque, and in Nicaragua; later, the deity 9-Wind became an aspect of Quetzalcoatl.[143] Mixtec rulers claimed descent from a deity they called 9-Ehecatl (called 9 Ehecatl Quetzalcoatl by one commentator).[144] Again, the importance of this evidence is in its implication that Quetzalcoatl provided the Aztecs with a ready-made discourse by which symbolically to appropriate the self-legitimation strategies of the elites of a very broad cultural and political terrain.

The symbolism of the Aztecs' installation ritual for the *huey tlatoani*, which culminated in the danced evocation of Quetzalcoatl at the moment of the monarch's apotheosis, was, in fact, ancient and widespread in Mesoamerica; similar installation rites were performed at Tenochtitlan, Tlaxcala, Huexotzingo, and Cholula in central Mexico, among the Quiche and Cakchiquels (in what is now Guatemala) and as far away as San Salvador and Nicaragua.[145] Wherever they were practiced, such ceremonies were essential for integrating (or asserting the integration of) political organization with the religious cult that legitimated power; at their heart was the connection between legitimate rule and the legendary Tollan.[146]

Although Quetzalcoatl's centrality in the ritual expressions of aristocratic legitimacy appears reasonably certain, it seems equally likely that those ritual displays were contested locally. In Tenochtitlan, where social stratification was highly organized and regulated, different status groups had their own cults and, where they came together in collective ritual, their own parts to perform.[147] The ruling class offered extensive patronage to artists whose distinctive productions reflect elaborate and innovative conceptualizations of the cosmos and its divinities.[148] Ritual objects marked social status. Objects meant for popular use in homes and fields portrayed different figures and were made from different materials.[149] Indeed, as the state cult grew more elite and exclusive within the increasingly closed spaces of the sacred precinct, popular cults were practiced in the streets and in open fields.[150] In Tenochtitlan as well as at distant sites in the Maya region, archaeological evidence suggests that this ritual pluralism was sometimes associated with tensions that erupted in violence against shrines, revitalization movements, and other forms of resistance.[151] Where the ritual expression of the Quetzalcoatl cult was sustained and highly coherent (as at Tenochtitlan just prior to the Spanish invasion), it seems reasonable to search for the strategies by which its celebrants managed to control such tensions.

Ritual pluralism was not always or only the result of urban class divisions. It was also inherent in the cultural diversity of Mesoamerica in the postclassic period. The interchange of ritual knowledge and practice mentioned earlier was only one element of the intense cultural exchange that characterized this period of Mesoamerican experience. The postclassic period in the Maya region was defined by a break from earlier architecture and traditions, followed by new styles that bear witness to external influence. The Long Count came to an end. Sometimes sites show evidence of depopulation or abandonment; more often, they show multiple styles in close proximity. Sometimes the new pluralism indicates radical change; sometimes only minor or gradual change. The Maya world shows evidence of multiple ethnic groups,[152] though, in general, the new styles can be associated with Toltec influence. The sources of that influence, whether, for example, invasion or shifting fashions, are in dispute and probably differed by locale. The main source appears to have been toward the western frontier of the Maya region, that is, closer to the sources of Toltec culture; however, evidence of a Toltec presence is best conserved farther from central Mexico, perhaps indicating less interplay or convergence of cultural influences in the outlying frontier zones.[153]

The forces that eventually transformed the Maya region were not new in the postclassic period.[154] What were new were political and cultural shifts that resulted in regional instability and a loss of former cultural coherence.[155] The alien cultural elements in the Maya region were marked by monumental ostentation, claims to political legitimacy, and the "Mexicanization" of ruling dynasties—a reference to Tula and Toltec stylistic influence.[156] Over the course of two centuries, the Maya resisted these claims to Toltecized bases of legitimacy, for their own sense of rulership rested on blood lines.[157]

During the postclassic period, Mesoamerica experienced a radical expansion of bases of authority and a sharply increased difficulty in establishing any one of them as a principle of rationalization. Political and religious ideas were in rapid circulation; commerce also connected the frontiers of Mesoamerica to its centers.[158] In some places, local elites confronted new elite groups; elsewhere, local elite solidarities collapsed.[159] Old infrastructures gave way or were abandoned in favor of new ones that linked the regions of Mesoamerica in new ways.[160] The Toltec influence that defined postclassic Mesoamerica was associated with a proliferation of new cults or variations of old ones.[161] In this context, Richard A. Diehl notes, "Quetzalcoatl's prominence increased tremendously, particularly in his guises as the Feathered Serpent and Ehecatl, the Wind God."[162] In practice, the boundaries of the Aztec empire were constantly changing, and within those boundaries, there was a constantly shifting cultural diversity.[163] Elsewhere in Mesoamerica, too, ethnic diversity expanded.[164]

Against this backdrop of accelerating diversity, the Aztecs' myth of migration and, in particular, the myth of Quetzalcoatl's return were articulate assertions of a generalized regional dominion and justifications of a particular regime. The Aztec myth and cult were selective in specifying Tula as their origin; given the extent to which evocations of Tula were bound up in other regimes' claims to rulership, the Aztecs' claim was, in effect, a claim to legitimacy wherever a Toltecized aristocracy ruled. The elected *huey tlatoani* of Tenochtitlan wielded a charismatic authority; that charisma was represented by the Aztecs as the replication or extension of Quetzalcoatl's piety and heroism.[165] At the same time, the Aztecs were careful to specify Quetzalcoatl's genealogical primacy as founder of the nobility and the ruling line in particular (and to specify the ancestry of Acamapichtli); perhaps this genealogy gave the Aztecs a lexicon for responding to challenges to Toltecized regimes on the basis of blood lines. Such challenges would have come not only from the Maya world but also from closer to home; the contest for control of the Valley of Mexico was never fully settled at core or periphery.[166] In that context, Sahagún's native informants described Mexico and Cholollan as "friends."[167] Perhaps this is evidence of how necessary the Quetzalcoatl cult was to the imperial Aztecs as an instrument with which to maintain their regional dominance. There is some evidence that all Mesoamerican rulers made a pilgrimage to Cholollan for sanctification.[168]

Archaeological evidence from the Yucatan and Quintana Roo suggests that there the Quetzalcoatl cult was involved in the mobilization of local populations around the new elites,[169] but the elites failed in their attempt to create a "Mesoamerican international culture."[170] David A. Freidel characterizes the context of that failure in terms that strikingly evoke the aftermath of the Spanish defeat of Mexico: "The general decline in the central control and deployment of social energy after Chichen Itza truly marks a dark age for a people no longer celebrating their own vision of the world and unable to accept a foreign one."[171] Indeed, Freidel's comment implies the extent to which the Spanish presence and mission were within the realm of what the Aztecs had previously experienced. Though the Spaniards were strangers to the indigenous populations of the region, they were not the only strangers. Mesoamerica was a diverse and dynamic world, in which elites in particular could maintain their claims to legitimacy only by learning to navigate the swift cultural and political crosscurrents of the region. Thus, it would seem that Motecuhzoma's reaction to Cortés should be comprehensible in terms of what he understood, rather than what he misunderstood.

I want to emphasize three main points: that it seems likely the Aztecs themselves came to Quetzalcoatl as foreigners, that their early encounters with highly organized Quetzalcoatl cults would likely have been at ritual centers in central Mexico which were in contact with Maya priesthoods knowledgeable about Quetzalcoatl's myth and veneration, and that in the postclassic period throughout the Mexican and Maya regions of Meso-america Quetzalcoatl was specifically involved in rulers' installation rituals and generally involved in the legitimacy of the new Toltecized aristocra-cies. These points suggest a broad cultural and political context in which Quetzalcoatl was already a focal point of contests over elite legitimacy (and, in the Aztec case, sovereignty) quite apart from whatever confusion might have arisen from Cortés's presence.[172]

Again, in each of these contexts, the manifold importance of Quet-zalcoatl to the imperial Aztecs included the representational means to assert the regime's own legitimacy to a very large and diverse audience in familiar terms and to profer that legitimacy as a rationalizing principle across eastern Mesoamerica. The results of that effort were at best incon-clusive at the time of the Spanish debarcation. Certainly, Cortés did not march across a unified empire. Nevertheless, if I have described with reasonable accuracy the context into which Cortés arrived, it is not sur-prising that Motecuhzoma should attempt to bring him into the empire using the same idiom as the Toltecized aristocracy, that of Quetzalcoatl's figure and signs. His own regime had successfully asserted itself using these very terms, if not in the Maya world, as I have suggested here, then at least among the Mexica. Motecuhzoma would thus have thought of Cortés not as a god but as a menace. The invasion was not an event meeting its awaiting interpretation as the conventional Western reading of cyclical times would suggest, but rather an event fully comprehended by the Aztecs whose actions were recorded at the time, people who un-derstood Cortés's challenge and responded accordingly.

Motecuhzoma and Quetzalcoatl

Before reconsidering Motecuhzoma's references to Quetzalcoatl in rela-tion to Cortés, let us return to Tenochtitlan as a site of political contest. I have already described how Aztec settlement at Tenochtitlan as well as the legitimacy of the royal line involved mythic references to Quet-zalcoatl, exiled from Tula in the myth but symbolically returned at the moment of each Aztec monarch's installation. Tlacaelel's famous refer-ence to the future return of the god[173] appears to have been a metaphori-cal reference to the temporariness of any monarch's incumbency. Further, "the Quetzalcoatl" was the priestly office equal in rank to that of the ruler within the sacred precinct.[174] In fact, Quetzalcoatl was symbolically in-volved in every aspect of Aztec celebrations of the foundation and succession of their kingship. The chronicles bear witness to the extent to which Quetzalcoatl also provided the narrative framework for these institutional processes.

And yet, it is essential to recall that Quetzalcoatl was not the only god or the most important. The Aztecs came to his veneration as aliens; they imported Huitzilopochtli as their patron and acknowledged many deities, among whom Quetzalcoatl was not supreme. Xiuhtecuhtli, the "old god," was the one most venerated.[175] What is important is that Quetzalcoatl was *already* the rationalizing principle of government in the Valley of Mexico when the Aztecs arrived. The Aztecs "symbolically acquired" his genealogy and efficacy by means of certain narrative strategies.

This sort of tactical symbolic appropriation and ritual eclecticism was commonplace in the capital. Richard F. Townsend notes that the "bonding of cults from different locations and sources was a well-known feature of religious life at Tenochtitlan and was part of an effort to create an imperial cult system."[176] The Templo Mayor was the setting for this effort, the site of many rituals besides the ones that legitimated the "state cult."[177] The great temple conserved ancient cosmological traditions, and the government itself was situated symbolically within the Aztec "cosmovision."[178] It was in this temple that Motecuhzoma was installed and where he made his last public speech.

The Aztecs' Huitzilopochtli cult was partially merged with a cult associated with Tezcatlipoca. Indeed, many of Quetzalcoatl's mythic acts of genesis are in partnership with either Huitzilopochtli or Tezcatlipoca.[179] Among his many aspects and mythic roles, Tezcatlipoca figures as the agent of Quetzalcoatl's exile in the myth of return. Tezcatlipoca was cunning; among his notable disguises was the aspect of a Huastec chili vendor.[180] He was also beguiling. In spite of Quetzalcoatl's famous self-discipline, Tezcatlipoca lured him into acts that made Quetzalcoatl wish for death, a death he denied himself by choosing self-exile from Tula instead.

Tezcatlipoca also figures importantly in post-Conquest narratives of the final days of Motecuhzoma's empire. Indeed, in Sahagún's chronicle of the last days, he is mentioned as many times as Quetzalcoatl.[181] When Motecuhzoma sent the regalia of Quetzalcoatl to the still-distant Spanish (widely read as evidence of his belief that Cortés was the returning god), he also sent that of Tezcatlipoca and other official regalia.[182] Sahagún's informants also tell of Motecuhzoma's subsequent efforts to forestall disaster by sending sorcerers against the Spanish army during a night before the fighting began; on the road, they met (and were turned back by) "the youth, Tezcatlipoca," disguised as a drunken Chalcan. Tezcatlipoca pointed to Tenochtitlan, already burning in spite of the fact that the fighting had not yet started.[183] Sahagún's informants detail omens that presaged Tenochtitlan's defeat, and these evoke "the reversal of cosmic order" in very specific ways.[184] The final one inverts one of Tezcatlipoca's emblems, the flute: "Suddenly the omen appeared, blazing like a great bonfire in the sky. . . . It . . . made loud noises, rumbling and hissing like a metal tube placed over a fire."[185]

These references, and the larger meanings of Tezcatlipoca, raise the possibility that it was not Quetzalcoatl's *return* that Cortés seemed to herald but, if anything, his *contest* with Tezcatlipoca or even his *exile*, again, at the hands of Tezcatlipoca. Be that as it may, the post-conquest chronicles seem to portray Tezcatlipoca as very much in control of the situation. Tezcatlipoca's centrality in indigenous accounts of the final struggle with Cortés's forces might imply that some Aztecs found words and images for these events in the mythic contest between Tezcatlipoca and Quetzalcoatl, not in a reincarnation of Quetzalcoatl. Whatever their personal beliefs, post-conquest authors found key metaphors and some of their narrative form in this titanic contest.[186] It should be viewed not as an *event* in the Aztec cosmos but as a representation of the circumstances of conflict which reveal rival sources of agency and the stakes in their multiplicity.

Motecuhzoma's own reported references to Quetzalcoatl raise somewhat different issues. Sahagún's informants record three instances when Motecuhzoma is said to have invoked Quetzalcoatl. The first is one that they ascribe to him, when he exhorts messengers from the coast to keep secret their encounter with the Spanish: "Thus [Motecuhzoma] thought—thus was it thought—that this was Topiltzin Quetzalcoatl who had come to land. For it was in their hearts that he would come, that he would come to land, just to find his mat, his seat."[187] This image of returning to the mat or the seat was central to the Aztec ceremonial discourse of royal succession. According to Sahagún's glossary, the mat, the reed mat, the seat are standard Nahuatl metaphors for the ruler's throne.[188]

The second reference, as the Spanish army approaches, is in the incident in which emissaries from Motecuhzoma carry four "arrays" to them as gifts, those of Quetzalcoatl, Tezcatlipoca, the lord of Tlalocan, and another set of Quetzalcoatl regalia.[189] Motecuhzoma subsequently sent additional gifts, this time poisoned foods and potions, in a failed attempt to destroy the Spanish.[190] I take this as evidence that the first set of gifts was sent not to a recipient whom Motecuhzoma thought to be a deity but to one he considered dangerous and a threat to his realm.

The third reference is in Motecuhzoma's final public speech, delivered in the presence of Cortés before a crowd of witnesses. I quote it in full from Sahagún's informants:

O our lord, thou hast suffered fatigue, thou hast endured weariness. Thou hast come to arrive on earth. Thou hast come to govern thy city of Mexico; thou hast come to descend upon thy mat, upon thy seat, which for a moment I have watched for thee, which I have guarded for thee. For thy governors are departed—the rulers Itzcoatl, Moctezuma the Elder, Axayacatl, Tizoc, Auitzotl, who yet a very short time ago had come to stand guard for thee, who had come to govern the city of Mexico. Under their protection thy common folk came. Do they yet perchance know it in their absence? O that one of them might witness, might marvel at what to me now hath befallen, at what I see quite in the absence of our lords. I by no means merely dream, I do not merely see in a dream, I do not see in my sleep; I do not merely dream that I see thee, that I look into thy face. I have been afflicted for some time. I have gazed at the unknown place whence thou hast come—from among the clouds, from among the mists. And so this. The rulers departed maintaining that thou wouldst come to visit thy city, that thou wouldst come to descend upon thy mat, upon thy seat. And now it hath been fulfilled; thou hast come; thou has endured fatigue, thou hast endured weariness. Peace be with thee. Rest thyself. Visit thy palace. Rest thy body. May peace be with our lords.[191]

Are these words addressed to someone whom the speaker believes to be a god? Two sorts of evidence suggest that they are not.

The first evidence comes from another public ritual context in which a principal actor is simultaneously addressed as god and man. Aztec coronation rites included many exhortations to the royal candidate for investiture, including one that emphasized the humanity of the candidate and the willing suspension of disbelief in his imminent apotheosis:

Although thou art human, as are we, although thou art our friend, although thou art our son, our younger brother, our older brother, no more art thou human, as we are; we do not look to thee as human. Already thou representest, thou replacest one. Thou callest out to, thou speakest in a strange tongue to the god, the lord of the near, of the nigh.[192]

The officiant at these rites was the *huey tlatoani* of Texcoco (who was present at Motecuhzoma's address to Cortés and turned away in anger when it was over). This speech marked the end of an extended phase of the investiture ritual which included autosacrifice (bloodletting) and human sacrifice.[193] The next phase of the rites followed a "confirmation war" in which victory confirmed the candidate. The central act of the coronation was the distribution of insignia of rank following the victory.[194]

In the events preceding Motecuhzoma's speech, there was indeed a sacrifice of Spanish soldiers at the Templo Mayor[195] and a brief period of fighting. I believe that this evidence supports the possibility that the context of the speech was that of an installation rite and that Motecuhzoma was attempting to assert a very public and comprehensive ritual confirmation of his own legitimacy as ruler in a strategic effort to transcend the political dimensions of the crisis precipitated by the Spanish presence.

In addition, there are significant parallels between Motecuhzoma's speech and the prayers and ceremonial speech recorded by Sahagún's informants after the Conquest. Sahagún's encyclopedia is comprehensive; only one volume (the famous volume 12) concerns the events of the conquest. Volume 6 is a compilation of Nahuatl sayings, speeches, and prayers, including eleven speeches or prayers for occasions related to the succession of the ruler and his official performance.[196] These are (in order):

> seeking help for the new ruler (chapter 4),
> seeking a successor to a dead ruler (chapter 5),
> begging for the death of a ruler who has performed his office badly (chapter 6),
> the ruler's prayer for revelation upon his installation (chapter 9),
> greetings to the new ruler (chapter 10),
> the response to the ruler's speech (chapter 11),
> ruler's thanks to his nobles (chapter 12),
> the ruler's first speech to the inhabitants of the city (chapter 13),
> the first response to the ruler's first speech (chapter 14),
> the second response to the ruler's first speech (chapter 15),
> the ruler's admonition to his sons (chapter 18).

The prayers for a successor (following the natural death or the malfeasance of the ruler) and the ruler's prayer for divine revelation (as well as several others in the collection) are addressed to the god Tezcatlipoca.

Motecuhzoma's speech appears to include elements of several of these prayers: the prayer for a successor, the prayer for revelation, and the ruler's address to the city. The opening section of the prayer bears strong figurative and rhetorical similarity to the opening of the prayer for an imminent succession, addressed to Tezcatlipoca. It is the only speech recorded by Sahagún's scribes which includes the genealogy of the rulers (as does Motecuhzoma's speech). Furthermore, like Motecuhzoma's speech, it also plays on the image of the god's return to the throne during its temporary vacancy. Motecuhzoma uses the first person where Sahagún's transcript uses the third person to refer to the dead ruler. The second person in both texts addresses the god:

Briefly, for a while, [he] hath come to assume thy troubles for thee on earth. . . .
For a day, for a while, he came to assume thy troubles for thee. And he came to

reap reward on thy reed mat, thy reed seat. . . . He knew, he hath followed our mother, our father. . . . And verily he hath approached, he hath known his great-grandfathers, his progenitors, those who had already gone beyond to reside, those who had come to establish the realm—the lords, the rulers, the lord Acamapichtli, [and] Ticoc [Tizoc], Auitzotl, Ueue Motecucoma [Motecuhzoma the Elder], Axayacatl, the one who hath here followed Motecucoma Ilhuicamina [Motecuhzoma II]. . . . And it hath been forever. . . . Hath he perhaps just gone somewhere to come back, to return, that once again the city may look upon his face?[197]

The next sections of this generic prayer detail the hypothetical effects of an extended vacancy on the common people; it concludes with a compact petition for a successor: "Give him as a loan for a little while thy reed mat, thy reed seat, and thy rule, thy realm."[198]

The next section, in the middle of Motecuhzoma's speech (beginning "I by no means merely dream . . ."), appears to be a reference to the opening line of a section of the generic ruler's prayer for revelation. In that passage, the generic ruler rhetorically stresses his dependance on Tezcatlipoca for guidance, lest he lead his realm to ruin:

Do I dream? Do I see in dreams? . . . What is the road I shall follow? What way shall I make? Do not conceal, do not hide the mirror, the torch, the light. May I not carry things into dangerous places. May I not direct, introduce the governed into the forest, to the cliff. May I not cause one to encounter, to see the way of the rabbit, of the deer.[199] And may something [evil] not move upon me; may warfare not move, unfold upon me. May hunger, may famine not befall me.[200]

The next paragraph of the same prayer recalls Motecuhzoma's reference to having been afflicted: "To what purpose . . . shall I deal with the governed? Where shall I take them? . . . Wretched have I become. What can I [do], I who am untrained, ignorant?"[201]

The illustrations (drawn by Sahagún's informants) accompanying the transcripts of the prayers to Tezcatlipoca show the speaker standing, whereas the speaker, particularly the ruler, is otherwise depicted as seated on a woven reed throne. In volume 12, Sahagún's chronicler is careful to describe Motecuhzoma's standing posture during his address: "Thereupon he [Motecuhzoma] arose; he arose to meet him [Cortés] face to face. He inclined his body deeply. He drew him close. He arose firmly."[202]

The generic ruler's response to his noblemen "in order to humble himself and in order to thank them" also includes a reference to dreams which leads rhetorically to the ruler's hyperbolic self-abasement: "Our lord [i.e., the god Tezcatlipoca] hath inclined his heart. Verily he hath mistaken me for another . . . for here I dream, I see in dreams. . . . What do they see [in me]? . . . for I am an imbecile. . . . And the truth is now that I have spent my life in excrement, in refuse."[203] The conclusion seems to share the concluding image of Motecuhzoma's speech before Cortés ("thou hast come. . . . Peace be with thee. Rest thyself."). Here, as in the other texts, the second person singular apostrophizes the god, not the witnesses:

And thou prayest for those who went guarding for you, those who went performing their office, their work, on the reed mat, on the reed seat—the lords, the rulers who have already gone beyond to reside, those who came to dispose, to order well for our lord, on the reed mat, on the reed seat. Peace be with thee. Be seated; rest thy hands, thy feet.[204]

Motecuhzoma's reference to having "gazed at the unknown place whence thou hast come—from among the clouds, from among the mists" appears to be conventional metaphorical language for someone who is "highly esteemed," "very rich," or "never before seen."[205] Sahagún's glossary notes that the phrase "from among the clouds, from among the mists" was applied to the Spanish to describe their strangeness, but that the phrase was also standard usage. If so, then Motecuhzoma is not, apparently, making a literal reference to heaven or a divine object.

The significance of these textual parallels is, of course, inconclusive. Perhaps the scribe who recorded Motecuhzoma's last speech telescoped a much longer address, using as a mnemonic aid these focal images, which do indeed play key roles in the rhetoric of the generic prayers and ceremonial speech recorded elsewhere. Perhaps Motecuhzoma himself drew on standard ceremonial narrative genres in improvising his remarks. My main point is that the imagery and form of Motecuhzoma's speech reveal strong parallels to the Aztec prayer repertoire specific to crises of imperial legitimacy and succession.

Sahagún's volume 6 does not include a generic abdication speech; possibly, Motecuhzoma's speech should be read as an abdication and unilateral conferral of his empire on Cortés. This interpretation might account for the angry reaction of the lords who shared the platform. If it was an abdication, there is no convincing evidence that Motecuhzoma imagined he was talking to Cortés as a god. He appears not to have addressed him at all; his apostrophe is addressed to Tezcatlipoca. It seems to me that the case is stronger for reading the speech as a carefully framed (if futile) rhetorical reassertion of Motecuhzoma's own legitimate rule, addressed to both Aztec and Spanish audiences. Either way, Motecuhzoma, far from welcoming Cortés as a returning god, appears to have used traditional speech forms to assert the continuity of imperial legitimacy in the profound extremity of the moment. The speech forms, built on the mythic representation of Tezcatlipoca and Quetzalcoatl, were consistent with the ceremonial and other actions aimed at Cortés, as well as Motecuhzoma's broader strategies of expansionary statecraft prior to the Spanish invasion.

In these early post-conquest references to Motecuhzoma's final efforts to ensure Mexico's survival, then, the ruler reveals himself to be an actor on the world stage even in this emergency. He responded to Cortés's presence as the Aztecs had to other strong alien presences: with an articulate effort to appropriate the alien element symbolically through assertions of a shared genealogy and authenticity.[206] That he should have turned to Quetzalcoatl for some of his motifs as Cortés approached Tenochtitlan is not surprising; the Spanish army posed a political crisis of a more or less familiar sort, and only later a more profound threat.

If the crisis drew Motecuhzoma's attention to the figure of Quetzalcoatl, it was not Quetzalcoatl alone but the struggle between that deity and Tezcatlipoca which provided him the framework and idiom with which to improvise his responses to events and mobilize efforts to survive them politically. The references to these gods in the chronicle of Motecuhzoma's last days of rule are not the record of a desperate individual's religious frenzy unless we imagine cyclical time itself to be a defect of reason. In this chapter, I have tried to suggest another reading.

Whether his final speech should be understood as an attempt to bring Cortés within his imperial influence or the reverse, I believe the broader evidence is against any interpretation of events that makes Motecuhzoma mistake Cortés for a deity. Cortés's first letter to Charles V, most often cited as evidence of the king's misidentification, also quotes Motecuhzoma at a moment when, as host, he seems to have been concerned to reassure his foreign visitor that he himself was not a god. Referring to his "enemies" in the states of "Cempoal and Tascalteca" along Cortés's itinerary to Tenochtitlan, Motecuhzoma said to Cortés:

"I . . . know that that they have told you the walls of my houses are made of gold, and that the floor mats in my rooms and other things in my household are likewise of gold, and that I was, and claimed to be, a god; and many other things besides. The houses as you see are of stone and lime and clay."

Then he raised his clothes and showed me his body, saying, as he grasped his arms and trunk with his hands, "See that I am of flesh and blood like you and all other men, and I am mortal and substantial. See how they have lied to you?"[207]

The cyclical time whose rupture the West was so quick to celebrate in the figure of the emperor betrayed by his own faith did not, I think, fail the Aztecs. Indeed, their conceptions of time and cosmos remained perfectly adequate to comprehend and express the full scale of Spain's challenge to them, and to act on them. Motecuhzoma's actions, culminating in his final speech, may have been an improvisation that failed, but that failure was not destiny. It was a defeat. Ironically, it is the Western advocates of linear time who in this famous case ignore the conquest as an event and instead assert that it was preinscribed in the world's true meanings.

6   Time, Life, and Law in the United States

ONE WAY OF summarizing this book so far is to observe that concepts of time represent diverse logics of cultural and social management. My main argument has been that social time has no reality apart from circumstances directly or indirectly involving claims of legitimacy and accountability. Throughout the volume, I have stressed how negotiable time concepts are in the institutional contexts in which those negotiations are embedded. Accordingly, I have dwelled on both the relevance of the institutional contexts for such negotiations and the implications of the fact that representations of time, though their adherents perhaps claim them as totalizing absolutes, are inevitably "about" multiple (including rival) temporal and social orders. In fact, temporality appears to be most useful as a matrix of political improvisation in precisely those contexts where the challenge to legitimacy comes in the form of diversity, as perceived by those challenged. I hasten to add that diversity means something different in each case.

For the Ch'in, the goal of unifying formerly independent kingdoms was explicit. Accordingly, whereas Legalist thought influenced Ch'in statecraft, it is important to acknowledge that Ch'in temporal innovations accommodated and absorbed Confucian ideas of the cosmos, among others. The materialization of time in the person of the emperor appears to have been the major Legalist contribution to the representation of time, but their ideas of temporality implied by new representational forms overlapped signficantly with those of other major philosophies. Indeed, my point is that it would not have served the Ch'in to invent a new kind of time, but it did serve their interests to invent a new means of reconciling social orders, and this is what they were able to achieve through their temporal innovations. Importantly, these innovations survived as part of the semiotic and ritual repertoire of empire long after the Ch'in dynasty collapsed.

In Mesoamerica, the temporality inscribed in the Quetzalcoatl myth provided Motecuhzoma with a political and rhetorical resource of considerable value in the context of Aztec contests beyond Tenochtitlan, including the emergency posed by the Spanish invasion. I have proposed a reading of Quetzalcoatl's mythic efficacy in terms broad enough to include Aztec expansionism as well as Motecuhzoma's response to Cortés. Even if one is inclined to be more cautious about Motecuhzoma's territorial ambitions, however, the figures of Quetzalcoatl and Tezcatlipoca remain symbolically potent in his direct contest with Cortés.

Representations of time also pose different problems of management in and of themselves. In China the effect of the Legalists' refinements of the temporal aspects of political legitimacy identified the emperor not only with time itself but also with the territory of China. Though I would not claim that these were intentional exercises in political symbolism, they were consistent with developments in the Chinese geopolitical sphere, that is, the consolidation of China under a single rule. In Mesoamerica, there was also a territorial dimension to time, though much more deeply embedded in Aztec concepts of succession, symbolized as the return of Quetzalcoatl and the ingathering of his diversified agency. In China and Mesoamerica these symbolic complexes and their associations with the reigning sovereign were articulated in public rituals on a large scale, as well as private rituals. As the Mesoamerican case illustrates with particular force, the problems of maintaining these symbolic associations are ultimately inseparable from the problems of maintaining the institutions whose vitality they are claimed to celebrate.

For different reasons and by different means, both Chinese and Mesoamerican conceptions of time drew a connection between time and space through the sovereign. In China the connection was through the emperor's person. The Aztecs appeared to have drawn the connection through the emperor's office. This is an important difference, since, as noted, the Ch'in materialized time in the imperial incumbent, and the Aztecs historicized time in the imperial succession. While both Chinese and Mesoamerican representations of time and space were conceptually fused in a number of ways, the sovereign's role vis-à-vis spatiotemporal representations in political ritual and rhetoric was different in each case. In the Chinese context, Ch'in symbolic manipulations of temporality made history the projection of the emperor's generative reality. Motecuhzoma's improvisations, by contrast, asserted not his own agency but that of Quetzalcoatl and more especially Tezcatlipoca with regard to his place in the Aztec succession of kings. In neither case should we imagine that the evidence tells us anything about how the First Emperor or Motecuhzoma actually regarded himself. Rather, it tells us what sorts of representations would be legible to their rivals and allies.

This chapter is about the United States, and again the subject is improvisation with temporal representations which have political consequences in contexts involving new forms of diversity. In this case, temporality emerges from participants' competition over the horizon between "politics" and "justice." Whereas the differences between these two terms might seem obvious as an everyday matter, several points bear special mention for my broader ethnographic purposes. First, "justice" has no explicit territorial referent in the United States, notwithstanding the particular character Americans might imagine the U.S. *system of justice* to have in relation to that of other countries or locales. Politics, of course, does have an inevitable territorial referent in a democracy, given its intrinsic connections to citizenship and representation. A second, parallel point is that "justice" has no explicit temporal referent in the United States, nothwithstanding fluctuations Americans might perceive in *access to justice* or *delivery of justice* in particular periods or instances. "Politics," however, is very much in the times, the stuff of the hourly news.

Given public and constitutional commitments, at least at the level of rhetoric, to democratic forms and meanings of representation, the judiciary faces specific cultural difficulties when faced with a vacancy. As recent times have repeatedly made clear for anyone watching the U.S. scene, judicial succession has fallen into a dialogue between standpoints that the public culture traditionally (at least until recently) made incommensurate; high federal discourses of politics and justice are not easily assimilated to each other. Federal judicial nominations come from the executive, and are confirmed (or not) by the legislature, the political branches par excellence. Yet, out of these representative branches, rooted to their own time and place, is supposed to come a justice—and justice. The case studies in this chapter explore how participants themselves identify and grapple with the terms of this contradiction.[1]

It would be misleading to suggest that the contradictions of politics and justice in the United States, or anywhere, are only discursive or symbolic incongruities. In this chapter, I draw on two judicial confirmation stories that were intensely controversial and, in important ways, remain so. The confirmation hearings on the appointments of Robert Bork and Clarence Thomas to the Supreme Court were historically significant in that they drew a heavy media presence and public attention. The context for the unprecedented publicity was a national political climate in which nominations to the Court were widely understood as components of the president's social and political agendas in specific ways; this much cannot be considered controversial, although the symbolism of the judiciary left Bork and Thomas supporters with only the most straitened rhetoric for acknowledging the extent to which their nominees should be viewed as representatives of particular legal and social philosophies. To be more accurate, this rhetorical embarrassment was clear in the Bork hearings in

1987, but by 1991 the idea that a judicial nominee should have to pass a "litmus test" of his or her opinions was no longer strange, although it remains deeply contested.

Certainly, presidential attempts to color the Supreme Court with particular views were by no means new or exceptional; the entire history of the Court can be understood in these terms. What were new were the intensity and explicitness of the effort to reinvent the Court as a representative branch. That effort failed with respect to the Bork nomination but succeeded in the Thomas case. The pressure to make the judiciary representative can be seen in the context of times in which two Republican presidents faced a Democratic Congress and substantial legislative opposition to a conservative Republican agenda, particularly to the goals of the ultraconservative fundamentalist Christian Right, the political legacy of the "Moral Majority" of the 1970s. The Bork nomination, under President Ronald Reagan, hinged crucially on Judge Bork's ideas about the constitutional protections for privacy, the legal basis of the right to abortion, which was in the late 1980s, arguably the major domestic political issue in terms of its claims on public attention and emotion.[2] By 1991 President George Bush's nomination of Judge Clarence Thomas still involved the abortion issue but was also more broadly focused substantively and symbolically on trimming the federal role in civil rights. Thus, the confirmation hearings for these two appointments can be understood as being about the boundary between politics and law, not just in the usual figurative sense of the political dimension of law but in the literal sense of defining the nature and limits of the judiciary in relation to the other branches of government.

My focus in this chapter is on the confirmation hearings themselves, since that setting provides a well-defined arena within which to observe the cultural mechanics of these maneuvers. Readers should be aware that both hearings were televised continuously for public viewing and drew large audiences. Such media coverage was unprecedented for a Supreme Court nomination; not long ago, nominees did not even appear before the Judiciary Committee while it considered confirmation.[3] Senators, nominees, and witnesses prepare extensively for the public hearings; however, preparation and opening statements notwithstanding, the dialogues at the hearings are spontaneous improvisations.

Thus, as we return to the question of how time is publicly constructed in different contexts, the question of symbols and how they work must be inseparable from the contests within and beyond the Senate hearing room in which fundamental issues of rights, social justice, and—a new word in the 1980s—multiculturalism dominated public representations of "the times" in the United States. The discussion in the next section offers a return of sorts to the issues with which this book opened, the preconceptions about the nature of time, life, and law which are also embedded in the anthropology of time.

The Indeterminacies of Linear Time

Since the Middle Ages, linear time has been the time of the nation-state, although its modes of rationalization (as technology and social control) vary with time and place. In Chapter 1, I considered one element of its appeal for Europe's emerging secular sovereigns, that is, the prior association of linear time with their necessary but rival institution, the church. But I have not yet considered what it is about linear time that does the state's work. There are extraordinary difficulties involved in applying linear time to the very context where it is claimed to be most natural, an individual life, and yet, those very difficulties themselves reveal the mechanics and the stakes of linear time—that is, the relationship of individual agency to the agency claimed for the nation. It is important to acknowledge that when I refer to "the state's interventions," I mean the rhetorical improvisations of ordinary people who happen to hold high public office (in this case, U.S. senators and the nominees themselves), and whatever is at stake in these.

In the previous chapters, we have seen some of the ways that linear time is drawn into the naturalization of large-scale institutions. For example, the historiographic tradition crediting Motecuhzoma's defeat to his misreading of events dates to the time of the conquest itself; the immanent power of linear time is, as it were, built into the self-legitimations and historiographic traditions of the West. China might be considered the opposite case, in which it was not the deficits but the surfeits of linear time which were blamed for the Legalists' downfall (again, in the Western historiographic tradition). Between too little and too much is the modern West itself, in which its own version of linear time (although in reality there would seem to be no one version) is held forth as both rational and attuned to the individual. In Part I, I described many routes by which these ideas about linear time are incorporated into social science—notably through ideas about social structure, death, law, literacy, and exchange. In their canonical forms, these share important assumptions about the irreversibility of time, the universal meaning of death, the (corresponding) significance of the interval, the individuality of agency, and the significance of agency as production. Any of these ideas is contestable on ethnographic grounds, but that is beside the immediate point.

My starting point in this chapter is the metonymy these canonical ideas about time, life, and law create between individual agency and the significance of on-going history of the collectivity, the nation itself. In particular, linear time does the state's (or any institution's) work by providing an idiom with which individual agency can be represented as flowing into the nation's. Furthermore, this metonymy permits the symbolic juggling that allows one person to claim to represent *an*other or *all* others in a democratic forum. And finally, this metonymy required considerable cultural work in the Bork and Thomas hearings, since neither "life" easily met the prerequisites that an individual's life have a clear linear trajectory, that it be tellable as a life story with a unified narrative structure. If personal history is to be fitted into national history, autobiography must be constructed out of the same elements as the collective story of progress modern nation-states claim for themselves. The case studies in this chapter provide an opportunity to consider these points in detail.

Linear time is conventionally said to be an advance over cyclical time, literally to reform it within its same general framework. As we have seen, from officialized Western perspectives, linear time reinvents cyclical time as a line, but misshapen into a circle, creating repetition where there is none.[4] This misreading would appear to be due to the habit, fostered by notions of linear time, of considering temporality only in terms of individual agency and restricting agency to production (of intentions, conduct, and so forth). This reformulation of cyclical time may be a misreading of cyclical time practices, but it facilitates the incorporation of cyclical time representations into those associated with linear time. This in turn requires that the crucial differences among time's forms can be effectively suppressed. Linear time accomplishes this suppression by stipulating the preeminence of the end points of life and then placing them beyond experience. For example, the difference between death as a source of life and death as the marker of an ineluctable ending and the difference between life as an event and life as a condition can be (and are) blurred by the cultural premise that places them beyond experience. Different formulations of linear time (as finite or infinite) can also be blurred. Thus, the competition among forms of time can be managed effectively since, in effect, their different claims cannot be put to a test.

In this sense, the indeterminacies of linear time (or any time form) are critical to its efficacy in absorbing or accommodating other formulations of agency at least to some degree. Linear time maintains two crucial kinds of indeterminacy vis-à-vis cyclical time in the West, one in the construction of the lifetime (both as the reciprocal of death and as a finite duration), and the other in the representation of the completeness time claims to represent (linear progress versus cyclical repetition).

But linear time also has meaning in relation to the larger "infinity" or "eternity" of which it is supposed to be the segment. The rhetorical landmarks of the transition from time to eternity include a metaphorical shift from geometry to genesis, a substantive shift from act to principle, and a shift of voice from the descriptive to the normative or oracular. It is tempting to consider that the ideas of fixed sacred texts and the instantaneous inscription of order on and in the world are not only ancient ideas but also modern ones, appropriated from the orality of priests and claimed for the literate mythos of law.

Linear time constructs its relationship to temporalities of indeterminate form (or without form) as if to a shapeless matrix. Western institutions maintain this distinction (between time and its authenticating source) in any number of basic dichotomies, for example, between law and justice, sense and truth, culture and nature, and so on. When secular sovereigns borrowed the church's temporal idiom for their own purposes in the fourteenth century, this major strategic innovation of statecraft was not the linear shape of time but the genetic relationship between time and eternity and the broad dispersal of agency implied in that genesis. By constructing time in relation to eternity, secular temporal discourse reified society by locating the end(s) of time outside any individual or collective experience. As we have seen, canonical social science notions of "society" or "social structure" recuperate and consolidate some of the agency thus dispersed.

The relationship between time and eternity was also at issue in European solutions to problems of royal succession. Secular monarchies eventually resolved the contradictions between an enduring kingship and a mortal king with the notion of "the king's two bodies," differentiating between the office of the king, with its enduring qualities and emblems, and the occupant of the office.[5] This conceptualization of incumbency is by no means unique to Europe, though it is not universal.[6] Before the idea of the king's two bodies was established, the king had already become the symbol of the state, as evidenced by the idea of treason, new in Edward III's time in England.[7] Treason acquired statutory definition in England before any other crime (in 1352), as if the symbolic status of the state had to be established before acts could be prosecuted in "its" name. The important point here is that this symbolic status was achieved by regularizing the temporal contradictions of kingship. When both the king's mortal person and the enduring kingship were embraced within a single institutional form, the state's claims to constitute in itself a body of enduring principles were insulated from the most unpredictable aspects of succession. This was an important conceptual innovation in this period of consolidation. Indeed, Europe's legal development was revolutionary in Europe in the medieval period according to the widely accepted scholarly assessment.[8]

By the time the modern period began, law had become the dominant image of conflict resolution, linking king and subject, at least hypothetically, in the integument of everyday life.[9] Extensive changes in European legal institutions and law were but one element of wider patterns of social and cultural change, including the development of cities, major changes in church doctrine, and profound changes in the structure of the economy.[10] By the end of the medieval period, Europe had the common law, written contracts, juries, and academic law, and in general, law was used more widely in the prosecution and defense of individual interests.[11] Legal institutions and their pattern of use, which look unfamiliar to the modern eye at beginning of the Middle Ages, increasingly reflected the symbolic consolidation of diffuse social relationships in the individual contract, a legal text.[12]

From this perspective, some of the meanings of the individual as a social unit can be seen to take shape against a background of highly indeterminate cultural concepts—society, kingship (and citizenship), and legality. This indeterminacy permits these concepts to be asserted as temporal constructions against a field of contested value. The history of European institutional commitments to resolving these indeterminacies is beyond the scope of this chapter. The general point is that institutional attempts to mobilize the relationship between time and eternity or (to put it in modern secular terms) history and principle involve basic cultural connections among the state, law, sovereignty, the individual, textuality, and the sacred. In the Western context, because of the institutional settings in which these ideas and technologies developed, a reference to any one of them is a reference to all of them.

The common law (which is also a product of the late Middle Ages) incorporates and responds to these indeterminacies in several significant ways. In some respects, it perfectly reflects a logic of linear time in its reliance on precedent, its commitment to reform, and its acknowledgment of individual persons and rights. But the common law also involves larger claims beyond linear time. Reasoning by analogy to precedent creates a false historicity in that it perpetually reclaims the past for the present. In theory, a current dispute can be settled by reference to cases from the beginning of the legal record almost a millennium ago. "The law" thus accumulates, but it never passes; at any instant, it represents a totality. It is by definition complete; yet its completeness does not preclude change. It is a human achievement; yet, by its reversible and lateral excursions and by its collective voice, it is not identifiably the product of any particular individual or group. "The law" is the work of a nation which, in this context, has a transcendent aspect imported to it through the symbolism of law and the judiciary.[13] In the symbolism of the modern liberal tradition, the common law in effect stands at the border between the two great themes of Indo-European myth: the human made (the anthropogonic) and the god made (cosmogonic). One implication throughout this chapter is that the symbolic fonts of the judiciary's cultural legitimacy are nourished in the discursive space created by the indeterminacy of the distinction between events in linear time (politics) and the significance of time itself (justice) in some larger scheme of things—or, conversely, depleted by the loss of that space.

Law has a mythic dimension in the West, in its self-totalization, its quality of being in time (in that it is a human product) but also out of time (where did it or does it begin or end?), and in its promise of systematic yet permutable meanings. This myth is essentially a temporal one. Specifically, at the level of its legitimating symbols, the law's implicit claim is to invoke the total system of its own distinctions simultaneously in a way that individualizes subjects/citizens and orients them toward particular forms of action. That such symbolism has been effective in the West only since the Middle Ages reveals the continued capacity of modern society to generate myth. At the heart of the mythic aspects of law are several key distinctions, such as those between law and interests, text and spirit, the ephemeral and the enduring, the political and the just. As the examples in this chapter illustrate, legal institutions reiterate the terms of these distinctions much more easily than they can operationalize them, since the myths of law—like any myth—fail to account for the nature of everyday practice. Moreover, the Reagan-Bush years appear to have substantially altered the mythic basis of law in the United States, through the Bork and Thomas hearings, among other means.

Law and Time in the United States

It is precisely in judicial succession that multiple temporalities, of the law, personal lifetimes, public lives, and larger structures of significance, as well as their indeterminacies, must be worked out. The controversies over the Bork and Thomas nominations only underscore this point. I must stress that I refer here to cultural representations of succession; in practice, many difficulties intervene, as we shall see. The law must juggle at least three essentially different forms of time. First, at least in public life, the dominant institutional culture stresses the linearity and infiniteness of time and, simultaneously, the finite irreversibility of any individual's lifetime. Thus, whereas modern secular thought suspends the beginning and end points of time as indeterminate, it nonetheless celebrates them in the "certainty" of time's "passage" from past to present and future. No moment repeats another, and the passage of time is both regular and regulated according to international standards.[14] This is the time of biographies and national histories, among other things.[15]

A second temporality is in the law itself, which involves the constant expansion of a linear time framework in the production and use of "precedent," but not in that sense alone. Its extension is a gesture toward the ultimate sociality of law. The end point of the law in time is neither fixed nor envisioned. It is symbolically coterminous with a national social life, and it symbolically represents that national life in temporal terms.[16] As mentioned earlier, the mythic aspects inherent in this arrangement of things set the law apart from the many other institutions in which conflicts can be resolved and the normative repertoire adjusted. Importantly, the mythic aspects of the law which inhere in its special expanded temporality are essential to both its claims to neutrality and the enduring validity (in its own terms) of its texts. If linear time is the time that connects individual interests to the state in some historical framework of events, then neutrality in a linear time idiom requires a larger symbolism of the infinite in which *all* interests and histories can be represented as pertaining to the social field in which the law operates.

The time of the law is distinctive not only for its cumulativeness but also for its reversibility. The law exists in reversible time in two senses: first, in that prior decisions can control present ones and, second, in that prior decisions can be reversed. The reversibility of the law is another important hallmark of its mythic nature. It symbolically underscores claims that legal institutions transcend any particular era of an individual's life. It also symbolically connects the law to nature itself. In the case of the United States, it is that peculiarly reasoned and authored nature of the late eighteenth century which made God, law, and reason share a single set of principles.[17] I argue later that the law's particular temporality generates key symbols of the American judiciary, even though the law has many sources, and modern skepticism has challenged the specifics (though not the symbols in civic culture) of the Enlightenment view.[18]

There is yet another kind of time in the law, and that is the judges' own lifetimes. In the starkest possible contrast to the law's self-totalizing, reversible, and boundless accumulations, judges' lives are finite. Indeed, any conception of time that has shape and direction focuses attention on the incongruities of sustaining the legitimacy of an institutional system while vesting individuals with its authority. In the special time of the law, which is multidirectional rather than nondirectional, qualification becomes a particular cultural dilemma as well as a practical problem that goes to the very heart of the judiciary's cultural legitimacy in the United States.

In the process of filling a vacant seat on the United States Supreme Court, all these aspects of time come vibrantly into play. A vacancy is ordinarily caused by the death of the incumbent or by age- or health-related decline of competence, actual or anticipated. Life tenure potentially secures long service from an individual justice, and yet his or her performance can involve no conspicuous apprenticeship. The new justice is selected by the two "other"—the two political—branches of government; the partisan aspect of confirmation has been increasingly explicit in recent years. That confirmation hearings for Supreme Court nominees are now televised and widely viewed in the United States reinforces several aspects of the process from a cultural perspective, particularly, the cultural distinction between offices and their incumbents.[19]

The special temporal symbolism of the law constructs a special "kind" of person, one who will find the law, not make it; know the law but not preach it; be a representative of the national community but have no causes of his or her own, except the law itself. In practice, these symbolic requirements can be made to fit an actual individual only with the deft management of essential temporal symbols, that is, by downplaying or suppressing altogether the particular aspects of a person's career, so that the judicial "career" can avoid any appearance of *becoming*. It is in becoming a judge that any tensions between a person's individuality and a judicial persona would be most evident.[20]

What is required of a person culturally considered to be qualified for the Supreme Court would probably not stir much controversy in the abstract; what follows is literally a textbook enumeration:

One, demonstrated judicial temperament. Two, professional expertise and competence. Three, absolute personal as well as professional integrity. Four, an able, agile, lucid mind. Five, appropriate professional educational background or training. Six, the ability to communicate clearly, both orally and in writing, especially the latter.[21]

Several things are striking about this set of criteria. They are presented, for example, as if they describe an exceptional individual; yet they evoke attributes that one might assume are widely and positively valued in society. The list is evenly balanced between general statements of professional experience and personal attributes that are not aspects of experience. The description implies that a judicial temperament is reinforced by the ability to reason. Furthermore, communication skills are clearly important but not the sort used in ordinary social conversation; rather, one's writing ability is key. Walter Murphy offers a metaphor for this personal and professional elite when he refers to the justices' "performance of their priestly duty of expounding the meaning of that holy writ [the U.S. Constitution]."[22] The priestly metaphor is perhaps at the heart of the matter: in the United States, the judiciary is the only robed branch. The robes, like those of American academics in procession, are those of medieval clerics.

The prescription for a Supreme Court justice might be clarified by any number of contrasts, but the different temporalities of the justices and the American presidents are most salient; they are each other's inverse. The president is elected every four years; justices are appointed for life. Presidential candidates campaign actively and in public; the campaign becomes part of their public story. If potential justices campaign, it is far from the public eye. Presidents, if they are popular, become the center of personal cults, for instance, in popular stylizations of their biographies; such cults appear to play no part in the popular cultural idealizations of a Supreme Court justice.[23]

The crux of these symbolic distinctions (and others) is the cultural distinction between politics and justice. Supreme Court justices belong to the temporality of justice, which symbolically claims to be totalizing, cumulative, and reversible in a way that the time of the presidential politics is not. The time of politics is the time of interests and their fulfillment, linear time. The time of justice, again, as culturally idealized, may borrow a linear time idiom, but it symbolically transcends it by virtue of the judiciary's claims to represent *all* interests and none.[24] The special temporality of "justice" centrally involves this mythic refusal to acknowledge the possibility that justices themselves might have interests or individuality outside the law itself.[25]

Elsewhere, I have explored the connections between these contrasting temporalities and the symbolic problems of American judicial succession, essentially focusing on the absence of a public inaugural ceremony for new justices as evidence of the cultural silence on the subject of justices' personal processes of "becoming."[26] The absence of a public ritual also provides key evidence of the symbolic relationship between the temporality of the judiciary and that of politics. The ceremonial form of the inauguration is preserved for and by the president. Its absence *is* the public ceremonial form of the justices and, *as an absence,* affirms the symbolic connection of justice with "transcendent things."[27]

In effect, in terms of the symbolic construction of their office, justices must literally embody neutrality; they are literally "judicial bodies." That their relationship to the law is metonymic rather than metaphoric implies important cultural constraints on the notion of representation as an aspect of the judicial role. In the case of the Supreme Court, a very particular kind of neutrality is culturally valued. Justices are accountable "to the people," but in a way that precludes any legitimate scope for public expression of their own interests or personal views. Indeed, they are "supposed" to have no interests; this renunciation of particular private interests symbolically inverts to become, in effect, a claimed ability to embrace all public interests.[28] The alternative (positing renunciation as an expression of ascetic otherworldliness) would contradict other cultural stipulations that a justice be an exemplary individual without being either a hero or a saint. A justice should reason without the exercise of will but with the application of rigorous discipline.[29] Justices must be the law, but they must also be society without representing either. Such are some the symbolic prescriptions of the judicial office of the Supreme Court.

In the symbolic schema of legal liberalism, justices are imbued with a special personhood at the moment of their becoming justices.[30] It may be that the past decade has brought this symbolic scheme to an end. Certainly, there now appears to be widespread cynicism about the possibility of judicial neutrality, although, to be fair, if this cynicism exists, it would not be due to the Bork and Thomas hearings alone. Be that as it may, such transformations occur in ritual seclusion all over the world, as Victor's Turner's work on rites of passage shows.[31] Justices are liminal as nominees (though not in office). Their liminal period was traditionally suppressed in terms of public display, but in the Bork nomination, it became highly public through print and television. A contextual factor that might have added to the atmosphere was the bicentennial of the United States Constitution, also in September 1987, and independently a focus of intense public ritual displays, directed by the former chief justice, Warren Burger. Although justices remain public figures and offer their signed "opinions" to the nation, justices' opinions are not their own in the usual sense of the term. Their menu of considerations is legally circumscribed (*stare decisis* symbolically and legally downplays the innovative and improvisatorial dimensions of judicial findings); their opinions are designated as *legal*, not *personal*. In any event, justices conventionally forbear from narrating their own decisions and indecisions as personal events. Their primary discourse is written, not spoken; their conversations with each other are strictly secret. As individuals, justices do not *represent* justice; they *are*, finally (which is to say, symbolically), justices. This metonymy is key.

Further evidence of the suppressed personal temporality of justices in favor of the more mythic temporalities of justice "itself" is in the virtual nonexistence of autobiography among Supreme Court justices. The only exceptions are memoirs by Justices Hugo Black, Earl Warren, and William O. Douglas. (Consider the inverse proportions of presidents who have written memoirs.)[32]

Although the prescription for eligibility to the Court is reasonably clear from a symbolic point of view, it is mute on the question of how and when an individual comes to be inscribed with judicial qualities. This is an important cultural silence, for at stake in it are other, larger questions about the nature of social life. For example, if justices are literally to be found, then the implication is that there is a natural hierarchy of men and women, some fit for service and others not, and the authority and power of the president and Senate are symbolically downplayed. On the other hand, if justices are made at the moment of their nomination—or confirmation, or installation—then claims of the democracy of the law symbolically enhance the authority and power of the president and Senate. These are among the issues in the Bork and, even more so, the Thomas hearings.

In effect, the structure of government in the United States places the judiciary and the other branches in competition for the key symbols of democracy. This problem becomes overt primarily in contexts of judicial vacancy. In normal times, Supreme Court justices reiterate their independence; public symbolism stresses the Court's accountability to the American people—an ancestral or mythic historical invocation. The mythicization of accountabilities corresponds to the transformed meanings of the justices as public persons, even their physical bodies. The illnesses of sitting justices are stikingly downplayed in the press compared to those of the president, for example. Their gender, until Justice Sandra Day O'Connor's appointment, was unmarked (male). Their race, until recently, was unmarked (white). Now, the refraction of this tradition creates new generic markers: the public might refer to a "Jewish seat" or a "black seat." More recently, the public refers to conservative and liberal seats and invokes a metaphor of dynamic balance (or lack of balance) in references to partisanship and "swing" votes on the Court.[33]

In the symbolic schema of liberal jurisprudence, the people who sit on the Supreme Court bench are not ordinary mortals who mature and decline; theirs is the mortality of gods, as if justices were born in fully mature form at the bench and died in full stride. For them, retirement is metaphorical death. The life of a justice is no longer the lifetime of the man or woman who became that justice. As noted, in the symbolism of the liberal tradition, all aspects, biographical and political, of becoming a justice are symbolically suppressed. Those are precisely the ones that would (though they cannot) resolve the indeterminacies linking the Court to the other branches of government; they are also the ones that emerge from the relationships of linear time to the larger temporality embedded in American public institutions. The Bork and Thomas hearings are culturally interesting precisely because they focus so very directly on the biographies of the nominees.

The case studies I develop here involve these and other symbolic claims and distinctions. In particular, they highlight the tensions between cultural understandings of biography and justice, interests and renunciation, profession and representation, politics and law—all juxtaposed here as involving irreconcilable constructions of time. My evidence derives almost exclusively from the published transcripts of the Senate Judiciary Committee hearings in 1987 and 1991. Though their outcomes were different, the cases are related in explicitly referring to the partisan contest over the nomination within the committee and the public and to the political battle between the White House and Congress to control the nomination process. Overall, it seems to me, the growing contest over judicial candidates' biographies and the increasingly public display of it shift traditional meanings of justice from transcendent neutrality to political representation. Indeed, by the end of the Thomas hearings, it appeared that the symbols of justice had not only shifted but had been proferred in an exchange, as the president himself appropriated the symbols of the transcendent "everyman," responsive by nature to all interests. The exchange of the symbols of legitimacy between the Court and the president during the Reagan-Bush years goes beyond the scope of this book. Nevertheless, it is possible to say that this exchange compels caution in concluding that a more representative court is inevitably a more democratic one.

Judge Bork and the Politics of Time

In 1987 with the resignation of Justice Louis F. Powell, President Reagan had a vacancy to fill on the United States Supreme Court. As is constitutionally required, his nominee was subject to confirmation by the United States Senate. I want to look here at the first set of what turned out to be hearings on three different nominees before Justice Anthony Kennedy was confirmed that fall. Specifically, I am interested in what has been called the "retraction problem,"[34] of the first appointee, that is, Robert Bork's public disavowal of specific writings from earlier in his career. What follows is in no way an attempt to explain why Bork's nomination failed or to speak directly to the abundant constitutional or partisan dimensions of the retractions or the nomination story.[35] The cultural problem is not to explain a particular outcome but rather to identify how major concerns came to be defined in the hearings. In any social setting, such concerns must be continually negotiated; they are never entirely settled or even determinate. Accordingly, my interest in the Bork hearings is in how the retractions—as Judge Bork presented them and as they were received—allow us to isolate a knot of crossed temporalities and thus to explore an interesting example of the role of temporal constructions in defining institutional processes, and vice versa.

The "retraction problem" focused on two articles Judge Bork wrote while on the faculty of the Yale Law School. The first of these, published in the *New Republic* in 1963, expressed reservations about the proposed Civil Rights Act.[36] The second, which appeared in the *Indiana Law Journal* in 1971, dealt with limitations on the scope of the First Amendment.[37] Each piece left a legacy of public retractions. He reconsidered both essays in 1973 at his confirmation hearings when he was appointed solicitor general; he also reconsidered the 1971 piece in 1982 at the Senate confirmation hearings on his nomination to the Court of Appeals) and again in 1984.[38]

In all three hearings (on his nominations to the positions of solicitor general in 1973, circuit court judge in 1982, and associate justice of the Supreme Court in 1987),[39] questions about Bork's revised opinions led to questions about the likelihood that his personal views might dominate his performance in public office and, more generally, about his future predictability. This line of questioning strategically evoked Bork as a "self" suspended between the past and the future. That the self should occupy this position may seem unproblematic; after all, the conventional definition of the present in linear constructions of time places "now" between a dynamic past and future.

Yet, if we take his testimony at face value, it seems clear that Bork resisted this construction of past, present, and future. In contrast to the linear time model implicit in the questioning, he situated his "self"—as academic, as advocate, as solicitor general, as judge—in a variety of professional contexts, past and present. While committee members seemed to expect to "meet" Bork somewhere on a continuous time line between his past and his future, he came to them from a discontinous past as an individual who had successfully fulfilled multiple professional roles and looked forward to the possibility of others. These different temporalities, which involve rather different constructions of "the self," structured the narratives that made up the hearings. Sometimes, these temporalities and the alternative meanings of the self which they implied were also the explicit subject of the hearings, as we shall see.

Let us begin with Judge Bork's own words. In 1982 while he was testifying at the Senate Judiciary Committee hearings on his nomination to the United States Court of Appeals for the District of Columbia, Bork was invited to discuss the 1971 article. In his response he distanced himself from that article by alluding to the nature of "theoretical argument" and emphasizing his view of the nature of an academic's writing generally:

[The] first amendment protects the free exercise of religion and the freedom of the press as well as speech. Within the speech area, I was dealing with an application of Prof. Herbert Wechsler's concept of neutral principles, which is quite a famous concept in academic debate. I was engaged in an academic exercise in the application of those principles, a theoretical argument, which I think is what professors are expected to do. . . . It seems to me in my putative function as a judge that what is relevant is what the Supreme Court has said, and not my theoretical writings in 1971.[40]

In 1973 he answered a similar question on the same article in a similar vein: "It was speculative writing which professors are expected to engage in, without meaning that that is what they believed for all time or that is what they think would be appropriate for some other organ of Government to pick up at that time and it is explicitly stated to be speculative in that sense."[41]

John Tunney, at these same 1973 hearings, asked Bork to comment on his earlier assessment of the Nixon administration's antitrust policy. Bork's reply distinguished academic analysis from law enforcement:

Senator, in my opinion, which is my opinion as an academic in this field, the conglomerate merger campaign was an antitrust mistake. However, it should be said that this administration, and this Justice Department, continues to enforce the antitrust laws vigorously. They have guidelines about conglomerate mergers. Those will be enforced, and should such a case come up to me, that case will be dealt with in line with that policy and not in line with my academic opinion I expressed in that article.[42]

Later, Tunney asked Bork to relate an excerpt from his 1971 article to "recent Supreme Court decisions relating to the freedom of speech." Bork replied, "[Let] me say that article is a theoretical exercise. As a professor, I am paid to speculate, and I do speculate."[43] Would Bork's actions as solicitor general be guided by his personal views, Tunney asked. "I think," Bork answered, "that whether I think the Supreme Court is likely to do it, whether to come down more in line with my views, or perhaps less in line with my views, if I have reason to believe the Supreme Court wants to consider the subject, it seems to me, as an officer of the court, I ought to bring that case up and explain the varying positions that are available."[44]

Bork's responses to such questions about his past views and his future predictability were entirely consistent from 1973 through the opening days of his Supreme Court interviews. Throughout that period, he responded to questions by detailing his understanding of the structural accountabilities and limits of the office he aspired to and the customary canons of ethics and etiquette each position involved. For example, in 1982, asked whether he would "feel [himself] obliged to follow Supreme Court precedent even though [he might] greatly disagree with its application in a particular case," Bork responded: "Mr. Chairman, it seems to me that a lower court judge owes a duty of absolute obedience to Supreme Court precedent. If that were not true, the legal system would fall into chaos, so that my personal views certainly cannot affect my duty to apply the law as the Supreme Court has framed it."[45] In 1973 Bork responded to a similar question from Gary Hart:

Q. What if the Government takes a position in the field of antitrust or civil rights that you think is wrong, and have said in the past is wrong, what do you do? *Mr. Bork.* What will I do? I will enforce the policy of the Government in antitrust as the Government defines it. I do not define it, Senator.

I might say that in practice both for defendants in antitrust cases and for plaintiffs in antitrust cases I frequently urged positions that as an academic I would criticize.[46]

Also in 1973 Tunney asked a related question:

Q. [Would] not you [*sic*] have wide room for imposing your own personal view of the law upon that appellate process even where you disagreed with the Attorney General or with the appellate division of the Justice Department? *Mr. Bork.* . . . I would like to point out that the Solicitor General has the degree of freedom that he does have by custom and tradition really on condition that he not abuse it. By law he is under the Attorney General's direction.[47]

Well into the 1987 hearings, Bork continued to invoke the separate offices he had held and might hold as more or less distinct professional and normative contexts. He distinguished among what academics, solicitors general, judges, and special masters *do* and *are expected to do* in order to account for the different positions he had brought to legal issues over time. In particular, Bork consistently relied on the sociological concept of the profession, particularly the academic profession, to make questions of his personhood (e.g., his personal opinions) rhetorically subordinate to issues of office.

The 1987 Hearings

I take at face value Bork's representation of his own career as involving discrete portfolios, his professional "voice" constituted as a serial multivocality in the various professional contexts in which he has been "paid"—to recall one of his more impatient references to the academic profession. I also take at face value the diffuse notion of renunciation which seems to be Bork's corollary to his concept of professional employ-ment, his consistent view that professions are not forums for the expres-sion of personal opinion but rather for the particular forms of textuality and substance appropriate to them. His concept fuses renunciation with subordination (to codes, clients, or higher levels of authority).

From the cultural point of view I am pursuing, Bork's responses changed significantly midway through the 1987 hearings. He stopped re-sisting the attempts of committee members to place him on the "line" between his past and his future; indeed, he ultimately used that temporal idiom himself.

There were essentially three different positions in the controversy, and each invoked a different temporal idiom. Critics who characterized Bork's retractions as "confirmation conversions" made their case by plac-ing all Bork's writings, utterances, and opportunities on the single time line of the political careerist, emphasizing their sequence and—by defini-tion of a time line—their consequences.[48] Linear time has provided the canonical form for personal investment and redemption ever since the theologians and manufacturers of the Middle Ages merged their meta-phors and their institutions of salvation and economy. Indeed, the mock-ing reference to "conversion" is a play on this canonical temporal form and its root metaphors.

Bork's advocates worked with a dual temporality, dividing the time line of Bork's life into two strands. One strand represented Bork the person, vital, growing, pruning, thriving: the metaphors were distinctly natural, even evolutionary.[49] The other strand, coextensive with but nei-ther explaining nor to be explained by the first, represented his career. The doubling of the time line gave Bork's supporters a rhetorical vantage point from which to respond to critics' charges of cynical retraction.

Bork himself employed neither of these temporal idioms in the hear-ings in 1973 and 1982. Through the opening questions in 1987, too, he resisted both the critics' single-strand linear time idiom, with its portrayal of his self-interest, and his supporters' double-strand time line, with its portrayal of his independence. He voiced the third possibility of plural professional engagements and their separate normative requirements. Particularly in reference to his writings while an academic, which were the focus of the retraction controversy, he insisted on a meaning of "the-ory" which set it at some indeterminate remove from "personal opinion."

The first sign that Bork's rhetorical resistance to both his critics' and his supporters' constructions of "interest" and "independence" had begun to soften came on the first day of the 1987 hearings. Edward M. Kennedy asked him when he had first "publicly" changed his position on the Civil Rights Act. Bork began his response with a reference to the classroom, whereupon Kennedy interrupted him, repeating the one word, "pub-licly." Apparently Kennedy was rejecting the idea of the classroom as a public space. Bork then said:

Well, I think it is implicit in some of the things that I wrote earlier, but I first said it, I think, where it was written down at least, in a confirmation hearing in 1973. But, one has to know the evolution of my thinking about political matters to understand where that article came from and why I no longer agree with it and have not agreed with it for a long time.[50]

Bork's reference to evolution is crucial here, since it is the first time he invoked the temporal metaphors of the double-strand time line, the one that braids together the evolving inner man and the committed public man, an author of "fixed texts."

A few minutes later, Bork responded to Kennedy's characterization of the time between his 1963 article and the 1973 public retraction by invert-ing, in a way, the ambiguity of the word "opinion," which can refer to either a person's self-expression or a judicial text. In doing so, Bork inev-itably (though implicitly) reiterated the metaphor of continuity in a way that he had heretofore resisted: "Senator, I do not usually keep issuing new opinions every time I change my mind. I just do not. If I re-visit the subject, I re-visit it, but I do not keep issuing looseleaf services about my latest state of mind."[51]

But the full conversion to the double-line time idiom seems to have come in an exchange with Dennis DeConcini, who asked him when he had ceased "being a libertarian."[52] Bork responded by narrating the cir-cumstances of his authorship of the *Fortune* magazine article while on sabbatical, only to discover in the classroom, through a colleague's chance observation, that he was no longer voicing the positions he had taken in print.

Eventually, even Bork's two-strand temporal idiom flattened into a single-strand time line. Whereas in the earlier hearings he had used the first-person singular pronoun only to situate himself as a professional, midway through the 1987 hearings he began to use it in a way that was, by comparison, crowded and personal. The self and the public man are shoulder to shoulder in the response to Charles Grassley's question about his predictability: "If I got on the Supreme Court and began to do any-thing else [other than what I have been saying for the last sixteen years], I would be a laughingstock. I would make a fool of myself in history for having done that. I suppose that is the best guarantee I can give you."[53] Later, he drew a more complete image connecting Bork as self, Bork as judge, the committee, and—through the news media—the American public:

[This] is a hearing which you gentlemen refer to [as] historic, you refer to it as one of the most complete and so forth. I have expressed my views here, and those views are now widely known, more widely known than any views of mine before have been.

It really would be preposterous for me to sit here and say the things I have said to you and then get confirmed and and get on the Supreme Court and do the opposite. I would be disgraced in history. Aside from everything else, I am not going to do that.[54]

This statement completes the rhetorical fusion of Bork as self and Bork the professional into a single time line. This is not the "I" of "I am paid to speculate." It is an "I" who can be made into a fool, disgraced. Bork's reference to "history" displaces his earlier references to the professions as the rhetorical means by which he could express his independence from a vantage point external to his self; however, whereas invoking his profession once refracted his personal temporality, invoking history now consolidates it.

Even after he adopted the unilinear temporal idiom for his self-presentation, Bork continued to invoke "theory," though with increasing difficulty, as the hearings progressed. Indeed, the unilinear model of a lifetime leaves no room for distancing theory from opinion. I believe it was this point that Kennedy was making in his response to Bork's attempt to distinguish views he might voice in a formal public setting from those he might express in an informal question-and-answer session with students. Kennedy concluded: "It is your life."[55] Again, Bork himself expressed the collapse of the distinction between his life as a self and his public life in an uncomfortable (if colloquial) poetics, noting that he had repeatedly had to "eat" his *Indiana Law Journal* article.[56]

At the very end of the hearings, when Alan Simpson asked him why he wanted to be an associate justice of the Supreme Court, Bork reinvoked a symbolic consumption: "I think it would be an intellectual feast just to be there and to read the briefs and discuss things with counsel and discuss things with my colleagues." He concluded by elaborating on the "reputation" he would hope to "leave."[57]

The multitemporality of his professional engagements which Bork invoked for so long is relevant because from a cultural point of view this temporal idiom approached but ultimately subverted the idealized model of justice I sketched earlier. It approached it in its implications of independence, renunciation, and responsibility; it subverted it by making "justice" a profession, like teaching, like other forms of work. In the tradition of American liberal jurisprudence, however, justice is not a profession but a distinct modality of being. Symbolically, justices are not supposed to have—I should say, *were* not supposed to have—autobiographies. Yet, the Bork hearings made it plain that they must. His failed nomination appears to have been the school for Thomas's successful candidacy. By the time of Thomas's confirmation, the old idea that a justice's public life should be entirely textualized in the law itself had been set aside in favor of a textualization of private life for public purposes.

Bork's multitemporal idiom almost fulfilled these cultural requirements by disengaging his past from his "putative" future as a justice and by acknowledging the special ethos of the Court. Early in the hearings, Bork distinguished between judicial activism and the "inevitable bias" that affects a judge "because each of us sees the world, understands facts, through a lens composed of our morality and our understanding."[58] This statement is entirely consistent with what appears to be Bork's concept of a profession. Indeed, from other perspectives, too, to the extent that the notion of "profession" retains any residuum of a calling, it is a symbolic "wick" by which the self is incorporated into an institution's causes.

By the end of the hearings, the image of incorporation was inverted, as Bork—as himself—borrowed the temporal idiom of his critics and envisioned the symbolic consumption of his time on the Supreme Court as if it were an "intellectual feast."[59] In context, it is an image that anticipates grateful and self-effacing delight, but it reveals something of the logic of unilinear time, which makes individuals larger than life, even in their humility. It is not the temporality of justice, which symbolically posits an individual justice's renunciation of personal interests and transcendence over all other interests. Unilinear time, by contrast, posits the individual's redemption and self-representation in time.[60] Whatever conversions might have preceded the hearings, the hearing process itself seems to have produced this one, emerging as it did from the battleground between Congress and the White House over the politicization of the Supreme Court and the particular litmus test issues that were part of the public climate surrounding Bork's nomination. The conversation I have analyzed here was an improvisation, but its improvisatorial quality only highlights the power of its specific tropes—temporality, personhood, professions, and the judiciary in general—and the intensity of the contests over them.

The Perils of Autobiography

I have focused on Judge Bork's "retraction problem" because it offers a productive juxtaposition of explicit cultural idioms of temporality and justice in a single institutional and historical context. I do not want to be misunderstood as implying that Bork's autobiographical difficulties were somehow the cause of his defeat. Explaining outcomes is no more the purpose in this chapter than it is in the others. Rather, I am interested in the nature of the difficulty with which a life story (as autobiography) is wrested out of life experience. Part of the difficulty arises, at least in the Bork and Thomas cases, from the conditions that make an individual's autobiography relevant in the first place, that is, to someone besides him- or herself. Once those conditions have been met, it seems that the protagonist has already lost considerable narrative freedom, since "the life" is preanalyzed as significant, in the literal sense of signifying something beyond the life itself.

The hearing process preanalyzed Bork's autobiography as significant of powerful interest groups or people to whom he was alleged to be indebted for his career. Thus, the hearings made his autobiography contested ground with respect to the ambiguities of his retractions in at least two ways: first, with respect to his *intentions* (sincere intentions were constructed in the hearing as unchanging or changing only incrementally) and, second, with respect to whether, in taking different points of view, he represented himself or others. This was not so much collaborative autobiography joining Bork and the committee as it was a loss of control over his autobiographical narrative in the face of committee pressure to reconstitute his life story as a sequence of personal choices, rather than a series of professional commitments.[61] By the end, Bork seemed to realize how limited his own narrative freedom was with respect to his professional autobiography.

Bork's experience and, even more so, Thomas's suggest that some modification is in order with respect to Mikhail Bakhtin's celebration of the temporal freedom authors bring to their work.[62] Bakhtin views as freedom the disjunction between an author's actuality in time and the times the author inserts in his or her creative work: "The author-creator moves freely in his own time: he can begin his story . . . at any moment of the events represented without violating the objective course of time in the event he describes. . . . [The] author-creator, finding himself outside . . . the world he represents in his work, is nevertheless not simply outside but as it were tangential to [it]."[63] In the hearings, it was Bork's critics and advocates who put him (and themselves) at the center of his story, as hero and antihero. Initially, Bork successfully situated himself tangentially, as the subject of his own narrative. The effect was of Bork, the author, *representing* a curriculum vitae that featured another Bork, *represented seriatum* by his professions.[64] But Bork was required to abandon this tangential position and place himself at the center of his own story.

Indeed, the idea of an author's temporal freedom is by no means the convention of autobiography. The autobiographical convention is singly centered in the self; it is self-referential, confessional, revelatory, and unilinear.[65] The canonical form for male autobiography in England and the United States since the nineteenth century is scriptural: apologia and revelation are its central motifs.[66] At first, the narrative form of Bork's self-presentation was markedly different from either of these, though his supporters invoked revelation and his critics parodied the apologia. Eventually, Bork deferred completely to this canon.[67]

In her book on race, gender, and "self-portraiture" in postcolonial literature, Françoise Lionnet borrows Edouard Glissant's term, *métissage* (creolization) to refer to narrative forms that are multicentered, multivocal, multitemporal, "braided," animated by a fusion of plural discourses. These narrative forms, she says, are critical and subversive in resisting and disrupting the "representational space" in which the discourses of domination are preserved and reproduced.[68]

Bork's evocations of the professions in 1973, 1982, and at the beginning of the 1987 hearings were not *métissage* in Lionnet's sense of the term, but the analogy (even with its flaws) suggests what is at stake when the "representational space" of an institution is addressed by a narrative form that disrupts its conventional terms of legitimation.[69] Convention demands the linear forms of apologia and revelation; the Senate committee in effect succeeded in enforcing deference to this convention so as to take their own measure of Bork's self-recognition and commitments. The initial pressure to reformat his life story came from his critics, in whose interest it was to portray him as serving others' political interests; his advocates came to his defense in terms that maintained that pressure. In successfully translating his self-presentation into conventional male autobiographical form, the committee reinterpreted his life story as one of successive engagements; his supporters and critics differed only as to their characterization of these engagements and his effectiveness in representing the interests they involved. The adversarial aspects of the hearings became, in this respect, a collaborative project to make Bork's life representative. In this way, the senators improvised a vocabulary that spoke directly through Bork to the contests between a conservative executive branch and a relatively more liberal legislative branch.

As the Bork nomination went down in defeat, one could still imagine that autobiographical convention effectively precludes judicial autobiographies; judicial autobiography in the United States is a null genre— or was, until the Thomas nomination. In the hearings on that nomination four years later, that subtext became explicit as the framework for the hearings. Certainly, the senators themselves stressed the partisan political contest between the president and Congress and within the Congress in relation to the nomination and confirmation "process," as they called it.[70] They also returned repeatedly to general checks-and-balances issues among the three branches.[71] By comparison, these issues were relatively muted in the Bork hearings, although they might have been no less decisive in that context. These constitutional and political contests, explicitly and starkly drawn as adversarial within the committee, set the stage. Once again, I am not concerned to explain the outcome of the hearings; that presumably could have been otherwise even if the record were the same. Rather, I am interested in the arrangement and rearrangement of cultural symbols of person, time, and social order, in particular, the symbolic and rhetorical technologies by which Thomas's autobiography was made central to his qualifications to serve on the United States Supreme Court.[72]

The Thomas Hearings

In some respects, the Thomas hearings began as the precise inverse of the Bork hearings, at least from the perspective of a social construction of a professional person situated in his own biography. Whereas Bork insisted on the separate accountabilities of his professional service when he was asked how his personal opinions might have shaped his professional performance, Thomas did just the opposite, at least initially. Whereas the committee resolved the ambiguities of Bork's self-representations privately, the Thomas hearings involved a reprise, a second set of hearings, to resolve publicly the truth questions in reports by a former associate that Thomas had harassed her sexually. Whereas Bork initially resisted the reformatting of his autobiography, Thomas cooperated fully, allowing autobiography and biography to unfurl in identical terms. I am interested primarily in the first hearings, for it was in these that the biographical "canon" was established for Thomas and explicitly drawn into the foreground of his qualifications. In particular, his biography was repeatedly invoked to assert that his identity as an African American was proof of his ability to represent, through memory, African Americans' struggles for civil rights and social justice in his future tenure on the Supreme Court.

Before Thomas took the stand for the first time on September 10, 1991, his life story had been given in condensed or extended form eight times that same day by different senators, most of whom spoke for his confirmation. Early on, Alan Simpson drew the contrast between the Bork and the Thomas candidacies, expressing the view that Thomas's prior confirmations would preclude challenges to his record ("That laundry has been well washed.")[73] But it was Sam Nunn, on that first afternoon, who made it explicit that Thomas's biographical litany could be used as a preemptive rhetorical strike against interest groups arrayed against him:

Our duty is not to create or deny another vote on abortion or sex discrimination or affirmative action or any other particular issue. Our duty, as I see it, is to confirm a Supreme Court Justice who, subject to good behavior under the Constitution, may serve for many years on the Court, indeed, may serve for life. I doubt seriously, Mr. Chairman, that many of today's—maybe most of today's—burning issues will still be raising the blood pressure of our nation seven years from now when Judge Thomas is 50, much less when he reaches the still relatively young judicial age of 60.[74]

The relevance of Thomas's life story, the "climb," as Nunn and others described it, from poverty and discrimination in Pinpoint, Georgia, to success and power in Washington, D.C., was well established in the hearings even before Thomas told it himself. Narrators stressed its comprehensiveness, repeatedly juxtaposing unpromising origins to present success. This aspect of his story was then rhetorically leveraged against the narrow interests of any particular group. His success was also invoked as an inspiration to others. But primarily, Thomas's life story was offered as the promise that in his future as a justice, he would bear memories that would inspire him to fight for "fairness and equal justice."[75] Significantly, making the life story the principal idiom of qualification was the work of Thomas's supporters. Thomas, unlike Bork, was a full participant in the collaborative narrative of his autobiography, to the point of referring to himself in the third person. At the beginning of his opening statement, "I hope these hearings will help to show more clearly who this person Clarence Thomas is and what really makes me tick."[76] It was his supporters who referred to him familiarly in the third person as "Clarence" (this was by his chief sponsor, John Danforth) or, more often, "Clarence Thomas"; his critics tended to refer to him more formally as "Judge Thomas."

The key themes these advocates evidently wished to stress in Thomas's life story were highlighted by a selective doubling of certain of its features. In the course of his welcome to Thomas, Judiciary Committee chair Joseph Biden made an offhand reference to the strong physical resemblance—a fictional twinning—between Thomas and his young son Jamal: "Jamal, welcome. You look so much like your father that probably at a break you'd be able to come back in, sit in there, and answer questions—so if he's not doing it the way you want it done, you just slide in that chair."[77] Just as the life story brought the young Clarence Thomas to the fore, what that young man looked like could now be seen in the hearing room.[78] At many junctures, Thomas was also provided (and provided himself) with another twin, his grandfather, whose aphorisms and experience Thomas cited with frequency and fervor. Occasionally, his grandfather was given a surrogate, another senior black male figure to whom Thomas was said to be heir, Associate Justice Thurgood Marshall.[79] The fictive kinship linking Marshall (as grandfather) and Jamal (as Thomas) lengthened the linearity of Thomas's life story. It also heightened its symbolic association with the national civil rights "story," an association intended and defended by Thomas and his advocates. But this double twinning also provided the basis for equating Thomas with both the senior and junior men—with Marshall, whose seat Thomas now occupies on the court, and with his "double," Jamal—as if Thomas's own life story in a sense could encompass both the past and the future.

Female members of Thomas's family were also important in setting the stage for the highly conventionalized narratives of his personal story.[80] Senators repeatedly made reference to the presence of his wife, sister, mother, and other family members throughout the hearing, and sometimes they addressed Thomas jointly with his family. Biden, for example, announced that he would explain the hearing procedure to Thomas and his family on the second morning of the hearings, as if the nominee were no more qualified than laypeople to understand the process.[81]

In context, these evocations and recitations of Thomas's life story by himself and others repeatedly referred to his physical presence as an African American, though in highly selective and patterned ways. His "race" as such was repeatedly dissociated from his candidacy and confirmation, although both supporters and critics, in very different ways, expressed the belief that his race had symbolic value. The prevalent direct racial references were to the past and future relevance of Thomas's identity as an African American—in the past, as a target of racist discrimination during his childhood in the South; in the future, anticipating how his memories of injustice might inspire him as associate justice. His future service on the Supreme Court was also evoked as the harvest of Justice Marshall's years on the Supreme Court.

Importantly, even when Thomas's "race" was not the subject of direct references, conventional stereotypes of African American men tended to frame the story of his personal upward mobility, his success contrasting with what were repeatedly said to be the stronger probabilities against it. For example, Thomas recalled watching a group of criminal defendants board a bus as he sat gazing from the window of his Equal Employment Opportunity Commission office and thinking, "But for the grace of God, there go I."[82] Thus, while Thomas's achievements were heralded as the bounty of his personal attributes and the civil rights era, these celebrations simultaneously called forth assertions of what were said to be more typical, and more typically negative, African American experiences and stereotypes.

At some points in the first hearings, Thomas's identity as an African American seemed to overtake the senators, derailing the substantive inquiry. For example, after reciting Thomas's life story in his own opening remarks, Arlen Specter shifted to an otherwise uncontextualized quotation from Martin Luther King:

> Mr. Chairman, it was 28 years ago that Martin Luther King stood on the steps of the Lincoln Memorial and gave a speech that I believe helped shaped [*sic*] the conscience of this nation. He said, "I have a dream that my four little children will one day live in a nation where they will not be judged by the color of their skin, but by the content of their character." We're here to learn more about the judicial philosophy of Judge Thomas, but I must say I am flatly and frankly impressed with the personal background and the character of Judge Thomas.[83]

In a related vein, Orrin Hatch made one of several references by senators and by Thomas to King and to Abraham Lincoln as advocates of natural law theory: "Well, . . . it seems to me it's apparent that you follow in the footsteps of Abraham Lincoln and Martin Luther King, Jr., who argued that natural law informs the Constitution. Do you agree with that? (Thomas:) I think it informs and inspires it the way we conduct ourselves in this country, Senator, in our political processes. (Hatch:) Well, I agree with that too."[84]

These patterned tacit allusions to race intensified toward the end of the first hearings, as senators sought some rhetorical means with which to sum up "the process" and the nominee. Howard Metzenbaum made direct reference to Thomas's race in dismissing race as the explanation for the intensity of the committee's scrutiny. Most others were less direct. Hatch evoked and inverted a powerful television image from the civil rights era, alluding to the possibility of a liberal filibuster over Thomas on the Senate floor and equating it with the conservative efforts to block the expansion of civil rights by filibuster a generation before.[85] In the same speech, he borrowed the rhetoric of choice from the context of the abortion debate and reintroduced it as the senators' "right of choice" in relation to accepting Thomas's testimony. Even more vividly, Hatch made metaphorical reference to Thomas's "working on the plantation" of the liberals or the conservatives.[86]

As already noted, the dominance of Thomas's life story, as it was told and retold in context, structured the hearings around conventional (and stereotypical) meanings of race and established Thomas as *one* African American man who had discarded the negative aspects of his identity ("there but for the grace of God") and kept the positive ones. These were rhetorically reduced to his "memory," his "sensitivity," and his potential as a role model for others, presumably younger African American men. The gendered aspects of Thomas's identity were much more explicit in the second hearings, but the relevance of his gender was established in the first hearings in relation to the conventionalized representations of his race and their relevance to his qualifications as a nominee.

Thomas's own references to his life story deepened his and his advocates' implicit and explicit claims that it was a frame within which all interests could find a touchstone.[87] More particularly, his own autobiographical references tended to broaden the context in which apparent changes in his positions on legal questions or questions of philosophy could be dismissed relatively easily. He stressed that his views were based on his life experience, which had permitted neither the time nor the context for theorizing: "I did not just simply sit around and spend time just trying to spin theories. I had certain experiences that prompted me to think about some of these issues, and with respect to the issue of having a right to—to run my grandfather's business, for example, I simply looked at what in theory was his right."[88] On several occasions, Thomas mentioned his grandfather or his own childhood perceptions when he was responding to questions about the development of his views on constitutional issues or specific matters of policy during his tenure on the Equal Employment Opportunity Commission (EEOC, the principal agency involved in enforcing civil rights law). For example, he recalled reflecting on the implications of gender discrimination at the age of eight.[89] Though some, such as Biden,[90] contested such references, others found them compelling. Specter said: "I do believe it is very important that Judge Thomas will serve as a role model for young African Americans and he brings a very different perspective to establishment positions and to the political process which is a by-product. Not a reason for supporting him, but in essence, I have more confidence and I pay more attention to his roots than to his writings, and I intend to vote for him."[91]

When relating details of his philosophy and views on policy, Thomas referred to his performance as an *employer* at the EEOC, although he also had policy-making responsibilities there. For example, asked by Kennedy if he believed women naturally lack interest in particular categories of employment, he referred to his promotion of women at the EEOC.[92] Later, in response to DeConcini's questions about the access of Hispanics to remedial forums at the EEOC, Thomas added a reference to his own promotion of Hispanics *within* the agency.[93] When Specter asked about his record against racism, Thomas cited his own EEOC performance as the substance of that record.[94] In this context, Simpson quoted Thomas's earlier interview with a journalist, who had asked him to anticipate the historical record of his achievements:

I just hope that whatever is said, whether someone agrees with me or disagrees with me, they don't waste a whole lot of time on nonsensical things like where I went to school and where I've worked and what I did before I came here; simply bottom line after everything is said, to hope that at least they say this was somebody who tried to do what was right. That's all. . . . Just that . . . when he came to this agency, he tried to do what was right.[95]

In other respects, Thomas's treatment by the committee—and, to some extent, his own references to himself—were strikingly disembodied. While critics made reference to "two Clarence Thomases"[96] or questioned the existence of an "authentic" Clarence Thomas,[97] his supporters also rhetorically separated the person from the nominee. For example, introducing Thomas to the committee on the opening day, Danforth claimed, "Other than the nominee himself, I know Clarence Thomas better than anyone who will appear before this committee."[98] In his own opening statement, Thomas also seemed to stand outside himself assessing his life: "I have grown and matured."[99] Under evident stress, Thomas (as well as most of the senators) often began statements of belief with such constructions as "I thought that I thought."[100]

The sense of detachment implicit in speakers' rhetoric and syntax was perhaps best conveyed in frequent use of optical metaphors from architecture, cinema, and stage. These pervaded senators' efforts to define Thomas's position as nominee in the confirmation process. For example, Patrick Leahy, speaking against Thomas, said he wanted "to kind of look into the window of your soul, if I could, although I find the shade down quite a ways."[101] Simpson, speaking for Thomas, rhetorically offered him "the Oscar on judicial temperament."[102] Later, Simpson characterized the entire confirmation process as having become a "very disturbing ritual" and "a charade" involving "caricature" and "cartoon."[103] On the Senate floor, Danforth defended the relevance of Thomas's life story (in opposition to the argument that the Supreme Court requires a legal scholar or theorist), declaring that the Supreme Court does not need a "bottled brain."[104] Hatch provided perhaps the most vivid evidence of Thomas's simultaneous absence and presence from the first hearings; he congratulated the nominee, "You've added a lot to these proceedings."[105]

As the first hearings were closing on September 27, when, it is now known, at least some of the committee members were aware of the sexual harassment report, the contest to characterize Thomas accelerated and changed shape several times. Critics tended to narrow the issues. For example, Leahy deflected the life-story canon by referring to Thomas's professional accountabilities.[106] More generally, critics reiterated themes of the balance of powers, the current state of the Supreme Court, and the criteria of judicial qualification. Supporters, on the other hand, tended to broaden the issues. Simpson referred to the quality of Judge and Mrs. Thomas as human beings ("I know what kind of quality people they are") and the unanimity of support for Thomas from people who knew him at the EEOC ("Not one person in this city that I have yet found knows this man and said a single negative thing").[107] In a effort to take a long view of the controversy that surrounded Thomas's nomination from the outset, Simpson asserted that partisan politics was inevitable in judicial confirmation: "We perform. We do it, I do it, the groups do it." Then, perhaps prompted by the refrain in his own improvised statement, he added what was perhaps an unintended parallel between partisan politics and heterosexual flirtation: "I remember the song of Eartha Kitt: 'Even all the birds and bees do it'—I believe that great piece of hers."[108]

In the first hearings, Thomas and his supporters invoked his life story as a way of defining African American identity as an identity of discrimination, celebrating Thomas's personal success, and expanding the conceptual frame around the substantive issues on which he might be challenged, to narrow and contain them. Senators explicitly described this tactic in their own statements. In particular, Thomas's life story centered prominently on his EEOC experience as the yardstick of his philosophy and capabilities as a lawyer and future judge. Both dimensions of this frame, the life story and the professional performance, were tightened around him considerably when the committee resolved to settle in public the ambiguities raised by the sexual harassment charges. These intensified the scrutiny Thomas and his supporters had initially deliberately focused on his personal life and professional conduct as the text of his record; however, they also substantially shifted that scrutiny to the life itself. When race dominated the life story narrative, Thomas's performance could be rhetorically distanced from his "self." When the second hearings took the same life story and reexamined it for its gendered and sexual content, such distancing appears to have been foreclosed. In this sense, the second hearings both extended and overturned the first.

It is worth noting that whereas the second hearings aimed at tightening the seams in Thomas's adult life story (Thomas's own metaphor was a lynching),[109] Thomas appears to have felt constrained by the single-strand approach to his life during the earlier hearings as well. Bork had essentially been forced to adopt the linear autobiography as a device to account (and to be held accountable) for his professional "paper trail." Thomas, however, was never pressed to cast his autobiography in professional terms; indeed, his repeated recourse to personal reminiscence and experience became the rationale for his silences when he chose to be silent. Although Thomas readily accepted (and offered) a narrative version of his life which stressed the sequence of his commitments, he was quick to express reluctance to permit his written and spoken record from one professional context to "speak for" another.[110] For example, anticipating confirmation, he declined to express his views on many legal issues on the grounds that they might compromise his impartiality later.[111] In the context of questions about constitutional guarantees of abortion, for example, Metzenbaum tried to distinguish an individual's belief from that individual's future vote on a case; Thomas consistently equated the two. These rhetorical efforts to create some space *within* his autobiography culminated in Thomas's references to the need to "strip down" (that is, refrain from expressing personal views) as a prerequisite to accepting a judicial position.[112] The autobiographical frame within which Thomas and his supporters presented his life as his career paradoxically highlighted Thomas's silences on these and other matters, providing ground for his critics' challenges on substantive policy and other questions. Thomas's silence, and these challenges, intensified in the second hearings, but they did not originate there.

Thomas's preference for silence on his professional record also extended to his use of others' writings. For example, one area of questioning involved Thomas's reference to an article by Louis Lehrman, a highly selective and incomplete reference, which Thomas claimed was useful in his effort to persuade conservatives to consider a natural law basis for civil rights (some senators contested this claim). In explaining his use of the article while denying that it could be read as reflecting his own views, he distinguished the *fact* of the article (which was his interest) from its *substance*; he explained that his interest in the essay's contents was "very, very limited."[113] Metzenbaum challenged this distinction, stating that words speak for themselves.[114] Eventually, Thomas asked to be evaluated on the basis of a textual record limited to his own speeches and writings while a judge.[115]

In taking this position, Thomas seemed to accept a view of his life as representative or perhaps exceptional—in either case, a life that could be taken as a comment on others' lives. At the same time, he resisted constructions of his life or his record which would involve some commentary *on* his life. Thomas opened the second hearings by telling the committee: "I will not provide the rope for my own lynching or for further humiliation. I am not going to engage in discussions nor will I submit to roving questions of what goes on in the most intimate parts of my private life or the sanctity of my bedroom. These are the most intimate parts of my privacy, and they will remain just that, private."[116] Bork failed to retain control of his life story; Thomas succeeded, even in adversity, as Biden's statement describes:

Your grandfather's right, you have no right to give up. . . . (One) of the arguments made against you constantly by those who opposed your nomination is here is a guy who sought this, he's suckered it, he's gone out and he's laid down for people for it, and he's not dumb; a guy who wanted this from the beginning. . . . Well, if you planned this in the late '70's and you did this, you're one of the dumbest people I've ever run across in my life. And you don't impress me as being dumb. Your defenders here haven't even been smart enough to figure out to make that defense for you.[117]

Overall, the collaborative construction of Thomas's life story appears to have prestructured the meanings, risks, and responses inherent in both hearings. Although several Senators lamented that the sexual harassment "charge" had derailed the confirmation, my point is that Thomas and his supporters had already defined the grounds of qualification as Thomas's personal life and conduct. The second hearings only increased the difficulty with which Thomas might return to the *legal* ground that in other contexts, his life had been claimed to represent. Life and law were connected in a historicized construction of race in a way they could not be when the terms of debate shifted to those of gender and personal conduct.

The Second Thomas Hearings

Anita Hill's charge of sexual harassment did not, in fact, involve an appeal for redress, although the committee claimed its role was to investigate and, *of necessity*, decide whether it was Thomas or Hill who was lying. Throughout the hearings, Thomas had justified his silences by distinguishing his life—his self—from the normative requirements of his past and future professional environments. Now, his supporters rejected the possibility that *Hill's* silence about harassment at the time of her employment by Thomas might have been necessary for *her* to survive the competing demands and accountabilities of her career. To do otherwise in either Thomas's or Hill's case would be to acknowledge the relevance of power politics, race, and gender within bureaucracies supposedly ordered by law, not to speak of acknowledging that the canonical form of autobiography leaves crucial aspects of men's and women's lives unaddressed.

The second hearings revealed some of the political risks of attaching autobiographies to judicial nominees and justices, but those risks are perhaps small in comparison to what is at issue in incorporating notions of representation and moral hierarchy so deeply and directly into the seat of justice. The cult of the life story once belonged to the other branches, the partisan branches, but the Bork and Thomas hearings redirected the temporality of the life story to a place where it is has never been, the Supreme Court bench. It is too soon to know what its future will be there.

Autobiography, Representation, and Diversity

If this were a full-scale study of temporal negotiations in contexts of judicial succession, it would be relevant to move from the Bork and Thomas hearings to those that intervened and followed, or to others in which a person's ascribed characteristics marked the nomination as unusual in some way (as in Justice Sandra Day O'Connor's case).[118] It would be interesting to compare Supreme Court confirmations to those of lower court judges as well. Why, for example, did Judge Bork's "retraction problem" or the harassment charge against Thomas become major issues only in the context of their Supreme Court nominations, rather than at the point of their nominations to lower courts? And it would be interesting, too, to compare the temporal discourse of appointed judges to the discourse of those who are elected after campaigning publicly for their judicial seats.

The larger context for this chapter is not the comparative study of judicial selection but the ethnological and ethnographic concerns that animate debates about the nature of the relationship among cultural conceptions of time and institutional discourses of legitimacy. The judicial confirmation hearings analyzed here demonstrate the impossibility of separating time's forms and meanings from the institutional contexts in which they matter. They also illustrate the power of temporal logics to sculpt public dialogue and understanding. Even when one "shape" of time is dominant or orthodox, questions about its form and meaning are never permanently settled. And even when a public institution's mandate is superficially secure, it is always productive to examine the daily negotiations over the terms of that mandate. Time acquires form and meaning in social interaction, and institutions whose legitimacy rests on one form of time or another must continually encompass or resist the challenges of the many alternatives that are inevitably available.

Because the temporal element was so explicit in them, the Bork and Thomas hearings are useful illustrations of the extent to which notions of judicial succession in the United States are highly charged with issues of individuality, nationhood, sacredness, and the nature of textuality, among other things. But there is more. The unprecedented relevance to confirmation of nominees' autobiographies must, I believe, be understood in relation to the public and highly politicized construction of the United States as a diverse and increasingly culturally fragmented society. The individual autobiographies were constructed in the hearings in such a way as to highlight particular issues and images associated, in Bork's case, with the intensely ideologized battles over reproductive choice in the middle to late 1980s leading up to the 1988 presidential election and, in Thomas's case, with the Bush administration's effort to confound liberal opposition by nominating an African American—and a conservative.

The ethnographic point is that the life story can do this work because it is constructed from the outside in, as it were. It is constructed out of forms and circumstances that are already legible, even before they acquire their particulars. A life story in linear form can never be personal, for the same reasons that the Bork and Thomas autobiographies could not be. The linear form converts conditions and commitments into a string of choices linked by a single principle (or perhaps punctuated by a single epiphany). In this sense, the life story, at least as constructed for Bork and Thomas in standard Anglo-American male terms, converts all significant experiences into demonstrations of personal agency. As we have already seen, agency is easily reclaimed and redistributed by the very notion of "society," making it available for other uses. This possibility of recycling is crucial, since it is what allows for the concept of representation in social science, democratic institutions, and other modalities. Of course, it is not the case that all individuals' life stories are immediately taken up by powerful institutions as the state's own. Furthermore, the metonymies of citizenship which link the time of the nation to the cultural construction of a lifetime are by no means equally distributed in current practices of recognition.

In this chapter, the central theme has been the connections, the cultural connections, between Western conceptions of temporality and the occasion the judiciary provides for the organization and reproduction of an essentially temporal myth. Linear time, which is the cultural preserve of national histories and the public institutions comprised in them, dominates those institutional settings only to the extent that the people who inhabit them (whether managers or employees, presidents or citizens) believe that linear time has a transcendent reality that allows it to absorb all the other, potentially rival temporal idioms that also suffuse daily life. The capacity of Western culture for that belief was established a thousand years ago or more, when institutional and social structural changes gave linear time a path from the sacred domain to the everyday. That is a path of power. "The law" is cultural not only, or not first, in its patterned processes and outcomes but in its constitution in multiple temporalities and their indeterminacies. Specifically, law, as an idea, carries cultural force because it engages these temporalities and their critical incongruities so directly. These incongruities are reinforced in the United States, where democratic rhetorics stress the capacity of public institutions to represent collective personal interests. The contemporary view of the United States as culturally divided adds to the premium and power of the symbols that fuse individual life stories to the linear time of the state.

This chapter has offered an analysis of some American symbols of "justice" as involving a constructed juxtaposition of temporalities—linear time in a variety of forms against something beyond linear time. Seen in this light, "justice" implies both progress for the world and a critique, that is, an imagined vantage point from which history itself might be judged. Although legal actors' claims to legitimacy might be conventionally or historically cast in terms of the connection between reason and fixed, timeless truths, the implication of this discussion leads in a different direction. The cultural interpretation developed here around issues of temporality situates the cultural force of the law not in its neutrality but in its engagement with multiple, mutually contesting possibilities—different limits—for inclusion. To say that the law is cultural does not by itself dismantle the force of the idea of justice.

Conclusion: Postmodernity This Time

WHEREVER TEMPORALITY IS given some determinate form, this formalism can be understood as arising from the political need to accommodate multiple formulations of agency within a single regime of legitimacy and accountability. The case studies in Chapters 4, 5, and 6 explore contexts in which such regimes were challenged by new forms of cultural diversity and political elites responded with innovations in the representation of time. "Social time" is built out of the codes for converting the pragmatic questions of the limits of authority into theoretical questions of cultural relativity. Some of these codes might be deeply inscribed in social practice; others might be improvisations. Whatever the case, such conversions are easily overlooked in part because classic ethnographic practice is itself so deeply inscribed with propositions about legality, temporality, agency, and the significance of scale.

In the seeming relativities of social time, anthropologists found the means to contemplate a critique of modernity (in taking seriously the other formulations of time) and refuse it (in privileging linear time as "really real"). The central implication of this book is that linear time is itself a formulation of social time. Specifically, the social character of linear time inheres in the efficacy of linear representations of time (as duration or interval) in bridging incommensurabilities of people's imaginations, sense, means, and ends. In practice, linear time represents agency as dispersed uniformly and universally across social space, but the geometry of time requires constant maintenance. The previous chapter shows some of the cultural work required to sustain the notion of individual agency *as a component* of the agency of larger institutions. Everyone, not just judicial nominees, is at risk of falling off the story line.

The broad dispersal of agency envisioned in canonical social thought does not by itself accomplish the institutional connection between the lives of individuals and the lives of societies, conventional notions of social structure notwithstanding. Rather, it is the condensations of individual agency intrinsic in the representations of time as an interval which guarantee the availability of any social unit as a metonymy in relation to others. This metonymic availability readily transgresses the usual considerations of scale. Large can "represent" small or the other way around. Indeed, this availability potentially transgresses any conceivable boundaries of time, space, or culture; linear time is highly "absorbent" because there are no a priori categorical limits to representation in the semiotic sense. In the previous chapter, the proximity and mutual permutability of representations of timelessness and linear time in the semiotics of the federal judiciary illustrates this point. In this chapter, I qualify the theoretical openness of linear time by considering how race and class affect constructions of agency in practice.

The general point about the form of time and the distributions of agency applies to other temporal forms, which, by contrast, appear to us to be more categorical or (alternatively) more unruly by virtue of their approaches to the dispersal of agency. Cyclical times, as we have seen, appear to be more categorical because they involve more restricted criteria for the dispersal of agency. Nongeometric forms of time appear to us to be timeless because their dispersals of agency are posited as occurring outside, though not necessarily prior to, the spheres of experience.

In different ways, then, any formal representation of temporality lends itself to service as a code of representation by which formulations of agency can be claimed in the service of other people's causes. Importantly, the efficacy of such claims is not inherent in the temporal forms themselves. Social time has no practical existence or intrinsic logic apart from its contexts of use. To put this another way, social time borrows the appearance of logic from the world of events, where accountability appears to be the most immediate experience of time. Accountability arises in a wide range of situations. I have related temporal representation to issues of political accountability (i.e., legitimacy), but the circulation of temporal representations ranges much more widely than this. The illustrative materials I have drawn on do not exhaust the relevant domains, by any means. My main point at this juncture is that social time is most accessible ethnographically in relation to contests over accountability.

The relationship between formal representations of time and their practical referents in the cultural organization of politics gives temporality its intrinsically modernist character. I have argued that social time is pluralist on ethnographic grounds. In particular, the temporal innovations at the heart of Part II are associated with particular problems of statecraft, specifically, the cultural legitimation of regimes confronted with challenges involving new forms of diversity. In Chapter 4, the temporal innovation was the materialization of time in the person of the emperor; its context was the first unification of China. In Chapter 5, the temporal innovation involved the mythic contest of Tezcatlipoca and Quetzalcoatl; its context was the Aztecs' cultural strategies for managing their dynastic succession. In Chapter 6, the temporal innovation made a public display of the autobiographies of candidates for the high judiciary; its context was the intensification of identity politics as a dimension of party politics in the United States during the Reagan-Bush years. In our own times, "postmodernity" has become the conventional term for acknowledging the relationship between schema of time and sociopolitical risks.

The inherent modernism of formal representations of social time provides the main theme for this Conclusion. By modernism, again, I mean the character of social time as a means of addressing diversity (whatever the situationally appropriate meaning of this term) by redefining incommensurabilities within a single representational system. Putting the matter this way does not eliminate the incommensurabilities *across* social times any more than representing time as circle or line can eliminate the incommensurabilities *within* societies. Most of the book has addressed issues arising from social time as a comparative problem. I want now to return those problems "to the ground" by exploring some of the connections between time and incommensurability within a society. My hope is to highlight the connection between social time and social contest which has been the varied refrain of the book. I develop this theme along two principal lines: the mythic nature of temporal forms and the contested nature of the contents of those temporal forms.

Modernism, Time, and History

Although early anthropological writings on time as such did not draw explicit connections to contemporary philosophical concerns with time, these no doubt provided some of the context in which ethnographic questions took shape. The nature of time, history, and modernity have been major intellectual concerns in the West since the nineteenth century.[1] While this is not the place to review the history of these concerns, it is relevant to underscore the extent to which philosophical concerns with subjectivity, epistemological pluralism, and the experience of time (through memory and historical consciousness) appear to frame the ethnographic debates outlined in Part I, if only tacitly.

At the turn of the twentieth century, when ethnography was new, some Western intellectuals sought the meanings of time in presuppositions about the nature of mortality and what seemed at least to some to be a daily rehearsal for death in the alienation of the self from one's own labor.[2] From this perspective, labor value and the hourly wage were essentially memento mori in a very personal sense, as if leaving one's home for work were a rehearsal for leaving one's life altogether. The ethnographic treatment of time—indeed, the very term "social time"—also offers a contrasting image of time as engagement rather than alienation. The very possibility that other people might "think" time differently, or not think about time at all, no doubt fascinated and promised liberation, if from a distance of longing. Indeed, other times were held out as the hallmark of other cultures, and checked there.

Closer to home, meanwhile, time was for the first time subject to large-scale legal regulation, in response to the growing structure of communications and high-speed travel. Ultimately, this response culminated in a world standard time, instituted in 1912.[3] The regulation of time by the state and international convention sharpened the sense of contrast between the inner experience of time and public time for those who were concerned with these questions. In making this point, Stephen Kern draws on the work of social philosophers, artists, poets, novelists, and cultural critics of the time in formulating his assessment: "The thrust of the age was to affirm the reality of private time against that of a single public time and to define its nature as heterogeneous, fluid, and reversible."[4] Anthropology's concerns with time took shape in this same context, a context that perhaps created an intellectual and even moral demand for some affirmation that there might exist pockets of humanity for whom public time was unregulated, still fluid, subjective, even reversible, and inextricably embedded in the most basic conditions of collective existence, or even for whom time was not a concern at all. As a speculative example, I might offer Evans-Pritchard's poignant comments on the good fortune of the Nuer people in lacking (in his view) a sense of linear time.

From the beginning, anthropologists have been committed to the idea that time provides at least a selective cultural text from which fundamental social values and visions of social order can be read. The commitment has been selective. It is generally the nonlinear time constructs that are read as cultural in this way, and generally with respect to non-Western societies. Correspondingly, linear time stands relatively unquestioned as self-evident, a social time but also "the time." Part of my own experiment has been to consider linear time as equally a social time, to demonstrate how reexoticizing linear time affects one's approach to other time forms elsewhere. Treating linear time as social time also reopens ethnographic questions closer to home, especially the question of what sorts of incommensurabilities linear time is (as it were) designed to bridge. We have seen how the conventions of linear autobiography transformed Judge Bork's multiple professional commitments to a sequence of choices, but we have yet to consider larger-scale contexts in which the pressures of linear time might be registered.

In *Islands in History*, Marshall Sahlins outlines the gains to be had by taking seriously "the heretofore obscure histories of remote islands."[5] He does not mean these islands' pasts, but rather their people's sense of the past. Sahlins points to Hawaii, Fiji, and New Zealand and indigenous peoples' simultaneous constructions of history and social structure. In this book, I have attempted the reciprocal move of redirecting attention to the representations of time at three centers of power (superpowers in their own context). That temporality and politics are packed with a dense cultural charge "even" among superpowers is, I think, inescapably clear. Sahlins's observation that "the use of conventional concepts in empirical contexts subjects . . . cultural meanings to practical revaluations" is as appropriate to emperors and senators in relation to their constituents as it is to the reaction of native Hawaiians to Captain Cook.[6]

It is obvious by now that I have not been able to follow the convention of ordinary language which distinguishes between time and history, not to speak of the various conventions of anthropology and history that distinguish between structure and history.[7] History, as Lévi-Strauss has written, "does not account for the present, but it makes a selection between its elements, according only some of them the privilege of having a past."[8] One implication of this book is that it is not the pastness of the past which makes history but the codes by which some "elements" are selected for special attention in particular circumstances. Understanding that these codes combine elements that are implicit and explicit, settled and improvisatorial, is the beginning of viewing history as a temporal formulation that is integral to social categories and hierarchies in both theory and practice.

Viewing history as time in this way underscores its particular mythic properties, as well as the cultural technologies by which the mythogenic properties of modern societies are conventionally denied. Lévi-Strauss insists on a distinction between totemism and history as complementary systems of classification. In his essay on anthropology and history, Lévi-Strauss refers to the "totemic void," that is, the dominance of history over totemic systems of classification in "the great civilizations of Europe and Asia": "The reason [for their totemic void] is surely that [they] have elected to explain themselves by history and that this undertaking is incompatible with that of classifying things and beings (natural and social) by means of finite groups." The principal antithesis between totemism and history, in Lévi-Strauss's view, is totemism's essential atemporality:

Totemic classifications no doubt divide their groups into an original and a derivative series: the former contains zoological and botanical species in their supernatural aspect, the latter human groups in their cultural aspect, and the former is asserted to have existed before the latter, having in some sort engendered it.

. . . The two series exist in time but under an atemporal regime, since, being both real, they sail through time together, remaining such as they were at the moment of separation. . . . In theory, if not in practice, history is subordinated to system.

When, however, a society sides with history, classification into finite groups becomes impossible because the derivative series, instead of reproducing the original series, merges with it to form a single series in which each term is derivative in relation to the one preceding it and original in relation to the one coming after it. Instead of once-for-all homology between two series, each finite and discontinuous in its own right, a continuous evolution is postulated within a single series that accepts an unlimited number of terms.[9]

The difference between totemism and history fades, however, when one considers that history (at least in Lévi-Strauss's colloquial usage here) is itself a central project for nations, national elites, and their aspiring rivals.[10] Paul Veyne looks to the nationalist agenda in his identification of history's mythic aspect. History "has never completely freed itself of its social function, that of perpetuating the memory of the life of peoples or of kings."[11] Veyne makes the additional important suggestion that it is the *function* of history which accounts for its form, not time. Specifically, the "convention" that unites "time and place" "binds history to the continuum and makes of it above all the biography of a national individuality."[12] In each of the cases in Part II, the reigning elites successfully (if temporarily) composed histories around themselves which concealed their human manufacture in the present circumstances *and* their innovative artifices.

But history is mythic not merely in its ritualizations or in proclaiming the significance of the pasts of modern nations. The mythic core of history is in the system of social distinctions which divides the past from the present *in the present*. In the modern United States, for example, racial and class differences are the canvas of myth in this precise sense. The totemic void Lévi-Strauss finds among the states and empires of the Old World is not a void but a virtual monopoly, so highly concentrated are the processes of social classification in the state itself: "nations," "natives," and "ethnic groups" are continuous with the distinctions Lévi-Strauss draws between the culturally designated "natural" world and the human forms it engenders among totemic societies. Only if we disregard the social and cultural processes by which such classifications as race, ethnicity, gender, and citizenship are invented and maintained at the level of the collective national society, and expressed *for* the collective society by *particular* actors in *particular* circumstances, can we say that totemic classification and history are mutually exclusive. The temporal strategies at the center of each case study involved a highly selective and partial domestication of difference in reference (and deference) to the regime in question.

The "totemic void" is filled at the level of the nation-state in its very claims to *be* a nation. It is this claim that commits modern states to making "difference" a matter for the state, in the sense that the cultural legitimacy of regimes and in some contexts the form of the state itself depend, at least in part, on the efficacy of their claims to encompass diverse groups. This is not to say that "nations" accomplish this work alone but that the processes by which social identity becomes real, and comes to matter, implicate the state in the existential conditions of personal life. In our own times, this interpellation (and inversion) of public and private cannot occur without the mythicization of identities—for example, ethnic and racial identities—as categorical personifications of "difference." This mythic operation, which in the United States makes key differences generic, and generic in the same way, is what makes a construction such as "the melting pot" (for example) conceivable.

In the case studies of Part II, the clearest connection between the mythic dimensions of historized identity and processes of statecraft is drawn in the Chinese example. There, the key temporal innovations of the Ch'in dynasty consisted of giving the idea of sovereignty dimensionality in time and space; the emperor was carefully linked symbolically to both of these dimensions, as the steward of time, the standard of social technology, and the itinerant guardian of the empire's full territorial extent. Thus, I agree with those who interpret the Legalists' sense of time and history as relatively modern in European terms, but I see the Legalists' modernity in their association of temporality with nationhood, not (as is conventionally held) in some linear notion of time. Their representation of time was, like ours, associated with sovereigns and sovereignty, but, unlike ours, it identified the sovereign with time's closure, not (as we claim for ourselves) with some infinite openness. How these claims were met by the emperor's constituents is an important question, which I could not answer from the evidence I had available. Still, the emperor's apparent effort to align all social forms with his reality and legitimacy is evident in his self-identification with temporality itself. Temporality was already the encompassing rubric of all social forms; the emperor's innovation was to identify himself as the preeminent sign of the times and, symbolically, claim a place in all social experience.

The modernist element of Aztec representations of time was articulated in the self-legitimating canons that involved a set of symbolic appropriations organized around the Quetzalcoatl myth. I have already considered possible links between the Quetzalcoatl myth and the Aztecs' expansionist designs against the Maya frontier, at least through an expanded sphere of influence that included the Maya region. In this sense, too, the mobilization of cultural diversity as a confirming feature of legitimacy and the identification of the ruling (or aspiring) elites with the forces that transcend or transform that diversity (from disruption to triumph), are legible here as modernisms among the Aztecs.

One implication of these case studies, if "modernism" is the right name for what is at issue in them, is that "modernist" states construct themselves in terms of both the manageability of diversity and, therefore, its potential subversiveness or disruptiveness. Implicitly or explicitly, the three cases involve such dual claims, although in very different ways. Importantly, the people whose texts and practices are the subject of those cases *themselves* heralded their own "moment" as distinctive, explicitly in the *e pluribus unum* claims of the Ch'in and the contemporary United States and more implicitly in the Aztec case. I repeat that what these modernities have in common is elites' assertions of categorical, local cultural differences as part of their very claims to legitimacy. In addition, each case situates these claims in contrast to representations of other temporalities, again in very different ways. They also involve more or less diffuse images of the future. Only the Aztec case offers some explicit prescription for the future, that in the event the incumbent fails to rule, the very cosmos will reverse itself to reclaim the legitimacy held only provisionally by the ruler.

Although the Chinese and U.S. cases lack such explicit references to hypothetical failures of legitimacy, contemporary Americans are inevitably familiar with political rhetorics that place the current administration (at any modern period) in a mediating position between order and disaster, both domestic and foreign. My general point is that modernity, as envisioned by the elites whose improvisations are at issue here, involves both a vocabulary of cultural diversity and a strong central administration, and links these as pluralism, different, it bears repeating, in each case.

I use the word "modernist" in spite of the two thousand or so years that separate the cases. Modernism conventionally refers to recent times, but it need not; instead, it might refer to the substance of these times.[13] These case studies suggest that modernism refers productively to any temporal representation that involves the simultaneous assertion and management of difference as core functions of central institutions. I propose that a modern political institution is one whose self-defined mandate rests at least in part on successfully defending its claims to stewardship in the transformation of difference into participation in the state, and vice versa. This is the strongest link among the case studies.

In stressing temporal representations as modernist expressions and expanding the meanings of modernism to include other, even ancient, temporal forms, my aim is to emphasize the contingent quality of elites' self-legitimations. In another context, Astradur Eysteinsson offers the metaphor of conversational interruption as a commentary on this aspect of modernism, that is, the simultaneity of the assertion and negation of critical differences:

> As a historical paradigm, . . . modernism is caught between the crisis or even breakdown of modern rational discourse and the attempts of that very discourse to critique its own social and ideological effects and functions. The various individual devices of modernist disruption or interruption are elements of a paradigmatic effort to interrupt the "progress" of rationality, and perhaps to initiate a "new" discourse, which we can, however, not really know, since it is (still) the negativity of the discourse in which we are immersed. It is the other (of) modernity, or, to put it differently, it is modernity held in abeyance.[14]

Eysteinsson's field is literature, but his observation is suggestive of the ways in which modernist movements might lend themselves to both expansions and contractions of the social bases of inclusion.

If there is a totemic void in the world's "great civilizations," it is continually under repair by the aspiring elites whose claims to legitimacy involve historical and mythic appeals to diverse constituencies. In each of the case studies, the simultaneity of difference among constituents or potential constituents is suspended, redirected, redefined and put to use in elites' claims to cultural legitimacy. In practice, in each case, difference is at least rhetorically central to elites' substantiation of the legitimacy of their rule in cultural terms. Their legitimating rhetoric renders all differences among citizens, subjects, or members incomplete and contingent. The case studies show, in very different ways, how cultural constructions of time offer elites a vocabulary for doing just this. Only in the U.S. case can we know with relative assurance how positive or negative was the response of constituents to these assertions: both nominations were intensely controversial, and the controversies underscored the corollary aspect of agency and temporality. Again, particularly with respect to formulations of time, one cannot assume that representations of time speak for the people to whom they are addressed.

One conclusion of this book is that modernity is not an epoch in time but a temporal situation in relation to configurations of political power and cultural diversity. The modern habit of viewing modernity as a period of time is only testimony to the long-standing self-legitimating claims of sovereigns and nations in the West which draw on the past. All formal temporal representations, not just linear time, involve modernist assertions; in practice, this is how "we" recognize them as temporal in the first place. Linear time entails the idiom of individual agency and choice; cyclical times offer other modernist idioms particular to their own formulations, as we have seen. Again, any explicit representation of time is a modernist assertion, for by definition temporal representations address the diversity of cultural forms and formulations of agency within a single set of rubrics.

Modernity in this sense entails a vision of its own undoing; that is part of its symbolic power. Inevitably, regimes that claim legitimation in modernist terms maintain continual contact with the terms of their own negation. In each of the case studies delegitimation scenarios are repeatedly replayed in actual or imminent violence. The violence is readily apparent in the Aztec and Chinese cases; both were military regimes. In the United States violence also plays a complicated role in consolidating the images and rhetorics of class, race, history, the future, and the role of law. I believe that modernism (or postmodernism; in this context the distinction does not matter) involves a constant proximity to violence or the risk of it. The relevance of violence as among the signs of the state's power is not only in the power to conquer or coerce but also in the power to contain and control the public relevance of personal and group difference.

The contact with the possibility of society's negation which appears to be central to modernity is also actively renewed through mythicized histories—of the Aztecs' wanderings as barbarians, of the Ch'in conquests and administrative achievements, of the U.S. melting pot. The placement of these mythic relations in the historic past is central to elites' claims to legitimate rulership. That is, elite claims to having overcome these pasts in the present are central to the cultural substantiations of their legitimacy, whereas their political authority actually derives from other sources, such as military and economic controls or the law. In such contexts, disorder is enlisted as confirmation of the mandate to rule.

From here, I return to the idea that myth and modernity are inextricably linked. Each of the case studies features an elite claiming to embody progress or a new era in thoroughly mythic terms. Indeed, modernism necessitates a rich repertoire of myth, as well as selective means of denying myth in the name of logic or other forms of realism.[15] Importantly, denials of myth need not be made on home ground; that is, a society need not deny its own myths; rather, as each of the case studies shows in a distinctive way, societies' self-serving denials of myth can just as effectively target the myths of an "other." This is true not only in the contemporary West, where exoticizings of the "other" are well documented.[16] The invention and exoticizing of the other also figures prominently among the Aztecs and the Chinese, whose elites also defined their home ground as the ultimate metropole in terms of time, space, and cultural content. The Legalists' parodies of the golden age, the Aztecs' claims to Quetzalcoatl's aegis, and the contest between the Senate and the president over judicial confirmation—each of these rests on a particular cosmopolitanism. In giving time and sovereignty the figure of the emperor, the Legalists explicitly rejected the mythic infrastructure of rival kingships. The American debates over the Bork and Thomas appointments were dominated by rival rhetorics, each of which took direct aim at what was constructed as the other's provincialism, as it were—Bork's extremism or Thomas's lack of judicial temperament, according to their critics.

The case studies also involve forthright denials of these denials, in contenders' claims that their own mythic charter is realism itself. The imperial Aztecs' claim to be descendants of Quetzalcoatl might be understood in this way; similarly, Thomas's supporters' claim that his life story would make him representative of other African Americans also offer myth (the American dream) as realism. Such denials are reproduced in the very distinction between modernity and tradition or between a familiarly rational "us" and an exotic "them," the present and the past. These are distinctly modernist denials, in that they juxtapose difference and commonality, particularity and generality, and cultural property and access to that property, and render these distinctions both categorical and generic in the name of order and progress.

In this context, it bears saying that the Aztec and Chinese cases feature in officialized Western constructions of modernity. Part of my interest in "rereading" those materials was for the chance to explore the specific ways in which they are explicitly treated as failed modernities in the West. The Legalists are conventionally said to have brought Chinese feudalism to an end and would have succeeded in introducing modern rationalism to Chinese society had they not been diverted by their own excessive rationality in the form of despotism. Similarly, the conventional reading of Motecuhzoma's downfall stresses his failure to understand the true nature of history as linear, rather than repetitive. In each case, my principal goal has been to explore the consequences of taking representations of time seriously without privileging linear time as some standard of meaning and action. In the U.S. context, where time is widely assumed to be linear, the case study serves the same purpose, to show the multiple ways in which the nature and meanings of time are indeterminate even in contexts where its representation is most explicit.

These are the themes of the following case study, which serves the dual purpose of illustrating the practical difficulties and stakes in linear time as a modernist expression, and offering some indication of where and how the ideas I have pursued here might take shape as ethnographic inquiry "in the field."

Time, Life, and Law (Reprise)

My final case study juxtaposes two highly public contexts in the United States. I have chosen them deliberately for their superficially extreme differences in order to illustrate how social time—here, linear time—helps us understand the porousness of institutions and cultural practices with respect to particular ideas of difference, agency, and social order. I begin with the press coverage of the events following the violence in Los Angeles in the spring, of 1992 after the acquittal of four white police officers accused of excessive force in apprehending an African American man named Rodney King. The trial galvanized national attention. Although the violence was quickly labeled "the King riots," it should be understood in the context of the verdict in the policemen's trial. Indeed, the question of what to call the violence—riot? uprising? civil unrest?—remains analytically and politically highly charged, as the editor's introduction to a collection of articles on the "L.A. disturbances" notes.[17] I pick up the story at the point when the violence was over and the newspapers became a forum for debating its implications for the future. That debate focused on the theme of racial diversity and its practical limits in a functioning society.

Next, I continue to explore the theme of diversity and the prerequisites of a functioning society by reviewing a selection of major civil rights texts from recent times. These are judicial opinions and legislation that abolished racial segregation and affirmed equal rights for all citizens. From a certain standpoint, the differences between the two cases are superficial. In fact, they *both* axiomatically associate diversity with violence and with a corollary need for active legal intervention. The interventions differ in form—police action in Los Angeles and judicial and legislative action in the civil rights context—but not in their operative premise that diversity is intrinsically uncivil without the intervention of the law. Thus, commentators identify a latent potential for violence that becomes manifest in Los Angeles; the legal texts claim to hold back such violence by the law's preemption of it.

The relevance of these scenarios for a consideration of social time is in the details of how time, difference, and state power operate *together* on the streets and in the law texts. From a cultural point of view, the materializations of state power (as police force in Los Angeles and federal civil rights law enforcement) depend on an implicit antithesis between racial diversity and a civil society. Commentators coded the "future" for particular applications of state power regardless of where they stood on the political spectrum. The meanings of "Los Angeles" were sharply contested, but that "Los Angeles" should have meaning beyond the participants in the events themselves was never contested. My purpose is to point out how the debates over meaning unfold around questions of commensurability and scale; these are the referents of linear time as a social time.

Within days of the end of the violence, the very name Los Angeles became a synonym for a confusing and volatile amalgam of race, class, ethnicity, law, and lawlessness; it became a genre. One heard media reports and conversations about other places becoming or not becoming "a Los Angeles." Los Angeles had already captured the "diversity" genre with futuristic overtones.[18] The new usage only switched the meanings of diversity from positive or neutral to negative, and of the future from dominating to vulnerable.[19] The accounts are complex, and I focus on just a few patterns that bear directly on the ways in which time becomes a canvas on which to portray, juxtapose, and assess the related possibilities of alterity, order, and disorder.

Once "the riots" had passed as an event, they lingered in a confusing temporal discourse that called the actuality of Los Angeles as a community into question. By this I mean that the violence seems to have unsettled everyday uses of chronology in the reporting of events. Certainly, the starting point of "the riots" became increasingly ambiguous: Was it the court verdict? the beating of King? the growth and poverty of the city's minority populations? Drawing on American histories of race and class, commentators described Los Angeles, or sometimes the nation itself, as exposed, as if violence revealed something underlying, latent or festering, beyond and before the King verdict.

Nor did the media portray "the riots" as being conclusively over. For example, two weeks after the violence a Los Angeles poll revealed that most people expected renewed violence, although they felt safe at present. In this sense, the event seemed to pool the past and the future together into the present. One essayist for the *Los Angeles Times* wrote of the "long overdue" "death" of the city's image as "THE city of the 21st century."[20] To borrow Anthony Giddens's language here, the commentaries contained vivid images of the past and future emptying their contents into the present. The future in particular was represented as empty; hopelessness was a recurring theme in the commentaries.

To put this another way, "the riots" were no longer discussed purely as an *event*, but as a *sign* of something latent in the city, nation, or world. Los Angeles similarly became the name of a place and a generic situation.

Commentators drew on images of race and class for an idiom with which to relate the causes and meanings of the violence in Los Angeles or specific neighborhoods to "cities" in general or the nation as a whole. There was great variation along these lines, but importantly for our purposes, it was race and class diversity that was tacitly invoked as the means for exploding the boundaries around "Los Angeles" as an event and turning it into a type of situation. The technology that accomplished this telescoping of scale was race and class diversity and the assumption that diversity is intrinsically destabilizing.

Although the interpretations varied, the terms of interpretation did not. On the one extreme, the *Los Angeles Times* eventually seemed to settle on an approach that reclaimed both time and place in very specific ways, identifying specific gangs, gang members, and their histories of violence in particular neighborhoods as the root cause of "the King riots." On the other extreme, the syndicated columnist Andrew Hacker generally found the causes of the riots in "white America" and its control of a zero-sum race-based competition for the future. In the same vein (although from a very different perspective), Vice-President Dan Quayle asserted a cause in what he implied were African Americans' abdications of self-control, referring to the "poverty of values" in the "inner city."[21]

The media assessment of the violence as the breakdown of community gave commentators a variety of idioms with which to articulate connections between social diversity (ethnicity, race, and class) and violence. Race and class provided the figurative ground on which the actual time and place of the violence could be rhetorically transformed into some more generic object lesson for the nation as a whole. To some extent, the lesson was that some groups are volatile; however, I believe the clearer lesson was supposed to be that groups become volatile when they mix, for example, as neighbors. That is, what is disorderly is not so much *difference* as *diversity*.[22] Furthermore, once the violence was identified as riot, the participants lost their particularity and became signs of more global social relationships in terms of which diversity acquires its modern referents. This elision of agency and significance is a fundamental taken-for-granted tenet that everyday social thought shares with academic social theory in the United States—that is, that individual actions signify the attributes of social groups. It is precisely this elision that compresses temporality and social categories into the same discursive space, particularly, it seems, with respect to racial and ethnic minorities.

In committing themselves to a view of the violence as literally significant, as a sign of something beyond itself, commentators repeatedly used the figures of race and class to move discussion away from times and places where violence occurred. I understand the oft-repeated references to the "reality" of Los Angeles (as opposed to the television or Holly-wood images of the city) in this way, as gestures toward the unspecified significance of the event. Vice-President Quayle's reference to the televi-sion character Murphy Brown (in the controversial speech I have cited) also played on the contrast between reality and television.

Not surprisingly, the law figured frequently in the news and commen-tary, particularly in the *Los Angeles Times* reports of local arrests and pros-ecutions. I leave aside the presentation of the jury verdict itself, which was universally cited as the precipitating event, if not the *cause* of the violence. In the aftermath, coverage of the arrest of the gang members, prosecution of individuals arrested for looting, and the arraignment for retrial of Laurence Powell, one of the four police officers charged with beating Rodney King, provided occasions for reiterating descriptions of the legal process as arbitrary and vulnerable.

Additional law-related themes involved the literal and figurative dis-placement of law. In a literal appeal for displacement, Powell's attorneys asserted that their client could not hope for a fair trial anywhere in or near Los Angeles, perhaps anywhere in the state of California. Mean-while, the *New York Times* reported a 50 percent increase in the sale of guns in California. In another more figurative vein, violence was attrib-uted to *people* who were out of place, as presidential candidate Pat Buchanan linked looters to patrol problems at the California-Mexico bor-der. In addition, stories on the history of Los Angeles noted increases in U.S. and foreign-born immigrants to that city, as if it were self-evident that these demographics contradicted the possibility of a viable commu-nity life.

In contrast to the deeply troubled images in which commentators in-terpreted the implications of racial and class diversity in Los Angeles, the language of recent civil rights law offers very different images of the positive potential in human associations. The legal developments I con-sider here were aimed at protecting citizens from the negative meanings of difference. Their strategy is to define the public space, community, as the meeting ground of a diverse population. The law represents its own part in these efforts as constitutive of the new relationships on that pub-lic ground. Federal civil rights law is by definition national in its scope, as permitted and delimited by the Constitution. In practice, the govern-ment's claims (through any of the three branches) to the constitutional power to make, adjudicate, or enforce civil rights law must always be explicit, and it is often contestable. For these reasons, the rhetoric of law is highly performative and is potentially as significant as any "bottom line" in terms of outcome.

I want to give four examples to show the figuration of "race" in relation to constructions of time in the efforts of the Supreme Court and Congress to defend federal interventions in the cause of civil rights. In effect, federal claims to civil rights powers required reinventing "the local" *in relation to* the federal government, primarily as the object of federal power. My examples come from four legal texts: *Brown v. Board of Education of Topeka* (74 Sup. Ct. 686), the Civil Rights Act of 1964, the Voting Rights Act of 1965, and the Civil Rights Act of 1991.

In *Brown v. Board*, the Supreme Court referred to "races" and racial distinctions in a general way, although the sole named racial distinction is the one between "Negroes" and "whites." This practice was consistent with a prevalent view at that time of American diversity in terms of two "races" or "castes" (the latter term is Lloyd Warner's). The Court repeatedly referred to the education of children and the education of white children but never to Negro children. When the parallel to "white children" was rhetorically necessary, the court referred to the education of Negroes, omitting the age marker, as if to draw the public's attention to the future when *these* children would be adults.[23]

The court wrote of a divided society, even a caste society, where people "are" either Negro or white. At the same time, the substance of the opinion evoked a collective society in which such distinctions are absent or not determinative. The Court envisioned removing "all legal distinctions among 'all persons born or naturalized in the United States.'" The collectivity, a United States without legal racial distinctions, was elaborated in a discussion of the central importance of education to the future of the United States. Though the opinion contained extensive references to the history of public education in the United States and, in particular, the social advances of African Americans, the rhetorical purpose of these references was to anchor the Constitutional issue firmly in the present:

In approaching this problem, we cannot turn the clock back to 1868 when the Amendment was adopted, or even to 1896 when Plessy v. Ferguson was written. We must consider public education in the light of its full development and its present place in American life throughout the Nation. Only in this way can it be determined if segregation in public schools deprives these plaintiffs of the equal protection of the laws.

The Court evoked the future through images of children, the benefits of education, and the fruits of citizenship.

Whereas the Supreme Court in *Brown* could defend its case with a diffuse evocation of Negro citizens as full participants in the vitality of the nation, subsequent developments tightened the relationship between federal civil rights powers and economic growth, and made it concrete. In the 1960s, as Congress labored over the Civil Rights Act of 1964, civil rights advocates defended the federal powers (which were by no means a settled question) by invoking the commerce clause of the Constitution.

Although the sociological reality behind federal intervention might have involved local grievances of citizens pleading for legal relief, the legal reality was the constitutional mandate to protect interstate commerce. Only by constructing the local as a site of both discrimination *and* commerce were civil rights advocates in practice able to secure federal power, bring it (in effect) over state lines, and apply it at the local level. As in Los Angeles, but even more directly, translocal commerce can be read (and, I believe, *is* read by the participants) as a materialization of the state's power to protect and enforce civility at the local level. Indeed, the conceptual separation between "local" and "federal" which is essential to modern civil rights law is a metaphorical spatialization based on the actual geography of interstate commerce. In this sense, "the local" is no more an actual place than is "the federal"; after all, the reality of people and actual places was not, in the political environment of the time, sufficiently constitutionally compelling to make the Civil Rights Act possible. Only the transformed reality of the local, as a node in interstate commerce, made it possible.

The Civil Rights Act of 1964 (Public Law 88-352; 78 Stat. 241) uses a somewhat different range of figures in guaranteeing new rights in the areas of voting, public accommodations and other public facilities, education, and so forth. In Title I, the reference is neutral and collective in its singularity; it refers to "any individual"; later, the reference is to "any person." In Title II, difference is offered as the "ground" of "discrimination or segregation"; these grounds are enumerated as "race, color, religion, or national origin." Modifying these terms for the specific contexts of their relevance gives them a startling flexibility in terms of scale; for example, Title VII, on equal employment opportunity, defines a person as "one or more individuals, labor unions, partnerships, associations, corporations, legal representatives, mutual companies, joint-stock companies, trusts, unincorporated organizations, trustees, trustees in bankruptcy, or receivers." In short, the Civil Rights Act of 1964 abandons the caste language of *Brown v. Board* and maintains the reality of race in an entirely different way.

The act envisions people who are selective victims of enumerated acts of discrimination—literacy tests, denials of access to public places, and so on—but whose identities are not limited to those experiences. In the act race is the name of an experience, not a "kind" of person. Furthermore, race figures as one among several grounds of illegal discrimination. Although there are timetables attached to specific legal procedures in the act, there is no explicit reference to the past, present, or future; its prohi-

bitions of discrimation are immediate, categorical, functional, and timeless.

The Voting Rights Act of 1965 (Public Law 89-110; 79 Stat. 437) collec-
tivizes "any citizen" and "persons" in its guarantee of protection against
denials and abridgments of voting rights "on account of race or color."
Like the Civil Rights Act of 1964, this act evokes racial groups only by
implication, as a social construction, that is, as people who have experienced the illegal discriminations enumerated in the text. As in the Civil
Rights Act, the temporality of the Voting Rights Act is immediate and
timeless; the focus is the immediate need for legislation. The future does
not feature in the act, which is preoccupied with "now." Again, the act
makes no direct or indirect reference to race as a classifier of populations;
the relevance of race is entirely social.

The Civil Rights Act of 1991 (Public Law 102-166; 105 Stat. 1071) offers
additional remedies and some modifications of existing protections in the
workplace. Its constructions of protected classes and its enumerations of
prohibited practices are markedly different from those of the other texts I
have been considering. There are virtually no references to "persons" or
"individuals," as in the older texts. Here, we read of "entities," "parties,"
and "employers." In Title II, called the "Glass Ceiling Act of 1991" the
protected population is named as a category, as "women and minorities."
These categorical distinctions stand in marked contrast to the *social* constructions of victims of discrimination by experience in the acts of 1964
and 1965.

This text suggests a more complicated world than the earlier ones.
Rather than identify the federal courts as the remedial agent, the act
gestures toward other venues—negotiation, alternative dispute resolution, and foreign legal systems. The public space is more crowded in this
act, not only with categories of people but also with sources of authority.
In the earlier acts, the federal government rhetorically claimed to monopolize the constitutive power of civil rights; here, that monopoly has been
to some extent redistributed to additional agencies and practices.

The most significant parallel among these four legal documents, taken
together, is their construction of public space as the literal and figurative
ground where the significance of difference is to be forged through law.
Importantly, except in the most general terms, they do not name the
groups whose protection they secure; in this sense, the texts rhetorically
focus on diversity, not difference. The law positions itself at the juncture
where timeless and timely social orders conceptually divide, that is,
where the issues of humans' "natures" (as racial, gendered, violent, weak,
and so forth) are separated from the cultural vision of a national story in
time. The texts create a space for the law's power at precisely the place

where differences might become volatile, taking over, as it were, from the forces of "nature" which are supposed to have made race. Law, in other words, constructs its own power as an agency capable of suspending the negative consequences of diversity, transforming diversity into civility.[24] This is the point at which the L.A. texts and the law texts converge.

In obvious ways, the newspaper accounts of life in Los Angeles and the civil rights law texts reveal different images of law, society, and the future. In other ways, though, they are similar in their construction of the public space as a site of engagement among "groups" and of the law as having a central role in mediating those engagements. These are crucial parallels between the current commentaries on Los Angeles and the legal texts. In Los Angeles, the engagement of "groups" is violent, and "law" means local police. The civil rights texts feature the federal judiciary as the agent of an orderly "diversity." Either way, the transformation of diversity into civility is the state's business, whether by protection from the consequences of difference through law (civil rights) or through law enforcement (policing).

The links between the negative and positive forms of community are particularly clear in the case of Los Angeles during its period of "recovery," cast by commentators as a transition from disturbance to health. "Recovery" is an interesting word choice ethnographically, since commentary inevitably isolates particular signs of community and traces their circulation around and across the former sites of violence, as well as offering tentative claims about their literal significance in time and space. But "recovery" is also a telling metaphor, focusing as it does on unhealthy (raced? classed?) bodies and the need for their transformation as a criterion of healthy social functioning.

Signs of the more positive meanings of community were taken (by the commentators) to be confirmed in the rapid commitment of public funds for relief and rebuilding, which won early bipartisan support. The need for literal rebuilding lent force to particular figurative images of reconstruction; rebuilding quickly took on vivid metaphorical meaning as moral reconstruction. This was not the only aspect of the city's recovery that claimed attention, but significantly, the commentary on investment situated it within the architecture of the state's control of urban space.

In such figurative contexts, private space ("values," for example) was also turned inside out, commoditized, and claimed as capital for use in the public domain. This particular inversion provided recurring imagery for politicians on both the Left and the Right. On the Left, for example, Tom Hayden envisioned the possibilities of a moral reengagement of white businessmen with Los Angeles' problems, although he was skeptical of the Ueberroth commission, which was appointed to lead planning for the city's recovery.[25] On the Right, Vice-President Quayle's equation of poverty with a poverty of values is a more generic inversion of the ordinary meanings of public and private. Literally and figuratively, then, in Los Angeles and in civil rights law, commerce emerges as an on-going materialization of the state's agency which, more episodically, takes up its vigil over the public space through law enforcement.

To summarize, civil rights law and public understandings of violence construct public space around the central axis of the state's role in the management of diversity in physical space—literally and figuratively, the common ground. On that ground, the ordinary meanings of diversity are negative, inherently uncivil. To the extent that the public space is *orderly*, racial and class diversity confirm the controlling power of rights. This ambivalence lends a particular ambiguity to the idea of community.

In the United States "community" is always an ambiguous (and sometimes unintended) evocation of an element of the constitutional structure of government which links suffrage to place of residence. The connection between representation and residence was itself the projection of the logic of powerful Enlightenment metaphor that drew parallels between "society" and "family." Thus, the household, a family in place, is the smallest civic unit in the political organization of the United States.[26] From there, all organizational relationships of parts and wholes are easily metaphorized as families and communities. We have just implied that the sliding metonymies of Western canonical social thought rely on cultural assumptions about the nature of racial and ethnic identity and their selective codings and recodings of individual agency as group attributes. These bear closer scrutiny.

In the United States "community" has both spatial and temporal components. The spatial element defines "community" as a social field and the temporal element defines "community" as the historically authentic or original local, regional, or national social form. A concept of community framed in these terms enlists the "other" in the deictics of time and space of the modern nation by making the "other" a hypothetical non-presence in the past, and a hypothetical non-absence in the present; this is the essence of the "melting pot."

Such hypotheses or prescriptions allow people to maintain a concept of "the nation" as culturally diverse while leaving "community" homogeneous by definition. This kind of spatial and temporal sleight of hand allows people to refer to "community" and "diversity" as if they were different social spaces even when local demographics are in reality mixed. This doubling is, in part, a temporal construction, as if the authentic community were homogeneous, and only the modern one diverse. In reality, it appears to be diversity that occasions the construction of a past "way of life," and not the other way around.[27] In other words, the distinction between the past and the present is built with the same tools—the antinomy of "diversity" and "community"—which conceptually separate state and civil society. These appear to be two different distinctions of different orders (one in time, one in the state itself) but they are actually one distinction (or set of distinctions) defining "race." Dividing "community" from "diversity" on these tacit racial grounds creates space for both the normal, negative meanings of diversity (as disorderly) and their transformed, positive meanings as the canvas of the state's agency ("law and order"). Importantly, though, race, temporality, and the legal order are inseparable ideas.

Part of the dynamics of these doublings and denials is the cultural allocation of agency, by which nonwhite individuals are denied substantial agency of their own at the local "level" as permanent "outsiders." One element of this social distancing is the ready elision of individual agency and group attributes, as I have mentioned. Another is that the history of the civil rights movement has made "minorities" icons of the state's agency. The iconic association of racial minorities with the state accounts in part for the broad-based materialization of state power in the "health" of "the community" in the case of Los Angeles (or "a" Los Angeles), as well as in the civil rights contexts where individuals' status in their home communities depends on federal intervention. In the previous chapter, Judge Thomas's life story was offered as the nation's civil rights story: the story of justice materialized as a justice. Such telescopings of scale are based on the "switches" by which individual agency is acknowledged or suspended in favor of collective attributes under particular circumstances.

In our own times, the story of the nation is predesignated as a linear story of progress, and in practice, this narrative form begs for a happy ending in which the future confirms the merit of the present. There is no parody in my making this observation; I am as hopeful as anyone. Rather, my point is that in practice the equal and universal dispersal of agency which linear time is said to involve (by its theorists and celebrants) requires the intervention of the state, given broad public assumptions about the nature of difference and, even more critical, race and class diversity. The imperatives of the future become those of state power because, in this context, the obstacle to the future is diversity; I trust it is clear that I am characterizing a world view here and not writing in my own voice.

In my own voice, I will add that invoking "the future" trains a spotlight on the state's legitimacy in relation to its fields of power in racial and class conflicts. Talking about the future draws attention to the cultural legitimacy of the state systems of law and social control; in this context, this is the meaning of "the future." The specifically mythic element in these scenarios is the codes of racial distinction by which individual agency is selectively converted into problems of jurisdiction and scale. It is this potentially incongruous proximity of agency and legality which temporal representations—in this case, "the future"— domesticate and, literally, normalize.

Postmodernity in the Here and Now

Giddens's recent discussion of postmodernity makes the loss of "community" a defining element of the here and now.[28] In that context, Giddens relates the existential condition of the self to global forces of technological and social change. One can accept his sense of the crisis surrounding public self-identity and still read his book as highlighting a certain romance of community, which also lingers ambiguously in others' more explicit calls for communitarian approaches to (post)modernity and diversity.

To the extent that scholars envision the present moment as a *departure* from a past time and place in which traditions were believed in and the self was wholly situated in viable community, they nourish a myth that makes community and difference into rivals. It is a pastoral myth, which has always existed in relation to its inverse, the myth of the city—or, to follow Peter Stallybrass and Allon White, the imaginary slum—even when the world was bigger, not yet "global."[29] One implication of the case studies in this book is that postmodernity is not about the end-state of history or the loss of "community's" social forms but about tensions between cultural diversity and the legitimacy of the *polis* (for want of a better general term).[30]

Indeed, Giddens himself links the acceleration of late modern social processes and institutions at the global level to the marked *de*acceleration of allowable affirmative expressions of difference. On the one hand, Giddens suggests that the institutions and politics of late modernity heighten discourses of collectivity—a culmination of Durkheimian solidarity, perhaps. On the other hand, Giddens also points out that the distinctive politics of late modernity undermines and disables affirmations of difference to the extent that expressions of difference are inherent challenges to the dominant and dominating discourse of a homogeneous community, be it the nation-state or communities of smaller scale. The commentary on Los Angeles illustrates these points—perhaps above all. The civil rights texts create a surrogate homogenous community from a heterogeneous population through the rights of citizenship.

Giddens's core image is a "colonising of the future." The phrase refers to the politics of late modernity, which, in his view, characteristically involves a pitched contest for control of the rhetorical meanings of the future. The very fact that the rhetorical power of the future is an object of open competition is a defining characteristic of "the late modern age," as Giddens calls it. In the late modern age, he suggests, time and space are unhinged from each other, and community is lost under the crushing pressure of a global mass culture. In that context, Giddens speaks of the "end of nature," but it would probably be more accurate to envision the "end of sociology" in this statement: "The 'emptying' of time and space set in motion processes that established a single 'world' where none existed previously. . . . late modernity produces a situation in which humankind in some respects becomes a 'we,' facing problems and opportunities where there are no 'others.'"[31] This other-less "we" is not a utopia; against it, rival first-person plurals have not breath enough to make their voices heard, nor a legitimate discourse for pressing their distinctive demands in public political arenas.

In the official forms of time in *our* world, the sequestering of the inner life from the world of action is part and parcel of the cultural story that makes the state, the workshop, the clock, the hourly wage, contracts, and private property roughly contemporary ideas since the late Middle Ages. From this perspective, the classic boundary between the social sciences and the humanities is a late vestige of the medieval contest between popes and secular sovereigns for dominion over souls and bodies, respectively.[32] One need hardly strain to adduce modern examples of the familiar cultural notion of personal virtue (or the lack of it) as the machine of history. These are the contexts in which the politics of nations and empires establish their own meanings of time and difference to sequester the human spaces where needs gather and acquire force as imagined, if unrehearsed, accountabilities. It is in this sense that the classic social science dichotomy of individual agency and social structure reproduces and reinforces the containment of difference which the state claims for itself. And it is for this reason that I have stressed, at least as a question, that cultural formulations of agency are only selectively acknowledged and accommodated by any particular institutional form. Social time reproduces these codes of selection. Their principal site of production and enactment is in the demand for and practices of recognition.

Examining the social lives of states from this perspective can illuminate how state forms *mis*recognize or altogether fail to acknowledge the formulations of agency they cannot accommodate. I take the term "resistance" to refer to these formulations of agency. The issue of resistance focuses our questions on the commensurability and incommensurability of cultural concepts of human agency within political situations, broadly speaking.[33] It also draws our attention to issues of hegemony. Given the evidence I have been able to consider, this book has more to say about hegemony than resistance. Both involve improvisation and creativity.

In particular, I want to stress the vital connection between hegemony and improvisation, as illustrated by the case studies of Part II. In theory, hegemony is associated with the settled or silent habits of power, but also with the discursive practices that, as "hegemonic forces," can accelerate and intensify in contexts of instability, as the Chinese and Aztec examples show in different ways. Hegemony also functions *within* state bureaucracies, as the Senate confirmation hearings illustrate. In the kaleidoscopic contingencies of political crisis, hegemony is potentially even more pressing as an ethnographic issue than when structures "work," since one must look for it in the improvisations that create, maintain, and defy inequalities.

"Hegemony" and "resistance," then, are not semantic parallels to "structure" and "agency," as they are often made to seem. Rather, they name the practices of recognition by which some forms of agency and some agents are acknowledged, while others are denied. Such denials are at the heart of whatever "postmodernity" might mean. Viewed from above, postmodernity involves the aestheticization of indeterminacy, fragmentation, and rupture; this is itself a mode of denial. Indeed, viewed from below, postmodernity involves myriad and not-always-systematic denials of the ways in which the state's self-legitimations are challenged in public and private, specifically insofar as nation-states by definition must claim to monopolize the agency of their citizens. In the United States these days, one hears a great deal about choices, values, contracts, commitments; these terms are deeply coded (as the voters seem to understand) for particular inclusions and exclusions. But it is not just in the United States that one listens in vain for some explicit recognition in national political discourses of the contests among cultural formulations of agency and hope.

Again, by agency, I mean people's goals, together with their broader sense of what is possible and of what relevance is about, even if their understanding of relevance excludes their own experiences from the story of the world. Others have made cogent and convincing appeals for considering resistance and knowledge practices as central ethnographic comparative and historical issues.[34] The effect of considering these as questions of agency, specifically as contests among different formulations of agency, reveals classic social science dichotomies to be built from incommensurate elements. "Structure," "agency," "hegemony," and "resistance" are shorthand for the different ways agency in practice is artificially constricted within broader theoretical and situationally relevant limits. By uncoupling structure and agency, we broaden the limits of ethnography past the comfortable domains where we can be assured that people's lives are equally acknowledged and redeemed in whatever institutions survive them. By loosening hegemony and resistance, we open more fully to view the ranges of epistemologies and practices of recognition that are the stuff of people's vulnerabilities and survival.

In the social sciences, the project of recovering those voices is traditionally identified with ethnography and, particularly recently, with postmodernist influence in anthropology. That influence is less in the form of methodological or epistemological postmodernism than it is a broader project of an ethnography of postmodernity. Interpretivism and the hermeneutic turns associated with the postmodern influence in ethnography fail to satisfy some critics, who claim that "art" cannot capture the world's violence and its relevance in social life among ordinary people.[35] One might dispute a view of art (if that is what interpretivism and postmodernism are) as simply decorative or as inevitably diverting attention from the reality of force and other things that matter. Still, the critique nonetheless underscores the extent to which ethnography has been relatively silent on the cultural production of the social classifications that make up "difference" on a large scale.[36] Expanding the limits of ethnography in this direction is important if we are to advance our understanding of the vulnerabilities and improvisations that are normally concealed by so-called ordinary circumstances.

The paradox of postmodern ethnography would seem to be that without attending to the cultural production of difference, the commitment to recuperating the voices of the silenced and oppressed itself renders these generic and contains them within a globalizing discourse. On the one hand, postmodernism calls to the foreground the raw material of political life, the arbitrariness of meanings, values, and interests and the ways this arbitrariness is made real in the practices that make up the experience of ordinary life at the grass roots. The relationship between local meanings and translocal social processes is an important and exciting new theme in contemporary ethnography.

On the other hand, the forces that generate and sustain these categorical statuses at the sites where they are themselves negotiated remain, for the most part, past the limits of the ethnographic gaze.[37] Thus, centers of state power, in the formerly colonizing world or elsewhere, tend to remain just past the horizon of inquiry, as they always have. As a result, there is not the empirical foundation that one might wish for as the basis for an ethnography of postmodernity (if that is what we are going to call it). We are left with the illusion that "local" and "global," for example, are spaces apart, rather than markets in which which people's value is measured in currencies of various kinds, both literal and figurative.

From a broad perspective, the possibility that ours is not the first or the only modernity adds some additional concreteness to current debates about postmodernity and its methodological implications in the humanities and social sciences. 'Postmodernity" may not be the right name for what we have on hand, but it is not bad as a reminder of the extent to which social struggles and their implications for the actual practice of power at the level of the state (and beyond) are aestheticized and reinterpreted as social time.[38] The "time-space compression" and "fragmentation" that are widely supposed to be features of postmodernity are examples of such aestheticizations well within the temporal schema of the nation-state. From the broader perspective I have attempted to achieve in this book, though, the compression in question is the reality or potentiality of a legitimacy crisis emergent from new politics within or beyond the state.

In this book, I hope to have encouraged others to view centers of power as lying within the horizon of ethnography, where they have been all along, latent in the very categories and experiences of difference which have traditionally inspired and informed ethnographic research. Like the places where anthropologists usually study, centers of power in the modern West and elsewhere are human spaces where cultural propositions and values are constantly invented and tested against the needs framed by fundamental, unresolved questions of structure, purpose, knowledge, and will. My approach in this book has been to explore these challenges and desires through the cultural representation of time, and the highly varied idioms time offers elites with which to assert and defend their own cultural legitimacy. Regrettably, the available evidence permitted only a one-sided focus on elites. If I were to take the anthropology of time to the field, the path this book has taken does not lead back to clocks and calendars but rather to the sites and practices in which ordinary people, whether they work in the state's name or not, are challenged directly or indirectly to assess their own roles as agents of justice. My purposes here are more preliminary. In this attempt to understand the meaning of the moment in different cultural contexts, I have hoped to connect anthropology's explorations of the "other" to both its potential for discovery closer to home and its efforts to come to terms with itself.

Notes

Introduction

   1. For example, see Toulmin and Goodfield 1965.

   2. On the temporal distancing of classic ethnology and ethnography, see Fabian 1983. On the temporal discourses of European nation-states in relation to local historical discourses, see Herzfeld 1991.

   3. Gell's 1992 study of the anthropology of time identifies this conundrum as the now-pervasive legacy of Durkheim's misreading of Kant.

   4. Strathern 1991, 2. My own focus is on the presumed connections between nature and cultural ideas about time, and I leave the other elements of this "logic" to the realm of implication. But these points are the subjects of significant critical literatures in their own right. On the problem of social wholes, for example, see Strathern 1988, 1991, 1992; on the problem of social reproduction, see Benhabib and Cornell 1987; Weiner 1980.

   5. Geertz 1973.

   6. Ortner 1984: 159.

   7. Harvey 1989; see also Bender and Wellbery 1991: 3.

   8. Giddens 1991: 27, and more generally, Giddens 1990.

   9. Chartier 1988: 5.

   10. Strathern (1988) addresses the interface of comparison and reflexivity. See also Herzfeld 1987 and Comaroff and Comaroff 1991, 1992, whose historical and ethnographic projects at the margins of power include a reflexive inquiry of anthropology and its contexts of production. Herzfeld's focus is on the conceptual reproduction of marginality in anthropology's resistance to European ethnography. The Comaroffs relate class and gender hierarchies in England to the complex asymmetries in European and indigenous solidarities and confrontations in southern Africa and to anthropology's relationship to history. Johannes Fabian's (1983) reflexive analysis of time in anthropology has also been important to ethnography's current self-critical moment.

1. Time, Life, and Society

   1. Goethe 1962: 84–85.

   2. Cullmann 1964; Le Goff 1960.

   3. Cullmann 1964: 51.

   4. Goody 1983: 33, 44–46.

   5. Le Roy Ladurie 1978; Le Goff 1977; Thompson 1967.

6. For an overview, see Huizinga 1924.

7. Mumford 1934; see Needham et al. 1986 on earlier timepieces in China and elsewhere.

8. Cullman 1964: 62–63; Le Goff 1960: 419.

9. Le Goff 1965: 169–248; Tawney 1962.

10. Gilson 1950: 64.

11. Dales 1982: 495–508; Leff 1967: 26; Le Goff 1965: 211–12.

12. Le Goff 1960: 420.

13. Gilson 1950: 385.

14. Ibid.

15. See Bloch 1964: 1; Gilmore 1952: 201; Le Goff 1965: 222.

16. Wolff 1962.

17. For contrasting interpretations of how the clock affected social consciousness, see Cipolla 1980: 182; Mumford 1934; also Thompson 1967: 56. For a modern study of time and social disciplinary regimes, broadly speaking, see Rutz 1992.

18. Le Goff 1977: 67. I do not mean to suggest that clocks and the popularization of linear time *determined* the nature and direction of Europe's changing social structure at this time; quite the contrary, it is the broader context and contests surrounding ideas about time which are relevant here, though this is not the place to examine these in any detail. The technological innovations with clockwork took place at the same time as the Hundred Years' War and the devastating pandemic of the plague; given the rarity of clocks in Europe at the turn of the fourteenth century (fewer than twenty, according to E. Pereira Salas), these ravages might have had more direct impact on people's consciousness of their individual mortality than theological canons. Wars, disease, and developments in the economic sphere sharply increased landlessness among peasants. Cicely Howell associates individualism with landlessness because exclusion from the land ruptured social ties that had formerly been critical to conceptualizations of personal identity. Pereira Salas 1966: 142; also Cipolla 1967: 66; Howell 1975; Wolf 1982; Thomas 1964.

19. Cipolla 1967; Pereira Salas 1966.

20. For additional data and discussion of these controversies, see Landes 1983; Needham et al. 1986. Lewis Mumford (1934: 14–17) ascribes the symbolic power of the clock to its dissociation of time from human events; in his formulation, timekeeping became timeserving.

21. Le Goff 1965; Tawney 1962: 44–55; Thomas 1964; Weber 1958.

22. See Wickham 1985: 54.

23. Leach 1961: 124.

24. For ethnographic examples, see Beidelman 1963; Firth 1967: 475–80.

25. See Wickham 1985 for discussion of factors contributing to the variability of such processes in Western Europe.

26. Le Goff 1977: 68–71; Thompson 1967.

27. Bhabha 1994: 139–70; Chatterjee 1993.

28. Frazer 1889: 431 n. 1.

29. Malinowski 1927: 203.

30. Nilsson 1920: 2.

31. Excellent guides to anthropological work on social time can be found in Gell 1992; Munn 1992; and Östör 1993.

32. Durkheim 1965: 22.

33. Ibid.

34. Ibid., 23.

35. Ibid., 23 n. 6, emphasis added.

36. Ibid., 489.

37. Ibid., 491.

38. Gell 1992: 3–14.

39. Ibid., 14.

40. Pitirim A. Sorokin and Robert K. Merton reiterated the importance of social time in their influential insistence on a mutually constitutive connection between time and social practices: "All calendrical systems have one characteristic in common. They arise from, and are perpetuated by, social requirements" (Sorokin and Merton 1937: 626). Sorokin and Merton condense the "social requirements" to motion, which they claim is at the root of the need for time (615). Jack Goody, too, naturalizes social time by making it "an aspect of experience, implicit in thought and speech" (Goody 1968c: 31). Such formulations leave ambiguously open the question whether time is understood and experienced differently from one cultural context to another, or whether it is the representation of time that varies contextually, or both.

41. Evans-Pritchard 1940; see also Evans-Pritchard 1939. Early reviews of *The Nuer* were Herskovits 1944 and Seligman 1941.

42. Evans-Pritchard 1940: 103.

43. Fortes 1949.

44. Ibid., 54.

45. Ibid.

46. Hallowell 1937: 647, 651.

47. Ibid., 670.

48. Leach 1961: 125.

49. Durkheim 1965: 23 n. 6.

50. All quotations are from Leach 1961: 125–27.

51. Lévi-Strauss 1969. For his discussion of time and social structure, see Barnes 1971. For an extended critique of Lévi-Strauss's writing on time and history, see Fabian 1983: 52–69. In general, Fabian finds that social anthropology uses temporality as a means of distancing "the other" from the West; the "denial of coevalness" is the focus of his brief. In particular, he explores anthropological schools, styles, and tropes, including Lévi-Strauss's structuralism, for the ways they suspend temporality as a dimension of ethnographic analysis.

52. Lévi-Strauss 1969: 15–16. In response to the analogy between music and myth, J. A. Barnes (1971: 550) observed that "we do not escape from time but rather conquer and domesticate it, so that its graph becomes a butterfly in our collection."

53. Geertz 1973: 393.

54. Bloch 1977: 282.

55. Ibid., 283.

56. Ibid., 285.

57. Ibid., 287, also 290.

58. Bourdillon 1978.

59. Howe 1981: 223, 231. Munn 1992 situates the debate joined by Geertz, Bloch, Bourdillon, and Howe more fully than I have here in a review of anthropological literature on social time.

60. On the confrontation of structuralism and history generally, see Sahlins 1981. Sahlins's claim is that "structural anthropology was founded in . . . a radical opposition to history" (3). Against this opposition, he undertakes a demonstration that there are "structures in history" (3). What anthropology can give to history is "the idea that the historical efficacy of persons, objects and events . . . arises as their cultural value" (7). Beyond this, "the great challenge to an historical anthropology is not merely to know how events are ordered by culture, but how, in that process, the culture is reordered" (8). Fernand Braudel considers the intersections of history and sociology as "one single intellectual adventure" (1980: 69) and turns to Lévi-Strauss's structuralism, a sociology of "the longue durée," as a reconciliation of anthropology and history. Paul Veyne looks to ethnography and sociology as the potential "salvation" of history, in that a "history of values" can be liberated from the strictures of "event-worthy history." Yet he also says that "complete history makes sociology useless: it does all that the latter does, and does it better" (1984: 286–87).

61. Humphreys 1981: 262, 269.

62. "Prenant une photographie de lui-même, l'Australien . . . dit: de la même façon que je suis cette photographie, je suis le kangarou." Sommerfelt 1938: 5 (my translation).

63. Meggitt 1962: 317.

64. Ibid.

65. Levy 1973: 232.

66. Leenhardt 1979: 9.

67. Woodburn 1982: 187.

68. Ibid., 202–3.

69. Bloch 1982: 213, 217.

70. Ibid., 213.

71. Ibid., esp. 217.

72. Ibid., 227.

73. Ibid., 226–27.

74. Indeed, the meanings of time are not denied by the symbolic equivalence of birth and death but asserted. Among the Hursu of eastern Indonesia, time is constructed around the marriage ties that link household circles. The ordinal memory of the creation of such ties makes up the Hursu sense of time. In Simonne Pauwels's (1990) analysis, the negation of time relocates time elsewhere. Brother-brother relations embody the negation of time in this sense, whereas brother-sister relations involve the passing of time, inasmuch as marriage is conceptualized as the exchange of women.

75. Aberle 1951: 20.

76. Schieffelin 1976: 25, 78.

77. Ortiz 1969: 41.

78. For ethnographic discussion of the abortion debate, see Ginsburg 1989.

79. Evans-Pritchard 1940: 95.

80. Ibid., 95–96.

81. Oliver 1974: 128–32; see also Sommerfelt 1938: 175–80 for comparable discussion of Australian Aranta.

82. Oliver 1974: 264. Several generations ago, Tahitians adopted Western time concepts, and while they have not completely abandoned their traditional system, Western time is increasingly relevant, in part because of the advent of transistor radios and the schedule of (and popular demand for) Tahitian-language broadcasts. Modern Tahitians told Levy that time is speeding up, pointing to evidence in the rapid aging of adults and the small size of today's children. Levy 1973: 251–53, 265–66.

83. Oliver 1974: 132.

84. Leenhardt 1979: 85–86.

85. Levy 1973: 504.

86. Ibid.

87. Leenhardt 1979: 87.

88. Ibid., 91.

89. Bohannan 1953: 260.

90. Rosaldo 1980: 40.

91. Ibid., 36.

92. Ibid.

93. Ibid., 58.

94. Ibid., 251.

95. Ibid., 58.

96. Ibid., 128.

97. Ibid., 276.

98. A classic example is Gluckman 1966: 1–26, "The peace in the feud."

99. Thornton 1980: 1.

100. Ibid., xv.

101. Ibid., 1.

102. Ibid., 10. Thornton suggests that much of what anthropologists conventionally take to be the functions of kinship are actually functions of territory in this sense. He traces the anthropological tendency to conflate the two meanings of territory to Sir Henry Maine, whose jurisprudential concepts of kin groups and sovereignty blurred the conceptual significance of territory.

103. Thornton 1980: 19.

104. Ibid., 171.

105. Ibid., 172–74, 180–81.

106. Stanner 1979: 23.

107. Bell 1993: 90–91.

108. Ritual performances are described throughout, e.g., ibid., 125–28.

109. Ibid., 93–94.

110. Ibid., 91.

111. Ibid., 91, 92.

112. Bohannan 1953: 260.

2. Relative Time and the Limits of Law

1. Portions of this section and the next are drawn (in amended and corrected form) from Greenhouse 1989a.

2. Goody 1968b: 32; 1968c: 48 n. 2.

3. Goody 1968a: 46–49; 1968c: 31, 39.

4. Ong 1977: 20; for a parallel view, see Goody 1968c.

5. Ibid., 233, 235.

6. See Carr 1991: 80–86, for discussion of the relationship between one's "ongoing projects" and death in the philosophy of Martin Heidegger and Wilhelm Dilthey.

7. Goody 1986; see also Goody 1977.

8. Goody 1986: 166.

9. Gough 1968: 159. My purpose in this discussion is to question not the scale of the impact of print (the subject Gough raises) but its locus, as it were. Writing more generally on nationalism in late colonial and postcolonial state formation, Benedict Anderson emphasizes the transformative power of print in terms not of literacy per se but of print capitalism and "print-as-commodity," new communities of readers, newly aware of each other (Anderson 1991: esp. chaps. 2–4). The importance Anderson ascribes to print capitalism as providing a medium from which nationalism might emerge as a communicative order is quite different from the aspects of literacy, as involving transformations of collective and personal cognition and rationality, which appear to interest Goody and Ong.

10. For their own linkages among these domains of activity, see Goody 1986: 127–70; Ong 1982: esp. 35.

11. For a related argument regarding Western cultural premises in scholarship on literacy, see Street 1984: 1–43. See also Boyarin 1993.

12. Goody 1986: 166.

13. Ong 1982: 31–77.

14. Ibid., 37–57.

15. Ibid., 175.

16. On gender, see ibid., 159–60 and, on civilization, 174–75. I am grateful to Nancy Ries for pointing out the parallels between Ong's discussion of orality and conventional characterizations of women's knowledge and speech.

17. Ong 1982: 175.

18. Clifford 1988: 277–346.

19. Ibid., 339–41.

20. Ibid., 328.

21. For a related critique, see Street 1993: introduction.

22. Wickham 1985.

23. Goody 1968b: 46–49, 69; 1968c: 34.

24. See Ong 1982: 175.

25. Noakes 1988: 214.

26. Chartier 1988: 19–52.

27. Ibid., 10; LaCapra 1985: 77.

28. For recent examples that follow and inform this tradition, see Ong 1982: 35; Goody 1986: 129.

29. Goody 1986: 127–70, quotation from 133.

30. Benveniste 1969: 2.

31. "C'est l' 'Ordre' qui regle aussi bien l'ordonnance de l'univers, le mouvement des astres, la périodicité des saisons et des années que les rapports des hommes et des dieux, enfin des hommes entre eux. . . . sans ce principe, tout retournerait au chaos" (Benveniste 1969: 2:100, my translation).

32. Ibid.

33. Ibid., 2:107, 110, 114, 140.

34. Ibid., 2:114.

35. "La manière 'habituelle' est en réalité une obligation de nature ou de convention" (ibid., 2:110, my translation).

36. Ibid., 2:14–15. The root is at the core of such terms as "direct," "rectify," and "regulate." The straight line (symbolized in the scepter, according to Benveniste) as a key symbol linking the cosmos to the world did not vanish from the West. For example, the discovery of optics and resulting accomplishments in the realm of perspective reinforced Renaissance notions of the line as both a symbol and the means of the diffusion of God's grace in the world (Edgerton 1975: 16–31, 60, 75). The straight line became a generalized symbol of moral superiority and dominion. Among its diverse materializations were the evocation of a "centric ray" in painting and, in some cities, restrictions to elites of access to straight boulevards (Edgerton 1975: 86–89).

37. Lincoln 1986: 140.

38. See Sorabji 1988 for an analysis of ancient ideas on this point.

39. "La fin du cycle . . . n'est pas dans le temps mais représente l'axe qui communique avec l'éternité" (Gaboriau 1982: 23, my translation).

40. On law use as contestation, see Lazarus-Black 1994 and Lazarus-Black and Hirsch 1994. For reviews of the anthropology of law and its internal critiques, see Cain and Kulscar 1981–82; Collier 1975; Comaroff and Roberts 1981; Just 1992; Moore 1970a and 1986; Nader 1965; Snyder 1981; and Starr and Collier 1989. The most recent overview of the field, concentrating on legal pluralism, is Fuller 1994. The question of whether legal anthropology defines some central *theorizing* project is a pervasive theme in these reviews.

41. My discussion refers especially to article-length assessments of the field by John Griffiths (1986) and Sally E. Merry (1988). Geertz (1983) addresses comparative and interpretive aspects of legal differentiation, but he does not refer to his subject as legal pluralism.

42. Griffiths 1986.

43. In taking this position, I differ in part with Chris Fuller (1994), who explores why legal pluralism is not currently a major anthropological question in Great Britain. He suggests that legal pluralism has been "taken over," as it were, by lawyers and that it must now be reclaimed by anthropologists. I suggest that there is little to be gained from a theoretical standpoint in taking it back unless anthropologists are prepared to include official law within their critical ethnographic frame. The central obstacle in the anthropological tradition in this regard is the tendency to conflate cultural difference with legal jurisdiction. The more interesting theoretical question is how signs of identity and difference cir-

culate in (and against) legal orders (so-called) as materializations of different forms of power and authority.

44. Griffiths 1986: 4.

45. Ibid., 29–37. Sally Falk Moore herself offers the concept of the semi-autonomous social field not as a theory of legal pluralism but as a methodology for the study of complex societies (Moore 1973).

46. Griffiths 1986: 38.

47. Merry 1988; see also Merry 1992.

48. See Assier-Andrieu 1993 for an analysis of the judicial use of anthropological knowledge in defining the legal status of indigenous nations in Canada.

49. Herzfeld 1986.

50. See also Gellner 1983.

51. Hobsbawm and Ranger 1983.

52. For a discussion of these, see Roberts 1978.

53. Malinowski 1926. On the debate over rules and processes, see Comaroff and Roberts 1981; Moore 1986.

54. See Von Benda-Beckmann 1988.

55. Geertz 1983.

56. Moore 1973, 1986.

57. "La loi pour exister doit être incessamment réinventée" (Assier-Andrieu 1987: 228, my translation). See also Assier-Andrieu 1993.

58. Greenhouse 1989b.

59. As we shall see, such formulations of agency are not universal. To my knowledge, the most detailed ethnographic assessment of cultural concepts of agency is Strathern 1988. The Melanesian concepts of agency she explores distinguish between causes and acts, acts and effects; they also involve contingencies of gender, alliances, ritual, and knowledge, among other things.

60. Perhaps this is what Jacques Derrida (1992: 20) means by his observation that "the temporality of time is not temporal"—which is a statement as much about the temporality in narrative as about the counterfeit temporal economies of modern life.

61. The term is borrowed from commodity exchange via Appadurai 1986.

62. I extrapolate, despite the meticulous caution with which Strathern refrains from generalization. See Strathern 1988: 309–39, esp. 326–28.

63. Strathern 1991: 2; see also Thomas 1994: 43, for a cautionary note against equating culture with governmentality.

64. The terms come from Comaroff 1980: 33. Comaroff's discussion is of ethnographic comparison, which he says cannot succeed at the level of "surface manifestations," such as jural systems. He argues for an approach to comparison at two levels, the "constituted order" and the "lived-in order," and the dialectical relationship between these. See also Comaroff and Roberts 1981 for an application of this approach in the field of Tswana law. Greenhouse and Greenwood (forthcoming) gives comparative ethnographic analyses of the relationship between state bureaucratic discourses and the construction of identity.

65. Importantly, though I refer to "colonialism" here, colonialism was not a single category or "totality," as Nicholas Thomas reminds us. Colonizing projects

involved "varied articulations of colonizing and counter-colonial representations and practices" (Thomas 1994: ix). Indeed, recent ethnographic and historical reassessments of colonial encounters move away from the standard dichotomy of colonizer/colonized, stressing individual agency and the highly varied nuances of consciousness (including resistance) within, or as, colonial orders. In addition to those cited by Thomas, major works include Comaroff 1985; Comaroff and Comaroff 1991; and Gordon 1992. For ethnographic works more specifically focused on law as a site of domination and resistance, see Lazarus-Black 1994; and Lazarus-Black and Hirsch 1994.

66. Marx 1981: vol. 2, chap. 2.

67. Appadurai 1986: 14.

68. Ibid., 13.

69. Ibid. For further discussion of the life course of commodities, see Kopytoff 1986.

70. Appadurai 1986: 13–14.

71. Ibid., 14–15.

72. Ibid., 15, emphasis added. Subsequently, Appadurai (1990) develops the idea of "cultural flows."

73. In general, this discussion draws on Bourdieu 1990a: 98–111.

74. Ibid., 108.

75. Ibid., 109.

76. Ibid., 108.

77. Ibid.

78. Ibid., 98, emphasis added.

79. Ibid., 99.

80. Ibid., 106–7.

81. Ibid., 110.

82. Ibid.

83. Ibid.

84. For Derrida, they are more than contestable; they are fictional, indeed, the essence of fiction. In his analysis, the interval between the gift and the countergift is the interval, or space, between the text and its reader and between the text and its supposed referent. Exchange, then, does not so much reveal time as strip away specific denials as to the nature of texts, reading, value, and law (as for Bourdieu). These domains wink in and out of view as Derrida considers the play of counterfeiting across or through them. Counterfeiting is a taking masked as donation; time is a forfeiture in this sense: "Time . . . gives nothing to see. It is at the very least the element of invisibility itself. It withdraws whatever could give itself to be seen. It itself withdraws itself from visibility. One can only be blind to time, to the essential *disappearance* of time even as, nevertheless, in a certain manner nothing *appears* that does not require and take time. Nothing sees the light of day, no phenomenon, that is not on the measure of the day, in other words, of the *revolution* that is the rhythm of a sun's course. . . . We will let ourselves be carried away by this word *revolution*. At stake is a certain *circle* whose figure precipitates both time and the gift toward the possibility of their impossibility" (Derrida 1992: 6). For Derrida, the inevitable forfeiture of time makes the inter-

val, of the gift or the written word, the sign of potential deception, or counter-feiting. If social time has a linear form but linear time is not presupposed to be "really real," then Derrida's discussion of forfeiture reveals instead the *impossibility* of confirming a "reality" to social time except in social terms.

85. The connection between practice and production is clearer in Bourdieu's theorizing of "symbolic capital," a "discourse" (and discourses are also practices) whose efficacy as performative language reveals a system of domination constituted in (literal) production. The term "symbolic capital" refers to the "recognition, institutionalized or not," that agents "receive from a group," giving them different "weight" or different levels of return in "the profit of distinction." Bourdieu continues: "The source of the profit of distinction . . . derives from the totality of the social universe and the relations of domination that give structure to it. . . . a discourse can only exist, in the form in which it exists, so long as it is not simply grammatically correct but also, and above all, socially acceptable, i.e. heard, believed, and therefore effective within a given state of relations of production and circulation" (Bourdieu 1991: 73, 76).

86. I rely on Munn 1983, 1986; Strathern 1988; Weiner 1976, 1980.

87. Weiner 1980: 71.

88. Weiner 1976: 8.

89. Ibid., 211, 213.

90. Ibid., 21.

91. Ibid., 221.

92. This idea is fully explored in Strathern 1988.

93. Munn 1983: 277.

94. Ibid., 279.

95. Ibid., 280.

96. The term "intersubjectivity" in this context is Munn's (1986: 14–16). Some feminist critics of Marx's emphasis on production also emphasize the importance of "intersubjectivity" (Benhabib and Cornell 1987: 2), "desire" (Irigaray 1987), and agency (Butler 1987) in their critiques of Marxist notions of reproduction as women's counterpart to work and production. (On this point specifically, see Nicholson 1987: 17–20.) Although their critiques are not ethnographically framed, these authors are alert to the dilemma of the sort raised by Strathern (1988) about the tensions between relativism (and its implicit essentialism) and imperialism. (See, e.g., Benhabib and Cornell 1987: 13–15.) According to Luce Irigaray, to understand sexual difference "we must reconsider the whole question of *space* and *time*" (1987: 119). In an important aside from her own discussion of agency, Strathern observes that agency should be distinguished from subjectivity and intersubjectivity, since "people can . . . have an effect on one another not registered through their minds at all" (Strathern 1987: 23–24).

97. Munn 1986: 10–11.

98. Ibid., 269.

99. Strathern 1988: xi–xii.

100. Ibid., 31.

101. Ibid., 342.

102. Ibid., 342–43.

103. Ibid., 344.

104. Ibid., 343.
105. See Alonso 1994: esp. 387–90.
106. Fabian 1983. See also the collections Hastrup 1992; and Wallman 1992.
107. See Strathern 1988.
108. Kristeva 1980: 65.
109. Ibid.
110. Time's relevance as a technology of "work discipline" (to borrow Thompson's famous phrase) is one major genre of ethnographic and historical writing on time. The classic example is Thompson 1967. Other influential ethnographic examples in the spirit of Thompson include Cooper 1994; Dubinskas 1988; Le Goff 1977; Rutz 1992. Critical explorations of social formations *in* and *as* time include Adam 1990; Bender and Wellbery 1991; Hastrup 1992; Thomas 1989; Ohnuki-Tierney 1990; Wallman 1992; Zerubavel 1985.

3. Agency and Authority

1. Giddens 1979: esp. 49–95. Agency emerged as an anthropological issue in the mid-1980s from several sources, among them ethnography, feminist theory, and sociology. In addition to Giddens, see Ortner 1984: esp. 159; Comaroff 1985; Fardon 1985; Strathern 1985, 1987: esp. 21–31, and 1988: 272–73.
2. Giddens 1979: 49.
3. Ibid., 53.
4. Ibid., e.g., at 4.
5. Ibid., 55.
6. Ibid., 56.
7. Ibid., 59: "The unintended consequences of action are of central importance to social theory in so far as they are systematically incorporated within the process of reproduction of institutions." There, "they become conditions of action also."
8. Strathern 1987: 23.
9. Giddens 1979: 59–65.
10. Giddens, optimistically perhaps, states that "social systems . . . *cease to be when they cease to function*; 'patterns' of social relationships only exist in so far as the latter are organised as systems, reproduced over the course of time" (Giddens 1979: 61–62). For another view, concentrating on the very systematic vulnerabilities of people who remain caught in social systems that no longer function in Giddens's (or anyone's ordinary) sense of the term, see Desjarlais and Kleinman 1994.
11. Giddens 1979: 63–64.
12. Ibid., 64.
13. Ibid., 73.
14. Ibid., 83.
15. Ibid., 80.
16. On consensus, see ibid., 76.
17. Ibid., 86.
18. Ibid., 95.
19. Comaroff and Roberts 1981.

20. For a discussion of the by-play of norms in judicial institutions, see Moore 1986.

21. I emphasize themes of supply and distribution (rather than the substance of agency) largely because the available evidence made these issues accessible.

22. Bourdieu 1977.

23. See Broda, Carrasco, and Matos 1987 on the Aztecs; and Wheatley 1971 on ancient China, for example.

24. Gilson 1950; for discussion of earlier periods in Europe, see Sorabji 1983.

25. For further discussion, see Edgerton 1975.

26. Fabian 1983.

27. Leach 1966: 126.

28. On Islamic "packets" of time, see Rosen 1977: 171–77. On Navaho "pulses," see Givens 1977.

29. Kern 1983: 132–39.

30. Anthropologists and others have begun to study these under the rubric of resistance; see Comaroff 1985; Nordstrom and Martin 1992; Scott 1990 for extended and influential examples.

31. Stanner 1979: 23. In this and other examples, the "timelessness" of indigenous thought tends to be presented negatively and constrastively by the ethnographer. I return later to the question of how time concepts serve as lenses for reading and misreading cultural difference.

32. For example, the Aranta (Sommerfelt 1938); the Canaque (Leenhardt 1979); the Murngin (Warner 1958); the Tahitians (Lévy 1973; Oliver 1974).

33. Lévi-Strauss 1966: 230–31.

34. Ibid., 235, my emphasis.

35. Leenhardt 1979: 91.

36. Ibid.

37. Ibid.

38. See Dumont 1986.

39. "L'homme, désormais, mesure à ses dimensions non seulement l'espace mais le temps. Le temps au Moyen Âge n'appartenait qu'à Dieu. . . . Pour le Moyen Âge, l'homme était une imitation, un raccourci du monde, un microcosme. Désormais le rapport est inverse. L'uomo è modelo dello mondo, dit Leonard de Vinci: 'L'homme est le modèle du monde'" (Le Goff 1965: 452).

40. Magnusson and Pálsson 1960: 349–51.

41. Leach 1966: 126.

42. Oliver 1974: 132.

43. Ibid., 128–32.

44. Ibid., 264, 268.

45. Turton and Ruggles 1978.

46. Ibid., 589.

47. Ibid., 587–88.

48. Ibid., 592.

49. Ibid., 592–93.

50. See also Burman 1981. Burman refers to the anthropological literature's

"somewhat overstretched dichotomies" of cyclical vs. linear time, and discontinuous vs. continuous change (251). Further, time concepts are not likely to be singular, and anthropologists should "look beyond those concepts that receive obvious formalised expression" (252).

51. See Kantorowicz 1957.

52. Van Gennep 1960; Turner 1969.

53. Kratz 1994.

54. Ibid., 210.

55. Ibid., citation omitted.

56. Ibid., 211.

57. Ibid., 210.

58. Ibid.

59. Bloch and Guggenheim 1981.

60. See Greenhouse 1986; Peacock and Tyson 1989.

61. See Fortes 1987: 94; Packard 1981: 24–32.

62. Packard 1981: 31.

63. Ibid., 34–42, for description and analysis.

64. Ibid.; see also Forde 1962.

65. Pocock 1964: 29.

66. I am indebted to James Boon for the phrase "multiplying times" in this context (personal communication).

67. Thompson 1967: 91.

68. Thomas 1964: 63–66. See also Le Goff 1965: 367–76.

69. Le Goff 1977: 69–71.

70. Thomas 1964; Le Goff 1977: 66–79.

71. Bourdieu 1977: 161–62.

72. Ibid., 162.

73. In this gesture, Bourdieu makes use of a musical analogy that is the inverse of Lévi-Strauss's famous characterization of myth and music as "instruments for the obliteration of time" (Lévi-Strauss 1970: 16).

74. Beidelman 1963: 11.

75. Ibid., 10–11.

76. Ortiz 1969: 84.

77. Fabian 1983.

78. Herzfeld 1990: 319.

79. Herzfeld 1990.

80. Herzfeld 1990: 319.

81. Reported in Greenhouse et al. 1994.

82. Kelly 1986.

83. Lévi-Strauss 1969: 16.

84. Leach 1961: 126.

85. Ibid.

86. Lévi-Strauss 1978: 40.

87. "[Il] ignore toute véritable division du temps. Il ne connaît ni année, ni mois, ne semaine. Il compte, dans la mesure ou il le fait, d'après les phases de la

lune. Il possède certaines designations de periodes marquantes de l'année" (Sommerfelt 1938: 175, my translation).

88. Oliver 1974: 132.

89. Ibid., 584.

90. Firth 1967.

91. Ibid., 29–31.

92. Ibid., 28.

93. Ibid., 26.

94. Ibid., 21, 24.

95. Ibid., 7. For an account of early mission activity, see Firth 1936: 43–50.

96. Firth 1967: 20, 475–80.

97. Rosaldo 1980: 60.

98. Ibid., 288.

99. Ibid., 276.

100. Bohannan 1953: 251.

101. Ibid., 262.

102. Ibid., 259.

103. Ibid.

104. Ibid.

105. Ibid., 251.

106. Ibid., 259.

107. Hugh-Jones 1979: 1.

108. Ibid., 13.

109. Ibid., 217–34.

110. Ibid., 200.

111. Ibid., 251–66.

112. Ibid., 266–74.

113. Ibid., 277, 280.

114. I do not mean to suggest that law, or the ethnology of law, is restricted to disputes and their consequences, nor do I intend to suggest some revival of "law" as a discrete domain of inquiry or theorizing. For discussion of the genesis of the "disputing paradigm" and its compelling critique in the anthropology of law, see Comaroff and Roberts 1981; Nader 1965, 1990; and Starr and Collier 1989. See also Just 1992. More generally, see Cain and Kulscar 1981–82.

115. These are primary structural variables in earlier comparative approaches to law developed in Koch 1974; see also Nader and Todd 1979. I do not give these features the same explanatory weight as did Koch; however, they remain relevant as comparative features, if only because state recognition of legal practices, or the refusal to grant recognition, necessarily involves these.

116. This was not the original rationale for privileging the third party as the central comparative issue in the ethnology of law; earlier generations focused on the third party because he (never she) was the evolutionary precursor of modern judges. In general, see Stein 1980 on evolutionary approaches to law in Western Europe since the eighteenth century.

117. On the Bedouin, see Peters 1967; on the Jalé, see Koch 1974; on the

Ilongot, see Rosaldo 1980; on Icelanders, see Magnusson and Pálsson 1960; on Scots, see Wormald 1983.

118. See Strathern 1972 and contributions to Epstein 1974.

119. For discussion of violence in contemporary contexts of political opposition, see Warren 1993. See also Nagengast 1994.

120. See Heider 1979; Rosaldo 1980; see also Strathern 1972: 144.

121. This will be an issue in the next chapter, in which the theorists of the Chinese state successfully improvised means of territorializing their representations of sovereignty. This was one aspect of the unification in the third century B.C.

122. On the Minj area, see Reay 1974; on the Mount Hagen area, see Strathern 1974.

123. Reay 1974: 239. Firth associates the individuation of social discourse with an increase in land disputes among the Tikopia. In other words, in addition to increased external pressure on land, the Tikopia also expressed a "sharper definition of land interest" (Firth 1959: 177). I am not suggesting that this development should be understood as the direct result of changing constructions of time (the Tikopia had had extensive contact with missionaries by then); rather, it should be seen as one element of a dynamic context in which ideas about agency, individuality, political authority, and territory were changing in relation to one another.

124. Strathern 1974: 273.

125. Moore 1970b.

4. Time and Territory in Ancient China

1. There is less consensus on where to place the modern end point of the continuum. Variously, it is put at the end of the Manchu dynasty in 1911, the revolution in 1949, or still ahead.

2. On Legalist ideas, there appears to be general agreement. I rely on the following sources in presenting these ideas, reserving the notes hereafter for references to particular details or areas of debate: Bodde 1967; Bodde and Morris 1967; C-Y. Chang 1983, 243–70; Ch'ü 1965, 226–80; Creel 1974, 1980: esp. 43–47; de Bary et al. 1960: 137–64; Duyvendak 1928; Escarra 1936, 31–57; Gernet 1982: 90–97, 103–17; Fung 1937, 312–36, and 1966 [1948]; Hulsewé 1981, 1985a; Loewe 1985, 1986a–d; Peerenboom 1993; Schwartz 1985, 321–49; Watson 1958, 1963a, 1963b, 1964. For discussions of the Ch'in state and empire, see also Idema and Zürcher 1990; Twitchett and Loewe 1986; also Bodde 1967; Hulsewé 1981, 1985a, b; Li 1985; and Schram 1985. For a discussion of tensions between Confucianism and Legalism in Korea, see Shaw 1980.

3. Hulsewé 1981.

4. Unger 1976: 86, and see 86–110, esp. 105–10.

5. Ibid., 87–88.

6. Ibid., 105.

7. Ibid., 106.

8. Ibid., 109. Unger brightens the distinction between the Confucians and Legalists by indexing them with *li* and *fa*.

9. Hulsewé 1985a, 1. Herrlee Glessner Creel (1980: 44), too, cautions against drawing too sharp a line between Legalist and Confucian ideas.

10. Fung 1966 [1948]: 165.

11. Van der Sprenkel 1962, 1966: 30.

12. For extensive discussions that emphasize the organic relationship of Legalist philosophy with other philosophical schools, including Confucianism, see Eno 1990; and Peerenboom 1993. See also Duyvendak 1928: 70; Wright 1957: 85. On connections between Legalism and Mohism, see Bodde 1967: 208; with Taoism, see Bodde 1967: 217, 220; and Schipper 1978: 357 (but see Creel 1974: 194 n. 121); with other philosophies, see C-Y. Chang 1983: 244; and Li 1985. For discussions of the contexts of Legalist thought in the geopolitical and social changes during the Warring States period, see Chan 1981: 188; Gernet 1968: 121; Hulsewé 1981: 1; and Peerenboom 1993.

13. For example, see Ronan 1978: 273–75.

14. On the terminological difficulties in reference to Legalists, see especially Loewe 1985: 242–43. See Wechsler 1980 for discussion of the varieties of Confucian thought and practice in the T'ang period (seventh and eighth centuries A.D.). For related discussions that urge caution (in highly substantive terms) about reifying other philosophical schools in China, see Sivin 1978 on Taoism and Zürcher 1982 on Chinese Buddhism. For general discussion of the difficulties in distinguishing among philosophical strands in the Han period, see Loewe 1982.

15. On Ssu-ma Ch'ien, see Hulsewé 1981: 1. The Chinese term is *fa chia*. See Creel 1974: 147–48, for a discussion of the difficulties of translating *fa chia*.

16. The golden age was a post hoc construction of complex relationships and influences which reduces them to coherent and opposed schools and periods. Post-Ch'in Confucians placed the golden age around the time of Confucius himself; other philosophical schools placed it earlier (Mohists) or at some indeterminate point prior to the development of human institutions (Taoists). The Legalists were distinctive in altogether rejecting the notion of a golden age. On pre-Ch'in Confucian thought, see Eno 1990.

17. For example, Fung (1966 [1948]: 160) observes that the Legalist "conception of history as a process of change is a common-place to our modern mind, but it was revolutionary viewed against the prevailing theories of the other schools of ancient China."

18. K. C. Chang 1983: 107. For additional sources on the Shang, see K. C. Chang 1980.

19. Keightley 1978: 214–19; Keightley 1979–80. See also K. C. Chang 1978.

20. Chan 1981: 182. On continuities from Shang to the succeeding dynasty, see Chan 1981: 181–84; Keightley 1978: 212. See also Wheatley 1971: 420.

21. Chan 1981: 180–94; Keightley 1978. See also Loewe 1986b: 664.

22. Cho-yun Hsu and Katheryn M. Linduff (1988: 54–55) discuss recent archaeology bearing on Chou dynastic claims of identification with the Hsia and suggest that the Chou claims involved contact or actual descent. On the cultural differences between the invading Chou and the Shang, see, in general, Bodde 1981: 113. See also Creel 1938: 46–47, on literacy and historical consciousness and

1980: 28–29, on law. See also Loewe 1986b: 664, on the distinctions between the Shang-ti cult and the Chou cult of heaven.

23. Hsu and Linduff 1988: 98–100.

24. Ibid., 109.

25. Ibid., 254.

26. Creel (1938: 32) writes: "It is doubtful that any people in the world had more of historical consciousness, than did the Chinese of the time of the beginning of the Chou dynasty." On the imperial interest in historiography, see Creel 1938: 97; Gardner 1961: 14; Han 1955: 1.

27. Hsu and Linduff 1988: xvii.

28. Bodde 1981: 165.

29. The doctrine was elaborated in considerable detail under the Han, and subsequently (Leban 1978; Loewe 1986c: 735–36). The Shang legacy was the principle of a single mandate (to an individual ruler), but later refinements stressed principles of dynastic continuity, criteria of qualification, and tests for the legitimacy of the incumbent. The mandate was revocable, in that a ruler could prove himself to be unqualified while in office. In the Ming and Ch'ing periods, there is evidence to suggest that rulers considered the heavenly mandate mutually reversible. Not only could heaven revoke the mandate of the ruler, but the ruler could also strip deities of their names and shrines as a means of coercing divine sanction (e.g., rain) when supplication failed. See A. Cohen 1978.

30. Chan 1981: 187.

31. In general, see Bodde 1986; Bodde and Morris 1967: 15–16; Hsu 1965; Hsu and Linduff 1988 and Li 1985; see also Creel 1970.

32. Hsu 1965: vii. Varying dates are given. See also Li 1985: 5.

33. Hsu 1965: 78. Several authors have compared Chou period feudalism to the feudalism of Europe's Middle Ages, e.g., Chan 1981: 185; Creel 1970: 3; Elvin 1973: 69.

34. Hsu 1965: 78.

35. Ibid., 88.

36. Ibid., 90.

37. Ibid., 92–93. Social changes accompanied these political changes. *Li*, the "code of conduct" that later came to mean "the code by which society was—or should be—governed" (Creel 1970: 335), at this period referred primarily to the aristocratic *courtoisie* of the ruling families, not general norms of behavior. By the end of the Warring States period, "nothing was socially impossible or improper anymore; the bonds of *li* had been loosened and the old regulated social order had broken down"—so at least it appears in post-Ch'in hindsight (Hsu 1965: 146).

38. Creel 1974; Hsu 1965: 94–95.

39. Rosen 1978: 99.

40. Chan 1981: 188; Hulsewé 1981: 1.

41. Bodde 1967; C-Y. Chang 1983: 22. See also Nakayama 1984: 37. One major debate at the time focused on the moral and administrative efficacy of the *pa* as a system of rule; for discussion of this debate in the state of Ch'in, see Schwartz 1985: 302–8, esp. 303.

42. Hsu 1965: 101.

43. For example, by Chan 1981: 190.

44. Chan (1981: 190) writes that Legalism "is not a comprehensive philosophy; rather it is primarily a set of methods and principles for the operation of the state."

45. I take the term *timeliness* in this context from Peerenboom 1993.

46. The phrase is from Gernet 1982: 90.

47. Creel 1980: 45; Hulsewé 1981: 2.

48. Bodde 1967: 166–67; Hulsewé 1981: 22, 1985a: 235.

49. Ch'ü 1965: 175.

50. Hulsewé 1981: 2–3. The phrase "political tool" in this context is also Hulsewé's.

51. Bodde 1981: 168.

52. Han Fei-tzu, quoted in Bodde 1967: 194.

53. See McLeod and Yates 1981 for discussion and translation of Ch'in regulations for processing and reporting disputes and other problems at the local level.

54. Hulsewé 1981: 22. The regulations to which Hulsewé refers in this statement were those of the state of Ch'in prior to the unification of China under the first emperor. The laws inscribed on bamboo strips which were discovered by a team of archaeologists in 1975 apparently represent a large but still incomplete portion of the Ch'in law codes. Overall, they reveal "an extensive corpus of administrative and criminal law, which was handled by a complex hierarchy of officials" (Hulsewé 1981: 21, and see 7–21). The Legalists did not have an economic program as such, and Legalist influence in the economy is difficult to identify (Hulsewé 1985b: 235). They saw agriculture as primary, and expressed "contempt" for merchants and workshop owners engaged in "secondary pursuits" (Hulsewé 1985b: 231–32; but see Gernet 1968, 1982 on the influence of merchants on Legalist thought and social technologies). Hulsewé (1955: 6) cautions against overestimating the effect of Legalist theory on social practice in the state of Ch'in or outside it.

55. Gernet 1982: 90.

56. Peerenboom 1993: chap. 5. The reference is to Han Fei-tzu.

57. Duyvendak 1928, 123.

58. Bodde 1981: 175. See Creel 1974: 147–48, on the difficulties of translating this word.

59. Creel 1938: 41–42.

60. Hulsewé 1955: 10. Later, in Han times, the words for law, statute, ordinance (*ling*) and ruling (*ko*) were used without distinction and were largely interchangeable, except that statutes appear to have been older than ordinances, and rulings were more specific to individual acts than law, which was an "indeterminate general name, applicable to all" (Hulsewé 1955: 9).

61. Derk Bodde (1981: 176) believes that this tradition historicizes gods of some earlier myth into secular heroes and kings. See also Bodde and Morris 1967: 12.

62. Bodde 1986: 31.

63. Bodde 1981: 176.

64. Bodde 1967: 193.

65. Hulsewé 1981: 4.

66. Bodde 1986: 26.

67. McLeod and Yates 1981: 130.

68. For example, Bodde (1981: 177–78) writes of Shu-hsiang, a "high dignitary," who sent a letter in 536 B.C. (long before the Legalists) to Tzu-ch'an, the prime minister of the neighboring state of Cheng, advising against promulgating written law: "As soon as the people know the grounds on which to conduct disputation, they will reject the [unwritten] accepted ways of behavior (*li*) and make their appeal to the written word, arguing to the last over the tip of an awl or knife. Disorderly conduct will multiply and bribery will become current. By the end of your era, Cheng will be ruined." Tzu-ch'an replied: "As to your statements, sir, I have neither the talents nor ability to act for posterity. My object is to save the present age. Though I cannot accept your instructions, dare I forget your great kindness?" For discussion of the significance Legalists attached to publication of legal rules, see Schwartz 1985: 325–27. Schwartz views Tzu-ch'an's goal in breaking the secrecy of the codes by publishing them as consistent with the belief that social control requires intimidation. On related issues of Legalist (and other contemporary) theories of social control, see also Peerenboom 1993: 140–47.

69. Luther Carrington Goodrich (1935) gives a history of book burning in China as a preface to his compilation of the edicts of the Ch'ing emperor Ch'ien-Lung commanding the destruction of specific works. The volume also contains reports from imperial agents in the field, advising the emperor of particular problems and successes in enforcing the edicts in individual cases.

70. Goodrich 1935: 1.

71. On the scale of losses, compare Creel 1938: 22–28, and Bodde 1986: 70. Bodde (1967: 160) notes that the book burning effaced ancient styles of script, accelerating Li Ssu's standardization of Chinese writing.

72. Bodde 1967: 201–2, 1981: 175–77. In general, see Creel 1980: 45.

73. Bodde 1981: 176.

74. See Bodde 1967: 160.

75. Bodde 1986: 40, 53–54.

76. Ibid., 53. See also Bodde 1967: 129–30.

77. Bodde 1967: 189–90.

78. Ch'ü 1972: 4; Hulsewé 1986: 542.

79. Duyvendak 1928: 41.

80. Bodde 1981: 173 n. 6.

81. Hulsewé 1985b: 235; see also Hulsewé 1981, 22.

82. Bodde 1967: 166–67; Duyvendak 1928: 57–58. Brian McKnight (1992: 22) doubts the Legalists invented the "cellular organization," but they did promote it. It continued into Sung times.

83. Bodde 1981: 172. Magistrates were not law-trained. There had been no legal profession under the Chou (Cohen et al. 1980: 12). See Miyazaki 1980 for discussion of the legal profession under the subsequent T'ang and Sung dynasties.

84. Hulsewé 1981: 21.

85. For discussion of the debates on this point, see Hulsewé 1955: 285–97.

86. Ibid., 285–86.

87. On anachronism, see Eno 1990. The Ch'in continued Chou legal principles and practices in their emphasis on rewards and punishments, their pragmatic rejection of "antiquity," their rare references to yin-yang principles, their commitment to promulgating laws, and so on. See Creel 1980: 43–45.

88. The phrase "unification of punishments" is Hulsewé's 1955: 285.

89. Bodde 1981: 182; Gernet 1982: 110. Hulsewé (1955: 285) notes that no one today knows how the Ch'in actually practiced their theories of unified punishments; however, Li (1985: 261) notes archaeological evidence confirming contemporary texts referring to corporal punishment of criminals.

90. Ch'ü 1965: 175. Shang Yang, a founding Legalist theorist of the state, was put to death by the king for practicing his theory of legal equality against the king's tutors while he was a prince (Ch'ü 1965: 174; Bodde 1986: 34). Shang Yang lived in the fourth century B.C., prior to the rise of the state of Ch'in over the empire.

91. Hulsewé 1981: 2.

92. Bodde 1986: 85–90. Later Confucian historians blamed the excesses of Legalist theory for the collapse. See, for example, Bodde 1986: 85–90. Hulsewé (1955, 6), however, cautions against crediting Legalist canons (or, one might add, any canons) for social practices that might appear to be in accord with them.

93. My principal sources on the Han dynasty are Ch'ü 1972 on society; Hulsewé 1955 on law; Loewe 1982 and Twitchett and Loewe 1986 on political history.

94. Hulsewé 1955: 5. On the retention of Ch'in Legalist ideas by the Han, see Bodde 1967: 237 and 1981: 168, 182; Ch'ü 1965: 10, 280; Creel 1980: 38–39, 44; Escarra 1936: 57; Hulsewé 1955: 297–98; Vandermeersch 1985: 14–16.

95. Bodde 1990: 38; Hulsewé 1981: 4.

96. For discussion of these claims, see Bodde 1986: 85–90.

97. Loewe 1982: 7; Wright 1957: 85.

98. Hulsewé 1981, 1985a.

99. Hulsewé 1988.

100. Han law also incorporated other strands; Hulsewé (1955: 5) calls some of them "archaic" "magico-mythical concepts."

101. Hulsewé 1955: 286–93.

102. Ibid., 295–97.

103. Ibid., 297.

104. Ibid., 298.

105. Loewe 1986c: 661–68.

106. Bodde 1990; Hulsewé 1986: 541, and 1955: 6–7.

107. Loewe 1974 and 1982: esp. 2–3; Vandermeersch 1990: 89.

108. Loewe 1982: 6; Cullen 1980–81; Harper 1980–81; Sivin 1969.

109. Creel 1938: 29–31. The Han also sought to recover the principles of symbolic architecture from the Chou period. See Maspero 1951 for detailed discussion of debate among Han literati as to the location and design of a reproduction of

the Chou *ming-t'ang*, a temple that would be the very site of the imperial connection with heaven.

110. Loewe 1982: 2–3.

111. Chan 1984: 21–22.

112. For an encyclopedic treatment of this issue and the larger question of Han imperial statecraft, see Twitchett and Loewe 1986.

113. Loewe 1982: 10.

114. Han 1955: 4; see also Kao 1981.

115. Wallacker 1978; see also Liu 1973.

116. Idema 1990: 191; see also Idema and West 1982.

117. Hulsewé 1981: 4.

118. The following pages draw on, expand, and amend Greenhouse 1989a: 39–41.

119. De Bary et al. 1960: 220–21.

120. Bodde 1975: 1.

121. Van der Sprenkel 1966: 127.

122. Bodde and Morris 1967: 14–15.

123. Ch'ü 1965: 230–31.

124. For discussion of the nature and scope of *li* in ordering human affairs (morally and temporally), see Loewe 1986c: 706–8.

125. Creel 1980: 39.

126. Johnson 1979: 14–15.

127. Ch'ü 1965: 209–10.

128. Van der Sprenkel 1966; Ch'ü 1965: 78–79.

129. "Le ciel ayant mis la loi naturelle dans le coeur de l'homme, le rôle du prince se limite à découvrir et à exalter cette loi en lui-même pour l'imposer à tous par son seul exemple. . . . La préservation de l'ordre universel est essentiellement le fait personnel du prince et ne doît rien à des règles abstraites." Escarra 1936: 31.

130. Ch'ü 1965: 9.

131. Bodde 1981: 178.

132. Ibid., 179.

133. Shen Pu-hai, a major fourth-century theorist, dismissed Confucian concerns with virtue. Shen Pu-hai is credited with founding the techniques of administration that, with Shang Yang's theory of punishments, became central to Legalists' contributions to Chinese society and statecraft. There is some debate as to whether Shen Pu-hai should be called a Legalist or not. Compare Creel 1974: 135; and Bodde 1986: 74.

134. Bodde 1980: 137.

135. Bodde's (1980) study of clemency in Ch'ing China reports that as many as two-thirds of young, old, and sick defendants received clemency at their trials.

136. Bodde 1980; McKnight 1981; Hulsewé 1955: 294, and 1981: 12–13.

137. Bodde 1981: 179.

138. I am indebted to Christopher Borstel (personal communication) for pointing out that another vital factor is in their *performance*.

139. Bodde 1981: 171, 180.

140. Ibid., 179.

141. Creel 1980: 39.

142. Bodde 1967: 212.

143. Eno 1990.

144. Bodde 1967: 211–15; Creel 1980, esp. 44.

145. Bodde 1967: 213. Mo tzu in "Against Confucius" had another reply to the Confucian veneration of the past: "The Confucians say: 'The superior man must use ancient speech and wear ancient dress before he can be considered benevolent.' But we answer: The so-called ancient speech and dress were all modern once, and if at that time the men of antiquity used such speech and wore such dress, then they must not have been superior men. Must we then wear the dress of those who were not superior men and use their speech before we can be considered benevolent? . . . someone must have invented the ways which the Confucians follow, so that in following them they are, by their own definition, following the ways of inferior men" (Watson 1963b, 127–28). Though these are playful examples, they are neat illustrations of how a progressive concept of history (modernity in these examples) displaces Confucian notions of the inherent superiority of antiquity.

146. In general, see Fung 1948: 158–62.

147. Duyvendak 1928: 238.

148. Creel 1980: 44.

149. Ibid.

150. Ibid.; see also Bodde 1967: 213.

151. See Bodde 1967: 211–15.

152. See Chan 1981: 185; Creel 1970: 3; Elvin 1973: 69.

153. For example, see Ronan 1978 on law; Ronan 1981 on astronomy; Sivin 1969 on mathematics and astronomy; Unger 1976: 86–109, on law.

154. In pre-Han times, yin-yang was not yet identified with Confucian philosophy (Bodde 1975: 37) or Legalism; however, it was a part of the cultural context of both. For discussion of the evolution of yin-yang, see Nakayama 1984: 93–94. For descriptions of yin-yang and the five agents, I draw primarily on Bodde 1981: 143; Chan 1984: 26–27; de Bary et al. 1960: 214–16; Loewe 1982: 41–42; and You 1994: esp. 464–68.

155. On cycles, see Lao 1982: xxii. Confucians called the succession of agents "mutual production" or "pulsations." Legalists preferred to speak of the "mutual conquest" of the elements. Loewe 1982: 41.

156. You 1994: 464 (Chinese terms and notes omitted).

157. Ibid., 466.

158. Ibid.

159. "Time is itself a series of cycles based upon the motions of the planets," de Bary and his colleagues note, and history is its counterpart. "The Chinese concept of history . . . was cyclical. This is only natural, since history is no more than a counterpart in the human sphere of the similar cycles of Heaven and earth, those in the planets and seasons" (de Bary et al. 1960: 220–21).

160. For discussion of agentive properties and emblems, see Loewe 1982: 41–42.

161. Gernet 1982: 98.

162. Chan 1984: 26.

163. Creel (1980: 54 n. 94) sounds an important cautionary note on this point, observing that important Legalist writings contain very few references to yin-yang.

164. Bodde 1986: 77, 96–97; Chan 1984: 27.

165. For detailed accounts of subsequent debates in the Han dynasty concerning their choice of a regnal element, see Chan 1984: 28–31; Loewe 1986d: 737–39; and in general Loewe 1974. The Han elaborated the imperial uses of the five agents theory considerably, notably in the context of Wang Mang's claims to rule (A.D. 9). See Chan 1984: 30–31; Loewe 1986c: 690–91.

166. For both perspectives, see Chan 1984: 19, 42.

167. Leban 1978: 317.

168. Ibid.

169. Loewe 1986: 737.

170. Wechsler 1985: 215–16; 222.

171. Ibid., 222; more generally, see Needham et al. 1960: 175.

172. C-Y. Chang 1983: 255; Wechsler 1985: 223.

173. Wechsler 1985: 223.

174. Ibid.

175. Loewe 1986: 686; see also Han 1955: 3.

176. Bodde 1981: 193; Loewe 1986: 677. It would be interesting to know whether and how calendars and sovereignty were conceptually fused in other respects, specifically, the localization of time. K. C. Chang (1978: 13) describes the Shang terms, called "heavenly stems" (*t'ien kan*), which were used both to provide one set of day signs (the Shang calendar intercalated two sets of signs) and posthumous names for an individual's ancestors. Perhaps this practice suggests one means by which Shang localized time without a territorialized concept of sovereignty. Cf. Keightley 1979–80: 26. There is a considerable literature on Chinese time reckoning and timepieces, but no timepieces survive from before the Han period. For descriptions of calendars, hours, days, weeks, and larger time cycles in later Chinese thought, see K. C. Chang 1978; Creel 1938: 39; de Bary et al. 1960: 221; Loewe 1974: 280; Needham et al. 1960; and Sivin 1969.

177. For his discussion of the lack of interest in chronology in Shang and Chou times, see Creel 1938: xx.

178. Keightley 1979–80.

179. Loewe 1986: 674.

180. Ibid., 673–82; Wheatley 1971: 419.

181. Loewe 1986: 680.

182. The phrase "ritual regime" is from Loewe 1982: 2–3.

183. Loewe 1974, 1982, 1985.

184. Hummel 1966: xiv–xv.

185. Bodde 1981: 179, 193; but see Vandermeersch 1985: 3. Peerenboom (1993) develops the tensions between natural and positive law in the Huang-lao school but does not treat these as dichotomies.

186. See Bodde 1986: 69–72.

187. Vandermeersch 1990: 91.

188. See Bodde 1986: 72 n. 78; see also Průšek 1971; Yang 1982 for discussions of Chou-period Chinese concepts of geography, frontiers, and ethnogenesis.

189. Yü 1964–65: 119–20.

190. Li 1985: 9.

191. Bodde 1967: 217.

192. Ibid., 220.

193. Creel 1974: 194 n. 121; see Sivin 1978 for more general cautions. Taoist writings symbolically conflated the emperor with China itself. See Schipper's (1978: esp. 357–58) discussion of Taoist metonymies of the ruler and the country and, more generally, the human body and territory. Taoists held that the ruler is the body's heart and his officials its viscera. The body of the ruler was the "ruling body," and his inner harmony was the territory's peace. Schipper dates the full development of these ideas to the late Han period, long after the period that concerns us here. In what may be a more relevant metonymy, one Chinese expression of the sovereign's ideal relationship to his subjects says his edicts suffuse the person and body politic "like sweat" (Vandermeersch 1985: 13–14). "Sweat" recalls Han Fei-tzu's reference to "morning dew"; the similes are obviously parallel in their references to water (the Ch'in sign) and in their rhetorical references to the sovereign's edicts as a natural and irreversible effusion, always latent, sometimes visible. The *Han Shu* (chap. 36, the biography of Liu Hsiang) explains the metaphor as "meaning that 'the orders (or decrees, etc.) are like sweat of the body, which once it comes out of the body, cannot be returned into the body.' The saying was given in the context that good orders from the emperor should be given time to be carried out and should not be withdrawn or changed abruptly. Otherwise, it would be like returning sweat into the body. The moral here is that the emperor should stick to his orders as long as they are good" (Thomas Lee, personal communication). I am indebted to Thomas Lee for locating and explaining this reference to the *Han Shu*.

194. Zürcher 1980: 124–25; see also Needham 1975; and Zürcher 1982. Loewe (1986c: 683) seems to date the horizontal plane of earth and heaven somewhat later than Zürcher, that is, at the first century B.C. The earlier concept, according to Loewe, was the "Dome of Heaven."

195. Wheatley 1971: 423–24.

196. Ibid., 425.

197. Gough 1968a: 77. In the next chapter, a central interpretive issue involves the question of whether the directional signs of the ancient Maya should be understood as involving cardinal directions. Ades and Brotherston 1975 and Brotherston 1976 use several sorts of evidence, including maps, to argue that ancient Mesoamericans conceptualized directions as interrelated forms of agency, not cardinal points. It seems plausible that a similar argument might be made in the Chinese context, where directions are defined as one scheme of differentiation within the larger system of five agents. In general, see Wheatley 1971.

198. Wheatley 1971: 428.

199. Ibid., 434.

200. Ibid., 431.
201. Bodde 1986: 82.
202. Ibid., 66–68.
203. On the Shang period, see Keightley 1979–80: 26.
204. Yü 1964–65: 89–90.
205. Ibid.
206. Needham 1975: 97; Yü 1964–65: 89.
207. Yü 1964–65: 119.
208. Ibid., 91.
209. Ibid., 94.
210. Wechsler 1980: 31; Bodde 1986: 68, and see 78; Loewe 1986c: 719–25. Chinese discourses of immortality changed significantly from the beginning of the Ch'in dynasty to the end of Han times. In the time of the First Emperor, *hsien* immortality and worldly longevity were two distinct, though interrelated, ideas. Three hundred years later, they were completely fused. For example, an individual's "translation" into *hsien* immortality could include his family and chattels (Yü 1964–65; see also Needham 1975: 100). Later Han-period Taoism (in the late second century A.D.) and Buddhist influence at the same time accelerated popular concerns with immortality and an afterlife. Earlier, however, otherworldly immortality was not a popular concern. Loewe (1986: 719) characterizes Ch'in and Han times as distinctly "this-worldly." Thus, the intensification of the ritual *hsien* activity at the beginning of the Ch'in dynasty and, in particular, the First Emperor's experiments with *hsien*, should be appreciated as innovations. Yü (1964–65: 94, 101) believes the First Emperor's personal ritual practices were motivated by a desire for permanent health but also notes (91) that he was the first prince to seek *hsien*.
211. Bodde 1986: 71; Loewe 1986d: 731.
212. Bodde 1986: 41–42.
213. Gernet 1982: 97.
214. For discussions of the meanings of "events" and "biography" to Chinese authors in later periods, see Liu 1961; Taylor 1978.
215. Langlois (1981: 165) ascribes central importance to this issue throughout Chinese legal history: "The primary issue in traditional Chinese jurisprudence was the setting of punishments. No other issue commanded equal attention by the greatest legal minds or aroused equally deep intellectual debate." One element of this debate was literacy, heralded by advocates as the safeguard of standards but decried by critics as undermining judicial discretion and moral probity.
216. Fung 1937: 325; see also Kroll 1990.
217. Creel (1970: 4–5) notes the Legalists' preference for mechanical metaphors generally.
218. Vandermeersch 1985: 3–4.
219. Bodde 1975: 1.

5. Time and Sovereignty in Aztec Mexico

1. But see Offner 1983: esp. 80–82; Offner's study of law and politics in Aztec Texcoco finds "striking parallels" between the Chinese Legalists and the "legal

architect" of Texcoco, Nezahualcoyotl, who, in Offner's view, tried to centralize "all legal and political power" in the person of the emperor. Both the first emperor of China and Nezahualcoyotl enlarged their bureaucracies, Offner believes, to accommodate the expanding powers of the state. In Texcoco, the context of bureaucratic expansion was the increasing "ethnic diversity" of the region. Offner concludes that "legalism seems to arise in a period of turmoil, with many different ethnic groups, societies, and cultures in contact, and with a relative breakdown of all modes of social control" (82). Moreover, legalism "requires a consolidating political agency that consciously seeks to center political and legal power in itself" (82). In general, I agree with the tenor of Offner's comparison, especially his exploration of law as a component of a regime's self-legitimation, if not the direct comparison of "legalisms" or the direct association of ethnic diversity with the breakdown of social control.

2. Pagden 1986: 85–87, 98–99. Pagden presents the sources and interpretive traditions ascribing Cortés's victory to Motecuhzoma's "mistake" at length and offers substantive historical and exegetical grounds for doubting Cortés's credibility. See Pagden 1986: 467–69 n. 42. Benjamin Keen (1971: 483–84) also notes Mexican scholars who are critical of this rendering of Motecuhzoma's reaction, notably Eulalia Buzmán and Ignacio Romero Vargas Iturbide. For an influential modern example of the conquest in these terms, see Todorov 1987a: 51–123, esp. 116–19; see also D. Carrasco 1982. For an extended critique of Todorov, see Obeyesekere 1992: 16–19.

3. Pagden 1986: 86.

4. Henry B. Nicholson (1971) calls them deity complexes. The details of the Quetzalcoatl myth (that is, with respect to the deity, apart from the conquest narratives) vary with the source. For a range of more detailed versions, see Aveni 1980: 186; Brundage 1979; D. Carrasco 1982; M. Miller 1986: 171; and Nicholson 1979.

5. Tollan is conventionally translated as Tula, Hidalgo, but see D. Carrasco 1982 for detailed consideration of alternatives.

6. Susan D. Gillespie (1989: 171–207) maintains that the legend of Quetzalcoatl as king is a post-conquest development. Specifically, she shows that Aztec historiography figures epochal closure and renewal in twinned "boundary figures," in this case, Quetzalcoatl and Motecuhzoma. From this perspective, her evidence suggests that both the king Quetzalcoatl and his symbolic association with Motecuhzoma were post-conquest constructions of the end of Aztec rule, consistent with Aztec historiographic conventions.

7. D. Carrasco 1982.

8. Sahagún quoted in Anderson and Dibble 1975: 12:9.

9. Ibid., 12:11–12.

10. Ibid., 12:44.

11. Ibid., 12:45.

12. Todorov 1987a: 86–87.

13. Obeyesekere 1992: 16–17.

14. Ibid., 17.

15. Todorov 1987a: 86.

16. For general readings of pre-Hispanic Mesoamerican time concepts and calendrical systems, see Aveni 1989; León-Portilla 1988; and Broda 1969.

17. The 260-day calendar was unique to Mesoamerica; Aveni 1980: 148.

18. Brundage 1979: 124; Nicholson 1979: 42.

19. Scholars have sought alternatives in the lunar cycles or in the heliacal risings of the sun at Copan, thought by some to be the site where the calendar originated (Aveni 1980: 148), as well as in other "natural" rhythms, such as human gestation. Johanna Broda dismisses all three hypotheses (1969: 15).

20. Broda 1969: 13.

21. Ades and Brotherston 1975: 291.

22. Aveni and Hartung 1986: 56.

23. Broda 1969: 14.

24. I take this partial list from Anthony Aveni's (1980: 186) reference to the Annals of Quauhtitlan. When Venus's risings occurred on the first days of these signs, the annals stipulate a target for Venus's rays; for example, when Venus rises on One-Reed, the target is kings. One of Quetzalcoatl's manifestations is as the rising Venus; another of his names is One-Reed, for the date of his birth.

25. Broda 1969: 14.

26. Ibid., 13.

27. Aveni 1980: 158.

28. Aveni (1980: 142) defines the long count as follows: 1 day = 1 kin; 20 kins = 1 uinal; 18 uinals = 1 tun (360 kins); 20 tuns = 1 katun (7,200 kins); 20 katun = 1 baktun (144,000 kins). After thirteen baktuns, the long count would begin again in a new "creation epoch" (Aveni 1980: 143). Thus, the "long count" counts the number of days elapsed since a fixed point in the past, a transit that Aveni metaphorizes as distance traveled on a road (Aveni 1989: 216). Broda's (1969: 62) cautionary note against using the long count as evidence that the Maya thought of time as finite would not necessarily preclude this metaphor; she suggests that the calendar's scale is governed by culturally determined calculation considerations. The earliest long count dates begin in the eighth baktun; the last is in the tenth. The end of the long count is widely taken as one marker of the end of the classic period. John Henderson dates the advent of the long count to the first century B.C., so as to include the highlands of the Pacific slope (personal communication).

29. Aveni 1980: 135.

30. Broda 1969: 65.

31. Ibid., 19.

32. But see ibid., 17–18, on the inappropriateness of the lunar analogy to the Mesoamerican calendrical units.

33. Ibid., 65.

34. Ibid., 36–44.

35. Brundage 1979: 21.

36. Ibid., Umberger 1987: 442.

37. Aveni 1980: 154; Brundage 1979: 26–27; Townsend 1979.

38. Umberger 1987: 441, and see 437–39; and Nicholson 1971 for descriptions of Aztec rituals.

39. Aveni 1980: 136.
40. Brundage 1979: 13.
41. Broda 1969: 65.
42. I am indebted to John Henderson for his observations on this point.
43. Broda 1969: 28.
44. Broda (1969: 62) cautions against inferring that the Maya conceptualized time as having a beginning and an end.
45. Brundage 1979: 26–27.
46. Broda 1969: 73; see also Tichy 1981.
47. See Aveni 1980, 1989, Aveni and Hartung 1986.
48. Broda 1969: 62.
49. Aveni and Hartung 1986.
50. D. Carrasco 1982.
51. Aveni 1989: 212.
52. I take the term "cosmovision" from Broda 1978.
53. Aveni and Hartung 1986: 57.
54. Marcus 1976: 17.
55. On the other hand, she does note other local variations in central Mexico, such as the celebration of monthly festivals within the 260-day count and the year beginnings; Broda 1969.
56. Chase et al. 1990: 550.
57. Ibid.
58. Aveni and Hartung 1986; see also Aveni 1980: esp. chap. 4. For example, they explore the significance of the shift in Maya architectural alignments from westward to eastward with the rise of Teotihuacan. The eastern "skew" prevails throughout Mesoamerica from the late formative period (i.e., with the founding of Teotihuacan) through the postclassic (Aveni and Hartung 1986: 10–11, 54). This detail might be relevant to the origins and extent of a Quetzalcoatl cult, which some scholars place at Teotihuacan and its very large zone of influence.
59. Tichy 1981.
60. Ades and Brotherston 1975: 301.
61. This is Eduardo Matos Moctezuma's (1987: 191) suggestion.
62. Broda 1987; Matos Moctezuma 1987.
63. The phrase "mountain cult" is Broda's (1987: 224).
64. Matos Moctezuma 1987; Broda 1987.
65. Matos Moctezuma 1987: 186–88.
66. Matos Moctezuma (1987: 188) records the thirteen heavens as follows: (1) the moon and clouds visible to all, (2) the stars, (3) the sun's path, (4) Venus, (5) comets, (6–7) green and blue, or black and blue, (8) storms, (9–11) gods, (12–13) Omeyocan (= "the place of duality").
67. Matos Moctezuma 1987: 188.
68. The term in this context is from ibid., 206.
69. Ades and Brotherston 1975: 280; but see Tichy 1981: 217, for reservations.
70. Aveni 1980: 135.
71. Brundage (1979: 3) refers to five cardinal points; Tichy (1981: 221) defines six—two in the east, two in the west, the zenith and the nadir. But see Broth-

erston 1976: 55–56, on the relativity of Mesoamerican concepts of above and below.

72. Ades and Brotherston 1975; Brotherston 1976. See also León-Portilla 1988: 161–205, for a summary of the controversy, and a critique of the "new interpretation," i.e., the Ades and Brotherston position. León-Portilla's critique draws a distinction between notation and cognition and develops the argument that the absence of directional glyphs does not necessarily imply the absence of directional thought.

73. Brotherston 1976: 49–50.

74. Ibid., 59.

75. Ades and Brotherston 1975: 299, and see 296–300. Similarly, celestial locations, stars, were significant in their own right, not as landmarks, so to speak, of celestial maps. Mesoamerican astronomy was not concerned with mapping the heavens; their constellations cannot be translated into European terms. Stars were not, it seems, understood as landmarks in space so much as signs in space-time (Ades and Brotherston 1975: 291).

76. Ades and Brotherston 1975: 286; their discussion is of the Maya book, the *Popol Vuh*.

77. Nicholson 1985: 145–46.

78. Brotherston 1976: 46.

79. Boone 1985.

80. Nicholson 1971: 428

81. Brundage 1979: 128.

82. Nicholson 1979: 38.

83. Ibid., 35.

84. Ibid., 37–38.

85. Ibid., 38.

86. Nicholson 1971.

87. D. Carrasco 1982: 102.

88. Ibid., 170–73; Klein 1987.

89. Brundage (1979: 55) refers to the Aztec gods as "qualities," not "entities."

90. An alternative interpretation of the complex of myth and ritual surrounding Quetzalcoatl which would be consistent with his putative absence might be one that treated these rites as commemorations of the departed man/god. In that case, the question would remain as to why Quetzalcoatl, uniquely among the gods, plays a *historicized* role as the object of remembrance. I follow D. Carrasco 1982, Nicholson 1979, and many others in reading Quetzalcoatl as myth in Lévi-Strauss's sense of this term (cf. Lévi-Strauss 1969, 1988). Lévi-Strauss emphasizes the distinctive properties of mythic thought, which entails a grammar and vocabulary related to, but not necessarily validated by, social experience. Myths imply their variants, just as language entails the availability of new, yet comprehensible speech. In that sense, myths are "about" the canonical forms within which human and cosmic relationships have meaning.

91. D. Carrasco 1982; however, as noted, the importance Carrasco places on Aztec historiography for an explanation of the defeat is less convincing.

92. Ibid., 157, citing Diego Duran, a sixteenth-century Spanish chronicler.

93. Ibid., 135.

94. Ibid., 3.

95. Ibid., 136–37.

96. Nicholson 1979: 39.

97. Cited in D. Carrasco 1982: 193.

98. For descriptions, see Broda 1978: 226–30; Townsend 1987; also Nicholson 1971: 435–36.

99. Erdheim 1978: 209.

100. Townsend 1987: 404.

101. Brundage 1979: 125. Ordinarily, the sounding of the drum marked the beginning and the end of the day. Commerce could take place only within these brackets. Thus, Quetzalcoatl divided day from night in time as in the creation myth. See Brundage 1979: 125.

102. Townsend 1987.

103. D. Carrasco 1982; Nicholson 1979.

104. D. Carrasco 1982: 170. On the history of the Huitzilopochtli cult, see Nicholson 1971: 426.

105. D. Carrasco 1982.

106. Broda 1987: 232; D. Carrasco 1982; Lopez-Austin 1987: 275; Matos Moctezuma 1987: 189, 196.

107. Ades and Brotherston 1975: 286. Although Ades and Brotherston (1975) address their discussion to "Mesoamerican description of space," it should be noted that this aspect of it refers to the Maya book, the *Popol Vuh*. When they turn to Mexico, it is to observe the absence of Mexican textual descriptions of space (instead, Mexican inscriptions refer to time). But then, Maya concepts of time were highly spatialized, as distance along a road (Aveni 1989: 216). Be that as it may, I refer to Ades and Brotherston's article in the Aztec context because of the prevalence of Quetzalcoatl in the Maya world; my contention is that part of the appeal of the deity in Mexico was political, derived from its essentially alien and cosmopolitan associations.

108. Aveni and Hartung 1986: 1; Aveni 1989: 261–65; see also Brotherston 1976: 44–45.

109. Brundage 1979: 11.

110. D. Carrasco 1982: 122. Matos Moctezuma (1987: 189) describes the Templo Mayor in similar terms. Teotihuacan reached its peak a thousand years before the Aztecs but it was the site of an elaborate Quetzalcoatl cult which survived the city's collapse.

111. Klein 1987: 343; but see also Nicholson 1979: 42.

112. Some of the imagery specifically associated with Quetzalcoatl invites intriguing comparisons elsewhere; by inference, these, too, suggest Quetzalcoatl's centrality and add further to the possibility that his centrality implied the reversibility of time. Pocock's (1964) extended discussion of Hindu concepts of cyclical time offers a partial parallel. Cycles of time accumulate to a certain point, then collapse; each cycle represents an age. One deity, distinctive for his temporal reversibility, which is only one of his features, moves both forward and back across the ages. The Hindu Nepalese celebrate an annual ritual cycle that has no

termini but is ruptured by a period of days during which cosmic forces struggle against each other in battle and the dead come to life. Marc Gaborieau (1982: 23) refers to this season as an "axis": "The end of the cycle . . . is not in time but represents the axis that communicates with eternity." In both cases, the axis representing the reversibility of time within a temporal order is important in the cultural construction of time and space as moral orders.

113. Henderson 1981: 205.

114. Umberger 1987: 444.

115. Nicholson 1979.

116. Broda 1987: 238.

117. Ades and Brotherston 1975: 286.

118. The phrase is Freidel's 1985: 300, 301.

119. For cultural histories of their political ascendancy, see Calnek 1976; and Rounds 1982.

120. I take this to be the implication of Freidel 1985: 300.

121. See Katz 1972 for the migration story; see also D. Carrasco 1982.

122. D. Carrasco (1982: 157) stresses the implicit nature of the political motive in the text.

123. Quoted in D. Carrasco 1982: 157.

124. Ibid.

125. D. Carrasco 1982: 77.

126. Brundage 1979: 108; Carrasco 1982; Nicholson 1979: 37–38. Though I refer to *a* Quetzalcoatl cult, there is no reason to assume that practices relating to his veneration involved a unified doctrine; indeed, even in imperial Tenochtitlan, where ritual practice in general appears to have been exceptionally elaborate and coherent (see, e.g., Broda 1978: 226–30; Townsend 1979, 1987), religious life was diversified and pluralistic (Townsend 1987: 393). Indeed, in this discussion, I am less concerned with the origins of a particular myth than I am with broadening the horizon along which that search might be conceptualized.

127. For a detailed survey of evidence, see D. Carrasco 1982.

128. D. Carrasco 1982; Nicholson 1979: 37–38. Tula was not implicated in the collapse of Teotihuacan; it was founded afterward (Diehl 1981: 293). For a vivid description of the archaeological evidence of Teotihuacan's ritual sites and their intentional destruction, see Millon 1981.

129. M. Miller 1986: 168 considers the Huastec hypothesis; Nicholson 1979: 38 considers the Gulf Coast route.

130. Nicholson 1979: 37–38.

131. M. Miller 1986: 163; see also Diehl 1983: 143. Karl Taube's recent study of the iconography of mirrors at Teotihuacan would seem to urge caution in associating circular buildings with Quetzalcoatl. Drawing on evidence from modern Huichols, for whom many circular emblems represent mirrors, Taube notes that pyrite mirrors were cult objects for both Teotihuacan and the classic Maya, although little is known about the Maya use of mirrors (Taube 1992: 198). Mirrors—bowls of water—were significant in the iconography of Teotihuacan for their associations with both fire and water (Taube 1992: 186). The association with flame linked mirrors iconographically to butterflies during the late post-

classic period. In other contexts, mirrors were associated with images of spider webs or netted disks, shields, the sun, caves, and supernatural passageways, and passageways were associated with serpents (Taube 1992: 185–97). Some, but not all, of these images are associated with Quetzalcoatl's emblems or manifestations (butterflies, serpents). Tezcatlipoca's name translates as "smoking mirror."

132. Linnea H. Wren and Peter Schmidt (1991) note the recent reassessments of Chichen Itza's date in relation to Tula and its Toltecization, as well as the significance of these reassessments for our understanding of the Maya. They suggest that the subordination of Chichen Itza in the postclassic period was not due to active opposition between the elites of two ethnic groups (Mexican and Maya), as had previously been thought, but rather a "cultural convergence." The convergence of Mexican and Maya cultural elements dates from an earlier period than had previously been thought.

133. Nicholson 1979: 38; see also Henderson 1981: 200–20. Wren and Schmidt (1991: 203) observe that the earlier date of Toltec influence in Chichen Itza would tend to leave greater scope for Chichen's control over the southern Maya.

134. Diehl 1976: 260.

135. Henderson 1981: 197; D. Carrasco 1982: 134.

136. Compare interpretations by Aveni 1989: 206–7; D. Carrasco 1982: 132; and Henderson 1981: 197.

137. Henderson 1981: 197.

138. D. Carrasco 1982: 134.

139. Klein 1987: 350–51. See also Gillespie 1989.

140. Klein 1987: 354.

141. Henderson 1981: 200, 201.

142. Ibid., 218–19.

143. Nicholson 1979: 40.

144. D. Carrasco 1982: 28.

145. Broda 1978: 230. For a description of the rites in Tenochtitlan, see Townsend 1987.

146. Broda 1978: 230–31.

147. Broda 1976: 38–39. For a comparative discussion of social organization at Tenochtitlan, see Calnek 1976.

148. Pasztory 1979.

149. Heyden 1987: 110.

150. Broda 1976: 47; see also Fry 1985: 134.

151. Fry 1985.

152. Wren and Schmidt 1991: 203.

153. Diehl 1983: 144. For detailed discussion of the Maya postclassic and current interpretive debates, see Chase and Rice 1985; Culbert 1973; Henderson 1981: esp. 196–220; Sabloff and Andrews 1986; Willey 1987.

154. Henderson 1981: 206; A. Miller 1986: 199.

155. A. Miller 1986: 199–200.

156. Ibid., 211–12; see also Pasztory 1979.

157. A. Miller 1986: 220.

158. See, for example, Brown 1985.

159. Yoffee 1991: 305.

160. Graham 1985: 228.

161. Diehl 1983: 141.

162. Ibid., 141.

163. Berdan 1978: 179.

164. Rice and Rice 1985: 182.

165. Klein 1987: 360.

166. D. Carrasco 1982: 186; Diehl 1976: 284.

167. Anderson and Dibble 1975: 12:29.

168. D. Carrasco 1982: 136.

169. For example, Fry 1985: 132, 139; more generally, see Rice and Rice 1985: 172; Wonderley 1985: 268; Freidel 1985: 308.

170. Freidel 1985: 308; see also M. Miller 1986: 179. Among the influences that are conventionally labeled Toltec or Mexican are round altars (as at Uaymil) and elements of ritual (e.g., new year rites), both associated with Quetzalcoatl's cult (Fry 1985: 132; Freidel 1985: 303). One apparent difference in the practice of the cult between Maya and the Aztecs is in the substantial popularization of the cults in at least some parts of the Maya region (Fry 1985: 139), along with, or in spite of, elites' pretenses to foreignness. Robert E. Fry (1985) explores the possibility of a revitalization movement at Uaymil; perhaps there were rival movements involving Quetzalcoatl in some locales. Given the distribution of Quetzalcoatl across Mesoamerica, it would not be surprising if new Toltecized practices met resistance from local groups whose vital communities identified with some aspect of this deity complex.

171. Freidel 1985: 309.

172. To these I would add the tangential and highly speculative point that it seems possible the contemporaneous intensification of the evidence of Quetzalcoatl and the disappearance of the long count in the Maya region are related developments if Quetzalcoatl can be taken as a hallmark of central Mexican influence during the postclassic period. Perhaps the long count was maintained by ritualists whose office was suppressed by the new Toltecized elites. In any event, it seems significant that the imperial Aztecs claimed Quetzalcoatl as the founder of the 260-day count that was common across Mesoamerica and that, closer to Tenochtitlan, that calendar was both more standardized and made more theatrical in its celebration in a host of public rites throughout the year (see Broda 1969).

173. D. Carrasco 1982: 193, citing Alvarado Tezozomoc.

174. Ibid., 172. The man identified as Quetzalcoatl in the myth of return may have held an office under this title at Tula, though not as the first incumbent; similarly, Kukulcan may have held this office at Chichen Itza (Nicholson 1979: 38–39).

175. D. Carrasco 1982: 189.

176. Townsend 1987: 393.

177. Broda 1987: 212–13.

178. Broda 1978: 222–23, 1987: 212–13.

179. Detailed by D. Carrasco 1982: 92–95.
180. Diehl 1983: 142.
181. See Anderson and Dibble 1975, vol. 12.
182. Ibid., 11–12.
183. Ibid., 33–35.
184. D. Carrasco 1982: 189–91.
185. Quoted in ibid., 190–91.
186. For examples and discussion, see D. Carrasco 1982: 191–204; see also Pagden 1986: 467–69.
187. Anderson and Dibble 1975: 12:9.
188. Dibble and Anderson 1969: 249.
189. Anderson and Dibble 1975: 12:11–12.
190. Ibid., 21–23.
191. Ibid., 44.
192. Dibble and Anderson 1969: 52; see also Townsend 1987: 401.
193. Townsend 1987: 398.
194. Ibid., 403–5.
195. D. Carrasco 1987.
196. Dibble and Anderson 1969.
197. Ibid., 21–22.
198. Ibid., 24.
199. That is, according to Sahagún's glossary of metaphors, may I not become a drifter or a fugitive because I have been ostracized from my parents' house (Ibid., 253).
200. Ibid., 42–43.
201. Ibid., 43.
202. Anderson and Dibble 1975: 12:44.
203. Dibble and Anderson 1969: 61.
204. Ibid., 62.
205. Ibid., 244.
206. Another chronicler, Bernal Díaz, who participated in the events of the conquest as a soldier in Cortés's army, reports Motecuhzoma's reference to the Spanish as being of "his own lineage" (quoted in D. Carrasco 1982: 173).
207. Pagden 1986: 86. Pagden's critical assessment of Cortés's reliability as a source extends to all his renderings of Motecuhzoma's words, including these.

6. Time, Life, and Law in the United States

1. The contradiction itself is not limited to the United States, or to the judicial context; however, the U.S. judicial context in recent years has made particular aspects of this contradiction especially clear. See also Greenhouse 1989b.
2. For an ethnographic perspective on the abortion debate in the 1980s, including observations of the impact of national "pro-life" organizations in local communities, see Ginsburg 1989.
3. Patrick Baude, personal communication.

4. In practice, cyclical time does not appear to dwell on questions of individual agency, but on the socially relevant sources of agency and their signs.

5. Kantorowicz 1957.

6. See Goody 1966.

7. Holdsworth 1927: 287–89.

8. See, for example, Gibbs 1949; Harding 1966.

9. Bossy 1983: 287.

10. Cipolla 1980: 143–49; Le Goff 1981: 9.

11. Bloch 1964: 1:113–20; Kagan 1983.

12. This is not the place to review the history of legal development in Europe, but some examples might be useful as illustrations of important discontinuities between medieval and modern legal institutions and law use. Anglo-Saxon law was kin-based (Pollock and Maitland 1959: 1:31). Land disputes were regularly resolved through trial by battle (Harding 1966: 41). The blood feud persisted in northern Europe until "well into the medieval period" (Wormald 1983: 101–2). An early role of the church in local dispute settlement in sixth-century Gaul was to intervene to end blood feuds; records from this period also show the legal use of ordeals and oaths (James 1983: 25, 32–33). The ancient law of Belgium and northern France distinguished family rights but not personal rights (Meijers 1956: 1:228). The same could be said of England, where the early state had to compete against the family (Pollock and Maitland 1959: 1:31). Under the Normans, legality was concentrated in the king through the enforcement of absolute liability (Pollock and Maitland 1959: 1:54). The regularization of law in England under the Normans is credited with resolving serious disorder that had persisted since the breakup of plural kingdoms in the eighth century (Gibbs 1949: 60). Carlo Ginzburg (1985) and Emmanuel Le Roy Ladurie (1978) offer extended documentary evidence of concepts of legality and trial practice in medieval Italy and France (respectively).

13. Berman 1983: 49–119; see also Herzfeld 1986.

14. Zerubavel 1982.

15. Henderson 1989; Kahn 1988: 509. In the United States, Phyllis Chock (1986) identifies linear time as an element of the structure of personal narratives of ethnic identity.

16. Kahn 1988: 508–16. See also Kahn 1987.

17. See Horwitz 1977: 7.

18. Robert A. Ferguson (1984: 15–16) notes that this particular equation (linking law, reason, and nature) emerged in American culture only after the Revolution. By the time Chief Justice John Marshall retired roughly fifty years later, in 1835, the Supreme Court had become "the great oracle of Americanism" (Ferguson 1984: 23).

19. Gitlin 1986: 31. At the same time, the media "transform the great silence of things into its opposite" by means of a narrative of "what's-going-on" (de Certeau 1984: 185). This publicity is radically at odds with the public silence the justices conventionally preserve about the development and negotiation of judicial opinions, and also at odds with the sort of narrative that make up legal opinions.

20. Ernst H. Kantorowicz (1957: 500) describes parallel debates over kingship in ancient Greece, as to whether the person who becomes king does so by receiving grace at the moment of installation or by imitating the divine.

21. Abraham 1985: 4.

22. Murphy 1964: 16.

23. But see Wilson 1983 on a posthumous Oliver Wendell Holmes cult in the United States: "The popular feeling about Holmes was illustrated in a striking and touching way in the reception by Eastern audiences, sixteen years after Holmes' death (in 1951), of a rubbishy film about him with the title *The Magnificent Yankee*. It was significant that what most moved these audiences were not the parts that were personal and sentimental but the scenes, all too few and inept, in which the hero's moral courage was shown. They seemed to be responding to these with a special enthusiasm of reassurance because they were made to feel—at a moment of the national life particularly uncertain and uncomfortable: the end of Truman's second administration—the Korean War, the Hiss trial, the rise of McCarthy—that here was a just man, a man of the old America who, having proved himself early in the Civil War, had persisted and continued to function through everything that had happened since, and had triumphed in remaining faithful to some kind of traditional ideal. But what *was* this ideal they applauded? . . . Independence and fair-dealing, no doubt; rectitude and courage as a public official; and a conviction that the United States had a special meaning and mission to devote one's whole life to which was a sufficient dedication for the highest gifts" (Wilson 1983: 554).

24. This symbolic evocation of a judge as the embodiment of principle and reason is by no means uncontested. See Cover 1986: 1628.

25. The symbolic representation of transcendence in no way implies that people do not want to know the details of a judicial candidate's life; a major theme in the early days after Justice David Souter's nomination to the Court in 1990 was how little was known about his private life and thought.

26. Greenhouse 1989b: 1642.

27. The phrase in this context is Geertz's 1983: 125. The inauguration ceremonies of the justices and the presidents to some extent extend the inversion of the temporalities their branches express. Presidents are inaugurated in a public festival, sworn in by the chief justice. Justices are installed in private ceremony. For example, Justice Souter's constitutional oath was administered at the White House by Chief Justice William H. Rehnquist; the next day, in accord with tradition, the Chief Justice administered the judicial oath to Souter before the bench at the Supreme Court. *New York Times*, October 10, 1990.

28. See Kahn 1987: 56–57.

29. Kelman (1987: 65) develops the distinction between desire and reason in liberal thought; desire individuates and reason universalizes. Later, Kelman (229) relates this world view to a vision of law and truth as being beyond history. See also Mensch 1982.

30. Again, this is a symbolic point, not one about public attitudes toward individual justices.

31. Turner 1969: 80–118.

32. Philippe Lejeune (1989: 4) excludes memoirs from the genre of auto-biography; however, from the perspective of the question of what forms of narra-tive are appropriate to Supreme Court justices, their first-person narrative pre-cludes them equally.

33. At the same time, such relevance is not monolithic. The examples in the text perhaps suggest the extent to which diversity on the court shifts the mean-ings of "seats" from the straight metonymy I have sketched to locuses of repre-sentation along gendered, racial, or political lines.

34. Rudenstine 1987: 9.

35. Nominations to the Supreme Court fail only rarely. Lawrence Sager (1990: 23) cites eleven.

36. Bork 1963.

37. Bork 1971.

38. Bork 1984.

39. Hereafter, I cite these as *SG Hearings*, *CA Hearings*, and *SC Hearings*, with page references to published transcripts of the proceedings, for the Senate Judiciary Committee confirmation hearings in the contexts of Bork's nominations to the positions of solicitor general, judge on the Court of Appeals, and associate justice of the Supreme Court, respectively.

40. *CA Hearings*, 1–2.

41. *SG Hearings*, 21.

42. *SG Hearings*, 11.

43. Ibid., 12.

44. Ibid., 13.

45. *CA hearings*, 5.

46. *SG Hearings*, 8.

47. Ibid., 11.

48. See, for example, Gillers 1987: 50.

49. See, for example, Rudenstine 1987: 9–10.

50. *SC Hearings*, 152.

51. Ibid., 153.

52. Ibid., 252.

53. Ibid., 262.

54. Ibid., 451.

55. Ibid., 667.

56. Ibid., 269.

57. Ibid., 854.

58. Ibid., 180.

59. The temporal idiom of Bork's book *The Tempting of America* returns to the double braid of the inner man reflecting on the public man's work. At the beginning of his chapter on the nomination and "the campaign" against him, Bork (1990: 271) writes: "This is not an autobiography." Nevertheless, he pro-ceeds to develop a narrative of his record along the lines of that given by his supporters, invoking a more or less double-stranded temporal model of his per-sonal and professional development.

60. Grassley invited Bork to compare himself to Justice Potter Stewart, who

dissented in the *Griswold* case and then joined the majority in *Roe* v. *Wade*: "*Grassley*. Do you see yourself able to make those sorts of changes? *Bork*. Well, I suppose I could if I became convinced, sure, that I was wrong the first time. I have changed my mind on cases— *Grassley*. But he necessarily says he was wrong the first time. It was a case of the passage of time" (*SC Hearings*, 264). The exchange places the confession (of wrong) squarely and explicitly at the center of a linear time representation of Bork's career.

61. The term "collective autobiography" is Paul Eakin's (1989: xvii).

62. Bakhtin 1981: 254–56.

63. Ibid., 255–56.

64. The metaphor of representation is a suggestive one here, since, as we have seen, it was Bork's plural self-representations that became the issue in the retraction controversy. It is tempting to consider that it was the representational dimension itself that was problematic, given the cultural proscription of justices as representatives. The model Bork initially seemed to hold of the judicial role as a professional one would be at odds with this cultural (and legal) proscription. As we have seen, different temporal idioms involve different possibilities for representation, depending on the quality and quantity of distance they evoke between a person's self and his or her public performance.

65. Lejeune 1989; Leverenz 1989; Ricoeur 1984: 52.

66. Henderson 1989.

67. His deference to the biblical narrative canon of male autobiography is perhaps illustrated by his allusion to the "feast" at the close of the hearings. In her analysis of Victorian autobiographical narrative, Heather Henderson (1989: 23) offers the example of John Henry Newman's sermon "The Gospel Feast," in which the audience is invited to feast on the Gospel texts themselves.

68. Lionnet 1989: 4.

69. The disruption also introduces a problem of reading analogous to the one Paul de Man (1979: 176) finds in Rousseau's *Pygmalion*: "The provisional syntheses that are achieved along the way in the course of the action do not necessarily mark a progression and it is the burden of the reading to decide whether the text is the teleology of a selfhood that culminates in the climactic exclamation 'Moi!' or a repetitive vacillation."

70. The term "process" was used by Joseph Biden 9/10: 32; Simpson 9/10: 42; Simpson 9/11: 77; Arlen Specter 9/13: 2–3; Kennedy 9/27: 4; Howard Metzenbaum 9/27: 7; Orrin Hatch 9/27: 10; Arlen Specter 9/27: 26; Hank Brown 9/27: 28. The dates and page numbers refer to the transcript of the Thomas hearings, as published by Lexis (United States Senate 1991). The Thomas hearings opened on September 10, 1991, and closed with the committee's roll-call vote on September 27. They reopened on October 11, 1991, to consider Anita Hill's report that she had been sexually harassed by Thomas while his employee. Those hearings closed on Sunday, October 13, 1991. For the later hearings, see U.S. Senate 1993.

71. Kennedy 9/10: 25–26; Specter 9/11: 28; Herbert Kohl 9/12: 6, 8; Patrick Leahy 9/27: 12; Grassley 9/27: 22.

72. Recent published analyses of the Thomas hearings, notably Toni Morrison's collection *Race-ing Justice, En-gendering Power* (1992) primarily address what have become known as "the Anita Hill hearings." These are historically and

culturally significant, but my own focus is on the first hearings, since it was there that the hearings' framework was fused to a canonical rendering of Thomas's autobiography.

73. Thomas hearings, 9/10: 44.

74. Ibid., 9/10: 3.

75. Nunn, ibid.

76. Ibid., 9/10: 11.

77. Ibid., 10.

78. The twinning also juvenilized Thomas, as was consistent with the paternalistic tone of his advocates in the first hearings.

79. This connection was made most directly by Hatch, Thomas hearings, 9/27: 8.

80. The conventional stories included Thomas's reference to his sister, whom he portrayed publicly (and erroneously) as an example of excessive dependency on the welfare system.

81. Thomas hearings, 9/11: 34.

82. Ibid., 9/12: 4.

83. Ibid., 9/10: 54, and see Strom Thurmond, 9/12: 24.

84. Ibid., 9/12: 70, and see Thomas, 9/11: 36.

85. Ibid., 9/27: 9.

86. Ibid., 9–11.

87. See also DeConcini, ibid., 21, for such a reference.

88. His reference to the press of concerns other than *Roe v. Wade* (which had legalized abortion in 1973) came in response to Leahy's question about Thomas's views of the case while he was a student at Yale Law School, ibid., 9/11: 5–6.

89. In response to Kennedy, ibid., 9/10: 28; for related references to childhood or youthful experiences in response to a range of policy questions, see also responses ibid., to Kennedy, 9/10: 24, Howell Heflin, 9/11: 19, Brown, 9/11: 26–27, Paul Simon, 9/11: 32.

90. Ibid., 9/10: 15.

91. Ibid., 9/27: 26.

92. Ibid., 27. This is a key issue in employment discrimination law, since if women naturally lack interest (e.g., in heavy construction work), a woman cannot successfully sue for employment on grounds of sexual discrimination. See Schultz 1990.

93. Thomas hearings, 9/11: 54.

94. Ibid., 14.

95. Ibid., 9/13: 36.

96. Simon, ibid.

97. Kohl, ibid., 43.

98. Ibid., 9/10: 7.

99. Ibid., 12.

100. For example, Thomas, ibid., 9/11: 38.

101. Ibid., 9/16: 40.

102. Ibid., 81.

103. Ibid., 9/27: 17.

104. Ibid., 10/3: 18–19.

105. Ibid., 9/13: 21.
106. Ibid., 9/27: 14.
107. Ibid., 16.
108. Ibid., 17.
109. Ibid., 10/11: 9.
110. In general, see Thomas, ibid., 9/11: 44, distinguishing between policy-making and judicial roles.
111. Ibid., 39.
112. Ibid., 9/12: 10.
113. Ibid., 9/11: 4.
114. Ibid., 9/12: 72–73.
115. Ibid., 9/13: 45.
116. Ibid.
117. Ibid., 10/12: 2.
118. I am grateful to Professor Terry Dworkin for this suggestion.

Conclusion: Postmodernity This Time

1. For a discussion and analysis of philosophical positions and debates, see Habermas 1987; for an interpretation of the effects of post-Darwinian concepts of chronology on ethnology, see Trautmann 1992.
2. On alienation and death, see Carr 1986: 18–44.
3. Kern 1983: 23; see also Zerubavel 1982, 1985.
4. Kern 1983: 34.
5. Sahlins 1985: 72.
6. Passage quoted is from ibid., 145.
7. Braudel 1980; Lévi-Strauss 1966, esp. chap. 9; Sahlins 1981, 1985.
8. Lévi-Strauss 1966: 231.
9. Ibid., 232–33.
10. In general, see Veyne 1984.
11. Ibid., 282, and see 272–82.
12. Ibid., 284.
13. For Habermas (1987: 2), "modernization" expresses a move from modernity as a temporal referent to a concept that capture social relationships specific to the forms of modern life. In effect, my suggestion is that the mythic aspect of modernity inheres in the *connection* between these two referents.
14. Eysteinsson 1990: 240.
15. In general, see Herzfeld 1985; see also Herzfeld 1990: 248–51.
16. Documented, for example, in Bernal 1987, on Africa; Fabian 1983, on "primitive peoples"; and Said 1979, on the Middle East.
17. *Contention* (Spring 1994). For source material and cultural analyses of the violence in Los Angeles, in addition to the *Contention* essays (Jackson et al. 1994; Sonenshein 1994; and Miles 1994), see contributions to Gooding-Williams 1993.
18. Rieff 1991.
19. In what follows, I draw on the *New York Times* and the *Los Angeles Times* from roughly two weeks following the violence, as the stories of the violence

gave way to related headlines in news and feature sections: *Los Angeles Times*, May 10–17, 1992; *New York Times*, May 10–21, 1992.

20. *Los Angeles Times*, May 13, 1992, pg. T3. Peter Stallybrass and Allon White (1986) write of the proximity of desire and revulsion in the urban landscape of nineteenth-century London. For discussion of class, caste, and the polarities of self-control and conflict, see Greenhouse 1992; Greenhouse et al. 1994; and Yngvesson 1993.

21. Reprinted in the *New York Times*, May 20, 1992. Quayle's linkage of poverty to poverty of values has older parallels in the classic anthropological literature on American concepts of class and caste. Greenhouse 1992 reviews this literature for its implications about the relationship between diversity and violence.

22. The phrase "disorderly difference" comes from Sarat and Berkowitz, forthcoming.

23. This implicit portrayal of children as future adults was the inverse of the L.A. photographs, which invited readers to think of today's adult "others" as former children by photographing children of mixed races or ethnicities together. Of course, the children were also a palpable sign of the hope for a better future.

24. I borrow this term from Susan Harding's (1984) analysis of the civil rights movement in the U.S. South as involving two phases, white civility and white supremacy. Her thesis is that the civil rights movement involved a renegotiation of the terms of white hegemony.

25. *Los Angeles Times*, May 13, 1992.

26. This is true primarily as a paradigm that accounts for the organization and content of the intense public debates over the theory and practice of individual interests and privacy within and beyond the family "unit," of which public debate over abortion is perhaps the most immediate but by no means the only salient contest.

27. Greenhouse 1986: chap. 6; Greenhouse et al. 1994: chap. 7.

28. Giddens 1991. From this perspective, David Harvey's (1989) perspective on postmodernism as arising from the mass standardization of Fordism and its corollaries in politics and social life is similar to Giddens's, the key parallel being their respective periodizations of modernity and postmodernity. By contrast, Zygmunt Bauman (1987, 1992) offers a leading example of a conceptualization of postmodernity in terms that refuse periodization. Instead, Bauman defines postmodernity as a crisis of legitimacy integral to liberalism's central claims to envision a social order that is both pluralist and centralist. My view is closer to Bauman's, in that I view postmodernity (and any representation of time) as a reference to the cultural legitimation of authority. Postmodernity might be more preoccupied with legitimacy, but this preoccupation does not mean that modernity has been superseded.

29. Stallybrass and White 1986: 125–48; Williams 1985. In modern times, the myth of community has been no less punishing of the categorical "others" whose presence seems always (though not always in the same way) to have implied the symbolic rupture (and literal disruption) of community. Color and class have always been implicit in the corollary that the myth of community draws between consensus and belonging. Indeed, invocations of community provide avenues by which specific propositions about the positive or negative meanings of race and

class can be imported into the analysis of social situations and materialized in social space without seeming to be (Harvey 1988 [1973]; Lawrence 1982a and b). This is not to say that it cannot be inclusive, but the invocation of community does not settle this question by itself.

30. Fredric Jameson (1991: ix), for example, opens his book on postmodernism with the claim that "it is safest to grasp the concept of the postmodern as an attempt to think the present historically in an age that has forgotten how to think historically in the first place." My own view is that the neglect (if that is what it is) of history is only the corollary of an even more entrenched refusal to think anthropologically, that is, to take difference both seriously and affirmatively. For an ethnographic argument linking ahistoricism and social conflict in a "community" context in the United States, see Greenhouse 1986.

31. Giddens 1991: 27.

32. For another view of social science as a residuum of ancient sacred holisms, see Dumont 1986.

33. Cf. Comaroff 1985: 260–63. In the current literature on resistance, there is some debate about how meaningful the term is in circumstances where there is no organized political action addressed to an oppressive group to organize resistance. For the reasons just discussed, restricting the term in this way limits the ethnography of politics to circumstances in which those in positions of power acknowledge the existence and legitimacy of others at the margins. Accordingly, I suggest that resistance should be conceptually uncoupled from its usual derivative connection to hegemony, at least insofar as either term implies an active social movement with an ideological charter.

34. Comaroff and Comaroff 1991: 20–22; Fardon 1985; Strathern 1988: esp. 272–73, 325–39.

35. For an example of this critque in the anthropology of law, see Moore 1986: 325–26; more generally, see Rosaldo 1990: 2.

36. This critique is not limited to ethnography; feminist assessments of postmodernism offer wide-ranging criticism of its failures to connect the idea of "difference" (in this case, gender) to lived-world hierarchies and options (see Bordo 1990; Di Stefano 1990). More broadly still, Bauman (1989: x) challenges sociology, by which he seems to mean social science, to confront the dangers of modern times: "The Holocaust was not simply a *Jewish problem*, and not an event in *Jewish history* alone. *The Holocaust was born and executed in our modern rational society, at the high stage of our civilization and at the peak of human cultural achievement, and for this reason it is a problem of that society, civilization and culture.*"

37. Notable exceptions include Chock 1991; Comaroff and Comaroff 1992: chap. 10; Herzfeld 1992; and Verdery 1993.

38. Bauman (1987, 1992) and Bruno Latour (1993) offer different arguments for "detemporalizing" postmodernity and instead using the term to refer to particular aspects of a legitimation crisis—for Bauman, the fragmentation of political authority and the resulting authority of a market discourse and, for Latour, a crisis of knowledge as the scientific paradigm of the Enlightenment yields to pervasive doubts. The paradigmatic discussion in these terms is Jean-François Lyotard's (1984).

References

Aberle, David Friend (1951). "The psychosocial analysis of a Hopi life history." *Comparative Psychology Monographs* 107 v. 21(1). Berkeley: University of California Press.

Abraham, Henry J. (1985) *Justices and Presidents: A Political History of Appointments to the Supreme Court.* 2d edition. Oxford: Oxford University Press.

Adam, Barbara (1990). *Time and Social Theory.* Cambridge: Polity Press.

Ades, Dawn, and Gordon Brotherston (1975). "Mesoamerican description of space I: Myths; stars and maps; and architecture." *Ibero-Amerikanisches Archiv* n.s. 1(4):279–305.

Alonso, Ana María (1994). "The politics of space, time, and substance: State formation, nationalism, and ethnicity." *Annual Review of Anthropology* 23:379–405.

Anderson, Arthur J. O., and Charles E. Dibble, trans. (1975). *Fray Bernardino de Sahagún, Florentine Codex: General History of the Things of New Spain*, book 12. 2d edition, revised. Monographs of the School of American Research, 14, part 13. Santa Fe: School of American Research and University of Utah.

Anderson, Benedict (1991). *Imagined Communities.* London: Verso.

Appadurai, Arjun (1981). "The past as a scarce resource." *Man* n.s. 16(2):201–19

—— (1986). "Introduction: Commodities and the politics of value." In Appadurai, ed., *The Social Life of Things: Commodities in Cultural Perspective*, pp. 3–63. Cambridge: Cambridge University Press.

—— (1990). "Disjuncture and difference in the global cultural economy." *Theory, Culture, and Society* 7:295–310.

Assier-Andrieu, Louis (1987). *Le peuple et la loi: Anthropologie historique des droits paysans en Catalogne française.* Paris: Librairie Générale de Droit et de Jurisprudence.

—— (1993). "In the eye of the law." *Journal of Legal Pluralism* 33:179–94.

Aveni, Anthony F. (1980). *Skywatchers of Ancient Mexico.* Austin: University of Texas Press.

—— (1989). *Empires of Time: Calendars, Clocks, and Cultures.* New York: Basic Books.

Aveni, Anthony, and Horst Hartung (1986). *Maya City Planning and the Calendar. Transactions of the American Philosophical Society*, vol. 76, part 7.

Bakhtin, M. M. (1981). *The Dialogic Imagination.* Ed. Michael Holquist. Trans. Caryl Emerson. Austin: University of Texas Press.

Barnes, J. A. (1971). "Time flies like an arrow." *Man* n.s. 6(4):537–52.

Bauman, Zygmunt (1987). *Legislators and Interpreters: On Modernity, Post-modernity, and Intellectuals.* Cambridge: Polity Press.

—— (1989). *Modernity and the Holocaust*. Cambridge: Polity Press.

—— (1992). *Intimations of Postmodernity*. London: Routledge.

Beidelman, Thomas O. (1963). "Kaguru time reckoning: An aspect of the cosmology of an East African people." *Southwestern Journal of Anthropology* 19(1):9–20.

Bell, Diane (1993). *Daughters of the Dreaming*. 2d edition. Minneapolis: University of Minnesota Press.

Bender, John, and David E. Wellbery, eds. (1991). *Chronotypes: The Construction of Time*. Stanford: Stanford University Press.

Benhabib, Seyla, and Drucilla Cornell (1987). "Introduction: Beyond the politics of gender." In Benhabib and Cornell, eds., *Feminism as Critique: Essays on the Politics of Gender*, pp. 1–55. Cambridge: Polity Press.

Benson, Elizabeth P., ed. (1981). *Mesoamerican Sites and World-Views*. A conference at Dumbarton Oaks, October 16–17, 1976. Washington, D.C.: Dumbarton Oaks.

Benveniste, Emile (1969). *Le vocabulaire des institutions indo-européennes* 2 vols. Paris: Minuit.

Berdan, Frances F. (1978). "Replicación de principios de intercambio en la sociedad mexica: De la economía à la religión." In Johanna Broada and Pedro Carrasco, eds., *Economía política e ideología en el Mexico prehispanico*, pp. 175–93. Mexico City: Nueva Imagen.

—— (1987). "The economics of Aztec luxury trade and tribute." In Elizabeth Hill Boone, ed., *The Aztec Templo Mayor*, pp. 161–83. A symposium at Dumbarton Oaks, October 8–9, 1983. Washington, D.C.: Dumbarton Oaks.

Berlo, Janet C., ed. (1992). *Art, Ideology, and the City of Teotihuacan*. Washington, D.C.: Dumbarton Oaks.

Berman, Harold (1983). *Law and Revolution: The Formation of the Western Legal Tradition*. Cambridge: Harvard University Press.

Bernal, Martin (1987). *Black Athena: The Afroasiatic Roots of Classical Civilization*. New Brunswick: Rutgers University Press.

Bhabha, Homi K. (1994). *The Location of Culture*. New York: Routledge.

Blacker, Carmen, and Michael Loewe, eds. (1975). *Ancient Cosmologies*. London: George Allen and Unwin.

Bloch, Marc (1964). *Feudal Society*. 2 vols. Trans. L. A. Manyon. Chicago: University of Chicago Press.

Bloch, Maurice (1968). "Astrology and writing in Madagascar." In Jack Goody, ed., *Literacy in Traditional Societies*, pp. 278–97. Cambridge: Cambridge University Press.

—— (1977). "The past and the present in the present." *Man* n.s. 12(2): 278–92.

—— (1982). "Death, women, and power." In Maurice Bloch and Jonathan Parry, eds., *Death and the Regeneration of Life*, pp. 211–30. Cambridge: Cambridge University Press.

Bloch, Maurice, and S. Guggenheim (1981). "Compadrazgo, baptism, and the symbolism of a second birth." *Man* n.s. 16(3): 376–86.

Bloch, Maurice, and Jonathan Parry, eds. (1982). *Death and the Regeneration of Life*. Cambridge: Cambridge University Press.

Bodde, Derk (1967). *China's First Unifier: A Study of the Ch'in Dynasty as Seen in the Life of Li Ssu 280-208 B.C.* Hong Kong: Hong Kong Press. First edition 1938.

—— (1975). *Festivals in Classical China* Princeton: Princeton University Press and Chinese University of Hong Kong.

—— (1980). "Age, youth, and infirmity in the law of Ch'ing China." In Jerome A. Cohen, R. Randle Edwards, and Fu-mei Chang Chen, eds., *Essays on China's Legal Tradition*, pp. 137–69. Princeton: Princeton University Press.

—— (1981). *Essays on Chinese Civilization.* Ed. Charles LeBlanc and Dorothy Borei. Princeton: Princeton University Press.

—— (1986). "The state and empire of Ch'in." In Denis Twitchett and Michael Loewe, eds., *The Cambridge History of China* 1:21–102. Cambridge: Cambridge University Press.

—— (1990). "The idea of social classes in Han and pre-Han China." In W. L. Idema and Erik Zürcher, eds., *Thought and Law in Qin and Han China*, pp. 26–41. Leiden: E. J. Brill.

Bodde, Derk, and Clarence Morris (1967). *Law in Imperial China.* Cambridge: Harvard University Press.

Bohannan, Paul (1953). "Concepts of time among the Tiv of Nigeria." *Southwestern Journal of Anthropology* 9(3):251–62.

—— (1957). *Justice and Judgment among the Tiv.* Oxford: Oxford University Press.

Boone, Elizabeth Hill, ed. (1985). *Painted Architecture and Polychrome Monumental Sculpture in Mesoamerica.* A symposium at Dumbarton Oaks, December 10–11, 1981. Washington, D.C.: Dumbarton Oaks.

—— (1987). *The Aztec Templo Mayor.* A symposium at Dumbarton Oaks, October 8–9, 1983. Washington, D.C.: Dumbarton Oaks.

Bordo, Susan (1990). "Feminism, postmodernism, and gender-scepticism." In Linda J. Nicholson, ed., *Feminism/Postmodernism*, pp. 133–56. New York: Routledge.

Bork, Robert H. (1963). "Civil rights—a challenge." *New Republic* (August): 22.

—— (1971). "Neutral principles and some First Amendment problems." *Indiana Law Journal* 47(1):1–35.

—— (1984). "Judge Bork replies." *American Bar Association Journal* February 1, 1984, p. 132.

—— (1990). *The Tempting of America: The Political Seduction of the Law.* New York: Free Press.

Bossy, John, ed. (1983). *Disputes and Settlements: Law and Human Relations in the West.* Cambridge: Cambridge University Press.

Bourdieu, Pierre (1977). *Outline of a Theory of Practice.* Trans. Richard Nice. Cambridge: Cambridge University Press.

—— (1990a [1980]). *The Logic of Practice.* Trans. Richard Nice. Stanford: Stanford University Press.

—— (1990b) *In Other words: Essays towards a Reflexive Sociology.* Stanford: Stanford University Press.

—— (1991). *Language and Symbolic Power*. Ed. John B. Thompson. Trans. Gino Raymond and Matthew Adamson. Cambridge: Harvard University Press.

Bourdillon, M. F. C. (1978). "Knowing the world or hiding it: A response to Maurice Bloch." *Man* n.s. 13(4):591–99.

Boyarin, Jonathan, ed. (1993). *The Ethnography of Reading*. Berkeley: University of California Press.

Braudel, Fernand (1980 [1969]). *On History*. Trans. Sarah Matthews. London: Weidenfeld and Nicolson.

Broda, Johanna (de Casas) (1969). "The Mexican calendar as compared to other Mesoamerican systems." *Acta Ethnologica et Linguistica* 15, Series Americana 4, Vienna.

—— (1976). "Los estamentos en el ceremonial mexica." In Pedro Carrasco, Johanna Broda, et al., *Estratificación social en la Mesoamerica prehispanica*, pp. 37–66. Tlalpan: Centro de Investigaciones Superiores Instituto Nacional de Antropología e Historia.

—— (1978). "Relaciónes políticas ritualizadas: El ritual como expresión de una ideología." In Broda and Pedro Carrasco, eds., *Economía política e ideología en el Mexico prehispanico*, pp. 221–55. Mexico City: Nueva Imagen.

—— (1987). "The provenience of the offerings: Tribute and *cosmovision*." In Elizabeth Hill Boone, ed., *The Aztec Templo Mayor*, pp. 211–56. A symposium at Dumbarton Oaks, October 8–9, 1983. Washington, D.C.: Dumbarton Oaks.

Broda, Johanna, Davíd Carrasco, and Eduardo Matos Moctezuma (1987). *The Great Temple of Tenochtitlan: Center and Periphery in the Aztec World*. Berkeley: University of California Press.

Brotherston, Gordon (1976). "Mesoamerican description of space II: Signs for direction." *Ibero-Amerikanisches Archiv* 2(1):39–62.

Brown, Kenneth L. (1985). "Postclassic relationships between the highland and lowland Maya." In Arlen F. Chase and Prudence M. Rice, eds., *The Lowland Maya Postclassic*, pp. 270–81. Austin: University of Texas Press.

Brundage, Burr Cartwright (1979). *The Fifth Sun: Aztec Gods, Aztec World*. Austin: University of Texas Press.

Burman, Rickie (1981). "Time and socioeconomic change on Simbo, Solomon Islands." *Man* n.s. 16:251–67.

Butler, Judith (1987). "Variations on sex and gender: Beauvoir, Wittig, and Foucault." In Seyla Benhabib and Drucilla Cornell, eds., *Feminism as Critique: Essays on the Politics of Gender*, pp. 128–42. Cambridge: Polity Press.

Cain, Maureen, and Kalman Kulcsar (1981–82). "Thinking disputes: An essay on the origins of the dispute industry." *Law and Society Review* 16(3):375–402.

Calnek, Edward (1976). "The internal structure of Tenochtitlan." In Eric R. Wolf, ed., *The Valley of Mexico: Studies in Pre-Hispanic Ecology and Society*, pp. 287–302. Albuquerque: University of New Mexico Press, School of American Research.

Carr, David N. (1991 [1986]). *Time, Narrative, and History*. Bloomington: Indiana University Press.

Carrasco, Davíd (1982). *Quetzalcoatl and the Irony of Empire: Myths and Prophecies in the Aztec Tradition*. Chicago: University of Chicago Press.

—— (1987). "Myth, cosmic terror, and the Templo Mayor." In Johanna Broda, Davíd Carrasco, and Eduardo Matos Moctezuma, *The Great Temple of Tenochtitlan: Center and Periphery in the Aztec World*, pp. 124–62. Berkeley: University of California Press.

Carrasco, Pedro, Johanna Broda, et. al. (1976). *Estratificación social en la Mesoamerica prehispanica*. Tlalpan: Centro de Investigaciones Superiores Instituto Nacional de Antropología e Historia.

Carrier, James G. (1992). "Occidentalism: The world turned upside-down." *American Ethnologist* 19(2):195–212.

Chan, Hok-lam (1981). "Ideologies and traditions of monarchy and government in imperial China." In A. L. Basham, ed., *Kingship in Asia and Early America*, pp. 179–216. 30th International Congress of Human Sciences in Asia and North Africa. Mexico City: El Colegio de Mexico.

—— (1984). *Legitimation in Imperial China: Discussions under the Jurchen-Chin Dynasty (1115–1234)*. Seattle: University of Washington Press.

Chang, Ch'i-yun (1983). *China's Cultural Achievements during the Warring States Period*. Trans. Orient Lee. Yangmingshan, Taiwan: Chinese Culture University Press, China Academy.

Chang, Kwang-Chih (1978). "*T'ien kan*: A key to the history of the Shang." In David T. Roy and Tsuen-hsuin Tsien, eds., *Ancient China: Studies in Early Civilization*, pp. 13–42. Hong Kong: Chinese University Press.

—— (1980). *Shang Civilization*. New Haven: Yale University Press.

—— (1983). *Art, Myth, and Ritual: The Path to Political Authority in Ancient China*. Cambridge: Harvard University Press.

Chartier, Roger (1988). *Cultural History*. Trans. Lydia G. Cochrane. Ithaca: Cornell University Press.

Chase, Arlen F. (1985). "Postclassic Peten interaction spheres: The view from Tayasal." In Chase and Prudence M. Rice, eds., *The Lowland Maya Postclassic*, pp. 184–205. Austin: University of Texas Press.

Chase, Arlen F., and Prudence M. Rice, eds. (1985). *The Lowland Maya Postclassic*. Austin: University of Texas Press.

Chase, Diane Z., Arlen F. Chase, and William A. Haviland (1990). "The classic Maya city: Reconsidering the 'Mesoamerican urban tradition.'" *American Anthropologist* 92(2):499–506.

Ch'en, Ch'i-yun (1986). "Confucian, Legalist, and Taoist thought in Later Han." In Denis Twitchett and Michael Loewe, eds., *The Cambridge History of China* 1:766–807. Cambridge: Cambridge University Press.

Chen, Fu-mei Chang (1970). "On analogy in Ch'ing law." *Harvard Journal of Asiatic Studies* 30:212–24.

Ch'en, Paul Heng-chao (1979). *Chinese Legal Tradition under the Mongols*. Princeton: Princeton University Press.

Chock, Phyllis P. (1986). "The outsider wife and the divided self: The genesis of ethnic identities." In Chock and June Wyman, eds., *Discourse and the Social Life of Meaning*, pp. 185–204. Washington, D.C.: Smithsonian Institution Press.

—— (1991). "'Illegal aliens' and 'opportunity': Myth-making in Congressional testimony." *American Ethnologist* 18(2):279–94.

Ch'ü, T'ung-tsu (1965). *Law and Society in Traditional China*. Paris: Mouton.
—— (1972). *Han Social Structure*. Seattle: University of Washington Press.
Cipolla, Carlo C. (1967). *Clocks and Culture, 1300–1700*. London: Collins.
—— (1980). *Before the Industrial Revolution*. 2d edition. London: Methuen.
Clifford, James (1988). *The Predicament of Culture*. Cambridge: Harvard University Press.
Clifford, James, and George Marcus (1986). *Writing Culture*. Cambridge: Cambridge University Press.
Codex Fejervary-Mayer (1971). Intro. C. A. Burland. Codices Selecti, v. 26. Graz: Academische Druck-u. Verlagsanst.
Coe, Michael (1987). *The Maya*, 4th edition. London: Thames and Hudson.
Cohen, Alvin P. (1978). "Coercing the rain deities in ancient China." *History of Religions* 17(3–4):244–65.
Cohen, Jerome A., R. Randle Edwards, and Fu-mei Chang Chen, eds. (1980). *Essays on China's Legal Tradition*. Princeton: Princeton University Press.
Collier, Jane (1975). "Legal processes." *Annual Review of Anthropology* 4:121–44.
Comaroff, Jean (1985). *Body of Power, Spirit of Resistance: The Culture and History of a South African People*. Chicago: University of Chicago Press.
Comaroff, Jean, and John L. Comaroff (1991). *Of Revelation and Revolution*. Vol. 1. Chicago: University of Chicago Press.
Comaroff, John L. (1980). "Introduction." *The Meaning of Marriage Payments*. London: Academic Press.
Comaroff, John L., and Jean Comaroff (1992). *Ethnography and the Historical Imagination*. Boulder, Colo.: Westview Press.
Comaroff, John L., and Simon Roberts (1981). *Rules and Processes: the Cultural Logic of Dispute in an African Context*. Chicago: University of Chicago Press.
Cooper, Frederick (1994). "Colonizing time: Work rhythms and labor conflict in colonial Mombasa." In Nicholas B. Dirks, ed., *Colonialism and Culture*, pp. 209–45. Ann Arbor: University of Michigan Press.
Coulton, G. G. (1919). *Social Life in Britain: From the Conquest to the Reformation*. Cambridge: Cambridge University Press.
—— (1925). *The Medieval Village*. Cambridge: Cambridge University Press.
Cover, Robert M. (1986). "Violence and the word." *Yale Law Journal* 95(8):1601–29.
Creel, Herrlee Glessner (1938). *Studies in Early Chinese Culture*. First series. London: Kegan Paul, Trench, Trubner.
—— (1970). *The Origins of Statecraft in China*. Vol. 1: *The Western Chou Empire*. Chicago: University of Chicago Press.
—— (1974). *Shen Pu-hai*. Chicago: University of Chicago Press.
—— (1980). "Legal institutions and procedures during the Chou dynasty." In Jerome A. Cohen, R. Randle Edwards, and Fu-mei Chang Chen, eds., *Essays on China's Legal Tradition*, pp. 26–55. Princeton: Princeton University Press.
Culbert, T. Patrick, ed. (1973). *The Classic Maya Collapse*. Albuquerque: University of New Mexico Press, School of American Research.
—— (1991). *Classic Maya Political History: Hieroglyphic and Archaeological Evidence*. Cambridge: Cambridge University Press.

Cullen, Christopher (1980–81). "Some further points on the *Shih*." *Early China* 6:31–46.

Cullmann, Oscar (1964). *Christ and Time: The Primitive Christian Conception of Time and History*. Revised edition. Trans. Floyd V. Filson. Philadelphia: Westminster Press.

Dales, Richard C. (1982). "Discussions of the eternity of the world during the first half of the twelfth century." *Speculum* 57(3):495–508.

Damon, Frederick H. (1982). "Calendars and calendrical rites on the northern side of the Kula Ring." *Oceania* 52(3):221–39.

Davies, Nigel (1980). *The Toltec Heritage: From the Fall of Tula to the Rise of Tenochtitlan*. Norman: University of Oklahoma.

De Bary, William Theodore, Wing-tsit Chan, and Burton Watson (1960). *Sources of Chinese Tradition*. New York: Columbia University Press.

De Certeau, Michel (1984). *The Practice of Everyday Life*. Berkeley: University of California Press.

De Man, Paul (1979). *Allegories of Reading: Figural Language in Rousseau, Nietzsche, Rilke, and Proust*. New Haven: Yale University Press.

Demieville, Paul (1986). "Philosophy and religion from Han to Sui." In Denis Twitchett and Michael Loewe, eds., *The Cambridge History of China* 1:808–72. Cambridge: Cambridge University Press.

Derrida, Jacques (1992). *Given Time: 1. Counterfeit Money*. Trans. Peggy Kamuf. Chicago: University of Chicago Press.

Desjarlais, Robert, and Arthur Kleinman (1994). "Violence and demoralization in the new world disorder." *Anthropology Today* 10(5):9–12.

Dibble, Charles E., and Arthur J. O. Anderson, trans. (1969). *Fray Bernardino de Sahagún, Florentine Codex: General History of the Things of New Spain*, book 6. Monographs of the School of American Research, 14, part 7. Santa Fe: School of American Research and University of Utah.

Diehl, Richard A. (1976). "Pre-Hispanic relationships between the Basin of Mexico and north and west Mexico." In Eric R. Wolf, ed., *The Valley of Mexico: Studies in Pre-Hispanic Ecology and Society*, pp. 249–86. Albuquerque: University of New Mexico Press, School of American Research.

—— (1981). "Tula." In Jeremy A. Sabloff, ed., *Archaeology: Supplement to the Handbook of Middle American Indians* 1:277–95. Gen. ed. Victoria R. Bricker. Austin: University of Texas Press.

—— (1983). *Tula: The Toltec Capital of Ancient Mexico*. London: Thames and Hudson.

Dietrich, Craig (1972). "Cotton culture and manufacture in early Ch'ing China." In W. E. Willmott, ed., *Economic Organization in Chinese Society*, pp. 109–35. Stanford: Stanford University Press.

Di Stefano, Christine (1990). "Dilemmas of difference: Feminism, modernity, and postmodernism." In Linda J. Nicholson, ed., *Feminism/Postmodernism*, pp. 63–82. New York: Routledge.

Dubinskas, Frank A., ed. (1988). *Making Time: Ethnographies of High-Technology Organizations*. Philadelphia: Temple University Press.

Dumont, Louis (1986). *Essays on Individualism: Modern Ideology in Anthropological Perspective.* Chicago: University of Chicago Press.

Durkheim, Emile (1965 [1915]). *The Elementary Forms of the Religious Life.* Trans. J. W. Swain. New York: Free Press.

Duyvendak, J. J. L., trans. (1928). *The Book of Lord Shang.* Chicago: University of Chicago Press.

Eakin, Paul (1989). "Foreword." In Philippe Lejeune, *On Autobiography*, pp. vii–xxviii. Minneapolis: University of Minnesota Press.

Edgerton, Samuel Y., Jr. (1975). *The Renaissance Rediscovery of Linear Perspective.* New York: Harper and Row.

Ekholm, Gordon F., and Ignacio Bernal, eds. (1971). *Archaeology of Northern Mesoamerica: Handbook of Middle American Indians.* Vol. 10. Gen. ed. Robert Wauchope. Austin: University of Texas Press.

Elvin, Mark (1973). *The Pattern of the Chinese Past.* London: Eyre Methuen.

Eno, Robert (1990). *The Confucian Creation of Heaven: Philosophy and the Defense of Ritual Mastery.* Albany: SUNY Press.

Epstein, A. L., ed. (1974). *Contention and Dispute: Aspects of Law and Social Control in Melanesia.* Canberra: Australian National University Press.

Erdheim, Mario (1978). "Transformaciones de la ideologia mexica en realidad social." In Johanna Broda and Pedro Carrasco, eds., *Economía política e ideología en el Mexico prehispanico*, pp. 195–220. Mexico City: Nueva Imagen.

Escarra, Jean (1936). *Le droit chinois.* Peking: Henri Vetch; Paris: Librairie du Recueil Sirey.

Evans-Pritchard, E. E. (1939). "Nuer time-reckoning." *Africa* 12(2):189–216

—— (1940). *The Nuer.* Oxford: Oxford University Press.

Eysteinsson, Astradur (1990). *The Concept of Modernism.* Ithaca: Cornell University Press.

Fabian, Johannes (1983). *Time and the Other: How Anthropology Makes Its Object.* New York: Columbia University Press.

Fairbank, John K., ed. (1957). *Chinese Thought and Institutions.* Chicago: Chicago University Press.

Fardon, Richard (1985). "Introduction: A sense of relevance." In Fardon, ed. *Power and Knowledge: Anthropological and Sociological Approaches*, pp. 1–20. Edinburgh: Scottish Academic Press.

Ferguson, Robert A. (1984). *Law and Letters in American Culture.* Cambridge: Harvard University Press.

Firth, Raymond (1936). *We, the Tikopia.* London: George Allen and Unwin.

—— (1959). *Social Change in Tikopia.* London: George Allen and Unwin.

—— (1961). *History and Traditions of Tikopia.* Wellington, N.Z.: Polynesian Society.

—— (1967). *The Work of the Gods in Tikopia.* 2d ed. New York: Humanities Press.

Forde, Daryll (1962). "Death and succession: An analysis of Yakö mortuary ritual." In Max Gluckman, ed., *Essays on the Ritual of Social Relations*, pp. 89–123. Manchester: Manchester University Press.

Fortes, Meyer, ed. (1949). "Time and social structure: An Ashanti case study." In Fortes, ed., *Social Structure: Essays Presented to A. R. Radcliffe-Brown*, pp. 54–84. Oxford: Clarendon Press.

——— (1987). *Religion, Morality, and the Person: Essays on Tallensi Religion.* Cambridge: Cambridge University Press.

Foucault, Michel (1980). *Power/Knowledge.* Brighton, Sussex: Harvester Press.

Frazer, J. G. (1889). "Questions on the manners, customs, religion, superstitions, etc. of uncivilized or semi-civilized peoples." *Journal of the Royal Anthropological Institute* 18(4):431–39.

Freidel, David A. (1985). "New light on the dark age: A summary of major themes." In Arlen F. Chase and Prudence M. Rice, eds., *The Lowland Maya Postclassic*, pp. 285–309. Austin: University of Texas Press.

Fry, Robert E. (1985). "Revitalization movements among the postclassic lowland Maya." In Arlen F. Chase and Prudence M. Rice, eds., *The Lowland Maya Postclassic*, pp. 126–41. Austin: University of Texas Press.

Fuller, Chris (1994). "Legal anthropology, legal pluralism, and legal thought." *Anthropology Today* 10(3):9–12.

Fung, Yu-Lan (1937). *A History of Chinese Philosophy.* Peking: Henri Vetch; London: George Allen and Unwin.

——— (1966 [1948]). *A Short History of Chinese Philosophy.* Ed. Derk Bodde. New York: Free Press.

Gaborieau, Marc (1982). "Les fêtes, le temps, et l'espace: Structure du calendrier hindou dans sa version indo-népalaise." *L'Homme* 22(3):11–29.

Gardner, Charles S. (1961). *Chinese Traditional Historiography.* Cambridge: Harvard University Press.

Geertz, Clifford (1973a). *The Interpretation of Cultures: Selected Essays.* New York: Basic Books.

——— (1973b). "Person, time, and conduct in Bali." In Geertz, *The Interpretation of Cultures: Selected Essays*, pp. 360–411. New York: Basic Books.

——— (1983). *Local Knowledge: Further Essays in Interpretive Anthropology.* New York: Basic Books.

Gell, Alfred (1992). *The Anthropology of Time: Cultural Constructions of Temporal Maps and Images.* Oxford: Berg.

Gellner, Ernest (1983). *Nations and Nationalism.* Oxford: Blackwell.

Gernet, Jacques (1968). *Ancient China.* Trans. Raymond Rudorff. London: Faber and Faber.

——— (1982). *A History of Chinese Civilization.* Trans. J. R. Foster. Cambridge: Cambridge University Press.

Gibbs, Marion (1949). *Feudal Order.* London: Cobbett Press.

Giddens, Anthony (1979). *Central Problems in Social Theory: Action, Structure, and Contradiction in Social Analysis.* Berkeley: University of California Press.

——— (1990). *The Consequences of Modernity.* Stanford: Stanford University Press.

——— (1991). *Modernity and Self-Identity: Self and Society in Late Modern Age.* Stanford: Stanford University Press.

Gillers, Stephen (1987). "The compelling case against Robert H. Bork." *Cardozo Law Review* 9(1):33–62.

Gillespie, Susan D. (1989). *The Aztec Kings: The Construction of Rulership in Mexico History.* Tucson: University of Arizona Press.

Gilmore, Myron (1952). *The World of Humanism, 1453–1517*. New York: Harper and Brothers.

Gilson, Etienne (1950). *The Spirit of Mediaeval Philosophy*. Trans. A. H. C. Downes. London: Sheed and Ward.

Ginsburg, Faye D. (1989). *Contested Lives: The Abortion Debate in an American Community*. Berkeley: University of California Press.

Ginzburg, Carlo (1983). *The Night Battles: Witchcraft and Agrarian Cults in the Sixteenth and Seventeenth Centuries*. Trans. John and Anne Tedeschi. London: Routledge and Kegan Paul.

—— (1985). *The Night Battles: Witchcraft and Agrarian Cults in the Sixteenth and Seventeenth Centuries*. Trans. John and Anne Tedeschi. New York: Penguin.

Gitlin, Todd, ed. (1986). *Watching Television*. New York: Pantheon.

Givens, Douglas R. (1977). *An Analysis of Navajo Temporality*. Washington, D.C.: University Press of America.

Gluckman, Max (1955). *The Judicial Process among the Barotse of Northern Rhodesia*. Manchester: Manchester University Press.

—— (1966). *Custom and Conflict in Africa*. Oxford: Blackwell.

—— (1967). *The Judicial Process among the Barotse of Northern Rhodesia*. 2d ed. Manchester: Manchester University Press.

Goethe, J. W. (1962) *Italian Journey*. [1786–1788]. Trans. W. H. Auden and Elizabeth Mayer. Harmondsworth, U.K.: Penguin.

Gooding-Williams, Robert, ed. (1993). *Reading Rodney King/Reading Urban Uprising*. New York: Routledge.

Goodrich, Luther Carrington (1935). *The Literary Inquisition of Ch'ien-Lung*. Baltimore: Waverly Press.

Goody, Esther, ed. (1982). *From Craft to Industry: The Ethnography of Proto-industrial Cloth Production*. Cambridge: Cambridge University Press.

Goody, Jack, ed. (1966). *Succession to High Office*. Cambridge: Cambridge University Press.

——, ed. (1968a). *Literacy in Traditional Societies*. Cambridge: Cambridge University Press.

—— (1968b). "Restricted literacy in northern Ghana." In Goody, ed. *Literacy in Traditional Societies*, pp. 199–264. Cambridge: Cambridge University Press.

—— (1968c). "Time: Social organization." In David L. Sills, ed., *International Encyclopedia of the Social Sciences* 16:30–42. London: Crowell Collier and Macmillan.

—— (1977). *The Domestication of the Savage Mind*. Cambridge: Cambridge University Press.

—— (1983). *The Development of the Family and Marriage in Europe*. Cambridge: Cambridge University Press.

—— (1986). *The Logic of Writing and the Organization of Society*. Cambridge: Cambridge University Press.

Gordon, Robert (1992). *The Bushman Myth: The Making of a Namibian Underclass*. Boulder: Westview Press.

Gough, Kathleen (1968a). "Implications of literacy in traditional China and India." In Jack Goody, ed., *Literacy in Traditional Societies*, pp. 70–84. Cambridge: Cambridge University Press.

—— (1968b). "Literacy in Kerala." In Jack Goody, ed., *Literacy in Traditional Societies*, pp. 133–60. Cambridge: Cambridge University Press.

Graham, Elizabeth A. (1985). "Facets of terminal to post-classic activity in the Stann Creek District, Belize." In Arlen Chase and Prudence M. Rice, eds., *The Lowland Maya Postclassic*, pp. 206–34. Austin: Univerity of Texas Press.

Graulich, Michel (1981). "The metaphor of the day in ancient Mexican myth and ritual." *Current Anthropology* 22(1):45–50.

Greenhouse, Carol J. (1982). "Looking at culture, looking for rules." *Man* n.s. 17(1):58–73.

—— (1986). *Praying for Justice: Faith, Order, and Community in an American Town*. Ithaca: Cornell University Press.

—— (1989a). "Dimensions spatio-temporelles du pluralisme juridique." *Anthropologie et Sociétés* 13(1):35–52.

—— (1989b). "Just in time: Temporality and the cultural legitimation of law." *Yale Law Journal* 98(8):1631–51.

—— (1992). "Signs of quality: Individualism and hierarchy in American culture." *American Ethnologist* 19(2):233–54.

Greenhouse, Carol J., and Davydd J. Greenwood, eds. (forthcoming). *Democracy and Difference*. Albany: State University of New York Press.

Greenhouse, Carol, Barbara Yngvesson, and David Engel (1994). *Law and Community in Three American Towns*. Ithaca: Cornell University Press.

Griffiths, John (1968). "What is legal pluralism?" *Journal of Legal Pluralism* 24:1–55.

Habermas, Jürgen (1987). *The Philosophical Discourse of Modernity: Twelve Lectures*. Trans. Frederick G. Lawrence. Cambridge: MIT Press.

Hallowell, A. Irving (1937). "Temporal orientation in Western civilization and in a preliterate society." *American Anthropologist* 39(4, 1):647–70.

Han, Yu-Shan (1955). *Elements of Chinese Historiography*. Hollywood: W. M. Hawley.

Harding, Alan (1966). *A Social History of English Law*. Harmondsworth, U.K.: Penguin.

Harding, Susan (1984). "Reconstructing order through action: Jim crow and the southern civil rights movement." In Charles Bright and Susan Harding, eds., *Statemaking and Social Movements: Essays in History and Theory*, pp. 378–402. Ann Arbor: University of Michigan Press.

Harper, Donald (1980–81). "The Han cosmic board: A response to Christopher Cullen." *Early China* 6:47–56.

Harvey, David (1988 [1973]). *Social Justice and the City*. Oxford: Basil Blackwell.

—— (1989). *The Condition of Postmodernity*. Oxford: Blackwell.

Hastrup, Kirsten, ed. (1992). *Other Histories*. London: Routledge.

Heider, Karl G. (1979). *Grand Valley Dani, Peaceful Warrior*. New York: Holt, Rinehart, Winston.

Henderson, Heather (1989). *The Victorian Self: Autobiography and Biblical Narrative*. Ithaca: Cornell University Press.

Henderson, John S. (1981). *The World of the Ancient Maya*. London: Orbis.

Herskovits, Melville J. (1944). Review of *The Nuer: A Description of the Modes of Livelihood and Political Institutions of a Nilotic People*, E. E. Evans-Pritchard. *American Anthropologist* n.s. 46:396–400.

290   References

Herzfeld, Michael (1985). *The Poetics of Manhood: Contest and Identity in a Cretan Mountain Village*. Princeton: Princeton University Press.

—— (1986). "Of definitions and boundaries: The status of culture in the culture of the state." In Phyllis Chock and June Wyman, eds., *Discourse and the Social Life of Meaning*, pp. 75–93. Washington, D.C.: Smithsonian Institution Press.

—— (1987). *Anthropology through the Looking Glass: Critical Ethnography in the Margins of Europe*. Cambridge: Cambridge University Press.

—— (1990). "Pride and perjury: Time and the oath in the mountain villages of Crete." *Man* n.s. 25(3):305–22.

—— (1991). *A Place in History: Social and Monumental Time in a Cretan Town*. Princeton: Princeton University Press.

—— (1992). *The Social Production of Indifference: Exploring the Symbolic Roots of Western Democracy*. New York: Berg.

Heyden, Doris (1987). "Symbolism of ceramics from the Templo Mayor." In Elizabeth Hill Boone, ed., *The Aztec Templo Mayor*, pp. 109–30. A symposium at Dumbarton Oaks, October 8–9, 1983. Washington, D.C.: Dumbarton Oaks.

Hobsbawm, Eric, and Terence Ranger, eds. (1983). *The Invention of Tradition*. Cambridge: Cambridge University Press.

Hogbin, H. Ian (1934). *Law and Order in Polynesia*. London: Christophers.

—— (1958). *Social Change*. London: Watts.

Holdsworth, W. S. (1927). *A History of English Law*. 3d ed. Vol. 3. London: Methuen.

Horwitz, Morton (1977). *The Transformation of American Law, 1780–1860*. Cambridge: Harvard University Press.

Howe, Leopold E. A. (1981). "The social determination of knowledge: Maurice Bloch and Balinese time." *Man* n.s. 16(2):220–34.

Howell, Cicely (1975). "Stability and change, 1300–1700: The socio-economic context of the self-perpetuating family farm in England." *Journal of Peasant Studies* 2(4):468–82.

Hsu, Cho-yun (1965). *Ancient China in Transition: An Analysis of Social Mobility, 722–222 B.C.* Stanford: Stanford University Press.

Hsu, Cho-yun, and Katheryn M. Linduff (1988). *Western Chou Civilization*. New Haven: Yale University Press.

Hugh-Jones, Christine (1979). *From the Milk River: Spatial and Temporal Processes in Northwest Amazonia*. Cambridge: Cambridge University Press.

Huizinga, Johan (1924). *The Waning of the Middle Ages*. London: Edward Arnold.

Hulsewé, Anthony François Paulus (1955). *Remnants of Han Law*. Vol. 1. Sinica Leidensia, 9. Leiden: E. J. Brill.

—— (1981). "The Legalists and the laws of Ch'in." In W. L. Idema, ed., *Leyden Studies in Sinology: Papers Presented at the Conference Held in Celebration of the Fiftieth Anniversary of the Sinological Institute of Leyden University, December 8–12, 1980*, pp. 1–22. Sinica Leidensia, 15. Leiden: E. J. Brill.

—— (1985a). *Remnants of Ch'in Law: An Annotated Translation of the Ch'in Legal and Administrative Rules of the 3rd Century B.C. Discovered in Yun-meng Prefecture, Hu-pei Province, in 1975*. Sinica Leidensia, 17. Leiden: E. J. Brill.

—— (1985b). "The influence of the "Legalist" government of Qin on the economy as reflected in the texts discovered in Yunmeng County." In S. R. Schram, ed., *The Scope of State Power in China*, pp. 211–35. European Science Foundation. London: School of Oriental and African Studies; Hong Kong: Chinese University Press.

—— (1986). "Ch'in and Han law." In Denis Twitchett and Michael Loewe, eds., *The Cambridge History of China*, 1:520–44. Cambridge: Cambridge University Press.

—— (1988). "The wide scope of *Tao*: "Theft" in Ch'in-Han law." *Early China* 13:166–200.

Hummel, Arthur W., trans. (1966). *The Autobiography of a Chinese Historian*. Taipei: Ch'eng-Wen.

Humphreys, S. C. (1981). "Death and time." In Humphreys and Helen King, eds., *Mortality and Immortality: The Anthropology and Archaeology of Death*, pp. 261–84. London: Academic Press.

Humphreys, S. C., and Helen King, eds. (1981). *Mortality and Immortality: The Anthropology and Archaeology of Death*. London: Academic Press.

Huntington, Richard, and Peter Metcalf (1979). *Celebrations of Death*. Cambridge: Cambridge University Press.

Idema, W. L., ed. (1981). *Leyden Studies in Sinology: Papers Presented at the Conference Held in Celebration of the Fiftieth Anniversary of the Sinological Institute of Leyden University, December 8–12, 1980*. Sinica Leidensia, 15. Leiden: E. J. Brill.

—— (1990). "The founding of the Han dynasty in early drama: The autocratic suppression of popular debunking." In Idema and Erik Zürcher, eds., *Thought and Law in Qin and Han China*, pp. 183–207. Leiden: E. J. Brill.

Idema, W. L., and Erik Zürcher, eds. (1990). *Thought and Law in Qin and Han China: Studies Dedicated to Anthony Hulsewé on the Occasion of His Eightieth Birthday*. Leiden: E. J. Brill.

Idema, Wilt, and Stephen H. West (1982). *Chinese Theater, 1100–1450: A Source Book*. Münchener Ostasiatische Studien, 27. Wiesbaden: Franz Steiner.

Ingham, John M. (1971). "Time and space in ancient Mexico: The symbolic dimensions of clanship." *Man* n.s. 6(4):615–29.

Irigaray, Luce (1987). "Sexual difference." Trans. Seán Hand. In Toril Moi, ed., *French Feminist Thought*, pp. 118–30. Oxford: Blackwell.

Jackson, M-R., J. H. Johnson Jr., and W. C. Farrell (1994). "An analysis of selected responses to the Los Angeles civil unrest of 1992." *Contention* 33:3–21.

James, Edward (1983). "'Beati pacifici': Bishops and the law in sixth-century Gaul." In John Bossy, ed., *Disputes and Settlements: Law and Human Relations in the West*, pp. 25–46. Cambridge: Cambridge University Press.

Jameson, Fredric (1991). *Postmodernism; or, The Cultural Logic of Late Capitalism*. Durham, N.C.: Duke University Press.

Johnson, Wallace, trans. (1979). *The T'ang Code*, vol. 1: *General Principles*. Princeton: Princeton University Press.

Just, Peter (1992). "History, power, ideology, and culture: Current directions in the anthropology of law." *Law and Society Review* 26(2):373–411.

Kagan, Richard L. (1983). "A golden age of litigation: Castile, 1500–1700." In

John Bossy, ed., *Disputes and Settlements: Law and Human Relations in the West*, pp. 145–66. Cambridge: Cambridge University Press.

Kahn, Paul W. (1987). "The Court, community, and the judicial balance: The jurisprudence of Justice Powell." *Yale Law Journal* 97(1):1–60.

—— (1988). "Reason and will in the origins of American constitutionalism." *Yale Law Journal* 98(7):449–517.

Kantorowicz, Ernst H. (1957). *The King's Two Bodies: A Study in Medieval Political Theology*. Princeton: Princeton University Press.

Kao, George, ed. (1981). *The Translation of Things Past: Chinese History and Historiography*. Hong Kong: Chinese University Press.

Katz, Friedrich (1972). *The Ancient American Civilizations*. London: Weidenfeld and Nicolson.

Keen, Benjamin (1971). *The Aztec Image in Western Thought*. New Brunswick, N.J.: Rutgers University Press.

Keightley, David N. (1978). "The religious commitment: Shang theology and the genesis of Chinese political culture." *History of Religions* 17(3–4):211–25.

—— (1979–80). "The Shang state as seen in the oracle-bone inscriptions." *Early China* 5:25–34.

Kelly, William W. (1986). "Rationalization and nostalgia: Cultural dynamics of new middle-class Japan." *American Ethnologist* 13(4):603–18.

Kelman, Mark (1987). *A Guide to Critical Legal Studies*. Cambridge: Harvard University Press.

Kern, Stephen (1983). *The Culture of Time and Space, 1880–1980*. Cambridge: Harvard University Press.

Klein, Cecelia (1987). "The ideology of autosacrifice at the Templo Mayor." In Elizabeth Hill Boone, ed., *The Aztec Templo Mayor*, pp. 293–370. A symposium at Dumbarton Oaks, October 8–9, 1983. Washington, D.C.: Dumbarton Oaks.

Koch, Klaus-Friedrich (1974). *War and Peace in Jalémó*. Cambridge: Harvard University Press.

Kopytoff, Igor (1986). "The cultural biography of things: Commoditization as process." In Arjun Appadurai, ed., *The Social Life of Things: Commodities in Cultural Perspective*, pp. 64–91. Cambridge: Cambridge University Press.

Kratz, Corinne A. (1994). *Affecting Performance: Meaning, Movement, and Experience in Okiek Women's Initiation*. Washington, D.C.: Smithsonian Institution Press.

Kristeva, Julia (1980). *Desire in Language*. New York: Columbia University Press.

Kroll, J. L. (1990). "Notes on Ch'in and Han law." In W. L. Idema and Erik Zürcher, eds., *Thought and Law in Qin and Han China*, pp. 63–78. Leiden: E. J. Brill.

La Capra, Dominick (1985). *History and Criticism*. Ithaca: Cornell University Press.

Landes, David S. (1983). *The Revolution in Time: Clocks and the Making of the Modern World*. Cambridge: Belknap Press, Harvard University Press.

Langlois, John D., Jr. (1981). "'Living law' in Sung and Yuan jurisprudence." *Harvard Journal of Asiatic Studies* 41(1):165–217.

Lao Tzu (1982). *Tao Te Ching*. Trans. D. C. Lao. Hong Kong: Chinese University Press.

Latour, Bruno (1993). *We Have Never Been Modern*. Trans. Catherine Porter. Cambridge: Harvard University Press.

Lawrence, Errol (1982a). "Just plain common sense: The 'roots' of racism." In Centre for Contemporary Cultural Studies, *The Empire Strikes Back*, pp. 47–94. London: Hutchinson.

—— (1982b). "In the abundance of water the fool is thirsty: Sociology and black 'pathology.'" In Centre for Contemporary Cultural Studies, *The Empire Strikes Back*, pp. 95–142. London: Hutchinson.

Lazarus-Black, Mindie (1994). *Legitimate Acts, Illegal Encounters*. Washington: Smithsonian Institution Press.

Lazarus-Black, Mindie, and Susan Hirsch, eds. (1994). *Contested States*. New York: Routledge.

Leach, Edmund R. (1961). *Rethinking Anthropology*. London School of Economics Monographs in Social Anthropology, 22. London: Athlone Press.

Leban, Carl (1978). "Managing heaven's mandate: Coded communications in the accession of Ts'ao Pei." In David T. Roy and Tsuen-hsuin Tsien, eds., *Ancient China: Studies in Early Civilization*, pp. 315–41. Hong Kong: Chinese University Press.

Leenhardt, Maurice (1979). *Do Kamo: Person and Myth in the Melanesian World*. Trans. Basia Miller Gulati. Chicago: University of Chicago Press.

Leff, Gordon (1967). *Heresy in the Later Middle Ages: The Relation of Heterodoxy to Dissent, c. 1250–c. 1450*. Manchester: Manchester University Press; New York: Barnes and Noble.

Le Goff, Jacques (1960). "Temps de l'église et temps du marchand." *Annales E.S.C.* 15(3):417–33.

—— (1965). *La civilisation de l'occident médiéval*. Paris: Arthaud.

—— (1977). *Pour un autre moyen âge: Temps, travail, et culture en occident*. Paris: Gallimard.

—— (1981). *La naissance du purgatoire*. Paris: Gallimard.

Lejeune, Philippe (1989). *On Autobiography*. Minneapolis: University of Minnesota Press.

León-Portilla, Miguel (1974). *La filosofía Nahuatl: Estudiada en sus fuentes*. Mexico City: Universidad Nacional Autónoma de Mexico, Instituto de Investigaciónes Historicas.

—— (1988). *Time and Reality in the Thought of the Maya*. 2d edition. Norman: University of Oklahoma Press.

Leroy Ladurie, Emmanuel (1978). *Montaillou: The Promised Land of Error*. Trans. Barbara Bray. New York: Braziller.

Leverenz, David (1989). *Manhood and the American Renaissance*. Ithaca: Cornell University Press.

Lévi-Strauss, Claude (1964). *Le cru et le cuit*. Paris: Plon.

—— (1966). *The Savage Mind*. Chicago: University of Chicago Press.

—— (1967). *Structural Anthropology*. Garden City: Anchor.

—— (1969). *The Raw and the Cooked: Introduction to a Science of Mythology*. Vol. 1. Trans. John and Doreen Weightman. New York: Harper and Row.

294   References

—— (1978). *Myth and Meaning*. London: Routledge and Kegan Paul.

—— (1988). *The Jealous Potter*. Trans. Bénédicte Chorier. Chicago: University of Chicago Press.

Levy, Robert (1973). *Tahitians: Mind and Experience in the Society Islands*. Chicago: University of Chicago Press.

Li, Xueqin (1985). *Eastern Zhou and Qin Civilizations*. Trans. K. C. Chang. New Haven: Yale University Press.

Lincoln, Bruce (1986). *Myth, Cosmos, and Society: Indo-European Themes of Creation and Destruction*. Cambridge: Harvard University Press.

Lionnet, Françoise (1989). *Autobiographical Voices: Race, Gender, and Self-Portraiture*. Ithaca: Cornell University Press.

Liu, Chih-chi (1981). "Understanding history: The narration of events." Trans. Stuart H. Sargent. In George Kao, ed., *The Translation of Things Past: Chinese History and Historiography*, pp. 27–33. Hong Kong: Chinese University Press.

Liu, James T. C. (1973). "How did a neo-Confucian school become the state orthodoxy?" *Philosophy East and West* 23(4):483–505.

Loewe, Michael (1963). "Some notes on Han-time documents from Tun-huang." *T'oung Pao* 50(1):150–89.

—— (1974). *Crisis and Conflict in Han China, 104 B.C.–A.D. 9*. London: George Allen and Unwin.

—— (1982). *Chinese Ideas of Life and Death: Faith, Myth, and Reason in the Han Period (202 B.C.–A.D. 220)*. London: George Allen and Unwin.

—— (1985). "Attempts at economic co-ordination during the Western Han Dynasty." In S. R. Schram, ed., *The Scope of State Power in China*, pp. 237–67. European Science Foundation. London: School of Oriental and African Studies; Hong Kong: Chinese University Press.

—— (1986a). "Introduction" to Denis Twitchett and Michael Loewe, eds., *The Cambridge History of China* 1:1–19. Cambridge: Cambridge University Press.

—— (1986b). "The Former Han dynasty." In Denis Twitchett and Michael Loewe, eds., *The Cambridge History of China* 1:103–222. Cambridge: Cambridge University Press.

—— (1986c). "The religious and intellectual background." In Denis Twitchett and Michael Loewe, eds., *The Cambridge History of China* 1:649–725. Cambridge: Cambridge University Press.

—— (1986d). "The concept of sovereignty." In Denis Twitchett and Michael Loewe, eds., *The Cambridge History of China* 1:726–46. Cambridge: Cambridge University Press.

Lopez-Austin, Alfredo (1987). "The masked god of fire." In Elizabeth Hill Boone, ed., *The Aztec Templo Mayor*. A symposium at Dumbarton Oaks, October 8–9, 1983, pp. 257–91. Washington, D.C.: Dumbarton Oaks.

Lyotard, Jean-François (1984). *The Postmodern Condition: A Report on Knowledge*. Trans. Geoff Bennington and Brian Massumi. Theory and History of Literature, 10. Minneapolis: University of Minnesota Press.

Macaulay, Stewart (1989). "Popular legal culture: An introduction." *Yale Law Journal* 98(8):1545–58.

Magnusson, Magnus, and Hermann Pálsson, trans. (1960). *Njal's Saga*. Harmondsworth, U.K.: Penguin.

Malinowski, Bronislaw (1926). *Crime and Custom in Savage Society*. Totowa, N.J.: Rowman and Littlefield.

—— (1927). "Lunar and seasonal calendar in the Trobriands." *Journal of the Royal Anthropological Institute* 57:203–16.

Marcus, George E., and Michael Fischer (1986). *Anthropology as Cultural Critique: An Experimental Moment in the Human Sciences*. Chicago: University of Chicago Press.

Marcus, Joyce (1976). *Emblem and State in the Classic Maya Lowlands: An Epigraphic Approach to Territorial Organization*. Washington, D.C.: Dumbarton Oaks.

Marx, Karl (1981). *Capital: A Critique of Political Economy*. Vol. 2. Trans. David Fernbach. New York: Vintage.

Maspero, Henri (1951). "Le Ming-T'ang et la crise religieuse chinoise avant les Han." *Mélanges chinois et bouddhiques* 9:1–71.

—— (1955). *La Chine antique*. New edition. Paris: Imprimerie nationale.

Matos Moctezuma, Eduardo (1987). "Symbolism of the Templo Mayor." In Elizabeth Hill Boone, ed., *The Aztec Templo Mayor*, pp. 185–207. A symposium at Dumbarton Oaks, October 8–9, 1983. Washington, D.C.: Dumbarton Oaks.

McKnight, Brian E. (1981). *The Quality of Mercy: Amnesties and Traditional Chinese Justice*. Honolulu: University of Hawaii Press.

—— (1992). *Law and Order in Sung China*. Cambridge: Cambridge University Press.

McLeod, Katrina C. D., and Robin D. S. Yates (1981). "Forms of Ch'in law: An annotated translation of the *Feng-chen shih*." *Harvard Journal of Asiatic Studies* 41(1):111–63.

Meggitt, M. J. (1962). *Desert People*. Sydney: Angus and Robertson.

Meijers, E. M. (1956). *Etudes d'histoire du droit*. 4 vols. Leiden: Universitaire Pers Leiden.

Mensch, Elizabeth (1982). "The history of mainstream legal thought." In David Kairys, ed., *The Politics of Law: A Progressive Critique*, pp. 19–26. New York: Pantheon.

Merry, Sally E. (1988). "Legal pluralism." *Law and Society Review* 22(5):869–96.

—— (1992). "Anthropology, law, and transnational processes." *Annual Review of Anthropology* 21:357–69.

Miles, Jack (1994). "The alternative to anarchy: A response to Maria-Rosario Jackson, James H. Johnson Jr., and Walter C. Farrell Jr." *Contention* 3(3):30–37.

Miller, Arthur G. (1986). "From the Maya margins: Images of postclassic politics." In Jeremy A. Sabloff and E. Wyllys Andrews V, eds., *Late Lowland Maya Civilization: Classic to Postclassic*, pp. 199–222. Albuquerque: University of New Mexico Press, School of American Research.

Miller, Mary E. (1986). *The Art of Mesoamerica from Olmec to Aztec*. London: Thames and Hudson.

Millon, René (1981). "Teotihuacan: City state and civilization." In Jeremy A. Sabloff, ed., *Archaeology: Supplement to the Handbook of Middle American Indians* 1:277–95. Gen. ed. Victoria R. Bricker. Austin: University of Texas Press.

Miyazaki, Ichisada (1980). "The administration of justice during the Sung dynasty." In Jerome A. Cohen, R. Randle Edwards, and Fu-mei Chang Chen, eds., *Essays on China's Legal Tradition*, pp. 56–75. Princeton: Princeton University Press.

Moore, Sally Falk (1970a). "Law and anthropology." In Bernard J. Siegel, ed., *Annual Review of Anthropology 1969*, pp. 252–300. Stanford: Stanford University Press.

—— (1970b). "Politics, procedures, and norms in changing Chagga law." *Africa* 40(4):321–44.

—— (1973). "Law and social change: The semi-autonomous social field as an appropriate subject of study." *Law and Society Review* 7(4):719–46.

—— (1986). *Social Facts and Fabrications: "Customary" Law on Kilimanjaro, 1880–1980.* Cambridge: Cambridge University Press.

Morrison, Toni, ed. (1992). *Race-ing Justice, En-gendering Power.* New York: Pantheon.

Mumford, Lewis (1934). *Technics and Civilization.* New York: Harcourt Brace.

Mundle, C. W. K. (1967). "Consciousness of time." *Encyclopedia of Philosophy* 7–8:134–39. New York: Macmillan.

Munn, Nancy D. (1983). "Gawan kula: Spatiotemporal control and the symbolism of influence." In Jerry W. Leach and Edmund Leach, eds., *The Kula: New Perspectives on Massim Exchange*, pp. 277–308. Cambridge: Cambridge University Press.

—— (1986). *The Fame of Gawa: A Symbolic Study of Value Transformation in a Massim (Papua New Guinea) Society.* Chapel Hill: Duke University Press.

—— (1992). "The cultural anthropology of time: A critical essay." *Annual Review of Anthropology* 21:93–123.

Murphy, Walter (1964). *Elements of Judicial Strategy.* Chicago: University of Chicago Press.

Nader, Laura (1965). The anthropological study of law." In Nader, ed., "The ethnography of law," Special issue of *American Anthropologist* 67(6, 2):3–32.

—— (1990). *Harmony Ideology: Justice and Control in a Zapotec Mountain Village.* Stanford: Stanford University Press.

Nagengast, Carole (1994). "Violence, terror, and the crisis of the state." *Annual Review of Anthropology* 23:109–36.

Nakayama, Shigeru (1984). *Academic and Scientific Traditions in China, Japan, and the West.* Trans. Jerry Dusenbury. Tokyo: University of Tokyo Press.

Needham, Joseph (1954). *Science and Civilization in China.* Vol. 1. Cambridge: Cambridge University Press.

—— (1975). "The cosmology of early China." In Carmen Blacker and Michael Loewe, eds., *Ancient Cosmologies*, pp. 87–109. London: George Allen and Unwin.

Needham, Joseph, Ling Wang, and Derek J. de Solla Price (1960). *Heavenly*

Clockwork: The Great Astronomical Clocks of Medieval China. Cambridge: Cambridge University Press.

—— (1986). *Heavenly Clockwork: The Great Astronomical Clocks of Medieval China.* 2d edition with supplement by John H. Combridge. Cambridge: Cambridge University Press.

Nicholson, Henry B. (1971). "Religion in pre-Hispanic central Mexico." In Gordon F. Ekholm, and Ignacio Bernal, eds., *Archaeology of Northern Mesoamerica: Handbook of Middle American Indians* 10:395–446. Gen. ed. Robert Wauchope. Austin: University of Texas Press.

—— (1979). "Ehecatl Quetzalcoatl vs. Topiltzin Quetzalcoatl of Tollan: A problem in Mesoamerican religion and history." *Actes du XLIIe Congrès international des américanistes, 1976* 7:35–47. Paris.

—— (1985). "Polychrome on Aztec sculpture." In Elizabeth Hill Boone, ed., *Painted Architecture and Polychrome Monumental Sculpture in Mesoamerica,* pp. 145–71. A Symposium at Dumbarton Oaks, December 10–11, 1981. Washington, D.C.: Dumbarton Oaks.

—— (1987). "Symposium on the Aztec Templo Mayor: Discussion." In Elizabeth Hill Boone, ed., *The Aztec Templo Mayor,* pp. 463–84. A Symposium at Dumbarton Oaks, October 8–9, 1983. Washington, D.C.: Dumbarton Oaks.

Nicholson, Linda (1987). "Feminism and Marx: Integrating kinship with the economic." In Seyla Benhabib and Drucilla Cornell, eds., *Feminism as Critique: Essays on the Politics of Gender,* pp. 16–30. Cambridge: Polity Press.

Nilsson, Martin P. (1920). *Primitive Time-Reckoning.* Lund: C. W K. Gleerup.

Nivison, David S. (1966). *The Life and Thought of Chang Hsueh-ch'eng (1738–1801).* Stanford: Stanford University Press.

Noakes, Susan (1988). *Timely Reading: Between Exegesis and Interpretation.* Ithaca: Cornell University Press.

Nordstrom, Carolyn, and JoAnn Martin, eds. (1992) *The Paths to Domination, Resistance, and Terror.* Berkeley: University of California Press.

Obeyesekere, Gananath (1992). *The Apotheosis of Captain Cook: European Mythmaking in the Pacific.* Princeton: Princeton University Press.

Offner, Jerome A. (1983). *Law and Politics in Aztec Texcoco.* Cambridge: Cambridge University Press.

Ohnuki-Tierney, Emiko, ed. (1990). *Culture through Time: Anthropological Approaches.* Stanford: Stanford University Press.

Oliver, Douglas (1974). *Ancient Tahitian Society.* Honolulu: University Press of Hawaii.

Ong, Walter J., S. J. (1977). *Interfaces of the Word.* Ithaca: Cornell University Press.

—— (1982). *Orality and Literacy: The Technologizing of the Word.* New York: Methuen.

Ortiz, Alfonso (1969). *The Tewa World.* Chicago: University of Chicago Press.

Ortner, Sherry B. (1984). "Theory in anthropology since the sixties." *Comparative Studies in Society and History* 26:126–66.

Östör, Akos (1993). *Vessels of Time: An Essay on Temporal Change and Social Transformation.* Delhi: Oxford University Press.

Packard, Randall M. (1981). *Chiefship and Cosmology: An Historical Study of Political Competition*. Bloomington: Indiana University Press.

Pagden, Anthony, ed. and trans. (1986). *Hernan Cortés: Letters from Mexico*. New Haven: Yale University Press.

Pasztory, Esther (1979). "Masterpieces in pre-Columbian Art." *Actes du XLII Congrès International des Américanistes, 1976*. 7:377–390. Paris.

—— (1987). "Texts, archaeology, art, and history in the Templo Mayor: Reflections." In Elizabeth Hill Boone, ed., *The Aztec Templo Mayor*, pp. 451–62. A Symposium at Dumbarton Oaks, October 8–9, 1983. Washington, D.C.: Dumbarton Oaks.

Pauwels, Simonne (1990). "La relation frère-soeur et la temporalité dans une société d'Indonésie orientale." *L'Homme* 30(116):7–29.

Peacock, James L., and Ruel W. Tyson Jr. (1989). *Pilgrims of Paradox: Calvinism and Experience among the Primitive Baptists of the Blue Ridge*. Washington, D.C.: Smithsonian Institution Press.

Peerenboom, Randall P. (1993). *Law and Morality in Ancient China: The Silk Manuscripts of Huang-Lao*. Albany: State University of New York Press.

Pereira Salas, Eugenio (1966). "Les horlogers au Chili a l'époque coloniale." *Annales E.S.C.* 21(1):141–58.

Peters, Emrys L. (1967). "Some structural aspects of the feud among the camel-herding Bedouin of Cyrenaica." *Africa* 37:261–82.

Pocock, David F. (1964). "The anthropology of time-reckoning." *Contributions to Indian Society* 7:18–29.

Pollock, Sir Frederick, and Frederic William Maitland (1959). *The History of English Law*. Vol. 1. Cambridge: Cambridge University Press.

Průšek, Jaroslav (1971). *Chinese Statelets and the Northern Barbarians in the Period 1400–300 B.C.* Dordrecht: D. Reidel.

Reay, Marie (1974). "Changing conventions of dispute settlement in the Minj area." In A. L. Epstein, ed., *Contention and Dispute: Aspects of Law and Social Control in Melanesia*, pp. 198–239. Canberra: Australian National University Press.

Rice, Prudence M., and Don S. Rice (1985). "Topoxte, Macanche, and the Central Peten postclassic." In Arlen F. Chase and Prudence M. Rice, eds., *The Lowland Maya Postclassic*, pp. 166–83. Austin: University of Texas Press.

Ricoeur, Paul (1984). *Time and Narrative*. Vol. 1. Chicago: University of Chicago Press.

Rieff, David (1991). *Los Angeles: Capital of the Third World*. New York: Simon and Schuster.

Roberts, Simon (1978). "Do we need an anthropology of law?" *Royal Anthropological Institute News* 25:4.

Ronan, Colin A. (1978). *The Shorter Science and Civilization in China: An Abridgement of Joseph Needham's Original Text*. Vol. 1. Cambridge: Cambridge University Press.

—— (1981) *The Shorter Science and Civilization in China: An Abridgement of Joseph Needham's Original Text*. Vol. 2. Cambridge: Cambridge University Press.

Rosaldo, Renato (1980). *Ilongot Headhunting, 1883–1974: A Study in Society and History*. Stanford: Stanford University Press.

—— (1990). *Culture and Truth: The Remaking of Social Analysis*. Boston: Beacon Press.

Rosen, Lawrence (1977). *Bargaining for Reality*. Chicago: University of Chicago Press.

Rosen, Sydney (1978). "Changing conceptions of the hegemon in pre-Ch'in China." In David T. Roy and Tsuen-hsuin Tsien, eds., *Ancient China: Studies in Early Civilization*, pp. 99–135. Hong Kong: Chinese University Press.

Rounds, J. (1982). "Dynastic succession and the centralization of power in Tenochtitlan." In George A. Collier, Renato I. Rosaldo, and John D. Wirth, eds., *The Inca and Aztec States, 1400–1800: Anthropology and History*, pp. 63–89. New York: Academic Press.

Roy, David T., and Tsuen-hsuin Tsien, eds. (1978). *Ancient China: Studies in Early Civilization*. Hong Kong: Chinese University Press.

Rudenstine, David (1987). "Foreword." *Cardozo Law Review* 9(1):5–13.

Rutz, Henry J., ed. (1992). *The Politics of Time*. American Ethnological Society Monograph Series, 4. Washington, D.C.: American Anthropological Association.

Sabloff, Jeremy A., ed. (1981). *Archaeology: Supplement to the Handbook of Middle American Indians*. Vol. 1. Gen. ed. Victoria R. Bricker. Austin: University of Texas Press.

Sabloff, Jeremy A., and E. Wyllys Andrews V, eds. (1986). *Late Lowland Maya Civilization: Classic to Postclassic*. Albuquerque: University of New Mexico Press, School of American Research.

Sager, Lawrence (1990). "Back to Bork." *New York Review of Books*, October 25, pp. 23–28.

Sahlins, Marshall (1981). *Historical Metaphors and Mythical Realities: Structure in the Early History of the Sandwich Islands Kingdom*. Ann Arbor: University of Michigan Press.

—— (1985). *Islands in History*. Chicago: University of Chicago Press.

Said, Edward (1979). *Orientalism*. New York: Vintage.

Sarat, Austin, and Richard Berkowitz (forthcoming). "Disorderly difference: Recognition, accommodation, and the American law." In Carol J. Greenhouse and Davydd J. Greenwood, eds., *Democracy and Difference*. Albany: State University of New York Press.

Schieffelin, Edward L. (1976). *The Sorrow of the Lonely and the Burning of the Dancers*. St. Lucia: University of Queensland Press.

Schipper, Kristofer (1978). "The Taoist body." *History of Religions* 17(3–4):355–386.

Schram, S. R., ed. (1985). *The Scope of State Power in China*. European Science Foundation. London: School of Oriental and African Studies; Hong Kong: Chinese University Press.

Schultz, Vicki (1990). "Telling stories about women and work: Judicial interpretations of sex segregation in the workplace on Title VII cases raising the lack of interest argument." *Harvard Law Review* 103(8):1749–1843.

Schwartz, Benjamin I. (1985). *The World of Thought in Ancient China*. Cambridge: Harvard University Press.

Scott, James C. (1990). *Domination and the Arts of Resistance: Hidden Transcripts*. New Haven: Yale University Press.

Seligman, Brenda Z. (1941). Review of *The Nuer: A Description of the Modes of Livelihood and Political Institutions of a Nilotic People*, E. E. Evans-Pritchard. *Man*, 91–92.

Shakespeare, William (1969). "King Henry IV, Part I." In *The Complete Pelican Shakespeare: The Histories and the Non-dramatic Poetry*, pp. 242–76. Gen. ed. Alfred Harbage. New York: Penguin.

Shaw, William (1980). "Traditional Korean law and its relation to China." In Jerome A. Cohen, R. Randle Edwards, and Fu-mei Chang Chen, eds., *Essays on China's Legal Tradition*, pp. 301–26. Princeton: Princeton University Press.

Sivin, Nathan (1969). "Cosmos and computation in early Chinese mathematical astronomy." *T'oung Pao* 55(1–3):1–73.

—— (1978). "On the word 'Taoist' as a source of perplexity, with special reference to the relations of science and religion in traditional China." *History of Religions* 17(3–4):303–30.

Skinner, G. William (1964). "Marketing and social structure in rural China, part 1." *Journal of Asian Studies* 24(1):3–43.

Snyder, Francis G. (1981). "Anthropology, dispute processes, and law: A critical appraisal." *British Journal of Law and Society* 8(2):141–80.

Sommerfelt, Alf (1938). *La langue et la société*. Oslo: H. Aschehoug (W. Nygaard).

Sonenshein, Raphael J. (1994). "What about politics?" *Contention* 3(3):23–27.

Sorabji, Richard (1983). *Time, Creation, and the Continuum: Theories in Antiquity and the Early Middle Ages*. Ithaca: Cornell University Press.

—— (1988). *Matter, Space, and Motion: Theories in Antiquity and Their Sequel*. Ithaca: Cornell University Press.

Sorokin, Pitirim A., and Robert K. Merton (1937). "Social time: A methodological and functional analysis." *American Journal of Sociology* 42(5):615–29.

Stallybrass, Peter, and Allon White (1986). *The Politics and Poetics of Transgression*. Ithaca: Cornell University Press.

Stanner, W. E. H. (1979). *White Man Got No Dreaming: Essays, 1938–1973*. Canberra: Australian National University Press.

Starr, June, and Jane F. Collier, eds. (1989). *History and Power in the Study of Law: New Directions in Legal Anthropology*. Ithaca: Cornell University Press.

Stein, Peter (1980). *Legal Evolution: The Story of an Idea*. Cambridge: Cambridge University Press.

Stoller, Paul (1989). *The Taste of Ethnographic Things: The Senses in Anthropology*. Philadelphia: Pennsylvania University Press.

Strathern, A. J. (1971). *The Rope of Moka*. Cambridge: Cambridge University Press.

Strathern, Marilyn (1972). *Official and Unofficial Courts: Legal Assumptions and Expectations in a Highlands Community*. New Guinea Research Bulletin 47. Port Moresby: Australian National University Press.

—— (1974). "Managing information: The problems of a dispute settler: Mount Hagen." In A. L. Epstein, ed., *Contention and Dispute: Aspects of Law and Social Control in Melanesia*, pp. 271–316. Canberra: Australian National University Press.

—— (1985). "Knowing power and being equivocal: Three Melanesian constructs." In Richard Fardon, ed., *Power and Knowledge: Anthropological and Sociological Approaches*, pp. 61–81. Edinburgh: Scottish Academic Press.

—— (1987). "Introduction." In Strathern, ed., *Dealing with Inequality: Analysing Gender Relations in Melanesia and Beyond*, pp. 1–32. Cambridge: Cambridge University Press.

—— (1988) *The Gender of the Gift: Problems with Women and Problems with Society in Melanesia*. Berkeley: University of California Press.

—— (1991). "Introduction." In Maurice Godelier and Strathern, eds., *Big Men and Great Men: Personifications of Power in Melanesia*, pp. 1–4. Cambridge: Cambridge University Press.

—— (1992). *After Nature: English Kinship in the Late Twentieth Century*. Cambridge: Cambridge University Press.

Street, Brian V. (1984). *Literacy in Theory and Practice*. Cambridge: Cambridge University Press.

—— ed. (1993). *Cross-cultural Approaches to Literacy*. Cambridge: Cambridge University Press.

Taube, Karl A. (1992). "The iconography of mirrors at Teotihuacan." In Janet C. Berlo, ed., *Art, Ideology, and the City of Teotihuacan*, pp. 169–204. Washington, D.C.: Dumbarton Oaks.

Tawney, R. H. (1938). *Religion and the Rise of Capitalism: A Historical Study*. Harmondsworth, U.K.: Penguin.

Taylor, Rodney L. (1978). "The centered self: Religious autobiography in the neo-Confucian tradition." *History of Religions* 17(3–4):266–83.

Thomas, Keith (1964). "Work and leisure in pre-industrial societies." *Past and Present* 29:50–62.

Thomas, Nicholas (1989). *Out of Time*. Cambridge: Cambridge University Press.

—— (1994). *Colonialism's Culture: Anthropology, Travel, and Government*. Cambridge: Polity Press.

Thompson, E. P. (1967). "Time, work-discipline, and industrial capitalism." *Past and Present* 38:56–97.

Thornton, Robert (1980). *Space, Time, and Culture among the Iraqw of Tanzania*. New York: Academic Press.

Tichy, Franz (1981). "Order and relationship of space and time in Mesoamerica: Myth or reality?" In Elizabeth P. Benson, ed., *Mesoamerican Sites and World-Views*, pp. 217–45. A conference at Dumbarton Oaks, October 16–17, 1976. Washington, D.C.: Dumbarton Oaks.

Todorov, Tzvetan (1987a). *The Conquest of America: The Question of the Other*. Trans. Richard Howard. New York: Harper and Row.

—— (1987b). *Literature and Its Theorists: A Personal View of Twentieth-century Criticism.* Trans. Catherine Porter. Ithaca: Cornell University Press.

Toulmin, Stephen, and June Goodfield (1965). *The Discovery of Time.* Chicago: University of Chicago Press.

Townsend, Richard F. (1979). *State and Cosmos in the Art of Tenochtitlan.* Washington, D.C.: Dumbarton Oaks.

Townsend, Richard F. (1987). "Coronation at Tenochtitlan." In Elizabeth Hill Boone, ed., *The Aztec Templo Mayor,* pp. 371–409. A Symposium at Dumbarton Oaks, October 8–9, 1983. Washington, D.C.: Dumbarton Oaks.

Trautmann, Thomas R. (1992). "The revolution in ethnological time." *Man* 27(2):379–97.

Turner, Victor (1969). *The Ritual Process.* Harmondsworth, U.K.: Penguin.

Turton, David, and Clive Ruggles (1978). "Agreeing to disagree: The measurement of duration in a southwestern Ethiopian community." *Current Anthropology* 19(3):585–600.

Twitchett, Denis, and Michael Loewe, eds., (1986). *The Ch'in and Han Empires, 221 B.C.–A.D. 220.* Vol. 1 of *The Cambridge History of China.* Gen. ed. Denis Twitchett and John K. Fairbank. Cambridge: Cambridge University Press.

Umberger, Emily (1987). "Events commemorated by date plaques at the Templo Mayor." In Elizabeth Hill Boone, ed., *The Aztec Templo Mayor,* pp. 411–49. A Symposium at Dumbarton Oaks, October 8–9, 1983. Washington, D.C.: Dumbarton Oaks.

Unger, Roberto Mangabeira (1976). *Law in Modern Society: Toward a Criticism of Social Theory.* New York: Free Press.

United States Senate (1973). *Nominations of Joseph T. Sneed to be Deputy Attorney General and Robert H. Bork to be Solicitor General. Hearings before the Committee on the Judiciary.* 93rd Cong., 1st sess. January 17, 1973. Washington, D.C.: U.S. GPO.

—— (1982). *Selection and Confirmation of Federal Judges: Hearings before the Committee on the Judiciary,* 97th Cong., 2d sess. January 27, February 12, 26, and March 11, 24, 31, 1982. Washington, D.C.: U.S. GPO.

—— (1989). *Nomination of Robert H. Bork to be Associate Justice of the Supreme Court of the United States: Hearings before the Committee on the Judiciary,* 100th Cong., 1st sess. September 15, 16, 17, 18, 19, 21, 22, 23, 25, 28, 29, and 30, 1987. Washington, D.C.: U.S. GPO.

—— (1991). *Nomination of Judge Clarence Thomas to be an Associate Justice of the Supreme Court of the United States: Hearings before the Committee on the Judiciary,* 102d Cong. 1st sess. September 10, 11, 12, 13, 16, 1991. Federal Information Systems Corporation; Federal News Service: Lexis/Nexis.

—— (1993). *Nomination of Judge Clarence Thomas to be an Associate Justice of the Supreme Court of the United States: Hearings before the Committee on the Judiciary.* 4 parts. Washington, D.C.: U.S. GPO.

Vandermeersch, Leon (1985). "An enquiry into the Chinese conception of law." In S. R. Schram, ed., *The Scope of State Power in China.* pp. 3–25. European Science Foundation. London: School of Oriental and African Studies; Hong Kong: Chinese University Press.

—— (1990). "Aspects rituels de la popularisation du confucianisme sous les Han." In W. L. Idema and Erik Zürcher, eds., *Thought and Law in Qin and Han China*, pp. 89–107. Leiden: E. J. Brill.

Van Der Sprenkel, Sybille (1966). *Legal Institutions in Manchu China*. London School of Economics Monographs on Social Anthropology, 24. New York: Humanities Press.

Van Gennep, Arnold (1960). *The Rites of Passage*. Trans. Monika B. Vizedom and Gabrielle L. Caffee. Chicago: University of Chicago Press.

Vasari, Giorgio (1965). *Lives of the Artists*. Trans. George Bull. Harmondsworth, U.K.: Penguin.

Verdery, Katherine (1993). "What was socialism and why did it fail?" *Contention* 3(1):1–23.

Veyne, Paul (1984). *Writing History: Essay on Epistemology*. Trans. Mina Moore-Rinvolucri, Manchester: Manchester University Press.

von Benda-Beckmann, Franz (1988). "Comments on Merry." *Law and Society Review* 22(5):897–901.

Wallacker, Benjamin E. (1978). "Han Confucianism and Confucius in Han." In David T. Roy and Tsuen-hsuin Tsien, eds., *Ancient China: Studies in Early Civilization*, pp. 215–28. Hong Kong: Chinese University Press.

Wallman, Sandra, ed. (1992). *Contemporary Futures: Perspectives from Social Anthropology*. ASA Monographs, 30. London: Routledge.

Warner, W. Lloyd (1958). *A Black Civilization: A Social Study of an Australian Tribe*. Rev. ed. New York: Harper.

Warren, Kay, ed. (1993). *The Violence Within: Cultural Opposition within Divided Nations*. Boulder, Colo.: Westview Press.

Watson, Burton, trans. (1958). *Ssu-ma Ch'ien, Grand Historian of China*. New York: Columbia University Press.

—— (1963a). *Hsun Tzu: Basic Writings*. New York: Columbia University Press.

—— (1963b). *Mo tzu: Basic Writings*. New York: Columbia University Press.

—— (1964). *Han Fei Tzu: Basic Writings*. New York: Columbia University Press.

Weber, Max (1958). *The Protestant Ethic and the Spirit of Capitalism*. New York: Charles Scribner's Sons.

Wechsler, Howard J. (1980). "The Confucian impact on early T'ang decision-making." *T'oung Pao* 66(1–3):1–40.

—— (1985). *Offerings of Jade and Silk: Ritual and Symbol in the Legitimation of the T'ang Dynasty*. New Haven: Yale University Press.

Weiner, Annette B. (1976). *Women of Value, Men of Renown*. Austin: University of Texas Press.

—— (1980). "Reproduction: A replacement for reciprocity." *American Ethnologist* 7(1):71–85.

Wheatley, Paul (1971). *The Pivot of the Four Quarters: A Preliminary Enquiry into the Origins and Character of the Ancient Chinese City*. Edinburgh: Edinburgh University Press.

Wickham, Chris (1985). "Lawyers' time: History and memory in tenth- and eleventh-century Italy." In Henry Mayr-Harting and R. I. Moore, eds., *Studies in*

Medieval History Presented to R. H. C. Davis, pp. 53–71. London: Hambledon Press.

Willey, Gordon R. (1987). *Essays in Maya Archaeology*. Albuquerque: University of New Mexico Press.

Williams, Raymond (1985). *The Country and the City*. London: Hogarth Press.

Wilson, Edmund (1983). "Justice Oliver Wendell Holmes." In Lewis M. Dabney, ed., *The Portable Edmund Wilson*, pp. 507–55. New York: Penguin Books.

Wolf, Eric R., ed. (1976). *The Valley of Mexico: Studies in Pre-Hispanic Ecology and Society*. Albuquerque: University of New Mexico Press, School of American Research.

—— (1982). *Europe and the People without History*. Berkeley: University of California Press.

Wolff, Philippe (1962). "Le temps et sa mesure au Moyen Age." *Annales E.S.C.* 17(6):1141–45.

Wonderley, Anthony W. (1985). "The land of Ulua: Postclassic research in the Naco and Sula valleys, Honduras." In Arlen F. Chase and Prudence M. Rice, eds., *The Lowland Maya Postclassic*, pp. 245–69. Austin: University of Texas Press.

Woodburn, James (1982). "Social dimensions of death in four African hunting and gathering societies." In Maurice Bloch and Jonathan Parry, eds., *Death and the Regeneration of Life*, pp. 187–210. Cambridge: Cambridge University Press.

Wormald, Jenny (1983). "The blood feud in early modern Scotland." In John Bossy, ed., *Disputes and Settlements: Law and Human Relations in the West*, pp. 101–44. Cambridge: Cambridge University Press.

Wren, Linnea H., and Peter Schmidt (1991). "Elite interaction during the terminal classic period: New evidence from Chichen Itza." In T. Patrick Culbert, ed., *Classic Maya Political History: Hieroglyphic and Archaeological Evidence*, pp. 199–225. Cambridge: Cambridge University Press.

Wright, Arthur F. (1957). "The formation of guild ideology, 581–604." In John K. Fairbank, ed., *Chinese Thought and Institutions*, pp. 71–104. Chicago: University of Chicago Press.

Yang, Lien-sheng (1982). "Historical notes on the Chinese world order." *Sinological Studies and Reviews* Shih-huo Pub. Reprinted from John K. Fairbank, ed., *The Chinese World Order*, pp. 51–66. Cambridge: Harvard University Press, 1968.

Yngvesson, Barbara (1993). *Virtuous Citizens, Disruptive Subjects: Order and Complaint in a New England Court*. New York: Routledge.

Yoffee, Norman (1991). "Maya elite interaction: Through a glass, sideways." In T. Patrick Culbert, ed., *Classic Maya Political History: Hieroglyphic and Archaeological Evidence*, pp. 285–310 Cambridge: Cambridge University Press.

You, Haili (1994). "Rhythm in Chinese thinking: A short question for a long tradition." *Culture, Medicine, and Psychiatry* 18:463–81.

Yü, Ying-shih (1964–65). "Life and immortality in the mind of Han China." *Harvard Journal of Asiatic Studies* 25:80–122.

Zerubavel, Eviatar (1982). "The standardization of time: A sociohistorical perspective." *American Journal of Sociology* 88(1):1–23.

—— (1985). *The Seven Day Circle: The History and Meaning of the Week.* New York: Free Press.

Zürcher, Erik (1980). "Buddhist influence on early Taoism." *T'oung Pao* 66(1–3):84–147.

—— (1982). "Perspectives in the study of Chinese Buddhism." *Journal of the Royal Asiatic Society* 1982(2):161–76.

Index

Acamapichtli, 159–60
Accountability. *See* Law; Power
Ades, Dawn, 153, 158
Agency, 83–84, 86–87; and autobiography, 209; Christian view of, 35, 89, 93; and community, 224, 230, 231–32; and constructions of the "other," 98–103; as cultural concept, 4–5, 6–7, 81–82; cyclical time distribution of, 86, 91–93, 212; defined, 1, 83; and eternity, 89, 181; and inscription, 80; and intention, 78, 80–81; and Legalist time concepts, 140–41; linear time distribution of, 35–36, 86, 88–91, 93, 179–82, 211–12; multiple sources, 93–96, 101; of Quetzalcoatl, 155–57; and resistance and hegemony, 97–98, 109, 233–35; ritual redistribution of, 94–96, 105–6; singularization of, 60–61, 80; and structure, 6, 61, 77–81, 103–4, 107, 233–35; and surplus authority, 106–10; and temporal pluralism, 96–98; "timeless" distribution of, 86, 87–88, 212; and time-space relationships, 71, 103–6; totalization of, 47; in yin-yang theory, 131–32. *See also* Closure; Individuals
Algeria, 97
Anderson, Benedict, 242n.9
Anthropology: and difference, 73–76, 235–36; and indeterminacy of cultural norms, 12–13; and legal pluralism, 54–55, 56–60, 243n.43; and postmodernity, 235–36; and study of time concepts, 1–4, 24–25, 213–16. *See also specific anthropologists*
Appadurai, Arjun, 62–63, 68–69
Architecture, Mesoamerican, 151–52, 156–57
Aristotle, 36
Ashanti society, 29–30
Assier-Andrieu, Louis, 59
Australia, 45–46, 87–88

Authority, surplus, 106–10. *See also* Legitimacy
Authors: alienation of, 51; readers' relationship to, 54, 75; temporal freedom of, 197–98
Autobiography, 180, 187–88, 208–10, 273n.32; Bork's, 196–99, 273n.59, 274n.64; Thomas's, 200, 203–4, 205–6
Aveni, Anthony, 149, 151, 157
Aztecs, 101, 143, 261n.1, 267n.131; calendars of, 146, 148–51, 263n.28, 269n.172; conventional reading of fall of, 10, 144–48, 221; cosmology of, 145, 153–57, 166–68; and cultural diversity, 163, 165–66, 217–18, 269n.170; expansionism of, 143, 158–60, 175–76, 217–18; historical concepts of, 156, 157–60; installation rites of, 156, 163, 169–70; modernity of, 217–18, 220–21; space-time concepts of, 148–53, 156–57, 265n.72, 265n.75, 266n.107. *See also* Motecuhzoma; Quetzalcoatl

Baka society, 37
Bakhtin, Mikhail, 75, 197
Bali, 33
Barnes, J. A., 239n.52
Bashu society, 95–96
Bauman, Zygmunt, 277n.28, 278n.36
Beidelman, Thomas O., 98
Bell, Diane, 45–46
Biden, Joseph, 200, 201, 203, 207
Birth, 240n.74; and personhood, 39; as social disruption, 38
Black, Hugo, 187
Bloch, Maurice, 33–34, 37–38
Bodde, Derk, 120, 121, 128–29, 136, 137; on Confucian view of cosmic harmony, 127, 141
Bohannan, Paul, 41, 104